Cuisine à la Vapeur

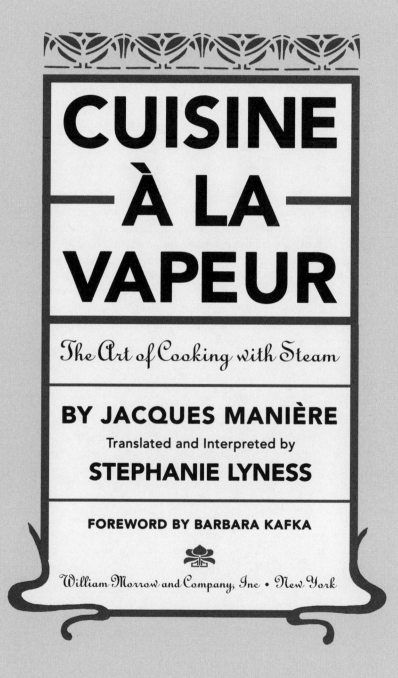

CUISINE À LA VAPEUR

The Art of Cooking with Steam

BY JACQUES MANIÈRE

Translated and Interpreted by

STEPHANIE LYNESS

FOREWORD BY BARBARA KAFKA

William Morrow and Company, Inc • New York

First published in French as *Le Grand Livre de la Cuisine à la Vapeur*
by Editions Denoël, Paris, 1985

It is the policy of William Morrow and Company, Inc.,
and its imprints and affiliates, recognizing the importance of preserving what
has been written, to print the books we publish on acid-free paper, and we
exert our best efforts to that end.

Library of Congress Cataloging-in-Publication Data

Manière, Jacques, 1923–1991
[Grand livre de la cuisine à la vapeur. English]
Cuisine à la vapeur = the art of cooking with steam / Jacques Manière :
translated and interpreted by Stephanie Lyness.
p.   cm.
Includes index.
ISBN 0–688–10507–6
1. Steaming (Cookery).   2. Cookery, French.   I. Lyness, Stephanie.
II. Title.   III. Title: Art of cooking with steam.
TX691.M3613   1995
641.7′3—dc20   94–32732
                                                       CIP

Printed in the United States of America

First Edition

1 2 3 4 5 6 7 8 9 10

BOOK DESIGN BY LINEY LI

CONTENTS

Foreword: Steamed Up for Manière BY BARBARA KAFKA . . . . *vii*

Preface . . . . *xi*

Notes About This Edition . . . . *xv*

The Basics of Steaming *1*

Vegetable First Courses and Side Dishes *19*

Fish and Shellfish *105*

Poultry *173*

Meats *223*

Desserts *269*

Mail Order Sources *299*

Translator's Acknowledgments *301*

Index *303*

FOREWORD
Steamed Up for Manière

One of the most exciting things about being a food writer is the discovery of a new talent and, sometimes, if one is lucky, sharing that talent with other people. Introducing the English-language edition of this book gives me the joy of three such discoveries and three such sharings. First, there is the original author, the brilliant and innovative Jacques Manière. Then, there is this book, equally brilliant and innovative. Finally, there is Stephanie Lyness, the talented and ardent young translator and adapter of the book. For me, it is a full plate of deep-tasting delights.

In 1967 in Paris, everybody—meaning the chefs and the eaters—was suddenly talking about Jacques Manière and his new restaurant, Le Pactole, which had opened a few months earlier, at the very end of 1966, on Boulevard Saint-Germain. Certain of the more astute gastronomes had, since 1959, found their way to his earlier version of Le Pactole in the working-class suburb of Pantin. Many had been led there by the raves of "La Reynière," the pseudonymous food critic of *Le Monde*.

I was late to get the message, but then I was very young at my work. As soon as I could I went to the small and simple Paris restaurant and met the vigorous, good-looking chef-owner, who, with his hair in a brush cut, reminded me and everyone else of Jean Gabin. I delighted in a dish that was to change the way great chefs cooked. It was Manière's *salade folle,* an opulent first course of tiny, lightly cooked haricots verts with foie gras and truffles. Today that sounds like a cliché, but only because it has been so often imitated. Manière was the cook and that was the dish that defined what was to become known as nouvelle cuisine. Unlike that of many others who followed in his footsteps, Manière's food was innovative without being outré. It was solidly based in the classic and regional cooking of France, particularly that of his native Perigord. Best of all, it was impeccably prepared and tasted wonderful.

At the time, it seemed revolutionary, as did the middle-aged chef, who had not even started to cook until he was thirty-two and had been a paratrooper and a salesman of the products of his region before coming to Paris in 1955. He was too revolutionary for the Michelin, which didn't give him even one star until 1978, by which time he had long been established in Gault-Millau, the voice of modern French cooking, with three toques (chef's hats) and eighteen out of a possible twenty points. Manière's irascible directness was as responsible as his cooking for the Michelin's shunning of him.

When he died in 1991 at the age of sixty-eight, he had left Le Pactole to his sous-chef and had opened a second restaurant, Dodin Bouffant, named for a fictional gastronome (the first had been named for a gold-bearing river in ancient Greece that had supposedly bathed Midas). Manière himself never had the golden touch; he spent too much on the best of ingredients and treating friends to wine and food. He also had a deep conviction that his food and wine should be affordable and charged much less than comparable restaurants, even at a time when popularity had him turning customers away. Later still—always ahead of the game—he said there should be a return to the full flavors of country cooking along with a more healthful way of cooking.

It would be impossible to write the history of French food since World War II without admiration of this extraordinary man who had so many young followers, so many memories of long nights drinking and chatting with other chefs, so many early-morning visits to the markets in search of that day's booty. He was the first to say that he couldn't tell you what was on the next day's menu because he didn't know what would be in the market, the first to have temperature-controlled saltwater tanks for live seafood (different for oysters and other bivalves), a perfectionist who said, "Twenty places [customers] is cuisine, thirty would be business," and who could insult friend, customer, and foe alike.

He said, "I work for the pleasure, for myself as much as for my customers." His pleasure was perfection; the customers often didn't live up to their end of the bargain: "In the dining room, the public doesn't always have talent." Having started the new movement, he could be hard on young chefs who he felt didn't have a mastery of their craft, a mastery he had learned on his own, having started with the expert cooking of his mother and what he felt was the brilliant innovativeness of his father: "The cuisine of young chefs is based on stereotypes. Beyond that, if you ask them stupidly to make a grilled turbot with béarnaise, nine times out of ten the turbot isn't bad; but as to the béarnaise, that's a failure. Or if you are in the country and if you tell them to make you a boudin [sausage], they reply: 'Oh, no, I don't have a good charcutier.' I make the boudin myself."

Today, years later, reading his menus still makes me want to rush out and eat his food. Reading his recipes in the book on steam cooking published in 1985 makes me want to rush into the kitchen and make his food—simple and luxurious by virtue of its excellence—and eat it. The ideas and recipes were formed and perfectly suited to him and the times when, in 1984, a handsome, white-haired sixty-one, he came out of retirement and took over a hotel-restaurant in the Ardèche. Interviewed at that time, he said: "Twenty years ago, I was the first to regularly use this way of cooking in great cuisine. Since that time, I have not ceased defending it. . . . It ensures at the same time a savory and healthy result." Coincidentally, he lost ten or twelve pounds.

He brought the same sense of history, balance, and excellence that had previously made him famous to his new endeavor, the book. He drank red wine—a little, but always the best. He appreciated the fact that the Chinese had been his culinary forebears. He researched the best way to flavor his foods with herbs, to reduce fat while adding some of its unctuousness to his sauces, to attain a totally simple and elegant cuisine that was easy to do, to invent new dishes, and to bring out and preserve the essential succulence and tastes of his ingredients. "Taste is like an accent, and products have the scent of their accent," he said. By this he meant the flavors of the place where things are grown and the dishes of that place.

It is this very special book that has brought to my attention Stephanie Lyness, one of the best young cooks and writers with whom I have been privileged to work in recent years. In the ensuing pages she explains how, resistant to Manière's ideas and discoveries, she became first a convert and then an enthusiast. I think you will also discover how well she has captured his spirit and enlarged on it while applying it to our ingredients—our "accents"—and current tastes for yet lighter food. Her work is a labor of love and intelligence that finally permits us to use and enjoy what the distinguished French food critic Michel Piot called a book that "gives us recipes for more than a hundred years and is as important in its genre as Escoffier was in the beginning of the century. If we could only have three cookbooks, this of Manière's would be one."

I hope you enjoy the triumvirate that I present to you as much as Piot and I. Good cooking.

—BARBARA KAFKA

PREFACE

When I began work on this translation of *Le Grand Livre de la Cuisine à la Vapeur* by Jacques Manière, I didn't know that I was going to fall in love. In fact, as my work progressed, the sentiment I experienced was often the opposite. I encountered many difficulties on the bumpy road to love, becoming in turn cranky and bewildered for a number of reasons: American steamers are not as large as those Manière used, our ingredients differ substantially from those available to the French reader, and since Manière died shortly after I began this translation, my dialogue with him was limited to what could be garnered from his recipes. His book was like a map for a buried treasure, with recipes for clues and Manière's visionary soul the ultimate bounty. I labored over the recipes daily, worrying at night that the prize might not be unearthed.

My first impression of the work was born while testing a recipe for tied boneless lamb shoulder, purchased after long negotiation with my butcher, whose American lamb shoulders were all much larger than their French cousins. I got the shoulder home, tied it, and steamed it medium-rare as Manière instructed, only to discover that, even steamed, a medium-rare American lamb shoulder is tough and nearly inedible. Frustrated, I put the shoulder back in the steamer and cooked it to well-done. I still didn't like it.

I told this story to my exacting mentor, Barbara Kafka, who grimaced at my lack of faith and, insisting I would be able to forge a partnership with my author, sent me back to work. I decided to give Manière another chance, and I moved on to the vegetable chapter. My relationship with him improved. Steaming brought out a wealth of flavors—sweet, bitter, salty, sharp—that astonished me. Manière was beginning to show his hand, and I loved his exquisite, unerring simplicity. A bite of his eggplant caviar was smooth and silky, with layer upon layer of flavors that broke like waves in my mouth. The six ordinary ingredients in his creamed cabbage combined to produce a dish that was masterfully delicate, refined, almost otherworldly. I began to steam vegetables as a matter of course, and even when I was too pressed to follow one of his recipes, my own meals almost always included a steamed vegetable, whether puréed, made into soup, or dressed simply in olive oil and lemon.

But it was in the fish chapter, somewhere between the cod and herring recipes, that I actually lost my heart. The fish was a delight. In these pages I could feel Manière's passion for each dish, and for the turbulent sea that spawned them. His food was at once familiar and unexpected, drawn from classic French cuisine but prepared with the deft hand and flash of a grin that are the elements of his genius. His instinct for flavor was invariably precise, never showing off or speaking too loudly. Finally I began to know Manière's food. I knew I'd prepared it properly when the ingredients were so seamlessly woven together that their individual tastes could no longer be pulled apart: Some flavors were clear and distinct, others subtle and hidden, but all resonated in delicious harmony.

I was in ecstasy, and followed Manière into the realm of the ocean. I began to steam virtually everything I could find in my local fish store, and found that while many of the recipes in the fish chapter were more elegant than for every day, I easily could use Manière's steaming techniques and simpler sauces for quick meals. Emboldened by my successes, I began teaching friends and even strangers to steam fish and was met with enthusiasm to match my own. My mentor smiled.

Thus I surrendered to Manière's teachings. As it turned out, my first experience with the lamb shoulder was an anomaly, for the steamed meats were eventually as successful as the fish. My challenge was to learn about the ingredients available to the American consumer and how best to use them within the context of the recipes. So while a whole steamed lamb shoulder is perhaps not the best use of our culinary resources, a steamed stew of shoulder pieces or a leg of lamb is right on the money. The dessert chapter also required quite a bit of experimenting to adapt Manière's custards, flans, and puddings to the American kitchen, but I was happy to discover steaming as an alternative to baking in a water bath. Manière used fruit to great effect in many of his desserts, so I threw myself into steaming the freshest produce possible and creating wonderful desserts and sauces.

By the end of this tremendous project, I had two or three steamers sitting on my stove at any given moment and, in my ardor, was steaming practically everything. The mountainous bags of steamed vegetables in my refrigerator (the result of timing experiments) often became soup, for no matter what went into the blender, the result was guaranteed to be delicious. When I entertained, I steamed the whole dinner even if it would have been easier to use the oven for a dish or two. One night I steamed a whole salmon and served it with artichoke hearts vinaigrette, an artichoke heart mayonnaise made with the pulp scraped from the steamed leaves, steamed broccoli, and new potatoes, followed by a dessert of steamed clafoutis. Another night, I made Manière's stupendous couscous.

Manière's genius was a given, but this is not to suggest that he was the epitome of delicacy and refinement. In fact, he was somewhat of a rebel, a daredevil who did nothing timidly or halfheartedly. He was a self-taught chef who never allowed himself to be limited by rules or convention, and he is still described by those who knew him as a larger-than-life figure. His former sous-chef told me a story that draws a vivid picture of the man. A diner once became impatient while waiting for his duck to be roasted, and complained to the waiter one time too many. Manière lost his temper and hurled the duck across the dining room at the patron. This was clearly a man with his own firm vision of how things ought to be done.

When I started work on this book, the original plan was simply to translate a selection of the four hundred or so recipes in Manière's edition and to adapt them for the American kitchen. I chose my favorite recipes and those that are most practical for American cooks. I dropped those that were very time-consuming or that used ingredients unavailable on our shores. I substituted ingredients where possible, but often it didn't make sense to push it: Manière's recipes for fillets of sole stuffed with sea urchin roe, or turbot with sea scallop roe sound delicious, but these fish and roe are too hard to find here, and there are no easy substitutes. I cut recipes from his game and offal chapters, as these foods are more common—and better appreciated—in France than in the United States. Finally, I culled recipes from some of Manière's separate chapters not included here, like those on egg preparations and sauces, and added them to the appropriate, complementary chapters of this edition.

Despite the recipe cuts, the project refused to stop growing. Each new discovery led to another. Each meeting with my mentor produced a new list of foods to test, a new batch of experiments to perform. I hope readers of this edition will embark on a similar odyssey with Manière. Use the information found in the Basics section, chapter introductions, and chapter endnotes to explore different types of steamers, steaming techniques, and ingredients—and you too will find yourself as enchanted as I by his spell.

—STEPHANIE LYNESS

NOTES ABOUT THIS EDITION

This book has ended up as a collaboration between two voices, each speaking, both figuratively and literally, a different language. Manière was a French restaurant chef writing for a French public; his recipes reflect the lifestyle of that public. I am an American chef and writer who is conscious of the demands of the American lifestyle because I live it. Manière had a large staff to do his kitchen prep, and while it is by no means true of all of his recipes, some are time-consuming, more suited to special occasions than to everyday cooking. I steamed a lot of everyday food in the course of testing this book and was always looking for ways to use steaming to simplify my life. As a result, this edition covers a lot of culinary ground, with both Manière's and my points of view represented.

Chapter Organization

The recipes in Manière's book are organized somewhat differently from those in most American cookbooks. With the exception of the dessert chapter, Manière didn't base chapters on the type of dish or its place in the meal (such as soups, salads, or appetizers), preferring instead to divide the chapters by raw foodstuff: vegetables, fish and shellfish, poultry, and meats. Within the chapters, the foods are arranged alphabetically and each chapter contains a variety of types of recipes: first courses, main courses, soups, and salads.

For the American edition, I've held on to Manière's chapter divisions; the recipes are not, however, always arranged alphabetically within the chapters. Don't be put off by this system: You'll find listings for soups, sauces, appetizers, vegetable side dishes, purées, and such in the Index.

The vegetable chapter in both Manière's and the American edition is arranged alphabetically by vegetable, starting with artichokes. Although somewhat unusual, Manière's system works well; by arranging the chapter this way, he directed our attention to the vegetable itself rather than to what's done to it. I've written a brief introduction to each vegetable, giving basic steaming times for each, in small and large quantities; simple recipes where appropriate; and whatever information I came across in my testing that might interest the reader—a description of the vegetable, steaming tips, and how to buy, prepare, serve, and/or embellish the vegetable. These recipes use vegetables in a wide variety of dishes: first-course soups, salads, and flans; main courses; side dishes; and purées.

It didn't really make sense to alphabetize the recipes in the fish chapter in this edition because, in America, we can't get many of the fish Manière used. The name of the game when steaming fish is substitution, so I grouped the recipes by method of preparation: steamed fillets and steaks; steamed fillets, steaks, and whole fish wrapped in aluminum foil packages (*en papillote*); and steamed whole fish. I give suggestions for substitution in each recipe. The shellfish recipes are arranged by type of shellfish. The poultry and meat chapters are arranged by the animal, as in American cookbooks. General technical information on how to prepare, bone, steam, and serve fish and shellfish, poultry, and meats, culled from Manière's book and my own experience, is at the end of each chapter. The dessert chapter is again grouped by preparation (custards, for example). I've included selected sauce recipes from Manière's sauce chapter in the appropriate chapters in this edition; you'll also find a listing for sauces in the Index.

Charts of Basic Steaming Times

One of the most useful elements of Manière's book is his collection of charts of basic steaming times. These charts, which precede the recipes in each chapter, expand the scope of the work enormously, giving the reader the possibility of steaming without using recipes. I've reworked and enlarged Manière's charts to reflect the foods available to us in America. Manière's original charts also include guidelines for the amount of water needed to steam each food; I didn't find these measurements to be critical to the success of the steaming and, given that no one in America will be using Manière's steamer, the quantities seemed unnecessary.

In the vegetable chapter of this edition, short charts of vegetable steaming times appear with the introductory information for each vegetable. Manière included timings for whole vegetables and certain cuts such as bâtonnets; I've added other cuts and shapes that I deemed useful to us in America.

In his fish and shellfish chapter, Manière listed times for whole and large pieces of fish, as well as for fillets and steaks where appropriate. I added steaming times for fillets and steaks for all the fish I could find at the Fulton Fish Market in New York City. (Unfortunately, the chart couldn't reflect all the fish found on the West Coast, notably lingcod and varieties of rockfish.) In addition, I found a reliable formula for steaming whole fish based on the thickness of the fish, and I give it in the introduction to the chart. To make substitution easier, the chart is divided into two categories: lean white-fleshed fish and darker-textured moderately fatty fish. The various fish in these two categories are further grouped by texture.

Manière's original poultry chart is for whole birds; I added timings for poultry parts. The French butcher meat differently from the way we do, so I adapted Manière's timing chart to American cuts. Once I discovered that steamed meat is great stuff, I steamed everything that made sense to try, particularly cheaper cuts that steamed well, and I added those times to the chart.

Finally, I created a chart of basic steaming times for bananas, pineapples, and available varieties of apples, pears, and grapes; it appears at the beginning of the dessert chapter in this edition.

Cuisine à la Vapeur

THE
BASICS OF
STEAMING

The technique of steaming is simplicity itself. The food is placed on a perforated rack (often on top of a bed of aromatics) over rapidly simmering water and covered with a tight-fitting lid. Then the food is steamed until done. That's really all there is to it.

How to Steam

When you're ready to steam, bring the water to a boil over high heat in the covered steamer pot and then reduce the heat as necessary until the water is at a brisk simmer and you can see steam escape energetically from under the lid. Then add the food on the steamer rack, cover the pot, and begin timing.

If you open the steamer while the food is cooking, either to check on the progress of the food or to replenish the water, raise the heat to bring the water back to a good simmer, then lower the heat again and continue timing.

Steaming Equipment

The right pot to steam in is any pot the food will fit into. The lid, whether a proper lid or an aluminum foil cover, mustn't touch the food. Following the ingredients list for each recipe, I give steamer suggestions. Chances are that you have suitable equipment for steaming in your kitchen right now. In the course of translating *Cuisine à la Vapeur,* I collected an assortment of steamers and improvised many more. Steamers are sold in hardware, department, and kitchenware stores. They range in price from cheap (one of my favorites cost a whopping $11.99) to quite pricey. Here's what's available.

✳ STACKABLE STEAMERS
These are three- or four-piece metal steaming units that include a solid bottom pot, one or two perforated stackable steamer com-

partments that sit above the pot, and a lid. These units are available in round and oval shapes, in varying sizes, and the pots can be deep or shallow. When you steam in two stackable compartments, the food in the top compartment steams slightly more slowly than the food in the bottom; add a few minutes to the times given in the timing charts.

Stackable steamers range in price from very inexpensive, for aluminum, to quite expensive ($100 or more) for stainless steel. Here are some specific examples of this type of steamer that can be ordered by mail:

Demeyere-Silvinox makes a heavy-gauge stainless steel stackable steamer in two sizes, roughly six-quart and three-quart capacities. Both have deep pots and two stackable steamer compartments. The design is similar to that of a *couscousière* (a specialized pot, traditionally earthenware, used for cooking couscous (see Manière's recipe on page 247). This Belgian-made steamer has an exceptionally good rubber seal between pot and steamer compartments and it steams food faster than any of my other stackable steamers. It holds a lot of food; the larger size holds an average chicken. The compartments are shallow, so it's easy to remove steamed fish fillets and steaks. This steamer is a pleasure to use, but on the expensive side. It can be ordered from Zabar's, in Manhattan (see page 299).

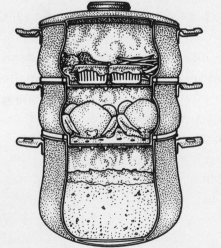

AMC makes an attractive heavy-gauge oval stainless steel steamer. It measures thirteen-and-a-half by eight inches, with a six-quart pot and a single steaming compartment. The compartment is long enough to hold a small whole fish and, if covered with an aluminum foil lid, can hold even a large chicken. The shallow pot doubles as a roasting pan. The steamer is sold with a serving tray. This is a lovely piece of equipment, and I like its shape, but it's on the expensive side. It can be ordered from AMC (see page 299).

Bridge Kitchenware in New York City sells high-quality oval and round Italian-made stainless steel stackable steamers in three-and-a-half- to six-quart sizes, also relatively expensive (see page 299).

A variety of lightweight aluminum and stainless steel stackable steamers in various sizes are sold in kitchenware stores in New York City's Chinatown: I've seen ten-inch, twelve-inch, and fourteen-inch versions. These have large pots, hold a lot of food (my twelve-inch pot can steam a large chicken and even a small fish), and have two steamer compartments. They are great for steaming festive dishes like couscous or a *grande aïoli* for a crowd, or food wrapped *en papillote,* which needs a lot of space. The lid on mine has begun to stick, and it steams some foods more slowly than other steamers of this type, but it's handy for its size and very inexpensive. Steamers of this type can be mail-ordered through Hung Chong Imports, Inc., in Manhattan (see page 299).

❋ PASTA COOKERS

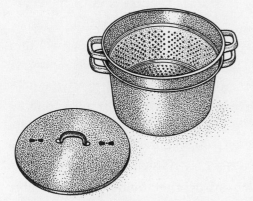

Pasta cookers are units that include a deep pot and a deep perforated insert that fits inside the pot. (Some manufacturers sell these inserts separately from the pots as well.) When the pasta is cooked, you simply lift the insert out of the pot, removing the pasta and draining it, in one operation. I use my nine-and-a-half-inch pasta cooker for steaming vegetables, poultry, meat, and shellfish. It's also great for steamed "stews" (see page 268), and I have used it to improvise a steamer for terrines such as the Carrot Terrine on page 57 that require a large steamer: Use an eight-inch Pyrex bread pan with handles at either end. Fill it with the terrine mixture and cover the pan with foil, as usual. Then, instead of setting the pan in the steamer insert, remove the insert from the pot and set the pan on top of the pot so that the handles sit on the rim; the foil covering helps to secure the pan. Then cover the whole thing with aluminum foil and steam it. A pasta cooker doesn't work for finfish fillets and steaks; it's too hard to get the fish out of such a deep insert. Pasta cookers are widely available and often inexpensive. Mine is thin stainless steel and comes with a second smaller insert with a wire handle that allows me to steam in two layers. Bridge Kitchenware sells a stainless steel Italian pasta cooker with a six-quart pot (see page 299). Chantal makes a pasta insert that fits inside its stockpot, as does Calphalon.

✳ STEAMER INSERTS

Steamer inserts, sometimes called pasta inserts, are shallow perforated inserts, sold separately, that fit into pots, like a pasta cooker. Bridge Kitchenware sells a stepped stainless steel Italian-made insert that fits into pots of various sizes (see page 299). Calphalon and All Clad, available from Zabar's and Williams-Sonoma (see page 299), make steamer inserts as well.

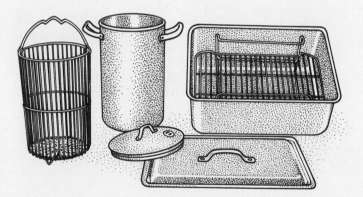

✳ ASPARAGUS STEAMERS

These steamers are made specifically to steam asparagus either standing up or lying down. The version intended to steam asparagus standing up is tall and narrow—like a bunch of asparagus—and, unless you're very creative or in a real pinch, is suited only to steaming asparagus because of its shape. It also holds very little water underneath the rack. The rectangular model features a deep, rectangular pot fitted with a wire rack to hold the asparagus horizontally and can be used to steam other foods as well. Bridge Kitchenware sells both types, in stainless steel (see page 299).

✳ COLLAPSIBLE STEAMER BASKETS

These ubiquitous stainless steel multipetaled baskets are sold in three sizes. They fold up on themselves for storage and expand to a diameter of nine and a half inches, ten and a half inches, or twelve inches for steaming. The baskets sit on legs about one inch high and have a center post for handling. The baskets can be set in many different types of steaming vessels; I've used a deep-lidded pot and a deep sauté pan. Either pan can be covered with aluminum foil (see Improvised Steamers, page 8) if the lid doesn't fit over the food. On some baskets, the center post can be removed so that the basket can hold a large ingredient, such as a chicken.

These baskets are versatile and they'll fit into a variety of different pots. I've used them to steam fish steaks and fillets and vegetables. Expanded to their maximum size, they hold a lot of food. They're very inexpensive and available almost everywhere. They should be a favorite piece of equipment, but oddly enough they're not—I find that I almost always choose a stackable steamer over a basket. Their short legs don't allow for much steaming water underneath, so they're better suited to steaming quick-cooking foods such as vegetables than a chicken; they're relatively hard to move around once loaded with food; and they tip easily in the steamer. I've never been able to take advantage of the ten-and-a-half-inch and twelve-inch baskets because I don't have a pot large enough to hold them expanded to their full size. It's not that I don't recommend them, but I do find other steamers more fun to use. And, the truth be known, it's often difficult to make any but the simplest of Manière's recipes in these baskets.

✳ ELECTRIC STEAMERS

There are a number of electric steamers on the market. Some Japanese companies, such as Zojirushi and Hitachi, make steamers that are for steaming rice only. (You can recognize one of these by its steamer bowl, which is solid, not perforated.) These companies and others such as Sanyo, Panasonic, and Sunbeam/Oster now also manufacture rice cooker/food steamers that are, at heart, rice cookers but include a perforated steaming plate so they can double as food steamers. With the perforated plate in place, these rice cooker/food steamers have only about a quarter inch of room for the steaming water, so they are not practical for steaming long-cooking foods.

Several other companies, such as Black & Decker, Waring, Rival, and West Bend, make all-purpose electric food steamers. I know people who swear by these steamers and use them every day to steam vegetables, fish, and poultry. I've used these four brands quite a bit; each is a little different. They all have an element that heats the water in a reservoir in the base of the unit. The Black & Decker, my preferred model, is round and is manufactured in two sizes, two- and four-quart. The Waring Deluxe Steam Cooker is oval and it is the only model of the four with two stackable compartments; the larger holds six quarts and the divided smaller compartment holds four quarts, two in each half. The Rival is oval and steams up to six cups of food. The West Bend model is oval and has about a six-cup capacity. The Black & Decker and West Bend both have timers. The Rival requires cleaning with vinegar after each use, which is impractical. All but the Waring use a drip tray—a separate tray or compartment to catch the juices from the food so that they don't fall into the steaming water. Some, like the Waring, allow stock or wine to be used as the steaming liquid. All turn off automatically when the steaming water has evaporated. These machines are convenient (you never have to worry about scorching a pan) and easy to use. Their disadvantage is that they are small and, when you are steaming meat, fish, and poultry, more suited to cooking for two than for four. Foods can take longer to steam in an electric steamer than in a stovetop model, so the steaming times in this book aren't really reliable for electric steamers.

✳ IMPROVISED STEAMERS: ROASTING PANS AND FISH POACHERS
Large, long foods like a leg or rack of lamb, a whole turkey or goose, or a whole fish need a big steamer. The only commercial steamers I've seen that are large enough to hold such foods are the stackable steamers sold in Chinatown (see page 5), and even those won't hold a whole large fish. Most people aren't interested in having a steamer for every occasion; here's the place to use a roasting pan or fish poacher instead. The only requirement of the pan or poacher is that it be large enough to hold the food comfortably—there should be about one inch of space between the food and the sides of the pan to ensure proper circulation of the steam. (If the food fills the steamer completely, it won't cook.) The pan

needn't have a lid; it can be covered with a sheet of aluminum foil. Press the foil tightly around the rim of the pan to hold in the steam. Make sure the foil doesn't touch the food—it won't cook properly where it's in contact with the foil. You may need to fold two pieces of foil together to get a piece large enough to cover the pan completely. I get a great sense of satisfaction from rigging up these improvised steamers. Even with all the fancy equipment I've collected, there are lots of foods I couldn't have prepared without these homemade jobs.

Roasting Pans with Wire Racks I use two roasting pans for steaming: One is an oval sixteen- by eleven-inch shallow enameled pan, the other an oval fifteen- by eleven-inch graniteware "ceramic on steel" dome-lidded pan. A rectangular roasting pan would work as well. At $11.99, the graniteware pan is a steal, particularly because it has the domed lid that accommodates big items. I bought an oval wire baking rack that fits easily into either pan, and I raise it off the floor of the pan with empty tuna cans or inverted cups placed under the rack (I've even used wadded-up balls of aluminum foil in a pinch—not very steady, but they did the trick) to allow more room for water. To give more room under the rack for making stock with bones (see page 221), use two stacked tuna cans for extra height. Shallow roasting pans can be covered with aluminum foil, as described above. The domed lid of the graniteware pan is high enough to fit over most foods; if not, the pan can be covered with foil. (An aluminum foil lid slows down the steaming marginally so I don't use it for steaming green vegetables.)

I use my roasting pan to cook large pieces of meat, whole poultry, whole small fish or larger fish cut in half, and large fish fillets and steaks. Depending on the rack, you may need to use a piece of aluminum foil to keep food from falling through the holes in the rack (see Steaming on a Foil Tray, page 163).

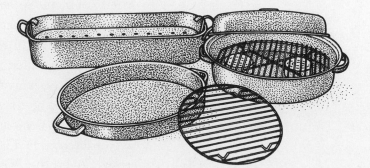

Fish Poachers When I started steaming large whole fish, I went shopping for a pan big enough to hold one. A huge roasting pan was impractical and expensive, so I bought a twenty-four-inch tinned-steel fish poacher for about fifty dollars. I raise the poaching rack off the floor of the pan with tuna cans, just as I do for the roasting pan, and cover the poacher with foil (with the rack sitting on the tuna cans, its handles surmount the top of the poacher and the lid no longer fits).

A fish poacher works beautifully for all but the largest fish; remember that you can have the fish store take the head and tail off if necessary. Set the poacher over two burners and make sure there is space between the sides of the poacher and the fish; a fish that is jammed in will take forever to steam. A fish poacher can of course be used to steam lots of different foods, but I never think of using it for anything but whole fish.

✳ BAMBOO STEAMERS

Early on in my testing I found that food typically takes about half again as long to steam in a bamboo steamer set over a wok as in a metal steamer. Since consistency of steaming times from steamer to steamer was a priority, I didn't use bamboo. I was also dismayed to find that no matter how careful I was, steaming in a wok inevitably removed the seasoning from the metal, and the wok rusted. Therefore, the steaming times in this book are for metal steamers only. However, as bamboo steamers are inexpensive, sturdy, easy to find, available in a variety of sizes, and so attractive that the food can even be served in them, you may want to use one anyway. Use the steaming times in the recipes and basic timing charts as a starting point but be aware that they won't be accurate.

✳ CONSISTENCY OF STEAMING TIMES IN DIFFERENT METAL STEAMERS

While metal steamers, as a group, give more consistent steaming times than bamboo, steaming times still do vary marginally among metal steamers. Some steamers seem to get hotter than others or to hold or conduct the heat better. While my Demeyere-Silvinox steamer, made of heavy-gauge stainless steel with a very good seal between steamer compartments, steams very fast, my aluminum stackable steamer works more slowly. The rate of steaming is certainly affected by the seal between the source of the steam and the steamer compartments, and by the fit of the lids; the timing may also be affected by the material the steamer is made of and even by its size. A steamer basket enclosed in a pot with a tight-fitting lid steams quickly because there's no loss of steam between the source (the simmering water) and the food. These variations in timing aren't critical; no cooking times are absolutely foolproof, and you'll get to know the personality of your steamer just as you get to know any piece of cooking equipment.

I used several different steamers for my testing, including pots covered with aluminum foil, as mentioned above. These steam more slowly than pots with lids because the seal is not as good. While steaming times varied slightly for some things, there wasn't a difference in the quality of the cooked food except with vegetables—which, as a rule, steam less consistently than other foods. While it's obvious to me that a vegetable will cook differently depending on season or its age, I'm continually amazed at how differently a vegetable can steam, even throughout the same season, and certainly in different steamers; I've had green beans that still weren't tender after twenty minutes and artichokes that took over an hour to cook. As a rule, I want to steam green vegetables fast, so I steam them in a steamer with a well-fitting lid. Fish, poultry, meats, and desserts, however, steam pretty much the same in all of my steamers, even the improvised ones.

✳ CHOOSING THE RIGHT EQUIPMENT

I can't point to any one piece of equipment as the best; I don't get everything I want in one steamer. I was fickle in my attentions and had brief love affairs with each pot: When I was testing whole fish, I adored my fish poacher, when testing leg of lamb, a large roasting pan with a rack was indispensable. Other steamers worked best for vegetables.

In my experience, the most important features of a steamer are its size and shape. I want a steamer to hold lots of different kinds of foods, including big things, and to have enough room between the bottom of the pot and the steamer rack so that I don't have to worry about the water evaporating. One of the advantages of steaming is that as long as the food is in one layer, the food cooks for the same length of time whether there's a lot of it or just one piece. That means that there's no advantage to buying a small steamer if you think you'll ever steam in larger quantities. An oval shape is more versatile than round. A shallow insert or pot is preferable to a deep one for steaming fish because it's very hard to get delicate fillets or steaks out of a deep pot in one piece. I prefer stainless steel to aluminum because aluminum discolors.

If I had to choose one steamer, I'd cheat. I'd buy one of the stackable steamers, preferably one with two compartments. But I'd also buy a roasting pan and a wire rack to do double duty for large foods.

The Finer Points of Steaming

✳ STEAMING WATER

The decision about how much water you need to put in the steamer is made as a compromise between how much space there is for water under the steamer rack and how long the food must steam. Optimally, you want to start with enough water so that you don't need to add more during steaming. (For this reason, I like stackable steamers with their deep steamer pots better than pasta cookers, which leave very little room for steaming water.) Long-cooking foods obviously require more water than quick-cooking foods. Also, water evaporates more rapidly from some steamers than from others, depending on how tight a seal there is between steamer compartment and pot and how tight-fitting the lid is.

I clocked the rate of evaporation of simmering water in a light-weight, stainless steel, nine-and-a-half-inch pot with a reasonably tight-fitting lid to get an idea of how fast the water evaporates. I found that three cups of water (a depth of five eighths of an inch) evaporated in fifty minutes, while four cups (seven eighths of an inch) took eighty minutes to evaporate.

Remember that the same quantity of water will evaporate much more quickly in a larger pot—or roasting pan—especially if covered with aluminum foil instead of a lid. You'll also find that some foods, whole chicken in particular, add juices and fat to the pot almost as quickly as the water evaporates. (Be careful when cooking duck and goose, which give off a lot of fat; the level of liquid won't go down much, but what's in the steamer will be fat, not water.) If the water level gets low, simply add more boiling water to the steamer. Whatever steamer pot you're using, it makes sense to have another pot of boiling water on the ready when steaming long-cooking foods.

For pots covered with aluminum foil, my suspicion is that as the water level gets very low, the food steams more slowly. Therefore, I try to keep at least half an inch of water in my steamers.

A good trick to keep from scorching the steamer pot is to put a couple of glass marbles in the bottom. When the water level gets low, the marbles will begin to jump around and make noise.

✳ PUTTING FOOD INTO THE STEAMER

There are two ways of getting the food into the steamer. If you're using a steamer unit with a compartment or insert—as opposed to a collapsible basket or a rack in a pan—arrange the food in the compartment or insert outside of the steamer, while the water heats in the pot. When the water has come to a boil, place the compartment or insert over or into the pot, cover, adjust the heat so that the water simmers briskly, and start steaming.

It's more difficult to transport a flimsy steamer basket or a rack loaded with food to the steamer pot. It works better to bring the water up to a boil with the basket or rack already in the steamer. Then turn off the heat so that you don't burn yourself and put the food on the basket or rack. Cover the pan, bring the water back to a boil, adjust the heat to a simmer, and start steaming. (Individual chapters give further instructions for handling specific foods.)

✳ TAKING FOOD OUT OF THE STEAMER

The most important point to make about taking the food out of the steamer is to beware of the steam: Steam burns badly. Always open the lid away from you and let some of the steam dissipate before looking into the steamer or putting your hands in it. Oven mitts will protect your hands.

When removing food from a steamer fitted with a compartment or insert, simply remove the entire compartment or insert holding the cooked food from the pot and set it on a plate to catch the drips. Then remove the food. If you're using a basket or rack, it's easier to leave the basket or rack in the steamer pot and remove the food from there.

A pancake turner is practical for removing cooked fish steaks and fillets and small pieces of meat and poultry from the steamer, and even custard molds, if the turner is sturdy enough. Firm meat and poultry can also be moved with sturdy kitchen tongs. A whole chicken can be picked up with two large forks, or by inserting a wooden spoon into the cavity and lifting. Move large pieces of meat with carving forks. Remove vegetables with a slotted spoon, to allow the moisture that condenses on them to drain.

✳ FLAVORING THE FOOD DURING STEAMING

Manière wrote that the steaming liquid doesn't flavor the food steamed above it; he liked to steam on a bed of aromatic vegetables and herbs so the food was actually in contact with the flavoring agent. My experience is that a bed of aromatics does indeed flavor far more effectively than a steaming liquid, but the liquid can impart flavor to mild-tasting food if it's strongly flavored enough.

Asian cuisine traditionally adds flavor by steaming the food on a deep plate with seasonings and herbs. The cooking juices are captured on the plate, while the food absorbs the flavor of the seasonings. The juices make a thin, tasty sauce. This method is possible in a bamboo steamer because the bamboo absorbs the condensation of the steam that would otherwise drip back into the plate and dilute the sauce. Manière stuck to his French culinary roots and got the same result by wrapping the food in aluminum foil, *en papillote* (see page 166). This system works in a metal steamer, for the foil protects the juices from the condensation that forms on the inside of a metal lid.

(see page 166)

Using the Steamer in Ways You May Not Have Considered

Once I really got steaming, one or another of my steamers was glued to the stove at all times, leaving its place only to be washed. I tried doing everything in the steamer and found it useful in ways I hadn't at first imagined.

I often put together quick and very simple steamed meals for myself and my young daughter, using a single steamer with one or two stackable compartments or two steamers, depending on what I was making. I started by steaming the foods that took the longest, adding the foods with shorter cooking times after an appropriate interval. I might start with small new potatoes, which take about twenty-five minutes, in the bottom steaming compartment, add the green beans fifteen minutes later, and then steam salmon fillets in the upper compartment during the final seven to eight minutes.

Steaming chicken or meat gave me a flavorful steaming liquid to play with. I might steam one or more vegetables in a second compartment or in another steamer while the meat or poultry cooked, and then purée the cooked vegetable with some of the meat or poultry steaming liquid to make soup, a vegetable purée, or a sauce to accompany the chicken or meat (see pages 100–102).

(see pages 100–102)

✻ REHEATING AND DEFROSTING
Other people use microwaves for reheating and defrosting; I use the steamer. It's excellent for reheating leftover fish, meats and poultry, vegetables, grains, burritos, pasta, stuffings—in short, practically anything—without drying the food out, as the oven will do. Fish, meat, poultry, and vegetables can be steamed as is. Foods such as grains, burritos, stuffings, and custards, which must be protected from the condensed steam that drips from the lid, should be wrapped in foil or steamed in a foil-covered heatproof container. I can make a large batch of rice at the beginning of the week and reheat it, covered, in the steamer throughout the week without the rice ever getting soggy. I use the same method selectively for defrosting frozen cooked foods such as sausages, chicken, and small pieces of meat.

✳ STEAMING FROZEN FISH FILLETS AND STEAKS

Manière's method also enables us to cook frozen fish in the steamer. I've tried this with fish fillets and steaks. Put the frozen fish in the steamer compartment and steam until cooked through as usual. You'll need to steam the fish one and a half to two times the Basic Steaming Time (see the chart on page 112) for that particular fish. Be careful not to overcook the fish; frozen fish dries out more quickly than fresh.

✳ KEEPING HOT FOOD WARM

Many recipes call for keeping food warm while you finish a sauce or an accompanying vegetable. Typically, we cover the food and set it aside, where it doesn't really stay warm, or put it in a low oven, where it can dry out. Manière kept poultry, meats (even rare meat), whole fish, and dense root vegetables such as carrots and potatoes warm without cooking further by placing them, sometimes wrapped in aluminum foil, in a steamer compartment set over low heat, with the lid slightly ajar. The only exceptions are green vegetables and fish steaks and fillets, which will continue to cook if held this way.

I use his system when I have roasted meat or poultry that needs to stay warm while I deglaze the roasting pan to make a sauce, to let steamed meat, poultry, or whole fish or roasted meat or poultry rest before carving, or when I'm reducing the steaming liquid to make a sauce for steamed meat, poultry, or fish. In this last case, I keep a pot of boiling water ready. Then, when the food is cooked, I pour the steaming liquid into another pan to reduce it and pour the boiling water in the steamer to keep the food warm.

Notes on Ingredients

Steaming doesn't transform food; rather, it uncovers its natural essence. Therefore, steaming demands a higher quality of food than other cooking techniques may allow. I found this out the hard way when I steamed a thawed frozen turkey one day. The flavor was unpleasantly strong, and so I thought I didn't like steamed turkey. A second turkey, however, tasted much better, and I realized that the problem was in the bird, not the steaming. If it had been under a crisp, tasty roasted skin, perhaps stuffed with a flavorful herb butter, I might not have noticed that the flesh of the turkey tasted a bit strong, but steamed, the bird didn't have a chance. This is doubly critical with fish, which has a shorter shelf life than meat or poultry. Manière said it beautifully: The steamer doesn't betray the flavors of the foods we offer it. It's a cuisine that speaks the truth. Its strength is in the way it exalts the flavor of food, and so it reveals the bad as surely as it shows off the good. Steaming obliges us always to choose the best vegetables, fish, poultry, and meats.

There are a few special ingredients that come up throughout the book and are worth discussing here in more detail.

✳ CRÈME FRAÎCHE

Crème fraîche is a thick, tangy, ivory-colored cultured cream that is used lavishly in classic French cooking. The joy of crème fraîche is its flavor; where regular heavy cream, particularly if ultra-pasteurized, has a mildly sweet, unprepossessing dairy flavor, crème fraîche is boldly rich and nutty with a mild acidity that gives food, particularly sauces, another dimension. In France, crème fraîche is sold everywhere, from special dairy stores to supermarkets. In America, you can buy it in specialty food stores and even some supermarkets, or you can easily make it yourself (see page 297).

Manière used crème fraîche in a great many of his recipes, more often than regular heavy cream. Crème fraîche really makes a difference in Manière's sauces; a sauce finished with crème fraîche has more life and more flavor than one made with regular cream. For other recipes, such as his potato-leek soup, both the crème fraîche and heavy cream versions are delicious. Adding lemon juice to heavy cream approximates the taste of crème fraîche by adding acidity; in most of these recipes, except where the quantity is very small, or there is already sufficient lemon juice in the dish, I've suggested a substitute quantity of heavy cream plus lemon juice as an alternative. For recipes that use only a little crème fraîche, the heavy cream plus lemon substitute or the heavy cream alone usually works fine. But for those that use a substantial amount of crème fraîche, and for the sauces in particular, it's worth buying or making your own.

✳ FROMAGE BLANC

Fromage blanc, or "white cheese," is a spoonable fresh cheese, something like cottage cheese but much smoother, available all over France. The French even sugar it and eat it as dessert. It can be made from whole or low-fat milk. Manière used full-fat *fromage blanc* in some poultry stuffings and nonfat *fromage blanc* as a low-fat alternative to cream in sauces and in vegetable flans and soufflés. Puréed cottage cheese is a good substitute, as is hoop cheese, a smooth fresh cheese available at some specialty food stores.

Any good produce store in France is stocked with at least those fresh herbs necessary to make the classic French combination *fines herbes:* tarragon, chives, parsley, chervil, and sometimes thyme. Ten years ago, it was hard to find anything beyond fresh parsley in American supermarkets, but today, with the exception of chervil, you're likely to find these herbs, perhaps even year-round, in your supermarket.

Fresh herbs should be wrapped in a damp paper towel and refrigerated; store parsley and basil like flowers in the refrigerator, with their stem ends in a glass of water and their tops covered with a plastic bag. Don't wash fresh herbs until you are ready to use them.

Fresh herbs are a delight to use—I find them indispensable for uncooked dishes—but dried herbs can be used in some of Manière's recipes as well. Some herbs, such as parsley, chives, and basil, don't dry well, losing their flavor; for these herbs it makes more sense to substitute what is available fresh (chopped scallion green for chives, fresh mint for basil), with the understanding that the finished dish will taste different, than to use a dried herb. Fresh chervil, for instance, a light green herb with delicate, faintly licorice-tasting fronds that blossom in tiny white flowers, is practically impossible to find unless you grow it yourself. I use a combination of chopped fresh tarragon and chopped fresh parsley rather than resorting to dried chervil.

Other herbs, such as thyme, tarragon, sage, marjoram, and oregano, do dry well, and you can use them in Manière's recipes as long as they're not so old that they've lost their flavor (most lose their flavor within six months). Dried herbs are stronger than their fresh counterparts; the standard proportion for substituting is one third the quantity of dried to fresh—one teaspoon dried thyme, for example, equals one tablespoon chopped fresh.

Fresh thyme is sold in large bunches, and unless I'm cooking a lot, I can't use it up before it blackens. So instead I dry it by hanging it by the window in my kitchen. Once it is dried, I store it in the refrigerator in a glass container with a good seal. Thyme dried this way has better flavor than most commercial dried thyme.

Manière often used fresh herbs as a bed for steaming fish, poultry, or meat. In this instance, dried herbs can be substituted for the fresh; the recipes give the information you'll need to do so.

A Brief Note on Measurements

The French don't use cups and tablespoons for measuring as we do in America; they measure liquid in liters and parts thereof, and they weigh dry ingredients. A liter is very close to a quart, and weight measurements are easily recalculated in cups; except in baking, a little bit over or a little bit under isn't critical. I had difficulty with one measurement that came up over and over in Manière's recipes: *cuillère à soupe,* or "soup spoon." This is often translated as a tablespoon. I found, however, when I was having trouble with a sauce, that a French soup spoon actually holds one and a half tablespoons of liquid. One-half-tablespoon measures are sometimes hard to find, but in using these recipes, if you don't have a half-tablespoon measure, simply remember that one and a half teaspoons is the same amount.

VEGETABLE

FIRST

COURSES

AND

SIDE DISHES

n the world of food, vegetables are the flowers." Jacques Manière often quoted this line, though he confessed he could no longer remember the author. He wrote that vegetables are as delicate, fragile, and multihued as flowers and should be as fresh. He had as little use for tasteless, underripe vegetables as for pretentious hothouse flowers, winter roses with no scent and a high price tag that have never known true soil or sunlight and only look real. He loved sturdy flowers toughened by a strong wind and earth-laden vegetables grown in the open field.

It's no wonder that Manière, a man who had such a passion for vegetables, was captivated by steaming, which is the perfect way to cook vegetables. Not only does steaming rob vegetables of fewer nutrients than any other cooking method apart from the microwave, but the subtlety and complexity of flavor that emerges is amazing; the dishes made from the recipes in this chapter gave me an experience of flavor for which years of cooking hadn't prepared me. Suddenly I tasted clearly the interplay of sweetness and bitterness in a sweet pepper, the hot spiciness and delicate sweetness of cabbage, and the bitter, salty, sweet richness of an artichoke. Steaming allows the pure taste of vegetables to speak for themselves; because their essence is so delicate and thus easily masked, it takes a cooking method—like steaming—that adds nothing to bring their exquisite flavor to life.

Manière gave us some superb recipes for vegetable soups, side dishes, hot and cold salads, first courses, and some dishes that are substantial enough to make a main course. None of these recipes is what people think of as fancy French food, yet none would be out of place at the most elegant table. They're all rooted in a tradition of great, simple French food and good cooking sense. Some are easy and quick enough to make for everyday, while others are more time-consuming. Green cabbage, steamed to a buttery sweetness and then tossed with cream, shallots, and fresh herbs (see page 53), takes under fifteen minutes to put together. A profusion of multi-colored vegetables, steamed and then marinated overnight in olive oil, garlic, coriander, and thyme (see page 74), takes more time but is not at all fussy. None of Manière's recipes is complicated. All speak directly, clearly, and simply and all have that quality of brilliant, jewel-like uniqueness and purity that is his hallmark.

Many of these recipes are practical for vegetarian meals. Manière served Artichokes Henry IV (page 34), artichoke bottoms stuffed with chopped mushrooms and topped with a poached egg, as a starter, but it's substantial enough to be a vegetarian main course. Without the ham, his Carrot Terrine (page 57) and Gratin of Endive (page 68) are also nourishing enough to eat as vegetarian main courses. The celery root, garlic, and spinach flans (see pages 66, 78, and 93) make tasty first courses—and are even more elegant sauced with a Chervil Butter Sauce (page 152), a Beurre Blanc (page 120), or a sauce made from a puréed steamed vegetable of contrasting color, as described on page 101.

Because vegetables are such a natural for steaming and Manière was so enchanted by them, this chapter is filled with useful information about how to cook them. He gave steaming times for many vegetables (see Using the Basic Vegetable Timing Charts, below), and I have added basic methods for cutting, steaming, and serving them. There are directions for finishing vegetables quickly with cream or butter. And there is additional information about vegetable purées, vegetable flans, soups, sauces, and grilled and stuffed vegetables at the end of the chapter (see pages 100–104).

Using the Basic Vegetable Timing Charts

Manière gave basic steaming times for all vegetables used in the recipes, and more that are not. I've added timings to cover other vegetables available to us in America. I also give timings for different cuts and sizes of vegetables. The timing charts are sprinkled through the chapter and, along with the general information about the vegetables and serving suggestions, introduce each vegetable. Steaming times in the charts are for vegetables arranged in roughly a single layer (see also Steaming Vegetables in Quantity on page 24).

I give a range of steaming times for most vegetables because vegetables differ so greatly in texture depending on age and size, and because individual preferences vary. Cooking times for vegetables have much greater ranges than those for fish, meat, or poultry. A really fresh stalk of asparagus need hardly be cooked at all, while one that is less fresh needs more time to develop flavor. Older turnips and celery root need more steaming time than younger vegetables and, in fact, if very woody, may never soften. I steam root vegetables to a softer state for a purée than if they are to be tossed in butter with steamed peas and pearl onions. Some vegetables, such as leeks and beets, get sweeter as they cook, and so I cook them until they are quite soft.

Refreshing Vegetables

Green vegetables can be refreshed by running them under cold water after steaming to set their color and keep them from cooking further. Almost any vegetable can be refreshed after steaming if it is to be served cold. Two exceptions are potatoes, which absorb water when refreshed, and asparagus, which loses its flavor in the wash.

If you are steaming a green vegetable for a dinner party, it's practical to steam it several hours ahead and refresh and refrigerate it until serving time. Then, just before serving, rewarm it quickly in the steamer or heat it in a little butter or olive oil in a frying pan over medium heat until warmed through.

To refresh vegetables after steaming, take the steamer rack out of the steamer and put it in the sink under a stream of cold water. Or transfer the vegetables to a bowl of cold water with a few ice cubes and let them sit in the water until cold, adding more cold water or ice as needed.

Finishing Vegetables with Butter or a Vinaigrette

The charts of basic steaming times give you the freedom to go beyond Manière's recipes. On a busy night, steam a vegetable and glaze it quickly in a pan with melted butter or toss with a simple vinaigrette. Use Manière's Basic Vinaigrette (page 26) or one of the three on page 24. Each of these three recipes makes one quarter cup vinaigrette, enough to lightly dress one pound of steamed vegetables. You can add a chopped fresh herb to any of them; use one to two teaspoons of chopped fresh parsley, chives, basil, chervil, or tarragon, or about half a teaspoon of the stronger or resinous herbs, such as thyme, rosemary, oregano, or marjoram. Don't add the vinaigrette to green vegetables until just before serving; the acid will turn the bright green color to drab olive. The vinaigrettes hold a week in the refrigerator.

Use Manière's method for making a vinaigrette (see page 26), or make the vinaigrette in a jar: Combine all the ingredients in the jar, cover, and shake to emulsify. For the red wine vinegar vinaigrette, shake the mustard with the vinegar before adding the oil.

LEMON VINAIGRETTE
Whisk together 1 tablespoon fresh lemon juice with ⅛ teaspoon salt and a pinch of freshly ground pepper. Whisk in 3 tablespoons olive oil.

RED WINE VINEGAR–MUSTARD VINAIGRETTE
Whisk together 1 teaspoon Dijon mustard, 1 tablespoon red wine vinegar, ⅛ teaspoon salt, and a pinch of freshly ground pepper. Whisk in 3 tablespoons olive or vegetable oil.

BALSAMIC VINAIGRETTE
Whisk together 1 tablespoon plus 1 teaspoon balsamic vinegar, ¼ teaspoon salt, and a pinch of freshly ground pepper. Whisk in 3 tablespoons olive or vegetable oil.

Finishing Vegetables with Cream

Manière sauced steamed vegetables such as zucchini (see page 96) and cabbage (see page 53) with reduced cream, fresh herbs, and chopped shallots. Not only are the vegetables more finished and richer this way, but they can also double as a sauce for steamed poultry or fish as Manière did with zucchini, saucing chicken. Any vegetable can be steamed and finished in this way.

Steaming Vegetables in Quantity

The basic vegetable timing charts throughout this chapter are for vegetables steamed in a single layer, except for those vegetables, such as greens or sliced cabbage, that would never be steamed in such a small quantity. Steaming in a single layer was practical for Manière because he used a large oval two-tiered steamer that held a lot of vegetables, even if in a single layer. For those of us using a small steamer or collapsible steamer basket, to steam a large quantity of vegetables (enough for four people), you'll likely need to pile the vegetables deeply in the steamer.

The steaming time is often, but not always, longer for vegetables steamed in quantity, because the steam doesn't penetrate as effectively. Foods hidden underneath other foods and insulated from the steam take longer to cook. Vegetables like green beans or carrot slices, which fall naturally into a compact shape, take longer to cook in quantity. Sliced zucchini also takes longer, because the vegetable slices form an almost impenetrable mass as they soften.

The shape of broccoli and cauliflower florets and potatoes means that there is naturally space open between them, and their steaming time is the same whether cooked in a single layer or in quantity. The density of the particular vegetable is also likely to have something to do with how the steaming time changes when steamed in quantity.

For many vegetables throughout this chapter, I have included notes about steaming vegetables in quantity (for four or more people, in more than one layer) so that you can adjust the steaming time accordingly. Even with the adjustment, the timing may vary depending on the age of the vegetables and on your steamer. Some vegetables, such as greens or green beans, need to be stirred halfway through the steaming time because the vegetables at the top cook faster than the vegetables underneath; this is noted where appropriate.

If you're not sure about the timing when steaming vegetables in quantity, steam them for the basic time given and then check them; if they're not cooked through, steam them half again as long. If the vegetables still aren't cooked, steam half again as long, one more time (so that the steaming time has been doubled). Most vegetables should be cooked at this point; if not, just keep steaming.

Steaming Several Vegetables Together

You may also want to steam a number of different vegetables in the steamer at the same time. In general, when doing so, start the longest-cooking vegetables first and add the other vegetables in order of their length of steaming time. If there are few enough vegetables that they lie in a single layer, each will steam exactly as it does when steamed alone, although you should add about thirty seconds to the steaming time each time you open the steamer. If the steamer is crowded and vegetables are piled on top of one other, the timing is trickier, because some vegetables steam more slowly when steamed in quantity, as mentioned above. It's possible to adjust for that, however; check the section on steaming in quantity for each vegetable you are using and follow the longer steaming time in the chart, if appropriate.

For example, I steam a combination of half a pound each of green beans and quarter-inch-thick slices of carrots, three quarters of a pound of cauliflower florets, and a quarter pound of broccoli florets, to serve four people. Broccoli and cauliflower steam the same in quantity as in a single layer; eight minutes for cauliflower and six to eight minutes for broccoli. Carrots and green beans take longer to steam in quantity; carrots take fifteen minutes, beans take twelve. Logically, then, I start steaming the carrots first, adding the beans after a few minutes and then the cauliflower and broccoli for the last eight minutes. In practice, however, I'm not so precise (nor was Manière, who often steamed a variety of vegetables together, all for the same length of time): The steaming times for the carrots and beans are close enough that I steam them together for four minutes and then add the other vegetables and steam eight more minutes.

If the timings of the different vegetables I choose are within a few minutes of each other, I pick an average time and put them all into the steamer together. Remember that steaming times are guidelines, not absolutes; if it's critical that the vegetables be cooked just right, you may want to steam each separately.

BASIC VINAIGRETTE

La Vinaigrette

This is Manière's simplest vinaigrette, along with variations. He directed us to dissolve the salt in the vinegar before adding the oil; once added, the oil coats the salt so that it won't dissolve properly.

MAKES ³/₄ CUP

3 tablespoons red or white wine vinegar

¼ teaspoon salt

½ cup olive, peanut, or vegetable oil, or a combination

⅛ teaspoon freshly ground pepper

 Combine the vinegar and salt in a medium bowl and whisk to dissolve the salt. Whisk in the oil in a steady stream, and then the pepper.

VINAIGRETTE FOR ASPARAGUS
Whisk 1 very fresh egg yolk—or 1½ tablespoons crème fraîche or 1½ tablespoons heavy cream mixed with ½ teaspoon fresh lemon juice—into the vinegar-salt mixture, and reduce the oil by 1½ tablespoons.

SAUCE RAVIGOTE

(for cold meats and fish or a warm French potato salad)

To the finished vinaigrette, add 1½ tablespoons chopped shallots or onion, 1 teaspoon tiny capers, 2 anchovies ground in a mortar and pestle or finely chopped (optional), and 1½ tablespoons mixed chopped fresh chives, tarragon, and chervil, if available. If using the anchovy, cut the salt to ⅛ teaspoon.

This makes enough vinaigrette to dress a potato salad to serve 8 to 10 people: Cut up and steam 5 pounds red-skinned new potatoes in their skins, according to the timings in the chart on page 89. Dress with the vinaigrette while still warm. If you like your potato salad vinegary, add another teaspoon of capers and another tablespoon of vinegar to the vinaigrette.

MAYONNAISE

La Mayonnaise

Manière wrote that cold is the enemy of a mayonnaise: It is critical that the egg yolk, oil, and bowl all be no cooler than about 65°F to 70°F, or cool room temperature.

MAKES ABOUT 1 CUP

1 large egg yolk

½ teaspoon Dijon mustard

1 teaspoon fresh lemon juice

¼ teaspoon salt

⅛ teaspoon freshly ground pepper, preferably white

¾ cup vegetable or olive oil

 Put the egg yolk in a medium bowl and whisk in the mustard, lemon juice, salt, and pepper. Whisk in the oil, drop by drop at first until thick and blended, and then in a steady stream until emulsified.

If the mayonnaise is too thick, thin it to the desired consistency with a teaspoon or so of boiling water.

Serve immediately, or press plastic wrap onto the surface of the mayonnaise and refrigerate for up to 2 days.

ARTICHOKES

Steamed artichokes are divine—I'll never boil an artichoke again. Steaming brings out their complex, nutty flavor, uncovering contrasting layers of sweetness and bitterness. Serve whole steamed artichokes with melted butter, Manière's Basic Vinaigrette (page 26), Mayonnaise (page 27), Béarnaise Sauce (page 35), or Lemon Butter Sauce (page 40), or any of the three vinaigrettes on page 24. Artichoke bottoms make graceful edible holders for poached eggs in Artichokes Henry IV (page 34) and for a stuffing in Artichoke Bottoms Barigoule (page 33).

In France, Manière could buy three different varieties of artichokes: the large, rounded *artichaut de Bretagne,* slightly flattened on top, with a large base and leaves tightly curved in against the body, and two pointy, open-leaved varieties (the leaves open out from the heart like an open rose). One of these is the violet artichoke of Provence—so called because the artichokes are a lavender color—which the French adore to eat raw when small and tender (see Artichokes à la Grecque, page 32). The Bretagne artichokes have particularly large bottoms and Manière would certainly have used them for recipes in which the bottoms are stuffed, such as Stuffed Artichoke Bottoms Barigoule and Artichokes Henry IV. Our California artichokes are similar to the rounded Bretagnes but have smaller bottoms; the visual effect is different but the flavor is just as good.

✳ ARTICHOKE HEARTS AND BOTTOMS

The terms *artichoke hearts* and *artichoke bottoms* are often used interchangeably, but they actually refer to different parts of the vegetable and call for different methods of preparation. Artichoke hearts are the entire central portions of baby artichokes, including the chokes and light-colored central leaves, all of which are edible. Artichoke bottoms are the trimmed bases of mature globe artichokes: The stems, inedible fuzzy chokes, and leaves are completely trimmed, leaving just the round bottom.

✳ ARTICHOKE PURÉE

Manière was a practical chef and wasted nothing. For artichoke purée, usually made just with the puréed bottoms, Manière used the entire vegetable: He steamed whole large artichokes, then pulled off the leaves and scraped the chokes from the bottoms. He scraped the pulp from the steamed leaves with a spoon and puréed the pulp along with the bottoms. (You can finish an artichoke purée with a little butter, olive oil, or cream, or with fresh cheese, as for Manière's Sunchoke Mousse on page 234.) He also used this pulp from the leaves on its own to make low-fat Artichoke Mayonnaise (page 31). You can use artichoke stems in a purée as well; pass them through a food mill after steaming to remove the fibers.

✳ PREPARING ARTICHOKES FOR STEAMING

The cut parts of artichokes blacken quickly when exposed to air. Rubbing lemon juice over the cut surfaces prevents this. Before you begin to prepare artichokes, whether they are to be steamed whole or trimmed to make hearts or bottoms, fill a bowl with water, cut a lemon in half, squeeze the juice into the water, and drop the lemon halves into the bowl. As you trim the artichokes, rub all the cut edges often with another lemon half. Hold them in the lemon water until ready to steam.

Whole Globe Artichokes Pull off the small, dark green leaves at the base of each artichoke and trim the stem close to the base so that the artichoke will stand securely. Or break the stem off entirely with a quick snap and trim the cut end. Cut off the top third of the artichoke so that the pale, purplish-white center leaves are visible. Cut off the sharp tips of the remaining leaves with kitchen scissors so you or your guests don't stab your fingers on the spines. Rub the cut parts of the artichoke with a lemon half and hold in a bowl of lemon water until ready to steam.

To cook, stand the artichokes upside down on the steamer rack so that condensation from the steam doesn't collect in the leaves. Steam whole artichokes until a leaf detaches easily and the bottoms are tender when pierced with a knife. Whole artichokes and bottoms needn't be refreshed.

Whole medium artichokes (³/₄ pound or under)...	25 to 30 minutes
Whole large artichokes (over ³/₄ pound)...	30 to 40 minutes

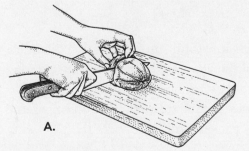
A.

Artichoke Bottoms To make artichoke bottoms from globe artichokes, snap off the stem of each one close to the base. (Reserve the stems to steam for purée, as on page 100.) Pull off all the outer green leaves until just the central light green cone of leaves remains. Lay the artichoke on its side on a cutting board. Use a large knife to cut off the remaining leaves just above the base (A) to expose the fuzzy choke. Rub all over with a lemon half. Using

B.

a sharp paring knife, trim off all the dark green outer skin from the sides and bottom of the artichoke to expose the whitish bottom (B), rubbing the cut edges often with the lemon as you work (C). Trim the bottom to make it smooth and round. Hold in a bowl of lemon water until ready to steam.

Steam artichoke bottoms, with the chokes, until the point of a small knife penetrates with no resistance. Scrape out the choke with a small spoon (D). (Steaming the bottoms with the chokes prevents blackening.) Artichoke bottoms needn't be refreshed.

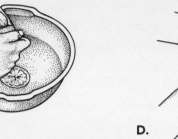

C.

D.

Artichoke bottoms..20 to 25 minutes

Hearts from Baby Artichokes To make artichoke hearts from baby artichokes, cut about an inch off the top of each one. Trim the bottom of the stem. Pull off the outer green leaves to expose the central cone of tender, yellow-green leaves. Then use a paring knife to trim all of the dark green outer skin from the base and the remaining stem. Rub all over with a lemon half, and hold in a bowl of lemon water until ready to steam.

Steam baby artichokes until the point of a knife penetrates with no resistance.

Baby artichoke hearts...20 to 25 minutes

✳ **STEAMING WHOLE ARTICHOKES IN QUANTITY**

To steam whole artichokes for four, use either a collapsible steamer basket or a vegetable steamer with an insert. If steaming more than four, if the artichokes are not tightly packed together and jammed against the sides of the steamer, the timing is the same as in the chart. Tightly packed artichokes take ten to twenty minutes longer to steam.

ARTICHOKE MAYONNAISE

Sauce à l'Artichaut

A clever French chef throws away very little food. Manière didn't like to waste the leaves from artichokes trimmed for their bottoms, so he made this lemony, low-fat sauce for a salad of steamed artichoke hearts and sweetbreads, using just the pulp scraped from the steamed leaves. Next time you need steamed artichoke bottoms for a recipe such as Artichokes Henry IV (page 34), take advantage of all parts of the artichokes: Steam them whole, then pull off the leaves and save them for this sauce. Trim the bottoms to smooth them and use as you normally would. If you haven't the patience to scrape the leaves, you can use puréed steamed artichoke bottoms and stems; be sure to pass the stems through a food mill to get rid of the tough fibers. This sauce is also delicious on sweetbreads, hot or cold steamed chicken, fish (particularly salmon), or veal, or serve it with hot or cold steamed artichokes or as a vegetable dip.

MAKES ABOUT 1⅓ CUPS

Pulp from the leaves of 4 steamed globe
   artichokes or ⅔ cup puréed artichoke
   bottoms and stems (from about 3
   steamed artichokes)
3 tablespoons low-fat fromage blanc or
   cottage cheese
Juice of 1 lemon (about 3 tablespoons)
1 teaspoon Dijon mustard
1 large egg yolk
1½ tablespoons olive oil
1½ tablespoons vegetable oil
Rounded ¼ teaspoon salt
¼ teaspoon freshly ground pepper

Put all of the ingredients in the bowl of a food processor and purée until smooth. Serve immediately, or press plastic wrap directly onto the surface of the mayonnaise and refrigerate for up to 2 days.

ARTICHOKES À LA GRECQUE
Artichauts à la Grecque

Manière took a typical Provençal starter of artichokes braised and marinated in a white wine and olive oil brine and made it better by steaming the artichokes above the brine, allowing them to develop their own rich, nutty flavor before they are marinated. The salty acidity of the brine is an exquisite counterpoint to the artichoke and doesn't muddy its taste. The coriander seeds soften enough during the steaming so that they can be eaten; they pop gently in the mouth with a burst of spice.

Traditionally, this dish is made with the violet artichokes of Provence called *poivrade,* harvested when they are young and small and the chokes are still completely edible. This is one of the rare vegetables that the French eat raw, sprinkled with salt and served with a vinaigrette or with a sauce speckled with crushed peppercorns (also called a *poivrade*). We sometimes get these little artichokes in America, but you can substitute baby artichokes in this recipe. *Poivrade* can be tough to find, even in France; Manière gave us the option of using globe artichoke bottoms, cut into eighths.

The artichokes must marinate twenty-four hours before serving. They hold three days, covered, in the refrigerator. For the brine, use three to four cups water, depending on how much liquid comfortably fits under the steaming rack. (My pasta cooker can hold only 3 cups water along with the wine and oil; any more and the simmering brine bubbles up over the rack.)

SERVES 4 AS A COLD FIRST COURSE

3 pounds poivrade or baby artichokes or
   8 medium globe artichokes

1 lemon

BRINE

1 cup olive oil

1 cup dry white wine

½ teaspoon fresh thyme leaves or
   ¼ teaspoon dried thyme

2 well-rounded teaspoons salt

3 to 4 cups of water (see headnote)

½ teaspoon black peppercorns
½ teaspoon coriander seeds

Pare baby artichokes for artichoke hearts, as directed on page 30, or globe artichokes for bottoms, as directed on page 29, holding the artichokes in lemon water while you work. Scrape the chokes out of the raw bottoms with a spoon. Cut artichoke hearts in half; cut bottoms into 8 wedges each. Hold the artichokes in the lemon water until ready to steam.

Make the brine: Combine the olive oil, wine, thyme, salt, and water in the steamer pot and bring to a brisk simmer. Put the artichokes on the steamer rack and set it over the simmering liquid. Sprinkle the peppercorns and coriander seeds over the artichokes. Cover the steamer pot and steam until the artichokes are tender, 20 to 25 minutes.

Remove from the heat, remove the lid, and let the artichokes cool for about 20 minutes. (During this time, the herb-flavored oil will rise to the surface of the steaming liquid.)

When the artichokes are cool, transfer them, along with the peppercorns and coriander seeds, to a serving bowl. Use a ladle to scoop up the oil from the surface of the steaming liquid and pour the oil over the artichokes. Cover and refrigerate for 24 hours. Bring to room temperature before serving.

STUFFED ARTICHOKE BOTTOMS BARIGOULE

Artichauts Façon Barigoule

Here, Manière has given us a brilliant variation on a classic French dish of stuffed artichoke bottoms. The traditional recipe has its roots in the peasant cookery of Provence, in a simple dish of violet artichokes (see page 32) stewed in olive oil and thyme. French haute cuisine transformed this relatively lean dish into a rich, more luxurious presentation, stuffing large artichoke bottoms with a ham and mushroom mixture and then braising them in stock.

Manière, in turn, transformed the classic by cleverly imprisoning a garlic-and-herb-flavored meat filling between two artichoke bottoms. The compact bundle is wrapped in fatback and steamed. The filling impregnates the artichoke with rich, meaty flavor, while the artichoke in turn perfumes the filling—and nothing is lost to a braising liquid.

If you can't buy ground veal and/or pork, pulse small cubes of lean meat in the food processor to grind your own. Manière wrapped each stuffed artichoke either with a thin strip of pork fatback or in a square of *crépine*—what we call caul fat—the fatty membrane that lines the stomach of a pig. Your butcher may have fatback; ask him to cut it very thin on the slicing machine. He may also be able to order caul fat. If you can't find either, use bacon, which adds a wonderful salty, smoky flavor that goes particularly well with the artichokes. The fatty wrapping keeps the artichokes moist during steaming. It can be removed before serving or eaten along with the artichokes.

(continued)

8 large globe artichokes

1 lemon

BARIGOULE STUFFING

7 ounces lean ground veal

7 ounces lean ground pork

½ cup fresh bread crumbs

1 clove garlic, minced

1½ tablespoons crème fraîche or heavy
cream

1 large egg

2 teaspoons chopped parsley, fresh
tarragon, or a combination of other
chopped fresh herbs (such as chervil,
thyme, and/or chives)

½ teaspoon salt

¼ teaspoon freshly ground pepper

Salt

Four 10-inch squares caul fat (see
headnote), four 12-inch-long and about
2-inch-wide strips fatback (see
headnote), or 4 strips bacon

Kitchen twine (if using fatback or bacon)

Steamer pot with insert, stackable
steamer, pasta cooker, roasting pan with
wire rack, or collapsible steamer basket

 Pare the artichokes to make artichoke bottoms, as directed on page 29, and scrape out the chokes with a spoon. Hold them in a bowl of lemon water until ready to steam.

Make the stuffing: Combine all of the ingredients in a bowl. Mix well with your hands or a fork.

Remove the artichoke bottoms from the lemon water and pat dry with paper towels. Place on a work surface, rounded sides down, and lightly sprinkle with salt. Divide the filling among 4 of the bottoms, mounding it in the centers, and cover with the remaining bottoms, rounded sides up. Wrap each package in a square of caul fat, or wrap each around its "equator" with a strip of fatback or bacon. Tie a piece of kitchen twine around the packages if using fatback or bacon, tying the string on top to hold the bottoms together.

Put the artichoke bottoms on the steamer rack, place over simmering water, cover, and steam until cooked through, about 30 minutes.

Remove from the steamer. Remove the string and remove the caul fat, fatback, or bacon wrapping if you like. Serve hot.

ARTICHOKES HENRY IV

Artichauts Henri IV

Manière wrote that although the length of this recipe seems intimidating, it's quicker to make than to explain. And, in any case, he assured us, such an elegant dish will get rave reviews. Plump poached eggs, sauced with a fresh tarragon Béarnaise, sit on a silken bed of creamy mushrooms in artichoke bottoms.

Manière had a clever way to use the steamer for both the poached eggs and the Béarnaise sauce, a tarragon-flavored variation of hollandaise. He poached the eggs in teacups half filled with vinegared water; it's a foolproof system and less work than the traditional method of poaching eggs. And for the Béarnaise, he whisked the egg-yolk mixture in a saucepan set in the steamer rather than over direct heat. It's tricky to beat the egg long enough to aerate it in the traditional way without overcooking and scrambling it, but the gentle heat of the steamer works perfectly.

Although there are a lot of different components to this dish, they can all be steamed, one at a time, using one steamer: The artichokes and filling are steamed first, and are served warm or at room temperature. The sauce can be made next, to be reheated just before serving. The eggs must be "poached" at the last minute.

S E R V E S   4   A S   A   F I R S T   C O U R S E

4 large globe artichokes
1 lemon

MUSHROOM FILLING
5 ounces mushrooms, trimmed
1½ tablespoons crème fraîche or
    1½ tablespoons heavy cream mixed
    with ½ teaspoon fresh lemon juice
1 large egg yolk
1 small garlic clove, peeled
1 teaspoon chopped parsley

BÉARNAISE SAUCE
8 tablespoons (¼ pound) unsalted butter
2 medium shallots, finely chopped (about
    3 tablespoons)
⅓ cup white wine vinegar
2 large egg yolks
1½ tablespoons water
¼ teaspoon salt
⅛ teaspoon freshly ground pepper
2 teaspoons chopped fresh tarragon or
    1 teaspoon each chopped fresh
    tarragon and chervil

4 large eggs

Stackable steamer with one or two
    compartments, steamer pot with
    shallow insert, or collapsible steamer
    basket with removable center post in
    a deep frying pan

 Pare the artichokes to make artichoke bottoms as directed on page 29, placing them in lemon water until ready to steam. Put them on the steamer rack, place over simmering water, cover, and steam until tender, 20 to 25 minutes. Scrape out the chokes.

Meanwhile, make the mushroom filling: Add the mushrooms to the steamer rack with the artichoke bottoms, or put them in a second steaming compartment, and steam 8 minutes.

Transfer the cooked mushrooms to the bowl of a food processor. Add the crème fraîche or cream and lemon juice, the egg yolk, garlic, and parsley and process to purée. Set aside.

Make the Béarnaise sauce: Melt the butter in a saucepan. Set aside.

Combine the shallots and vinegar in a small nonaluminum saucepan and bring to a boil over medium-high heat. Reduce until almost dry. Remove from the heat and let cool slightly. Then whisk in the yolks and water. Put the saucepan on the steamer rack, place over simmering water, and whisk until the eggs are doubled in volume and warm. Reheat the butter until boiling and gradually add it to the warm egg mixture, pouring the butter in a thin stream and whisking constantly. Whisk in the salt, pepper, and herbs. Cover and set aside in a warm place.

Poach the eggs in the steamer, as directed on page 36, and drain them on a towel.

If the sauce has cooled, return the saucepan to the steamer rack over simmering water and whisk until warm.

To serve, put the artichoke bottoms on individual plates and fill with the mushroom filling. Top with the poached eggs and spoon some of the sauce over the eggs. Serve the rest of the sauce in a sauceboat on the side.

EGGS POACHED IN THE STEAMER

Recette de Base pour les Oeufs Pochés

It's easier to make "poached" eggs in the steamer, as Manière did, than in the traditional way: The heat of the steamer is constant so there's no need to regulate it, the eggs needn't be touched once they're in the steamer, and steaming is less messy.

The key to steamed poached eggs is the shape of the cups in which they are steamed. A container that is relatively narrow at the bottom and shaped like an inverted dome is called for. Manière recommended a teacup; I use cups with a base about one and a half inches in diameter, widening to three and a half inches at the top. Ramekins or Pyrex custard cups won't work; the egg spreads too much and the yolk overcooks.

MAKES 4 POACHED EGGS

¾ cup water

¼ cup white vinegar

4 large eggs

4 teacups

Stackable steamer, steamer pot with
shallow insert, roasting pan with wire
rack, or collapsible steamer basket

 Bring the water to a boil in a small saucepan. Add the vinegar.

Put the teacups on the steamer rack and place over simmering water. Pour ¼ cup of the boiling vinegared water into each cup and break an egg into each one. Cover the steamer and steam 4 minutes. Remove the steamer rack from the pot and let stand, covered, for 3 minutes.

Fold a clean towel in thirds (or use a triple layer of paper toweling) and place it on a plate. Remove the eggs from the cups by carefully scooping them out with a spoon and slide them off the spoon onto the towel or paper toweling to drain.

ASPARAGUS

In France, asparagus is traditionally peeled, bundled together, and blanched in boiling salted water. The bundling protects the stalks and makes moving the vegetable in and out of the water easier.

By steaming, Manière revealed a delicate, concentrated flavor in asparagus that we don't taste after blanching, which waterlogs the vegetable, particularly if it has been peeled. Manière's method also made cooking asparagus easier, because steamed asparagus needn't be bundled; instead, the spears are arranged horizontally on the steamer rack so that they all lie in one direction. Once cooked, they are removed from the steamer with tongs or a large spoon.

Freshly picked asparagus is tender and very sweet. As it ages, it loses its sweetness and dries out, so that it feels tougher and more fibrous in the mouth. Look for compact, tightly closed tips and firm stalks; the tips of older asparagus begin to open and sprout and the stems look dry and, eventually, wrinkled. The white bottoms of asparagus spears are inedibly tough and fibrous and must be trimmed, if they are not to be peeled.

Very fresh steamed asparagus hardly needs adornment, but you can serve it hot or cold sauced with Manière's Vinaigrette for Asparagus (page 26), Hollandaise (page 38), Mousseline Sauce (page 39), Lemon Butter Sauce (page 40), or Lemon Vinaigrette (page 24). Manière also used asparagus tips in mixed vegetable dishes (see page 188).

✳ WHITE, GREEN, AND RED ASPARAGUS

You can find both white and green asparagus in France; Manière used the white for his Warm Asparagus with Soft-Cooked Eggs and Lemon Butter (page 40). White asparagus are grown under a covering of earth to "blanch" them, or keep them white. They are more fibrous than the green and must be peeled. The stalks of white asparagus range in color from pink to white to green; Manière preferred greenish ones. In America, most white asparagus is imported and is rarely really fresh. And it often is bitter. So-called "red" asparagus (actually more of a deep violet color) is available seasonally in America; the flesh is greenish-white and tastes identical to green asparagus.

✳ PEELING ASPARAGUS

Manière used thick asparagus in these recipes, and he always peeled his stalks. A bouquet of peeled white or green asparagus is gorgeous on the plate and absorbs the flavors of a vinaigrette or sauce especially well. In my experience, thick stalks are more tender and delicate-flavored when they are peeled, but medium stalks needn't be peeled unless you are inclined to do so. It may be impractical to peel pencil-thin asparagus, which is almost always rendered fully tender and flavorful by a few minutes of steaming alone.

✳ PREPARING ASPARAGUS FOR STEAMING

For thick green and white asparagus, peel the stalks: Lay each stalk on the work surface and hold the tip steady with your thumb and forefinger. Keeping the stalk flat on the surface, peel it deeply with a vegetable peeler, starting just below the tip. Then trim off half an inch to an inch from the bottom of the stalk with a knife.

For medium and "pencil" asparagus, simply bend each stalk

until it breaks, about two thirds of the way down the stalk, to remove the woody ends.

Steam asparagus in a single layer until a spear bends slightly when you hold it at one end and yields a bit when squeezed between your fingers. Asparagus is rarely refreshed, because the refreshing water leaches out flavor, particularly from peeled asparagus.

Thick (about ¾ inch) asparagus, peeled	6 to 7 minutes
Medium asparagus	5 to 6 minutes
"Pencil" asparagus	4 to 5 minutes
Asparagus tips	3 minutes

✷ STEAMING ASPARAGUS IN QUANTITY

Two pounds of asparagus will serve four generously. Use an asparagus steamer, a roasting pan, a steamer with an insert that is wide enough to accommodate the asparagus (an oval steamer works well), or a collapsible steamer basket. If the asparagus is deeper than a single layer, add a minute or two to the steaming times in the chart. If the asparagus is piled several inches high in the steamer, gently rearrange it with a spoon or tongs halfway through the steaming time for even cooking, bringing the bottom stalks up to the top.

HOLLANDAISE

Sauce Hollandaise

This classic sauce is made much like a mayonnaise, in that fat is whisked into the egg yolks to make an emulsion. The difference is simply that a hollandaise uses a hot fat, melted butter, instead of oil. According to Manière, the airiness of a hollandaise comes from the action of the boiling butter, which sets the molecules of air trapped in the beaten egg yolk. Like a Béarnaise (page 35), the sauce can be made an hour or so in advance and reheated in the steamer over simmering water.

8 tablespoons (¼ pound) unsalted butter

2 large egg yolks

1½ tablespoons water

1½ tablespoons fresh lemon juice

⅛ teaspoon salt

Pinch of freshly ground pepper, preferably
    white

Any shallow steamer or a roasting pan
    with wire rack

 Melt the butter in a medium saucepan. Set aside.

Combine the egg yolks, water, lemon juice, salt, and pepper in a nonaluminum heavy-bottomed medium saucepan. Put the saucepan on the steamer rack, place over simmering water, and whisk until the yolks are doubled in volume and warm. Reheat the butter until boiling and gradually whisk it into the warm egg mixture, pouring the butter in a thin stream and whisking constantly. Serve immediately or hold in a warm place until ready to serve.

LEMON MOUSSELINE SAUCE

Sauce Mousseline au Citron

Manière served this fluffy, lemony, butter-rich sauce with salmon, but it's superb on asparagus as well.

11 tablespoons unsalted butter

3 large egg yolks

1 tablespoon fresh lemon juice

½ teaspoon grated lemon zest

1 tablespoon dry vermouth, such as Noilly
    Prat

1 tablespoon water

¼ teaspoon salt

⅛ teaspoon freshly ground pepper,
    preferably white

¼ cup crème fraîche or heavy cream

 Melt the butter in a medium saucepan. Keep warm over very low heat. Combine the egg yolks, lemon juice and zest, vermouth, water, salt, and pepper in a nonaluminum heavy-bottomed medium saucepan. Place over low heat and whisk until frothy, thick, and doubled in volume, 2 to 3 minutes. (This is called a *sabayon*.) Reheat the butter if necessary so that it is very hot, then, keeping the sabayon over low heat, slowly pour in the melted butter, whisking constantly. (You now have a lemon hollandaise.) Set the sauce aside in a warm place. It will hold for at least an hour.

Whisk the crème fraîche or cream to soft peaks (not too much, or you'll make butter). Fold into the sauce and serve immediately.

WARM ASPARAGUS WITH SOFT-COOKED EGGS AND LEMON BUTTER

Asperges Tièdes à la Coque

This is one of Manière's simplest but most exquisitely satisfying creations; if you are to defy, just once, the current wisdom about the evils of cholesterol, let it be here. The dish has three parts: warm (not hot) asparagus, soft-cooked eggs, and a luscious, lemony butter sauce. Eat the asparagus with your fingers, drenching it first in the sauce and then dipping it into the soft egg.

Use this sauce to dress up other green vegetables (broccoli, artichokes, green beans), or serve it with lean white fish or shellfish, such as monkfish, cod, snapper, flounder, sole, or scallops.

The eggs steam at the same time as the asparagus, so you'll need a large stackable steamer with two steaming compartments or two steamers.

SERVES 4 AS A WARM FIRST COURSE

2½ pounds thick or medium asparagus

1 teaspoon sugar

4 large eggs

LEMON BUTTER SAUCE

3 tablespoons crème fraîche or heavy
 cream

¼ teaspoon salt

⅛ teaspoon freshly ground pepper,
 preferably white

Juice of ½ lemon (about 1½ tablespoons)

6 tablespoons unsalted butter, cut into
 bits

4 egg cups

Large stackable steamer with two
 steaming compartments, or two of the
 following: stackable steamer,
 asparagus steamer, roasting pan with
 wire rack, or collapsible steamer
 basket

 Peel the asparagus if necessary and trim it as directed on page 37. Spread the asparagus on the steamer rack, all facing in one direction, and sprinkle with the sugar. Place over simmering water, cover, and steam until the asparagus bends slightly when picked up and yields when squeezed between two fingers, 5 to 7 minutes, depending on size.

While the asparagus is cooking, in a second insert or another steamer, steam the eggs for 4 minutes.

Meanwhile, make the sauce: Bring the crème fraîche or cream to a boil in a small saucepan over medium-high heat. Remove from the heat and add the salt and pepper. Add the lemon juice, and then the butter, return to the heat, and whisk until the sauce just returns to a boil. Remove from the heat, taste for salt and pepper, and adjust the seasoning if necessary.

To serve, divide the sauce among four small bowls. Put the eggs into the egg cups. Using tongs or two large spoons, transfer the asparagus to a serving platter. Let each guest crack the shell and remove the top of the egg. Dip the asparagus spears first into the sauce and then into the soft egg.

BEANS

There are innumerable kinds of beans on the market, both fresh and dried, all shapes and colors. Fresh beans divide loosely into two categories—those in which the pod is edible (green beans and yellow wax beans) and those in which it is not (such as fresh lima beans, cranberry beans, and fava beans), often lumped together under the heading of shell beans. This grouping is handy but not altogether accurate; fava beans are actually broad beans, another family.

✳ GREEN BEANS, WAX BEANS, AND HARICOTS VERTS

Manière used haricots verts, a type of green bean commonly available in France, as a vegetable side dish or in salads, such as his Gourmet Salad (page 44). Picked young, haricots verts are slender and dark, no more than about four inches long. Haricots verts are available in some specialty food stores here. If you can find them, do steam them—they have exceptional taste. They take longer to cook than other varieties of green beans, but on the other hand, they do not get mushy as quickly. Don't undercook them; they need their full cooking time to develop flavor, or they taste grassy.

Dress warm beans with Lemon Butter Sauce (page 40), Basic Vinaigrette (page 26), or any of the three vinaigrettes on page 24. Or refresh them as directed on page 23 and serve them cold, with one of the same vinaigrettes or with Fresh Herb and Cream Vinaigrette (page 45), as a salad. Don't add the vinaigrette until just before serving—the acid will dull the bright green color of the beans.

Preparing Green and Wax Beans and Haricots Verts for Steaming Trim the ends of the beans.

Steam the beans until they bend slightly and yield when squeezed between thumb and forefinger.

Green or wax beans	7 to 9 minutes
Haricots verts	8 to 10 minutes

Steaming Green or Wax Beans or Haricots Verts in Quantity One pound of beans will serve four. When steaming more than a single layer of beans, count on about twelve minutes steaming time for green or wax beans and twelve to fourteen minutes for haricots verts, and stir once during the steaming—the beans on top cook more quickly than the beans on the bottom. Steam beans in a stackable steamer, pasta cooker, steamer pot with an insert, or collapsible steamer basket.

✳ SHELL BEANS

Steaming is a terrific way to prepare fresh shell beans; they cook to a perfectly tender, velvety texture without the risk of their bursting or falling apart, as they sometimes do when boiled. Manière served fresh white beans hot with tomatoes and onions as a vegetable (see Fresh White Beans Brittany-Style, on page 43) or cold, as a first course, drizzled with hazelnut or walnut oil and vinegar (one tablespoon vinegar to three tablespoons oil) and sprinkled with chopped parsley.

Two pounds of cranberry beans in the shell will yield about one pound, or three cups, shelled beans. Two and a half to three pounds unshelled fava beans will yield about three quarters of a pound, or about two and a half cups, shelled beans. (The volume of shelled beans varies with the size of the bean.)

Preparing Fresh Shell Beans for Steaming To prepare fresh shell beans for steaming, split open the pods and strip out the beans with your thumb. Shelled fava beans have a tough outer skin that must be removed. Manière removed it before steaming—use your nail to pierce the skin (see illustration below) and then pull it off—but the beans may also be skinned after steaming.

Steam shell beans until meltingly tender all the way through. Shell beans needn't be refreshed.

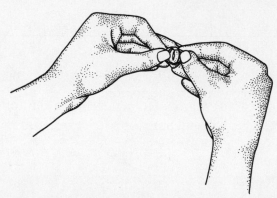

Cranberry beans	20 to 25 minutes
Fava beans, skins removed	10 to 12 minutes
Lima beans	10 to 12 minutes

FRESH WHITE BEANS BRITTANY-STYLE

Haricots Frais (Blancs ou Flageolets Verts) Écossés "Bretonne"

Here, Manière took a rustic recipe of white beans stewed with tomato, onion, and stock, traditional to the northwest coast of France, and refined it. He steamed the beans so they become tender but stay perfectly whole and plump. Then he simmered the beans for a few minutes in a tomato sauce made with water rather than stock, so that the taste of the tomato and beans speaks clearly and cleanly.

The recipe calls for fresh white beans or light green flageolet beans. Fresh flageolets are rarely available in this country, but fresh red-speckled cranberry beans (they lose their red color in cooking), available several months out of the year, are a delicious substitute. So are dried flageolets; soak them overnight, boil them in water to cover until tender, then finish the recipe as below.

Five tablespoons of butter makes these beans absolutely fabulous, but three tablespoons won't disappoint. You can use olive oil instead of butter to give the dish a Mediterranean flair. Serve the beans with lamb or pork.

SERVES 4 AS A VEGETABLE SIDE DISH

1 large round or 3 large plum tomatoes or
    1 cup drained chopped canned
    tomatoes
2 pounds fresh shell beans, such as
    cranberry, shelled (about 3 cups)
5 tablespoons unsalted butter
1 small onion, chopped
2 medium cloves garlic, minced
1½ tablespoons chopped parsley
½ teaspoon salt
⅛ teaspoon freshly ground pepper
¾ cup water

Stackable steamer, steamer pot with
    insert, pasta cooker, or collapsible
    steamer basket

 If using fresh tomatoes, make a tomato concassé (see page 98).

Put the beans on the steamer rack. Place over simmering water, cover, and steam until tender, 30 to 35 minutes.

Meanwhile, melt the butter in a medium saucepan over low heat. Add the tomato concassé or chopped canned tomatoes, the onion, garlic, parsley, salt, pepper, and water. Bring to a boil, then reduce the heat and simmer gently while the beans steam, about 20 minutes.

When the beans are tender, add them to the tomato mixture and gently stir together. Simmer 1 to 2 minutes over low heat. Serve hot.

GOURMET SALAD OF GREEN BEANS, CHICKEN LIVER, SHRIMP, AND MUSHROOMS

Salade "un peu folle"

I imagine that Manière called this playful, extravagantly colorful first-course salad *un peu folle*—"a little crazy"—because salad for the French is traditionally just a simple dish of mixed greens and it's only served after the main course.

This recipe is a good example of how steaming can make life easier. Because all of the ingredients can be steamed in the same pot, Manière simply started with the ingredients that take the longest time and added the more quickly cooking foods at the appropriate times, adding a few minutes to the steaming times to adjust for the quantity of vegetables in the pot. Using the basic steaming times for vegetables in this chapter and the timing charts for fish on page 112, poultry on page 182, and meats on page 228, we can use this salad as a model to make any number of salads, depending on what's in season, what's in the refrigerator, or what we have a yen for. Leftover bits of fish, poultry, or meat, rewarmed in the steamer, also make good salad additions. (See Steaming Vegetables in Quantity on page 24 for information about steaming a number of different vegetables in the same steamer.)

To steam correctly, protein must be in contact with the steam; the chicken livers and shrimp in this dish won't cook if sitting on top of the vegetables. If your steamer isn't big enough to hold the livers and shrimp in a single layer on the rack, steam them in a second steamer or steaming compartment of a stackable steamer, or steam the vegetables first, and then steam the liver and shrimp in the same steamer while you refresh and dress the vegetables.

SERVES 4 AS A COLD FIRST COURSE

4 chicken livers

¼ pound haricots verts or green beans, ends trimmed

1 small celery root (about ¼ pound)

2 medium carrots, peeled and coarsely grated

3 stalks celery, peeled and cut into julienne (see page 104)

12 medium to large (16/20) shrimp (see page 171), in the shell

4 mushrooms, thinly sliced

Cut off the white veins and yellow-orange fatty tissue from each liver where the two lobes join. Set aside.

Put the beans on the steamer rack, place over simmering water, cover, and steam for 8 minutes.

Meanwhile, trim and peel the celery root as directed on page 64 and grate it. (The celery root will discolor once grated, so either grate it just before cooking or put it in a bowl of lemon water, as for holding artichokes on page 29, if preparing in advance.)

Add the grated carrots and celery root to the steamer rack along with the celery, livers, and shrimp, if possible, and steam for 3 minutes.

Remove the livers and shrimp from the rack and let cool.

FRESH HERB AND CREAM VINAIGRETTE

¼ cup crème fraîche or ¼ cup heavy
    cream mixed with 1 teaspoon fresh
    lemon juice
1 teaspoon strong Dijon mustard
Juice of 1 lemon (about 3 tablespoons)
¼ teaspoon salt
⅛ teaspoon freshly ground pepper
¼ cup plus 2 tablespoons olive oil or nut
    oil, such as walnut or hazelnut

1 teaspoon chopped fresh tarragon
1 teaspoon chopped fresh chives

Stackable steamer with one or two
    steaming compartments, steamer pot
    with insert, pasta cooker, or
    collapsible steamer basket

Refresh the vegetables (on the steamer rack) under cold running water and drain them well on paper towels.

Put the vegetables in a bowl. Add the mushrooms.

Peel and devein the shrimp and set aside. Slice the livers into 3 slices each.

Make the vinaigrette: Whisk the crème fraîche or cream and lemon juice with the mustard, lemon juice, salt, and pepper in a small bowl. Add the oil in a thin, steady stream, whisking constantly until emulsified. Pour the vinaigrette over the vegetables. Add the chopped herbs and fold gently to mix.

Arrange the vegetables in a mound on a serving platter. Place the sliced livers around the vegetables, alternating with the shrimp, and serve.

BEETS

Manière didn't include a recipe for steamed beets because the French always buy them already cooked and vacuum-packed in plastic. In America we're not so lucky; we need to cook our own.

Steam beets whole and unpeeled to prevent them from bleeding and leaching out flavor, then cut them to the desired size. I cook them until very soft, the way the French prefer them, because their sweetness develops as they cook. Young beets, just out of the ground, need less cooking than winter beets.

If you find beets with the greens still attached, cut off the greens and steam them too, as directed on page 80.

✳ PREPARING BEETS FOR STEAMING

Wash the beets or scrub them gently with a vegetable brush, being careful not to break the skin. Trim the stem ends to about 1 inch, and leave the roots on.

Steam the beets until a knife penetrates with absolutely no resistance (like soft butter). Beets needn't be refreshed.

Whole medium beets (about 2 inches in diameter)............................30 to 35 minutes

Whole large beets (2½ to 3 inches in diameter)..............................35 to 40 minutes

BELL PEPPERS

Steaming concentrates the natural sweetness of bell peppers so that we clearly taste the play of sweet and bitter. This duality comes through even in green peppers, which are more bitter than sweet. I've never liked green peppers as much as in Manière's Provençal-Style Marinated Peppers (page 47).

✳ PEELING BELL PEPPERS

Manière steamed bell peppers, either whole or halved, to loosen the skins for peeling, as for tomatoes. He used peeled peppers in his sparkling first-course salad of marinated peppers and puréed them to make a bright orange-red sauce for lobster (see page 156). It's a little more work to peel peppers that have been steamed rather than roasted (green are particularly tough), but it's worth it: The soft, buttery texture is very like that of roasted, but the delicate, pure "pepperness" comes through more distinctly because it's not muddied by smoke.

Steam the peppers, let cool for about ten minutes, then peel off the skins with your fingers or a knife. (You may need to cut off the skin in places where it is recalcitrant.)

✳ PREPARING PEPPERS FOR STEAMING

You can steam bell peppers whole. Or cut out the stems with a paring knife, cut the peppers in half through the stem ends, shake out the seeds, and cut or pull off the white ribs with your fingers. Cut the peppers into smaller pieces if you like, and steam until the tip of a knife penetrates the flesh with no resistance.

Whole or halved peppers...	**15 minutes**
Peppers sliced ½ inch thick..	**10 to 15 minutes**

PIPERADE

Piperade

Piperade is a traditional Basque stew made with bell peppers and tomatoes, the latter steamed to remove their skins. Manière used it as a flavoring for scrambled eggs; it's also excellent as a thick sauce or relish with steamed chicken and fish. Piperade will keep two to three days in the refrigerator.

MAKES 1½ CUPS

4 plum tomatoes (¾ pound) or 4 small
round tomatoes
3 tablespoons olive oil
1 medium onion, halved lengthwise and
thinly sliced
1 medium red bell pepper, cored, halved,
seeds and ribs removed, and thinly
sliced
2 medium cloves garlic, chopped
1½ tablespoons chopped parsley
¼ teaspoon salt
¼ teaspoon freshly ground pepper

Make a tomato concassé with the tomatoes (see page 98).

Heat the oil in a medium saucepan over medium-low heat. Add the onion and bell pepper, cover, and cook gently until softened, about 5 minutes. Add the tomato concassé, garlic, parsley, salt, and pepper and simmer gently over low heat, uncovered, until the tomatoes are almost a purée and the vegetables are very soft, 10 to 15 minutes. Taste for seasoning. Serve hot.

PROVENÇAL-STYLE MARINATED PEPPERS

Poivronnade Provençale

Colorful dishes of smoky grilled red and green bell peppers, peeled and marinated in olive oil, are abundant in Mediterranean cuisines. Manière's version is startlingly different from those we're used to because he steamed the peppers. Without the smokiness of the fire, the delicate sweet-and-bitter flavor stands out. Steaming keeps the flesh meaty and luscious in texture, and there's no danger of the pepper's burning or drying out.

Start this dish a day in advance, as it needs to marinate overnight. Use a good-quality olive oil; it will really show up here. You can steam all the peppers at the same time in a large roasting pan or a stackable steamer with two steaming compartments; if using a smaller pan or a steamer basket, steam them in batches.

(continued)

3 medium red bell peppers, cored,
   halved, and seeds and ribs removed

3 medium yellow bell peppers, cored,
   halved, and seeds and ribs removed

3 medium green bell peppers, cored,
   halved, and seeds and ribs removed

8 medium cloves garlic, minced

¾ teaspoon salt

⅔ cup virgin olive oil

1½ tablespoons black peppercorns

½ teaspoon fresh thyme leaves or
   ¼ teaspoon dried thyme

Aluminum foil

Stackable steamer with one or two
   steaming compartments, roasting pan
   with wire rack, or collapsible steamer
   basket

 Put the pepper halves on the steamer rack, place over simmering water, cover, and steam 10 minutes. Put the garlic on a small square of aluminum foil, place it on the rack, and steam 5 more minutes.

Remove the peppers from the steamer and let cool slightly. Then peel them, as directed on page 46, and cut them into ¼- to ½-inch-wide slices. Put the peppers in a shallow, heatproof serving bowl and sprinkle with the salt.

Combine the oil, steamed garlic, peppercorns, and thyme in a small saucepan and heat over medium heat until just hot. Pour over the peppers and toss gently to coat. Let marinate overnight in the refrigerator. Bring to room temperature before serving.

BROCCOLI

We can steam broccoli in four forms: florets only, sliced peeled stalks only, florets and peeled stalks, and broccoli bouquets (florets with two to three inches of stalk attached). Steaming works best when the stalks are peeled so that they and the florets cook at the same rate; I prefer to steam a combination of florets and one-quarter-inch-thick rounds of sliced stalks. When steaming bouquets, I peel the stalks unless the broccoli is indisputably fresh; unpeeled stalks never get as tender as peeled, and if the broccoli is not fresh, the peel stays very tough.

Serve steamed broccoli with melted butter, Manière's Lemon Butter Sauce (page 40), Hollandaise (page 38), or Basic Vinaigrette (page 26), or any one of the three vinaigrettes on page 24. Steamed broccoli turns a brilliant green; if you're dressing it with vinaigrette or with lemon juice, wait until just before serving to add it, because the acid will dull the color. If you're serving broccoli cold with a vinaigrette, refresh it to hold the color.

✳ PREPARING BROCCOLI FOR STEAMING

For florets and peeled stalk pieces, cut the heads off the stalks and then cut them into bite-sized florets. Cut the tough one to two inches off the bottom of the stalks. Peel the stalks deeply with a knife. Cut the peeled stalks on the diagonal into quarter-inch-thick slices. (Cutting on the diagonal exposes the maximum amount of interior for the fastest cooking time.)

For broccoli bouquets, cut the heads into florets with two to three inches of stalk. Unless the broccoli is very fresh, peel the stalks with a knife so that they will cook at the same rate as the tops.

Steam broccoli until the florets are tender and/or a knife penetrates the stalks easily. Serve immediately, or refresh (see page 23) to serve later.

Bite-sized broccoli florets	5 to 7 minutes
Peeled broccoli stalks, cut into 1/4-inch-thick slices	5 to 7 minutes
Broccoli bouquets	8 to 10 minutes

✳ STEAMING BROCCOLI IN QUANTITY

Two pounds of broccoli will serve four. Steam in a stackable steamer, pasta cooker, steamer pot with insert, or collapsible steamer basket. Even if the broccoli is deeply piled, the steaming time is the same as indicated in the chart. Broccoli needn't be stirred during steaming.

BRUSSELS SPROUTS

Manière didn't include any recipes for Brussels sprouts, but I've found they're a good substitute for the cabbage in his Cabbage with Cream and Shallots (page 53). Steamed Brussels sprouts are divine with Manière's Basic Vinaigrette (page 26), with toasted walnuts and a drizzle of walnut or hazelnut oil, or with crumbled sautéed bacon and a warm bacon-mustard vinaigrette: Use the recipe for Red Wine Vinegar–Mustard Vinaigrette on page 24, but replace some of the oil with hot bacon fat.

✳ TO PREPARE BRUSSELS SPROUTS FOR STEAMING

Trim the stem ends of the sprouts and remove any damaged leaves. Cut a small "x" in the base of each end so that the sprouts cook faster.

Steam Brussels sprouts until the tip of a knife penetrates easily, with just a bit of resistance; they shouldn't be mushy. Brussels sprouts needn't be refreshed.

| Whole medium Brussels sprouts...11 to 12 minutes |
| Halved medium Brussels sprouts..10 minutes |

✳ STEAMING BRUSSELS SPROUTS IN QUANTITY

A one-pint container of Brussels sprouts will feed two sprouts lovers or three light eaters. The sprouts usually vary in size. The timing in the chart is for the average size; cut larger sprouts in half through the cut end and steam for the same time as whole medium sprouts. Quantity doesn't change the steaming time for Brussels sprouts. Steam Brussels sprouts in any steamer that will hold them.

CABBAGE

Cabbage is so quick and so good when steamed that I find myself eating a lot more of it than I used to. While it is reputed to have a very strong, almost bitter flavor that is only accentuated by cooking, steaming brings out its sweetness and a surprisingly delicate taste. The French prefer to use the milder-tasting, crinkly-leaved Savoy cabbage in cooking, but it is not always available in American supermarkets. Our smooth-leaved green cabbage tastes stronger and sweeter than Savoy but works perfectly well in Manière's recipes. You can also substitute the elongated Napa cabbage in recipes that call for Savoy; it is spicier than both green and Savoy. The steaming time for all three is the same except when whole leaves are steamed; the leaves of Savoy and Napa cabbage are thinner and more papery than those of green cabbage and so steam faster.

The French also use red cabbage, most often in salads. Red cabbage has a milder, mellower flavor than green or Savoy cabbage. Red cabbage is generally prepared with a little vinegar to set the color. Don't be concerned if it looks grayish when it comes out of the steamer—a little vinegar will brighten it considerably.

Manière's steamed cabbage sauced with cream and shallots (page 53) is a personal favorite, though I also like to dress steamed cabbage with the Red Wine Vinegar–Mustard Vinaigrette on page 24. I've used Manière's creamy cabbage as a bed for steamed monkfish, salmon, or cod fillets or for leftover steamed pork or ham, duck, chicken, or goose. (While testing the goose recipes in this book, I often had a steamed goose leg in the freezer. I could have an amazing meal in less than half an hour by defrosting the leg directly on a bed of raw cabbage in the steamer—thus flavoring the cabbage with the goose while the two steamed—and then finishing the cabbage with cream and shallots, as in Manière's recipe. Sometimes I added sliced raw potato to the steaming cabbage, and sometimes I had a frozen piece of smoked pork or slab bacon to add.)

✳ PREPARING CABBAGE FOR STEAMING

Manière steamed cabbage both in strips and as whole leaves, to make a delicate, edible wrapping for fish, poultry, and meat stuffings (see below).

Cabbage Strips Pull off the tough outer leaves and any that are damaged. Quarter the cabbage through the stem end and cut out the core. Lay each quarter, one cut side down, on the work surface, and cut lengthwise into thin strips. Manière used a serrated knife and a sawing motion to make slicing easier.

Rinse the cabbage: Manière rinsed, drained, and then steamed cabbage strips all in the steamer compartment of his stackable steamer. We can do the same in a steamer insert, pasta cooker, or collapsible steamer basket.

Steam cabbage strips just until wilted and tender. Cabbage needn't be refreshed.

½-inch-wide cabbage strips (6 to 12 cups)..15 minutes	
⅛- to ¼-inch-wide cabbage strips (6 to 12 cups)............................10 to 12 minutes	

Steaming Cabbage Strips in Quantity The timings in the chart are for a large quantity of cabbage strips (six to twelve cups; twelve cups is about one large head). One medium head, or ten cups raw cabbage, wilts to eight cups cooked, enough to serve six people. Six cups, or half a large head, of raw cabbage feeds four people conservatively (see the recipe on page 53); eight cups is better if the cabbage is dressed less richly.

Use a stackable steamer, a pasta cooker, a steamer pot with an insert, or a collapsible steamer basket. It's not necessary to stir cabbage during steaming.

Whole Cabbage Leaves When steaming whole cabbage leaves for stuffing, you must first pull the whole leaves off the head, but it's hard to do this without ripping the leaves. To make it easier, cut out the core in a conical section with a small knife. Steam the entire head for two to three minutes to wilt the leaves slightly, and then pull off the leaves. If they are hard to remove when you reach the center of the head, steam two to three more minutes and then remove them.

Steam whole cabbage leaves just until wilted.

Whole leaves (green and red cabbage)..7 to 9 minutes	
Whole leaves (Savoy cabbage)..4 to 5 minutes	

✳ STUFFING WHOLE CABBAGE LEAVES

Manière used steamed whole cabbage leaves to enclose stuffings in several recipes, including Herring Wrapped in Cabbage Leaves with Mint (page 133), Stuffed Cabbage with Kasha (page 236), and "Green Chicken" (page 253).

To prepare whole cabbage leaves for stuffing, steam and then pull off the whole leaves as described above. Pare down the raised center rib of the cabbage leaves to make them flat, keeping the leaves whole: Lay each leaf on a work surface with the raised side of the rib facing up. Hold the knife parallel to the work surface and shave off the raised part of the rib (see illustration below).

To wrap a filling in the cabbage leaf, first steam the trimmed leaf for two minutes to soften it. Lay the leaf on the work surface and place the filling across the center. Fold the bottom edge of the leaf up over the filling. Fold over the sides of the leaf, and then roll the cabbage over to enclose the filling.

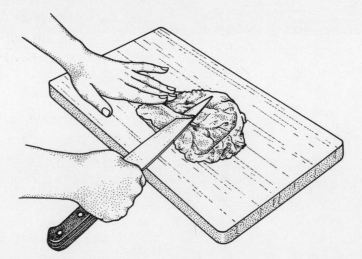

CABBAGE WITH CREAM AND SHALLOTS

Chou Croquant

Manière called this dish *croquant,* or crunchy, to indicate that we should steam the cabbage just long enough to take the rawness out of it, leaving it with a delicate bite, a lovely sweetness, and only a hint of the stronger flavor that develops with longer cooking. This luscious pale-green and white dish is a wonderful accompaniment to simple roasted or steamed poultry and fish; you don't need to sauce the fish or poultry, because the cabbage is saucy enough.

If you have a half-head of cabbage left from this recipe, use it to make the Warm Sweet-and-Sour Cabbage Salad (page 54).

SERVES 4 AS A SIDE DISH

½ medium head or 1 small head green cabbage, preferably Savoy

¼ cup crème fraîche or ¼ cup heavy cream mixed with 1 teaspoon fresh lemon juice

1 shallot, chopped (about 1½ tablespoons)

1½ tablespoons chopped parsley

¼ teaspoon salt

⅛ teaspoon freshly ground pepper, preferably white

Stackable steamer, steamer pot with insert, pasta cooker, or collapsible steamer basket

 Trim, quarter, and core the cabbage and cut it into ½-inch-wide strips with a serrated knife as directed on page 51. You should have about 6 packed cups cabbage strips. Put the cabbage onto the steamer rack and rinse it. Place over simmering water, cover, and steam 15 minutes.

Remove the steamer basket or insert, place it in the sink, and let the cabbage drain. Empty the water from the steamer pot, add the crème fraîche or cream and lemon juice, and bring to a boil over medium-high heat. (This is very little cream in a large pot; swirl it around as it heats to keep it from scorching.)

Return the cabbage to the pot, along with the shallots, parsley, salt, and pepper. Stir to combine, then simmer, uncovered, for 5 to 6 minutes to reduce the cream and marry the flavors. Taste for salt and pepper and serve.

WARM SWEET-AND-SOUR CABBAGE SALAD

Salade Tiède de Chou Vert, Sauce à l'Aigre-doux

Spicy, sweet, barely cooked cabbage is delicious with a warm sweet-and-sour vinaigrette. Manière purposely gave quantities to make twice as much vinaigrette as needed because the vinaigrette holds for several days at room temperature (or up to two weeks in the refrigerator). He recommended using the extra sauce with Napa cabbage prepared the same way as the green.

Manière suggested making this dish into a main-course salad by adding steamed chicken livers (see chart on page 182) or gizzards. I find that steaming toughens gizzards, so I poach them in the steaming liquid while a chicken steams. You can slice the cooked livers or gizzards, and then brown them in a hot frying pan (about one minute). Manière also used confit of pork tongue, available in France from a *traiteur*—a shop that sells prepared foods. This last is, unfortunately, not practical for the American cook, but we can use smoked sliced beef tongue, available in most delicatessens.

I have also made this recipe with red or with a combination of red and green cabbage. The purplish-red cabbage makes a very pretty salad.

SERVES 4 AS A WARM SALAD

1 heart Savoy cabbage or ½ medium
    head or 1 small head green cabbage

SWEET-AND-SOUR VINAIGRETTE
¼ cup sugar
½ cup wine vinegar or sherry vinegar
1 tablespoon strong Dijon mustard
¼ teaspoon salt
¼ teaspoon freshly ground pepper
1 cup peanut or vegetable oil

1 medium clove garlic, minced
1½ tablespoons chopped parsley

Stackable steamer, steamer pot with
    insert, pasta cooker, or collapsible
    steamer basket

 Clean, quarter, and core the cabbage and cut it into fine strips with a serrated knife, as directed on page 51. You should have about 6 packed cups cabbage strips. Rinse the cabbage strips and put them on the steamer rack. Place over simmering water, cover, and steam 4 minutes. Remove the basket or insert from the steamer pot and set it in the sink. Let the cabbage drain while you make the vinaigrette.

Make the vinaigrette: Put the sugar and 2 tablespoons of the vinegar in a medium heavy-bottomed nonaluminum saucepan. Bring to a boil over medium-high heat and cook until you smell the sugar beginning to caramelize, 2 to 3 minutes. Immediately remove the pan from the heat and carefully add 2 more tablespoons vinegar. (Stand back, because the vinegar will sputter.) Reduce the heat to medium, return the pan to the fire, and heat to melt the caramel that has formed. Remove from the heat.

In a small bowl, whisk together the mustard, the remaining ¼ cup vinegar, the salt, and pepper. Whisk in half of the oil until emulsified. Then whisk in the hot caramel, and finally the remaining oil.

Put the drained cabbage in a heatproof serving bowl and add the garlic and parsley. Add half of the vinaigrette and toss to coat. Serve warm.

Refrigerate the remaining vinaigrette for another meal.

CARROTS

Manière used standard-sized mature carrots as well as baby carrots in his recipes. He cut mature carrots into bâtonnets (see page 104), steamed them, and then sautéed them in oil and butter (see page 56; we can add a green vegetable for color). He puréed steamed carrots for a soufflé-like carrot and Gruyère cheese terrine (see page 57). He sauced baby carrots with parsley and butter to serve with veal (see page 242) or tossed them with other steamed young vegetables and butter to serve with chicken (see page 188). If you can't find baby carrots, cut larger carrots diagonally into slices or into bâtonnets, or buy peeled and trimmed two-inch carrots, sold in one-pound packages as "baby" or "mini" carrots; these carrots are shaped like small, short cylinders and are cut flat at each end, rather than coming to a natural point.

Manière steamed grated carrots just long enough to intensify the flavor and used them in a salad (see page 44). Or you can toss steamed grated carrots with Manière's Basic Vinaigrette (page 26), his Cumin Vinaigrette (page 86), or one of the three vinaigrettes on page 24. Or toss in reduced cream with additional flavorings, as in Manière's Cabbage with Cream and Shallots (page 53).

You can steam and purée carrots for a carrot flan, replacing the celery root in Manière's Celery Root Flans (page 66) with the same weight of carrots. For a puréed carrot soup, adapt the recipe for Leek and Potato Soup (page 90) by replacing half the potatoes with an equal weight of carrots. Or simply purée steamed carrots and potatoes very well in a blender and thin the mixture with stock, milk, or cream, as on page 100.

If you can find carrots with fresh-looking green tops, they are likely to be fresher than the carrots packaged in plastic bags. Cut the tops off when you get home; if left on, they will continue to grow, draining the carrots of flavor and sweetness.

✳ PREPARING CARROTS FOR STEAMING

For mature carrots, trim the ends and peel.

Manière always peeled baby carrots, but they can just be scrubbed. Trim the tops to leave one to two inches of green.

Steam carrots until the tip of a small knife penetrates easily; the carrots should be tender but still have "tooth." If the carrots are to be puréed, however, steam them until very soft. Carrots don't need to be refreshed after steaming.

Carrot bâtonnets ($^1/_4$ by $1^1/_2$ inches)..7 to 10 minutes

$^1/_4$-inch-thick carrot rounds...7 to 10 minutes

Whole baby carrots..10 to 15 minutes, depending on size

"Mini" carrots...10 to 15 minutes, depending on size

✳ STEAMING CARROTS IN QUANTITY

Steam carrots in a stackable steamer, a steamer pot with an insert, a pasta cooker, or a collapsible steamer basket. One to one and a half pounds of baby or mature carrots (or eight to ten medium mature carrots) feeds four people. Allow fifteen minutes' steaming time for sliced carrots steamed in more than a single layer, fifteen to twenty minutes for baby or "mini" carrots. Carrots needn't be stirred during steaming.

SAUTÉED CARROTS WITH PARSLEY

Garniture de Carottes Sautées

Here is a simple dish of sautéed carrots to accompany meat, fish, or poultry. If you like, you can replace half the carrots with another firm vegetable such as cauliflower, green beans, pearl onions, or turnips for color.

Manière was handy with a knife so cutting bâtonnets was child's play for him. For most of us it's a lot of work; this dish loses nothing if you simply slice the carrots.

1¾ pounds carrots if cutting bâtonnets or
    1¼ pounds if slicing
3 tablespoons unsalted butter
⅓ cup peanut or vegetable oil
Salt and freshly ground pepper
1½ tablespoons flat-leaf parsley leaves

Stackable steamer, steamer pot with
    insert, pasta cooker, or collapsible
    steamer basket

 Peel the carrots and cut them into ¼-inch by 2-inch bâtonnets (see page 104), or slice them crosswise into ¼-inch-thick rounds. Put the carrots on the steamer rack, place over simmering water, cover, and steam 5 minutes. Drain well on towels.

Melt the butter with the oil in a large frying pan over medium-high heat. Add the carrots and sauté for 5 minutes, or until lightly browned all over. Sprinkle with salt and pepper to taste and put the carrots in a serving bowl. Sprinkle with the parsley and serve hot.

CARROT TERRINE

Pain de Carottes

Manière served this as a vegetable side dish for four, but I find it substantial enough to serve as many as six to eight. It accompanies simple grilled, roasted, or steamed meats and poultry beautifully. The terrine also works as a first course for six to eight or, without the ham, as a vegetarian main course for four. For a richer, more elegant dish, serve it with Chervil Butter Sauce (page 152) or Tarragon Butter Sauce (page 254).

You can steam the terrine in a soufflé dish or charlotte mold on a rack in a dome-lidded roasting pan or in a large stackable steamer. Or my favorite way: in a Pyrex loaf pan with handles at either end that can be used to suspend the pan in a deep nine-and-a-half-inch pot (see page 5).

(continued)

Unsalted butter, softened, for buttering
the soufflé dish and foil

5 large carrots (1¼ pounds)

THICK BÉCHAMEL SAUCE
⅔ cup whole milk
2 tablespoons unsalted butter
3 tablespoons all-purpose flour
½ teaspoon salt
¼ teaspoon freshly ground pepper,
preferably white
⅛ teaspoon freshly grated nutmeg

½ cup finely grated Gruyère cheese
3 large egg yolks
½ cup diced ham
2 large egg whites

Aluminum foil
1½-quart soufflé dish or charlotte mold
or 8½- x 4½-inch loaf pan (see
headnote)
9½-inch pot (see headnote), large
stackable steamer, or roasting pan
with wire rack

 Brush the soufflé dish, charlotte mold, or loaf pan with softened butter.

Peel the carrots and cut them in half lengthwise. Then cut them crosswise into 1-inch pieces (you should have about 3½ cups). Put the carrots on the steamer rack, place over simmering water, cover, and steam until very tender, 15 to 20 minutes. Purée in a food processor or blender and set aside.

Make the sauce: Bring the milk to a boil in a small saucepan.

Meanwhile, melt the butter in a medium heavy-bottomed saucepan over medium heat. Whisk in the flour and cook, whisking, until the mixture (roux) puffs slightly and bubbles, about 30 seconds.

Remove the roux from the heat, pour in the hot milk all at once, and whisk until smooth. Return the pan to the heat and cook very gently over low heat for 5 minutes, whisking often and reaching into the edges of the pan to keep the sauce from burning. Remove the sauce from the heat and whisk in the salt, pepper, and nutmeg.

Whisk the grated cheese, egg yolks, and carrot purée into the béchamel. Stir in the diced ham.

Beat the egg whites until stiff. Fold into the warm carrot mixture. Pour into the prepared mold and cover with a piece of buttered aluminum foil, buttered side down. Press the foil around the rim of the container to seal.

Put the terrine on the steamer rack, place over simmering water, cover, and steam until just barely set (a knife inserted into the center should come out wet), 25 to 30 minutes. Don't overcook.

Remove from the steamer and let stand for 10 minutes. Turn the terrine out onto a serving plate and cut into slices. Serve warm.

CAULIFLOWER

Manière included two very unusual recipes for cauliflower, both Indian in mood. We can also steam cauliflower to serve in combination with other vegetables, as in Manière's vegetable medley served with rack of lamb (see page 244), or replace the celery root in his Celery Root Flans (page 66) with the same weight in cauliflower and serve the individual cauliflower flans with roasted or steamed meats, poultry, or fish.

Simpler still, steam the florets and toss them with butter heated until lightly browned and nutty-tasting, brightened with a squeeze of lemon and a handful of chopped parsley. Or sauce steamed florets with the Lemon Butter Sauce on page 40.

✳ PREPARING CAULIFLOWER FOR STEAMING

Cut off the leaves and trim the stem close to the base of the head. For florets, use a small knife to cut out the core in a conical section, and then cut the head into bite-sized florets.

Steam until the tip of a knife penetrates the cauliflower easily. Cauliflower needn't be refreshed unless it is to be served cold (see page 23).

Whole cauliflower head..	15 to 20 minutes
Cauliflower florets...	8 to 10 minutes

✳ STEAMING CAULIFLOWER IN QUANTITY

One large head of cauliflower serves four people. Steam cauliflower in a stackable steamer, a steamer pot with an insert, a pasta cooker, or a collapsible steamer basket. Steaming cauliflower florets in more than one layer doesn't increase the steaming time, and the cauliflower needn't be stirred during steaming.

PICKLED VEGETABLES WITH CURRY

Achards de Légumes au Curry

The recipe for these crisp, colorful pickles is in Manière's collection of what he called *semi-conserves,* cozy, homey foods that are not canned, but are packed away for several days or up to a few weeks to mellow in the cupboard or refrigerator. The recipe takes two days to make because the vegetables must first sit overnight in salt. Manière calls for the vegetables to marinate one week in the vinaigrette, so count on eight days before serving.

Manière used a strong curry vinaigrette here. Since curry powders vary in strength, try two tablespoons to begin with and then taste—if the curry flavor isn't strong enough, add more. Remember also that the flavors will mellow as the pickles age.

The pickles hold up to three weeks in the refrigerator. Bring to room temperature before serving, and serve with chicken or a cold pork roast.

MAKES ABOUT 2 QUARTS AS A SIDE DISH

½ small celery heart

1 medium head cauliflower, cored and cut into bite-sized florets

4 medium carrots, peeled and cut into bâtonnets (see page 104)

4 medium turnips, peeled and cut into bâtonnets (see page 104)

½ pound green beans, ends trimmed and cut into ½-inch pieces

2 medium lemons, thinly sliced

1 lime, thinly sliced (optional)

2 tablespoons coarse salt

CURRY VINAIGRETTE

3 tablespoons strong Dijon mustard

2 to 3 tablespoons curry powder

1 teaspoon ground ginger

⅛ teaspoon cayenne pepper

⅛ teaspoon ground cloves

⅔ cup white wine vinegar (or to taste) or juice of 2 lemons (about 6 tablespoons)

2 cups olive oil or 1 cup olive and 1 cup peanut or vegetable oil

2-quart glass jar

Stackable steamer with one or two compartments, steamer pot with insert, pasta cooker, or collapsible steamer basket

Trim the celery heart, remove the strings from the stalks with a paring knife (see page 63), and thinly slice crosswise; you should have just under 2 cups.

Put the vegetables, lemon slices, and lime slices, if using, into a large shallow bowl or a deep serving platter and toss with the salt. Cover and let stand in a cool place or in the refrigerator for 24 hours.

Put the vegetables and citrus slices on the steamer rack. (Use both layers of the steamer if there are two.) Place over simmering water, cover, and, if using a steamer with two compartments, steam 3 minutes; if using a steamer with a single compartment, steam 6 minutes. Remove the lid and continue steaming another 3 minutes, or until the vegetables are barely tender. Refresh under cold running water, drain well, and put the vegetables and citrus slices in a bowl.

Make the vinaigrette: Whisk together the mustard and spices in a small bowl. Whisk in the vinegar or lemon juice, and whisk in the oil until emulsified. Pour the dressing over the vegetables and toss well to coat. Transfer to a 2-quart glass jar and refrigerate 1 week before using. (Manière used a jar to ensure that the vegetables were completely immersed in the vinaigrette. You can use a bowl, but make sure that the vinaigrette covers the vegetables.)

INDIAN-STYLE VEGETABLE CUTLETS

Côtelettes de Légumes

In a chapter called *"Tour du Monde"* ("Around the World"), Manière presented foods from countries other than France. These spicy meatless cutlets are Indian in inspiration; they taste like a moist, cakey Indian bread stuffed with peas and green beans. Serve them with Fresh Tomato-Basil Sauce (page 62) or a store-bought bottled chutney.

Steam the vegetables in a pasta cooker, a stackable steamer, or a collapsible steamer basket. Although the foil-wrapped "cutlets" can overlap slightly on the steamer rack, they still call for a large steamer, so I use a roasting pan with a wire rack or a stackable steamer with two steaming compartments.

SERVES 4 AS A MAIN COURSE

2 medium waxy potatoes (about 7 ounces total), scrubbed and cut in half

¼ pound cauliflower florets (2 large florets, each about 3½ inches across)

¼ pound haricots verts or green beans, ends trimmed

1 cup fresh or frozen green peas

¾ cup plus 1 tablespoon all-purpose flour

½ teaspoon ground ginger

¼ teaspoon cayenne pepper

½ teaspoon salt

⅛ teaspoon freshly ground pepper

2 large eggs, lightly beaten

Unsalted butter, softened, for buttering the foil

Fresh Tomato-Basil Sauce (page 62)

Aluminum foil

Stackable steamer with one or two compartments, pasta cooker, collapsible steamer basket, and/or roasting pan with wire rack (see headnote)

 Put the potatoes on the steamer rack, set it over simmering water, cover, and steam 10 minutes. Add the cauliflower and steam 10 more minutes. Add the green beans and the fresh peas, if using, and steam 10 minutes longer. If using frozen peas, add them for the last 5 minutes of steaming. (If the potatoes need a little extra time, remove the other vegetables and continue steaming the potatoes until cooked through.) Remove the vegetables from the steamer and let stand until cool enough to handle.

Cut the beans into ¼-inch lengths and set them aside with the peas.

Peel the potatoes. Put the potatoes and cauliflower into the bowl of a food processor and pulse just until finely chopped, but not completely smooth. (Potatoes get gummy if overprocessed.) Add the flour, ginger, cayenne, salt, pepper, and eggs and pulse to mix. The purée should not be completely smooth; there should be flecks of potato in it. Transfer to a bowl and stir in the beans and peas. Taste for salt and pepper.

Cut four 12- by 12-inch rectangles of aluminum foil. Spread them on one side with butter. Mound a quarter of the vegetable batter in the center of one half of each piece of foil. Use a fork to flatten each mound into the shape of a large cutlet about 1 inch thick. Fold the other sides of the foil rectangles over the "cutlets" and fold the open sides over two or three times in ¼-inch folds to seal.

Put the foil packets on the steamer rack(s), overlapping them by about 1 inch if necessary. Place over simmering water, cover, and steam 8 minutes. Set the lid ajar and steam 5 minutes longer.

Open the packets and transfer the "cutlets" to plates. Serve hot with the sauce.

FRESH TOMATO-BASIL SAUCE

Coulis de Tomate au Basilic

Manière served this cold sauce with his Vegetable Cutlets (page 61), Stuffed Zucchini (page 96), and cold steamed fish.

MAKES ABOUT 2 CUPS

6 small round or plum tomatoes (about
    1¼ pounds total)
1 teaspoon strong Dijon mustard
3 tablespoons wine vinegar or sherry
    vinegar
⅜ teaspoon salt
⅛ teaspoon freshly ground pepper
½ cup peanut or vegetable oil
1½ tablespoons chopped fresh chives
1½ tablespoons chopped fresh basil
1½ tablespoons chopped fresh chervil or
    1 teaspoon chopped fresh tarragon

 Make a tomato concassé with the tomatoes (see page 98), straining and saving the juices in a medium bowl.

Add the concassé, mustard, vinegar, salt, and pepper to the juices in the bowl and stir to mix. Then stir in the oil and herbs. Taste for salt and pepper. Refrigerate. Serve chilled.

CELERY

Celery is underrated as a vegetable in America, where we esteem it primarily for its raw crunch in tuna or potato salad. Celery prepared in the French way—the hearts, the tender, light-colored inside stalks of the plant, braised in white stock with a little butter and seasoning—has another dimension entirely; the flavor deepens so it tastes almost like celery root. The heart has a milder flavor than the thick, outer stalks. Steaming, like braising, uncovers a richness of flavor in celery; but, unlike braising, in steaming there is no competition from other ingredients.

Manière didn't often cook branch celery, preferring to use celery root. When he did steam celery, he cut it into bâtonnets. Having rediscovered this "new" vegetable, I steam the hearts either in whole stalks or in two-inch lengths and serve them drizzled with Lemon Vinaigrette (page 24), sometimes with shavings of Parmesan cheese as well.

Steamed and grilled celery has a wonderful deep, smoky flavor. Steam whole stalks as below and then grill them as directed on page 102, about two minutes on each side.

Celery leaves are spicy and fresh-tasting. Chop them to add to salads or steamed vegetables, or use them as a bed on which to steam fish (see page 161).

✳ PREPARING CELERY FOR STEAMING

Unless you're cutting the celery into small bâtonnets, as Manière did, use celery hearts instead of large branch celery; even peeled, steamed branch celery is tough. Steam the heart in whole stalks or cut into pieces, or steam it cut in half through the root end. Celery needn't be refreshed after steaming.

Celery Stalks Trim the leafy tops and the stem ends and peel the stalks deeply with a vegetable peeler or a paring knife to remove the strings. (No matter how long the celery steams, the strings remain tough and unpleasant.) Steam until the tip of a knife penetrates the celery easily.

Celery bâtonnets (¼ by 1½ inches)	5 to 7 minutes
Whole celery stalks	15 to 20 minutes
Celery stalks cut into 2-inch pieces	15 to 20 minutes

Celery Hearts Remove any large outer stalks and save them for soup or stock, or peel them and steam them too. Trim the bottoms of the hearts, but leave enough of the root end to hold the stalks together. Trim the tops so that the heart is about five inches long. Cut the trimmed hearts in half lengthwise. Steam until the tip of a knife penetrates the celery easily.

Small to medium celery hearts, halved	20 to 25 minutes
Large celery hearts, halved	25 to 30 minutes

CELERY ROOT (CELERIAC)

Celery root is the large, bulbous, robust-flavored root of a particular variety of celery. We don't eat the scrawny green, leafy stalks that grow out of the bulb of this variety; they're trimmed off and discarded. Celery root is popular in France and becoming more available in America. The flavor is reminiscent of ordinary celery but stronger and richer, and steaming accentuates its appealingly peppery bite.

Eat celery root raw as a salad, as the French do, finely julienned and dressed with mayonnaise (see page 27) flavored with enough strong Dijon mustard to make the mayonnaise hot, or with a rémoulade sauce (see page 100). I often add grated apple or carrot to the salad. For a more unusual variation, dress the julienned celery root with the Cumin Vinaigrette on page 86.

Steamed celery root, combined with some milk or cream, makes a velvety, ivory-colored purée. Manière added steamed potato to bind and smooth the purée, then enriched it with milk and butter (see page 65). Puréed with steamed apple instead of potato, it makes a lighter, less starchy purée. Steamed celery root also makes a delicious winter soup, puréed on its own with stock, water, or cream or in combination with other root vegetables, such as potato, carrot, turnip, and rutabaga.

Celery root blackens quickly when exposed to the air, so either cut the vegetable just before steaming or hold it in a bowl of lemon water as for artichokes (see page 29) until ready to steam. Buy small celery roots, if possible; the larger ones can be woody. Old celery root is spongy and tough (like old turnips) and grainy when steamed. The best way to guarantee good celery root is to buy it when it is in season, in late summer.

You will lose about half the weight of the celery root in cleaning it, so buy twice the "cleaned weight" (see page 101) you need.

✳ **PREPARING CELERY ROOT FOR STEAMING**
Wash the bulb well (the skin usually holds a lot of dirt) and then cut off the stem end, the tough brown skin, and the small roots with a paring knife. Pare off the brownish, yellowish flesh just beneath the skin to the white below.

Steam celery root until the tip of a knife penetrates the flesh easily. The timing depends enormously on the age of the celery root. Old celery root takes longer to steam; if very old, it never gets soft. Celery root needn't be refreshed after steaming.

³/₄- to 1-inch cubes celery root...15 to 20 minutes

CELERY ROOT AND POTATO PURÉE
Purée de Céleri et Pomme de Terre

Manière served this with steamed *andouillette,* French tripe sausage. It's also delicious with poultry, particularly duck, and with pork and fish.

SERVES 4 AS A SIDE DISH

2½ pounds celery root (1¼ pounds
    cleaned weight)
¾ pound small waxy potatoes
1⅓ cups whole milk
4 tablespoon unsalted butter
½ teaspoon salt
¼ teaspoon freshly ground pepper,
    preferably white
Pinch of freshly grated nutmeg

Stackable steamer, steamer pot with
    insert, pasta cooker, or collapsible
    steamer basket

 Trim the celery root and cut off all of the tough brown skin, as directed on page 64. Cut the bulb into ¾- to 1-inch cubes. Scrub the potatoes and leave them whole if very small; cut them in half if large, or quarters if very large.

Put the vegetables on the steamer rack, place over simmering water, cover, and steam until tender, about 20 minutes.

Meanwhile, heat the milk just to a simmer. Cover and keep warm.

Put the celery root, warm milk, and butter in the bowl of a food processor and purée until very smooth. Peel the potatoes and add to the celery root. Pulse just to purée; potato gets gummy if overworked. Add the salt, pepper, and nutmeg and pulse to mix. Add a tablespoon or so of water if the purée is too thick. Serve hot.

CELERY ROOT FLANS
Petits Flans de Céleri

These little individual flans don't take long to put together, they look very elegant, and they are delicious. Manière served them with fish in place of rice, the traditional accompaniment to fish in France. We can also serve them with roasted or steamed meats and poultry or as a meatless first course with a sauce such as Chervil Butter Sauce (page 152) or Tarragon Butter Sauce (page 254).

Try this recipe with other vegetables. Use the same "cleaned weight" (see page 101) of carrot, turnip, or cauliflower to replace the celery root.

For a low-fat version of the flans, replace the two whole eggs with four lightly beaten egg whites and the crème fraîche with a low-fat fresh cheese, such as *fromage blanc,* hoop cheese, or low-fat cottage cheese. (If using cottage cheese, purée it with the celery root until very smooth before adding the egg whites.) I like this version a lot. It's a little lighter in texture and loses nothing in the flavor—which in fact comes through even more purely and clearly than in the full-fat recipe.

If using a collapsible steamer basket to steam the flans, make sure that the pot you are using allows the basket to expand completely—and take care not to start by setting just one flan on the basket, or it will tilt to one side.

S E R V E S 4 A S A S I D E D I S H / F I R S T C O U R S E

Unsalted butter, softened, for buttering the ramekins and foil

¾ pound (1 medium or 2 small) celery root (6 ounces cleaned weight)

¼ cup crème fraîche or heavy cream

2 large eggs, lightly beaten

¼ teaspoon salt

⅛ teaspoon freshly ground pepper, preferably white

Aluminum foil

Four 4-ounce ramekins or 4 Pyrex custard cups

Large stackable steamer, steamer pot with insert, pasta cooker, roasting pan with wire rack, or collapsible steamer basket

Generously brush the ramekins or custard cups with softened butter.

Trim the celery root and cut off all of the tough brown skin, as directed on page 64. Then cut the bulb into ½- to ¾-inch cubes. You should have about 2 cups.

Put the cubes on the steamer rack, place over simmering water, cover, and steam until very soft, 15 to 20 minutes. Let cool slightly.

Purée the celery root in a food processor or blender with the crème fraîche or cream. Add the eggs, salt, and pepper and process or blend until very smooth.

Divide the mixture among the prepared ramekins or cups. Press a small square of buttered aluminum foil, buttered side down, over the top and around the rim of each to seal. Put the flans on the steamer rack, set over simmering water, cover, and steam until just set and a knife inserted in the centers comes out clean, about 10 minutes.

Remove the flans from the steamer and let stand 1 to 2 minutes. Then remove the foil, invert the flans onto serving plates, and serve.

THE CHICORY FAMILY

Crisp, bitter greens such as chicory, escarole, *chicorée frisée,* and Belgian endive are often lumped together with lettuces, but they belong to a separate family of greens called *chicories* (see page 79 for other greens, page 92 for spinach). There are beautiful red-leafed varieties as well, which fade in color in cooking. It's tough to keep the names of the chicories straight because they change from country to country. In America, chicory is a long-leafed head with long, slender stalks topped by jagged leafy greens. Escarole has a shorter, wider head with fat ribs and broad green curly leaves that lighten to yellow in the center of the head. Both are quite bitter.

What we call Belgian endive, known as chicory in England and *endive* in France, is a smooth yellow- and white-leafed small chicory with a tightly closed head; it is sweeter-tasting than escarole and our chicory. Belgian endive is "blanched" like white asparagus: It's grown under the earth to keep it white and sold wrapped in blue paper to keep out the light, which would turn it green and bitter.

The gorgeous jagged, lacy-leafed chicory called *chicorée frisée* in France is sold as curly endive in England and America. It's crisp and delicate with a gentler bitterness than escarole or American chicory. Manière used the yellowish-white heart of frisée in warm skate and guinea hen salads (see pages 123 and 196). The inner, lighter colored escarole leaves can be substituted for frisée in Manière's recipes. The French use frisée in salads dressed with a warm vinaigrette to wilt the leaves.

I like to eat chicory, escarole, and endive sliced, briefly steamed, and tossed with a warm vinaigrette as a first-course salad, or seasoned with one of the vinaigrettes on page 24. Manière sprinkled Belgian endive with sugar before steaming to counteract its bitterness. His Gratin of Endive with Ham and Gruyère Cheese (page 68) is saucy, savory, and substantial enough to serve as a main course. A lighter gratin can be made with halved endive, steamed over chicken broth or other steaming liquid saved from steaming a chicken (see page 220). Reduce the broth, now sweet from the endive, to concentrate the flavor, and pour the broth over the endive in a gratin dish, to cover by about half. Sprinkle with dried bread crumbs and Parmesan cheese, dot with butter, and brown in a hot oven.

To prepare chicory and escarole for steaming, pull off the leaves and trim the stem ends. Wash the leaves well and cut crosswise into 1-inch pieces. Steam just until wilted.

Chicory leaves, sliced into 1-inch strips	2 to 3 minutes
Escarole leaves, sliced into 1-inch strips	2 to 3 minutes

To prepare Belgian endive for steaming, trim the stem end and remove any wilted leaves. Steam whole or cut in half lengthwise until tender or thinly sliced crosswise until wilted.

Whole Belgian endive	25 minutes
Belgian endive, cut in half	13 to 15 minutes
Belgian endive, thinly sliced crosswise	5 to 6 minutes

GRATIN OF ENDIVE WITH HAM AND GRUYÈRE CHEESE

Endives à la Flamande

This gratin combines soft, juicy, mildly bitter endive, salty ham, rich, almost gooey sauce, and crusty Gruyère cheese. Manière served it as a main course, and we can also enjoy it as a side dish with hot or cold poultry or as a first course, substantial enough to serve six to eight people.

Manière made this wonderfully rich, luscious classic French dish even better by steaming the endive instead of blanching it. Steaming concentrates the flavor of the endive and ensures that the béchamel isn't diluted by any blanching water trapped in the leaves of the vegetable.

Unsalted butter, softened, for buttering
    the gratin dish

4 Belgian endive, trimmed and halved
    lengthwise
1 teaspoon sugar

MEDIUM BÉCHAMEL SAUCE
1 cup whole milk
3 tablespoons unsalted butter
1 tablespoon all-purpose flour
½ teaspoon salt
⅛ teaspoon freshly ground pepper,
    preferably white
⅛ teaspoon freshly grated nutmeg

1 large egg yolk
1½ tablespoons crème fraîche or heavy
    cream
4 thin slices boiled ham, halved crosswise
⅓ cup finely grated Gruyère cheese

10-inch oval or square gratin or baking
    dish
Large stackable steamer, roasting pan
    with wire rack, or collapsible steamer
    basket

 Butter the gratin or baking dish.

Put the endive in a single layer (or overlapping slightly) on the steamer rack and sprinkle with the sugar. Place over simmering water, cover, and steam for 25 minutes. Remove from the heat and let cool slightly.

While the endive is steaming, make the béchamel sauce: Bring the milk to a boil in a small saucepan.

Meanwhile, melt the butter in a medium heavy-bottomed saucepan over medium heat. Whisk in the flour and cook, whisking, until the mixture (roux) puffs slightly and bubbles, about 30 seconds.

Remove the roux from the heat, pour in the hot milk all at once, and whisk until smooth. Return the pan to the heat and cook very gently over low heat for 5 minutes, whisking often and reaching into the edges of the pan to keep the sauce from burning. Remove from the heat and whisk in the salt, pepper, and nutmeg.

Whisk together the egg yolk and crème fraîche or cream in a small bowl, and whisk into the hot sauce.

Preheat the broiler.

Roll each endive half up in a half-slice of ham. Place side by side, seam side down, in the gratin or baking dish and pour the sauce down the center. Sprinkle the cheese over the sauce and broil for 4 to 5 minutes, until golden brown. Serve hot.

CORN

Corn is still an exotic food in France, so much so that Manière called for canned corn in recipes that use the vegetable. Steaming takes slightly longer than boiling corn, but it is worth the time; very little of the sweet freshness of the corn is lost to the cooking water.

Buy corn as fresh as possible, which means locally; the less distance the corn has to travel, the more likely it is to be fresh. The sugars in corn turn to starch as the corn ages. The corn kernels should be plump and firm, not wrinkled. (Jab a kernel with your fingernail—it should be full of a milky juice; if it is dry, the corn is old.)

Steam corn as is, or coat it with an herb-flavored butter: Stir one or two tablespoons chopped fresh herbs such as tarragon, chives, parsley, chervil, basil, or summer savory or two to three teaspoons chopped fresh rosemary or thyme into four ounces softened unsalted butter and season to taste with salt and pepper. Wrap the buttered corn in aluminum foil before steaming (the foil slows down the steaming substantially).

✳ PREPARING CORN FOR STEAMING

Remove the husks and corn silk. Steam the corn on the cob, or cut off the kernels with a large knife and steam just the kernels.

Steam corn until the kernels yield slightly when pressed with a finger.

Whole ear of corn..10 minutes

Whole ear of corn with herb butter wrapped in foil (see above)............................22 minutes

Corn kernels..4 to 5 minutes

✳ STEAMING CORN IN QUANTITY

Steam ears of corn in a stackable steamer, a steamer pot with an insert, a pasta cooker, or a collapsible steamer basket. When steaming corn for a crowd, you may need to break the ears in half so that they fit more easily into the pot. Stacked in layers, whole (unwrapped) ears of corn take about fifteen minutes to steam.

CUCUMBERS

Steaming gives cucumbers a translucent, bright green color and brings out a sweetness that their raw taste only suggests. Serve them warm with butter, salt and pepper, and a sprinkling of chopped fresh chives, parsley, chervil, basil, or cilantro, or with reduced cream, as Manière did with cabbage (see page 53). Or serve them cold, in a salad with mint and yogurt (see page 71).

Manière used the longish European hothouse cucumber in his recipes, but the American cucumber can also be used. The European variety has a denser, less watery flesh and more flavor; the American variety has a sweeter, almost melonlike taste and an appealing crispness when steamed. Both kinds should be peeled, particularly the American variety, the skin of which is often waxed. The smaller kirby cucumbers, which are generally used for pickling, aren't waxed and have a thinner skin, which is pleasant to eat.

❋ DEGORGING CUCUMBERS

Cleverly putting the steamer to good use, Manière used the rack to degorge sliced cucumbers before steaming, as the French do to remove the bitterness. He tossed the cucumbers with salt on the rack and placed it over a bowl to let them drain for an hour. Then he rinsed the cucumbers, still on the rack, under running water, before steaming.

❋ PREPARING CUCUMBERS FOR STEAMING

To prepare American or European hothouse cucumbers for steaming, peel and halve lengthwise. Scrape out the seeds with a small spoon or the end of a swivel-type vegetable peeler. Cut into the desired size or shape. Degorge as above, if you like.

Steam cucumbers until they are translucent and a knife penetrates easily; the cucumbers should be tender but still with a firm "tooth." The steaming times for American and European hothouse cucumbers are the same. Cucumbers needn't be refreshed after steaming unless they are to be used for making a salad (see page 23).

¹/₄-inch-thick slices cucumber..	5 minutes
Cucumber bâtonnets..	5 minutes

CUCUMBERS WITH MINT AND YOGURT
Concombres à la Menthe et au Yaourt

Manière believed that steamed cucumber is easier to digest than raw, but he made this quick, clean-tasting, refreshing salad with either. I prefer steaming the cucumbers because it improves the flavor and makes them gleam.

For a low-fat version of this recipe, substitute nonfat yogurt for the higher-fat varieties. The lower-fat yogurts, particularly nonfat, make the sauce very tangy.

(continued)

3 medium American or 2 medium
   European hothouse cucumbers,
   peeled, halved, seeded, and cut
   crosswise into thin slices
1 tablespoon coarse salt

YOGURT-MINT SAUCE
3 tablespoons white wine vinegar or
   juice of 1 medium lemon (about
   3 tablespoons)
⅛ teaspoon freshly ground pepper,
   preferably white
¾ cup plain whole-milk or low-fat yogurt
3 tablespoons peanut or vegetable oil
2 teaspoons finely shredded fresh mint

Mint leaves, for garnish

Stackable steamer, steamer pot with
   insert, pasta cooker, or collapsible
   steamer basket

 Put the cucumber slices on the steamer rack and degorge them: Toss them with the salt, set the rack in a bowl, and let drain for 1 hour (no longer, or they will become too salty).

Meanwhile, make the sauce: Combine the vinegar or lemon juice and pepper in a small bowl. (The sauce doesn't need salt because the cucumbers absorb enough in degorging.) Whisk in the yogurt and then the oil. Add the shredded mint. Refrigerate.

Rinse the cucumbers (in the steamer rack) under cold running water to remove excess salt.

Place the steamer rack over simmering water, cover, and steam 2 minutes. Refresh under cold running water and pat dry with a towel.

Toss the cucumbers in a serving bowl with the yogurt sauce. Garnish the salad with mint leaves and serve chilled.

EGGPLANT

Steaming uncovers a surprisingly mild sweetness in eggplant, and Manière's recipes superbly exploit this flavor. Traditional recipes cook eggplant in a lot of oil, which obscures the taste of the vegetable. Manière used oil as a seasoning to augment and enhance the flavor of the eggplant rather than to hide it. Steamed eggplant can be substituted for sautéed in many conventional recipes, by steaming peeled or unpeeled chunks or slices and then tossing them in a minimal amount of oil for flavor. Once steamed, the eggplant will absorb much less oil than usual because it is already moist. (If you choose not to peel your eggplant, you'll get the added bonus of tender purple skin that helps hold the flesh together.)

Chinese eggplants are a small, slender variety, pale lavender in color. They have fewer and smaller seeds than the larger varieties and a higher skin-to-flesh ratio, and, as a result, a slightly firmer texture when cooked. There is very little difference in flavor between the Chinese and larger eggplants except that Chinese eggplant is somewhat less bitter.

Although eggplants vary in bitterness, common wisdom is to salt and drain them before cooking. Manière's recipes don't salt—and I have never had steamed eggplant that tasted bitter.

✳ **PREPARING EGGPLANT FOR STEAMING**
Manière steamed eggplant whole for purée (see Eggplant Caviar, below) and in cubes for lamb stew (see page 246).

Whole Eggplant Wash the eggplant and steam, unpeeled, until very soft when squeezed.

Whole small to medium (up to 1 pound) eggplant..................................30 to 40 minutes	
Whole large (over 1 pound) eggplant..................................40 to 45 minutes	

Eggplant in Chunks Trim and peel the eggplant or not, as you like, and cut it into chunks. Steam until the chunks are just tender when pierced with the tip of a knife but still hold their shape. Steamed eggplant does not need to be refreshed.

2-inch cubes purple eggplant, with or without peel..................................5 to 7 minutes	
2-inch cubes Chinese eggplant, unpeeled..................................7 minutes	

Eggplant caviar
Caviar d'Aubergines

Eggplant spreads are a dime a dozen; most taste the same and none really tastes like eggplant to me. Manière's, however, is extraordinary. The smooth, subtle taste of the steamed eggplant fills the mouth, and the olive oil caresses the flavor without masking it or making it heavy. Manière served his eggplant caviar cold, on warm croutons. It's equally delicious hot, as a bed for grilled swordfish or tuna or steamed salmon.

Steamed eggplant is milder than grilled or roasted eggplant because it's not smoky from the fire. The quality of olive oil makes a difference in this recipe; an elegant, peppery Tuscan oil works especially well.

This keeps at least two days in the refrigerator. The recipe makes more than Manière's usual four servings, so that it can be on hand for another occasion.

. . . .

S E R V E S   6   T O   8   A S   A   C O L D   F I R S T   C O U R S E
(M A K E S   4   C U P S)

. . . .

1 medium head garlic, cloves separated
   but not peeled
2 medium eggplants
1 teaspoon salt
1 tablespoon freshly ground pepper,
   preferably white
1 tablespoon sweet Hungarian paprika
1½ tablespoons Dijon mustard
1 large egg yolk
⅔ cup good-quality olive oil
Hot toasted bread slices, for serving

Stackable steamer, steamer pot with
   insert, pasta cooker, or collapsible
   steamer basket

 Put the garlic and eggplants on the steamer rack, place over simmering water, and steam 40 minutes.

Remove the vegetables from the steamer and let cool a few minutes. Cut the eggplants in half, scoop out the flesh, and put it into the bowl of a food processor. Squeeze the garlic out of the skins and add it to the bowl. Add the salt, pepper, and paprika, and process to purée. Add the mustard and egg yolk and process to blend. With the machine running, add the oil in a thin stream. Refrigerate until well chilled.

Serve with hot toasted bread slices.

MARINATED VEGETABLES WITH CORIANDER AND THYME
Méli-Mélo de Légumes à la Grecque

. . . .

This is a stunning dish with its variety of colors, flavors, and textures—including the playful pop of the coriander seeds and peppercorns that soften enough in the steaming to make them completely edible. Standard recipes for *à la Grecque* preparations are time-consuming and require a lot of little pots. Each vegetable must simmer and then marinate separately in an olive-oil-and-coriander-flavored brine so that each can take on the taste of the marinade without being muddied by the flavors of the other vegetables.

Manière took advantage of the fact that steaming doesn't marry flavors by steaming all of his vegetables together above the brine. While he used only the oil from the steaming liquid to marinate the vegetables, I use some of the liquid too; it has a lot of flavor and it makes the dish a little lighter. Save the marinade after the vegetables have been eaten; drizzled over other steamed vegetables, it adds zip.

The vegetables must marinate twenty-four hours before serving, so start them a day ahead. They hold at least one week in the refrigerator; Manière purposely wrote the recipe for more than four servings to have some extra on hand.

Cut the carrots, eggplant, and zucchini on the diagonal, both to expose the maximum amount of interior and to make a pretty presentation.

5 medium carrots, peeled and thinly
   sliced on the diagonal

1 medium eggplant, trimmed and cut on
   the diagonal into ¼-inch-thick slices

3 medium onions, sliced into thin rounds

1 tablespoon salt

1 tablespoon coriander seeds

1 teaspoon black peppercorns

1½ tablespoons chopped parsley

1 teaspoon dried thyme leaves

2 whole cloves

6 medium cloves garlic, minced

4 small zucchini, thinly sliced on the
   diagonal

2 small red bell peppers, cored, halved,
   seeds and ribs removed, and cut into
   1-inch strips

1⅓ cups olive oil or a combination of
   olive and peanut or vegetable oil

Large stackable steamer, steamer pot
   with insert, pasta cooker, or
   collapsible steamer basket

 Put the carrots on the steamer rack, then the eggplant, and then the onions, sprinkling each vegetable with some of the salt. Sprinkle with the coriander seeds, peppercorns, parsley, thyme, cloves, and garlic. Add the zucchini and sprinkle with salt. Add the peppers and sprinkle with the remaining salt. Place the steamer rack over simmering water, cover, and steam 5 minutes.

Pour about ⅓ cup of the oil over the vegetables, replace the lid, and steam 5 more minutes. Pour another ⅓ cup oil over the vegetables, replace the lid, and steam 5 more minutes. Repeat two more times, until all the oil has been used and the vegetables have steamed a total of 25 minutes.

Use a slotted spoon to gently transfer the vegetables to a large shallow bowl. Let the steaming liquid cool and then, using a ladle, scoop the oil from the top of the liquid and ladle it over the vegetables. Ladle over some of the steaming liquid as well if you like (see headnote). Let the vegetables cool, then cover and refrigerate for 24 hours.

Bring the vegetables to room temperature before serving. (Remove only as much as you'll eat from the refrigerator; the peppers will ferment if left at room temperature for too long.)

FENNEL

Fennel is a versatile vegetable that can be eaten a number of ways. Raw, it is sweet and crisp with a distinct anise flavor. When it is sautéed or braised, in the French way, the sweetness gives way to luscious warm tones and a melting texture. Steamed fennel is something in between. It's clean-tasting with a concentrated warm anise flavor that hints at the sweetness of the raw vegetable.

I enjoy fennel either steamed until tender, as Manière preferred it, or thinly sliced and steamed just two to three minutes, to barely wilt. Still-crunchy fennel makes a fresh first course or cold salad dressed with Lemon or Balsamic Vinaigrette (page 24), along with a chopped fresh herb, chopped garlic or thinly sliced red onion, and shaved Parmesan cheese.

✳ PREPARING FENNEL FOR STEAMING

Cut off the fingerlike stalks on an angle that follows the shape of the bulb. Remove any browned or withered parts. Trim the root end of the bulb. If the bulb is large, peel the outside with a potato peeler. Cut the bulb in half through the root end. Cut it in half again through the bottom to quarter it, or lay the halves cut side down and cut slices lengthwise through the root end.

Steam the fennel until tender but not mushy—the tip of a knife pierces the vegetable with a little resistance. (The times in the chart are to cook the fennel completely; steam slices for two to three minutes just to wilt.) Fennel needn't be refreshed unless it is to be used in a cold salad.

Medium fennel, quartered	20 to 25 minutes
1/8- to 1/4-inch-thick fennel	8 to 10 minutes

FENNEL FANS WITH ZUCCHINI AND GARLIC
Fenouils à la Bohémienne

This dish is equally good hot or at room temperature, with fish. Serve the still-sealed foil packets on dinner plates, then slit the top of each with kitchen scissors so that guests can open their own to the pleasure of the delicious smells that escape.

SERVES 4 AS A SIDE DISH

2 small bulbs fennel, trimmed and halved
   lengthwise
2 small (slender) zucchini, trimmed and
   halved lengthwise
1 small onion, sliced into thin rounds
4 medium cloves garlic, minced
Salt and freshly ground pepper
1 tablespoon plus 1 teaspoon olive oil
1½ tablespoons chopped parsley

Aluminum foil
Large stackable steamer with two
   steaming compartments or steamer
   pot with insert, pasta cooker, or
   collapsible steamer basket for the
   vegetables and roasting pan with wire
   rack for the foil packages

 Put the fennel on the steamer rack. Place over simmering water, cover, and steam 5 minutes. Add the zucchini and onion slices to the rack. Put the minced garlic on a little round of aluminum foil to keep it from falling through the rack and add it to the steamer rack. Cover and steam 5 more minutes. Remove the vegetables from the steamer.

Cut four 7- by 10-inch rectangles of aluminum foil. Place the fennel halves, cut sides down, on a cutting board. Starting about an inch from the root end and cutting at an angle, cut four slits in each fennel half to make fans. Press down gently on each fennel half with the palm of your hand to flatten and open the fans.

Place a fennel fan, cut side down, on one half of each aluminum foil rectangle. Cut each zucchini half crosswise into 4 pieces. Slip one zucchini piece into each of the "slices" in the fennel fans, so that each fan holds 4 zucchini pieces. Distribute the onion and garlic evenly over the fennel fans and sprinkle with salt and pepper. Drizzle each fan with 1 teaspoon oil and sprinkle with the parsley. Fold the other sides of the foil over the fans and fold over the edges three or four times in ¼-inch folds to seal the packages.

Put the packages onto the steamer rack in a single layer, place over simmering water, cover, and steam 15 minutes. Place the packages on plates and let your guests open them.

GARLIC

While raw garlic is hot and sharp, steaming mellows it to a mild and velvety sweetness. Its pungency is so gentled by cooking that we can use a lot of it; the Eggplant Caviar on page 73, for example, calls for an entire head, and the Garlic Flans on page 78 use two. Manière believed that steaming removed most of the oxalic acid that can make garlic hard to digest.

Puréed steamed garlic has a creamy starchiness that works as a low-fat thickener for vegetable soups, purées, and sauces (see pages 100–102). Manière exploited this quality in the sauce for the veal kidneys on page 262.

✳ **PREPARING GARLIC FOR STEAMING**

Manière steamed whole garlic cloves for purée. He also steamed sliced or minced garlic when he wanted that sweetness in a vegetable mixture (see Fennel Fans, page 77) or stew (see Smothered Lamb with Eggplant, page 246).

Separate the cloves but do not peel. For older garlic, cut the cloves in half and, if there is a white or green sprout in the center, pull it out. (The sprout is hot and bitter.) Steam until the cloves are very soft when squeezed.

Unpeeled whole garlic cloves...15 to 18 minutes
Unpeeled halved garlic cloves..12 to 15 minutes

GARLIC FLANS
Flans d'Ail

Steamed puréed garlic gives these elegant little individual flans a rich, full taste that has none of the harshness of raw garlic. The base of the flan is similar to that of the Celery Root Flans on page 66, but Manière replaced one egg yolk with potato starch so as not to mask the sweetness of the garlic. Potato starch, a tasteless starch that looks something like cornstarch, is available in health food and some specialty food stores. Manière used it to give the flans a somewhat firmer texture. It's worth trying if potato starch is readily available, but the flans will hold together without it.

Manière served the flans with lamb and pork; I like them with poultry as well, or as a meatless first course sauced with Tarragon Butter Sauce (page 254). Manière's low-fat version of the dish replaces the crème fraîche with low-fat *fromage blanc* or a low-fat fresh cheese such as hoop cheese or low-fat cottage cheese. (If you use cottage cheese, purée it with the garlic until very smooth before adding the eggs.)

If using a collapsible steamer basket to steam the flans, make sure that the pot you are using allows the basket to expand completely—and take care not to start by setting just one flan on the basket, or it will tilt to one side.

S E R V E S   4   A S   A   S I D E   D I S H / F I R S T   C O U R S E

Unsalted butter, softened, for buttering
   the ramekins and foil

2 medium heads garlic
5 tablespoons crème fraîche or heavy
   cream
1 large egg
1 large egg white
1 teaspoon potato starch (optional)
¼ teaspoon salt
⅛ teaspoon freshly ground pepper,
   preferably white

Aluminum foil
Four 4-ounce ramekins or 4 Pyrex
   custard cups
Stackable steamer, steamer pot with
   shallow insert, or collapsible steamer
   basket

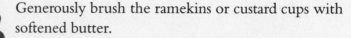

Generously brush the ramekins or custard cups with softened butter.

Separate the garlic cloves, peel, halve, and remove the center sprouts, if any. Put the garlic cloves on the steamer rack, place over simmering water, cover, and steam until very soft, about 15 minutes. Let cool slightly.

Purée the garlic with the crème fraîche or cream in a food processor or blender. Lightly beat the whole egg and egg white and add to the purée along with the potato starch, if using, and the salt and pepper. Process or blend until smooth.

Divide the garlic mixture among the prepared ramekins or custard cups. Cover each with a small square of buttered aluminum foil, buttered side down, pressing the foil around the rims to seal. Put the flans on the steamer rack, place over simmering water, cover, and steam until just firm and a knife inserted in the centers comes out clean, about 10 minutes.

Remove the flans from the steamer and let stand for 1 to 2 minutes. Remove the foil, invert the flans onto serving plates, and serve hot.

GREENS AND LETTUCES

Sautéed, blanched, or stewed greens such as kale and mustard, collard, and beet greens are familiar to Americans. The French eat cooked lettuces and chicories (see page 67) as well, as vegetables or added to soups and custards. All greens can be steamed, as Manière did. Steam tender greens such as watercress, Swiss chard, and beet and mustard greens in whole leaves (see also Spinach, page 92). I cut tougher greens, such as kale and collard greens, into strips before steaming. Eat the greens as is with a good olive or nut oil and lemon juice or one of the vinaigrettes on page 24. Or finish them in a sauté pan with oil and chopped garlic, onion, shallot, leek, or fresh ginger or hot red pepper flakes.

The French relish the fleshy stems of Swiss chard as much as the leaves; in some parts of France, the stem is preferred to the leaves. Steam the stem cut into two-inch pieces, then cover with a medium béchamel sauce (page 69) in a buttered gratin dish, adding small pieces of ham, if you like, and brown under the broiler, as for the Gratin of Belgian Endive with Ham and Gruyère Cheese on page 68.

✳ REFRESHING GREENS

Greens such as chard, kale, and collard greens are steamed past the point at which they turn bright green to make them tender, so they don't need refreshing after steaming. Spinach, on the other hand, is often refreshed (see page 23).

✳ PREPARING GREENS FOR STEAMING

The timings in the charts are for greens for two to four people, measured in packed cups, steamed in a steamer pot with an insert. Count on about half a pound of raw greens for each person. Stir halfway through the steaming.

To prepare Swiss chard, kale, or mustard, collard, or beet greens for steaming, hold the leaf in one hand, folding it in half lengthwise with the veiny side out, and strip off the tough stem with your other hand. (For small beet greens, it is sufficient just to trim off the stem even with the leaf.) Wash the leaves well. Cut kale and collard greens into strips; leave beet and mustard greens and chard whole. Steam until wilted and tender. Kale and collard greens will lose their bright green color, but if undercooked, they are tough and harsh-tasting.

Beet greens, whole leaves (2 bunches, 5 to 6 cups, to serve 2)..........................7 to 8 minutes

Kale, sliced $1/2$ inch thick (6 to 8 cups, to serve 4)......................................15 minutes

Mustard greens, whole leaves (1 small bunch, 6 cups, to serve 2)..................9 to 10 minutes

Collard greens, sliced $3/4$ inch thick (1 large bunch, 5 cups, to serve 4)..................15 minutes

Swiss chard, whole leaves (1 bunch, 5 to 6 cups, to serve 2)............................7 to 8 minutes

The fleshy stems of Swiss chard are edible. Cut them into two-inch pieces and steam them separately, as they take longer to cook than the leaves.

Swiss chard stems, cut into 2-inch sections	8 to 10 minutes

✳ STEAMED WATERCRESS

Manière used watercress, a small, dark-green-leafed member of the mustard family with a spicy, peppery taste, for a puréed soup (see below). It's also very good as a vegetable and needs less cleaning and trimming than other strong greens. Three bunches of watercress (eight to nine cups raw) feed four people. Trim about one inch from the stems and steam until wilted. Season to taste with salt and pepper and toss with a little butter or olive oil, if you like.

Watercress (2 bunches)	5 minutes
(4 bunches)	7 to 8 minutes

CREAM OF WATERCRESS SOUP
Crème de Cresson

This peppery light green soup is quick to make and not too rich because it uses milk instead of cream. Use the recipe as a model for other soups by replacing the watercress with another vegetable (a steamed head of cauliflower; a bunch of broccoli, trimmed and steamed; four cups steamed cubed peeled carrots or celery root). Manière served the soup with croûtons sautéed in butter. If you prefer, toast the bread triangles, without butter, in a 400-degree oven until lightly browned, about 10 minutes.

(continued)

1 medium waxy potato, halved

2 bunches watercress (5 to 6 packed
    cups), washed and tough stems
    trimmed

Salt and freshly ground pepper,
    preferably white

1 quart whole milk

CROÛTONS

4 slices white bread

2 tablespoons unsalted butter

Stackable steamer, steamer pot with
    insert, pasta cooker, or collapsible
    steamer basket

 Put the potato on the steamer rack, add the watercress, and sprinkle with salt and pepper. Place over simmering water, cover, and steam until the potato is tender, about 20 minutes.

Meanwhile, bring the milk to a boil. Remove from the heat, cover, and keep warm.

Make the croûtons: Cut the crusts from the bread slices and cut each slice on the diagonal into 2 triangles, then cut each triangle in half again. Melt the butter in a medium frying pan over medium heat. Add the croûtons and sauté until lightly browned, about 2 minutes on each side.

When the vegetables are cooked, put the watercress into the bowl of a food processor and purée, adding some of the hot milk if necessary. Peel the potato and add to the watercress. Pulse to finely chop the potato. The purée should not be completely smooth; potato gets gummy if overworked. Whisk the vegetable purée into the hot milk and then stir in 1½ teaspoons salt and ¼ teaspoon pepper. Taste, and add salt if necessary.

Ladle the soup into bowls, float the croûtons on top, and serve hot.

KOHLRABI

Kohlrabi is a member of the cabbage family, although it looks nothing like its relatives. It is a bulblike vegetable with a thick, light green skin, topped by long, slender, leafy stems. It looks like a root vegetable but it isn't. The bulb is simply the swollen, lower part of the stem, which appears above the ground. Kohlrabi is usually about the size of an orange but can be even larger, depending on the variety.

The flavor of kohlrabi is sweet and nutty and mildly cabbage-like. Young kohlrabi can be eaten raw (it tastes a lot like raw broccoli), but in America it's generally cooked. Serve it dressed with melted butter or cream, puréed with a little cream or stock (see page 100), or with any vinaigrette or seasonings you like with steamed broccoli.

✳ **PREPARING KOHLRABI FOR STEAMING**
Cut off the stems and leaves. Tender sprouts and stems can be cooked along with the bulb, but save the rest for soup—or discard. Peel the bulb with a small knife and cut it into bâtonnets (see page

104) or slices. Steam until the tip of a knife penetrates the vegetable easily. Kohlrabi needn't be refreshed after steaming, unless it is for a cold salad (see page 23).

Kohlrabi bâtonnets	10 to 12 minutes
¼-inch-thick slices kohlrabi	10 to 12 minutes

THE ONION FAMILY

Manière occasionally steamed standard yellow onions in stew-type dishes (see page 259), with other vegetables (see Fennel Fans with Zucchini and Garlic, page 77), or to flavor sauerkraut (see pages 128 and 255). But he was more likely to steam leeks, pearl onions, or spring onions when he wanted to serve an onion, or its relative, as a vegetable.

✳ SPRING ONIONS AND SCALLIONS

Spring onions are red or white onions with green tops, like scallions but with a rounder bulb. They come in different sizes, some as big as a standard yellow onion; the ones Manière used were small, the size of a pearl onion. He used sliced spring onions to flavor salads (see page 85) or as part of assorted spring vegetable combinations to serve with steamed chicken (see page 188), lamb (see page 244), and liver (see page 260). If you can't find spring onions, use scallions or pearl onions.

Preparing Spring Onions and Scallions for Steaming To prepare small spring onions for steaming whole, cut off all but about one inch of the green tops and trim the root ends. Pull off the outer layers of skin, if damaged. Steam until tender when pierced with the tip of a knife.

To prepare scallions, trim the root ends and pull off the outer layer of skin, if damaged. Cut off most of the green tops. Steam until tender when pierced with the tip of a knife.

Small spring onions (less than 1 inch in diameter)	10 to 12 minutes
Scallions	15 minutes

❋ PEARL ONIONS

Manière used pearl onions in Veal Blanquette (page 240), with fresh peas (see page 87), and for a sweet-and-sour jam (see page 193). Pearl onions are smaller and milder-tasting than yellow onions. Red, yellow, or white, the flavor is the same. Steamed pearl onions are mild, sweet, and delicious. Serve them tossed in butter, salt, and pepper, with other steamed vegetables.

Peeling Pearl Onions Traditionally, pearl onions are blanched for a few minutes to loosen the skins for ease in peeling. Manière steamed them instead: Steam 1 minute, and then peel with a paring knife.

Preparing Pearl Onions for Steaming Peel pearl onions as above. Steam them until a knife penetrates the onions with no resistance.

Small to medium pearl onions	10 to 15 minutes
Large pearl onions	15 to 20 minutes

❋ LEEKS

Like asparagus, leeks get watery when blanched. Steaming concentrates their elegant, delicate onion flavor. The French typically eat leeks as a cold first course, drenched in a vinaigrette, braised in stock, or in a soup, such as Cream of Leek and Potato Soup (page 90). Manière also used leeks, trimmed of their green tops, as a hot vegetable to accompany steamed tarragon-scented chicken (see page 190). Use the tops in stock or soup.

Eat whole steamed leeks, drizzled with butter or olive or nut oil and sprinkled with fresh herbs, as a hot vegetable or first course. Bedded side by side under a blanket of cheese and béchamel sauce, leeks make a savory gratin. Use the recipe for Gratin of Endive with Ham and Gruyère Cheese (page 68) as a guide, replacing the endive with steamed leeks trimmed of all but about an inch of the green tops. If you like, substitute grated Parmesan cheese for half the Gruyère. In the summer, steamed leeks rolled in olive oil, seasoned, and grilled over a wood fire are wonderful on their own or in combination with other grilled vegetables (see page 102).

If possible, buy slender or medium-sized leeks rather than large, fat ones.

Preparing Leeks for Steaming Trim the root end of the leeks, cutting off as little of the white part as possible. Pull off any yellowed or damaged leaves. Then, starting about one inch from the root end, quarter the leeks lengthwise, through the green part, so that they are slit open but held together at the root end. Wash the leeks well in warm water; they're usually very sandy. Depending on the season, leeks may have a hard, yellowish-white core. If so, cut the leek completely in half lengthwise and remove it.

Leeks may be steamed whole or sliced. The French usually trim off the green tops and save them for stock or soup, unless they are serving whole leeks cold with a vinaigrette.

Steam leeks until the tip of a knife penetrates the white part with no resistance. Manière gave longish steaming times for leeks because their sweetness develops as they cook.

Slender whole leek	10 to 15 minutes
Medium whole leek	15 to 20 minutes
Large whole leek	20 to 25 minutes
Leeks (white part only) cut crosswise into 2-inch pieces	15 to 25 minutes, depending on size

Warm chick pea salad with spring onions

Pois Chiches aux Oignons Nouveaux

This salad can be put together almost instantly using canned chick peas, as Manière did, to save us the peeling. (Dried chick peas are covered with a thin, tough skin that should be removed after cooking.) Whole cumin seed has a warm, spicy flavor that complements the nutty, velvety-soft chick peas; spring onion or scallion sweetens both. Spring onions are sold in bunches, with their green tops still attached. Mild, sweet scallions are a fine substitute.

(continued)

If your cumin seed has lost its scent with age, you can rejuvenate it by heating it in a dry sauté pan over medium heat until you can smell its fragrance, three to five minutes. Be careful not to burn it.

Two 1-pound cans chick peas, drained and rinsed

CUMIN VINAIGRETTE
3 tablespoons white wine vinegar
½ teaspoon cumin seed
½ cup olive oil
⅛ teaspoon salt
⅛ teaspoon freshly ground pepper

3 small spring onions, trimmed and thinly sliced, or ½ cup thinly sliced scallions
1½ tablespoons chopped parsley

Stackable steamer, steamer pot with insert, pasta cooker, or collapsible steamer basket

 Put the chick peas on the steamer rack, place over simmering water, cover, and steam 5 minutes, or until warmed through.

Meanwhile, make the vinaigrette: Whisk together the vinegar and cumin seed in a large bowl. Whisk in the oil, then the salt and pepper.

Add the warm chick peas and the onions or scallions to the vinaigrette and toss gently to mix. Scrape into a serving bowl, sprinkle with the parsley, and serve warm.

PEAS

Manière was very fond of peas. He used them in a variety of ways: tossed with butter, pearl onions, and fresh mint (see page 87); as sweet, bright green accents to vegetable assortments; with shellfish (see page 160); and with poultry (see page 188).

Fresh, tender, small peas in the pod may be hard to find if you don't grow them yourself. Older, larger peas get starchy and lose their sweetness. Manière's recipe for minted peas is a good way to cook older peas because the relatively long cooking time gives them time to soften, and the mint and onion perfume them. Frozen petite peas can be substituted for fresh in Manière's recipes.

Manière always used green shell peas, or peas in the pod, which need to be shelled. We also have edible pod peas, such as snow peas and sugar snap peas, both of which usually need to be strung. Sugar snap peas are plump and very sweet; they should be steamed just to wilt them so as not to diminish their sweet flavor. Snow peas have a flat pod and are a less vibrant green color than green or sugar snap peas.

✳ PREPARING GREEN PEAS FOR STEAMING

Shell the peas by grasping the little top stem with one hand and pulling down the side of the pod to open it. Shell peas just before cooking so that they don't dry out. Steam until just tender.

One pound of green peas in the pod yields one third to one half pound of shelled peas, or one and a third to one and a half cups. (The yield varies greatly depending on the size of the peas.)

Manière prepared four pounds of shell peas to serve four people, but this is very generous; two to three pounds is more usual.

Shelled green peas	8 to 10 minutes

✳ PREPARING SUGAR SNAP AND SNOW PEAS FOR STEAMING

Strip off the strings and steam until the color is vibrant and the peas are crisp-tender; longer steaming makes them less sweet. Refresh sugar snap and snow peas (see page 23) unless they are to be eaten immediately. One pound of snow or sugar snap peas serves four to six.

Sugar snap peas	3 to 5 minutes
Snow peas	3 to 5 minutes

PEAS WITH PEARL ONIONS AND MINT
Petits Pois à la Menthe

Pearl onions are a traditional accompaniment to peas in French cooking, the classic example being *petits pois à la française,* peas stewed in butter with pearl onions and julienned lettuce. Manière steamed peas with pearl onions and fresh mint, perfuming the peas with the flavor of both, then tossed them in cream and butter. (I confess to steaming more onions than Manière called for because I love them in this dish.)

The lavish combination of cream and butter makes this recipe wonderfully rich, but the cream can be omitted for those concerned about fat. Let the butter come to room temperature in the serving bowl while the peas steam.

SERVES 4 AS A SIDE DISH

4 pounds peas in the pod, shelled

8 pearl onions, peeled (see page 84)

3 sprigs fresh mint

Generous ⅛ teaspoon salt

2 tablespoons unsalted butter

3 tablespoons crème fraîche or
    3 tablespoons heavy cream mixed
    with 1 teaspoon fresh lemon juice

Stackable steamer, steamer pot with
    insert, pasta cooker, or collapsible
    steamer basket

 Spread the peas in an even layer on the steamer rack. Put the onions and sprigs of mint on top of the peas. Sprinkle with the salt. Place over simmering water, cover, and steam 20 minutes.

Meanwhile, put the butter and crème fraîche or cream and lemon juice in a serving dish.

When the peas and onions are cooked, remove the mint. Transfer the vegetables to the serving dish and very gently, so as not to mash the peas, toss with the butter and cream until the butter has melted.

POTATOES

Potatoes come in many varieties, and the steaming time and use vary according to type. Potatoes can be roughly divided into two categories: those that are mealy or floury in texture, called baking potatoes (like the Idaho Russet), and those that are denser and more finely textured, called boiling or waxy potatoes (such as red-skinned potatoes). The difference is determined by starch content; mealy potatoes are starchy, waxy potatoes are less so. Potatoes that fall in between the two are called all-purpose potatoes.

Mealy potatoes are fluffy and dry and fall apart easily. They are best baked or mashed, or used in vegetable purées (see page 100) or in rough soups, where their starch thickens the broth. Waxy potatoes are firm-textured and don't fall apart when boiled or steamed, unless overcooked. Use waxy potatoes if you particularly want the potato to hold together, in dishes such as boiled potatoes, potato gratins, and sautéed potatoes. All-purpose potatoes, as the name suggests, can be used in any potato preparation. Manière probably used a medium-starch yellow-fleshed potato with a velvety texture; Yukon Golds, an all-purpose potato available in some markets, is a good choice here.

Depending on their starch content, potatoes steam differently. The less starchy the potato, the faster it cooks. Idaho potatoes take longer to steam than waxy potatoes. This is important to know when steaming whole potatoes, as Manière did in many recipes. If the potato is large or a type that cooks slowly, the outside overcooks and falls apart before the inside is cooked through. When Manière's recipes call for whole steamed potatoes, use all-purpose or waxy potatoes weighing about three to four ounces each, or cut the potatoes into smaller pieces.

✳ PURÉEING POTATOES

In his recipes for soups, Manière used a food processor to purée steamed potato into the soup to thicken it. But hot potatoes get gummy and elastic if overworked in the food processor. So it's best, when puréeing a potato for Manière's recipes or for vegetable purées, to process the other ingredients first and add the potato last. Then add the potato and pulse until it is very finely chopped, but not completely smooth (there should be some specks of potato in the mixture).

FRENCH POTATO SALAD

Unlike the all-American potato salad, French potato salad is a warm salad of cut-up potatoes dressed with a vinaigrette, rather than with a mayonnaise. Count on about half a pound of waxy potatoes per person; red-skinned are a good choice, for the color. Cut the potatoes into one-and-a-half-inch pieces and steam them with the skin on. Then remove the skin or not, as you like, and dress them, while still hot, with Sauce Ravigote (page 27), a vinaigrette flavored with capers, onion, and anchovy.

✳ PREPARING POTATOES FOR STEAMING

Scrub the potatoes and steam them whole or cut up, unpeeled, until a knife penetrates to the center with no resistance.

Whole small waxy potatoes (2 to 3 ounces)	25 to 35 minutes, depending on variety
Whole medium waxy potatoes (4 to 5 ounces)	35 to 45 minutes, depending on variety
Waxy potatoes cut into 1½- by 2-inch pieces	20 minutes
Waxy potatoes cut into 1½- by 1½-inch pieces	15 minutes
Idaho potatoes cut into 1½- by 2-inch pieces	25 minutes

Steam potatoes in a stackable steamer, a steamer pot with insert, a pasta cooker, or a collapsible steamer basket. Potatoes steamed in more than one layer take the same amount of time to steam as in a single layer.

CREAM OF LEEK AND POTATO SOUP

Crème à la Mustel

Manière noted that this soup, created in 1906 by the chef Albert Chavallier, was called *Mustel* to honor the eighteenth-century Chevalier de Mustel, a captain of the dragoons who left the army to study agriculture and potato farming. Like Parmentier, with whom he was friends, Mustel helped popularize the potato in France; he published a treatise on potatoes in 1767, four years before Parmentier published his own.

This is a rich, creamy soup served in natural "bowls" created by hollowing out the steamed potatoes. Use well-shaped oval potatoes with unblemished skins, and make sure not to puncture the skins while scooping out the steamed flesh. This soup can also be made with stock (see page 101), milk, or half milk and half cream.

The potato "bowls" are small, so you'll have soup left over after the potatoes are filled. But the soup is rich enough that just a little will satisfy your guests, and the leftovers will be even better the next day.

SERVES 4

4 large red-skinned or all-purpose potatoes (4 to 5 ounces each), scrubbed

1 medium leek, white part only

½ teaspoon salt

¼ teaspoon freshly ground pepper, preferably white

2 cups crème fraîche or heavy cream

1½ tablespoons fresh chervil leaves or 1 teaspoon each chopped fresh tarragon and chopped parsley

 Wrap each potato in a square of aluminum foil and put them on the steamer rack. Place over simmering water, cover, and steam until tender, about 40 to 45 minutes. About 15 minutes before the potatoes are cooked, add the leek and steam until tender.

Remove the potatoes and leek from the steamer, cut open the foil, and let the vegetables cool for 10 minutes. Then take the potatoes out of the foil and set each potato in its most stable position. Cut the top quarter off each potato; reserve these little "hats." Scoop the pulp out of the potatoes with a small spoon, leaving a shell about ¼ inch thick, taking care not to break the skins. Save the pulp.

Aluminum foil

Stackable steamer, steamer pot with
insert, pasta cooker, or collapsible
steamer basket

Put half of the potato pulp (reserve the remainder for soup or a vegetable purée, see pages 100–101), the leek, salt, and pepper in the bowl of a food processor and pulse briefly until the potato is finely chopped but not completely smooth (if overworked, potato gets gummy).

Transfer the purée to a heavy-bottomed saucepan, add the crème fraîche or cream, and bring to a boil over medium-high heat, whisking constantly and reaching into the corners of the pan to keep the soup from burning. Taste for salt and pepper.

To serve, place each potato shell in a shallow bowl that has been warmed slightly in the oven. Fill with the soup, sprinkle with the herbs, and set the "hats" on top. Serve immediately.

TWICE-COOKED POTATOES

Pommes de Terre au Gruyère

Serve these with the Pork with Garlic and Sage on page 251. The egg yolks bind and enrich the purée, but if you're concerned about fat, it holds together fine without them.

SERVES 4 AS A SIDE DISH

4 medium red-skinned or all-purpose
potatoes (3 to 4 ounces each),
scrubbed

3 tablespoons unsalted butter, at room
temperature

3 tablespoons crème fraîche or sour
cream

2 large egg yolks

½ cup finely grated Gruyère cheese

¼ teaspoon salt

⅛ teaspoon freshly ground pepper

⅛ teaspoon freshly grated nutmeg

Stackable steamer, steamer pot with
insert, pasta cooker, or collapsible
steamer basket

 Put the potatoes on the steamer rack, place over boiling water, cover, adjust the heat as necessary, and steam until tender, 40 to 45 minutes. Remove from the steamer and let cool slightly.

Preheat the broiler. Cut the potatoes in half lengthwise. Carefully scrape out the pulp with a spoon without breaking the skins.

Transfer the potato pulp to a bowl. Add the butter, crème fraîche or sour cream, egg yolks, half the cheese, the salt, pepper, and nutmeg, and mix well. Taste for salt and pepper.

Fill the potato skins with the potato mixture and sprinkle with the remaining cheese.

Arrange the stuffed potatoes in a baking dish or on a broiler pan and broil, rearranging them as necessary in the dish, until the tops are an even golden brown, about 5 minutes. Serve hot.

Steaming is a practical way to cook spinach: The color stays a vibrant green and the spinach doesn't get waterlogged. Manière puréed steamed spinach to make flans flavored with mushrooms (see page 93). I steam it and then sauté it in butter or olive oil (see below) or purée it for a low-fat sauce (see page 100).

✳ REFRESHING SPINACH

Spinach needn't be refreshed if it is to be eaten immediately, but if you're holding it at all before serving, sautéeing it as in the basic recipe below, or puréeing it as in the recipe on page 93, it must be refreshed under cold water (see page 23) and then squeezed well to get out as much water as possible. If you are serving steamed spinach at a dinner party, it's practical to steam and refresh it early in the day, refrigerate it, and then reheat it in butter or olive oil (see below) just before serving.

✳ PREPARING SPINACH FOR STEAMING

Hold each leaf in one hand, folding it in half lengthwise with the veined side out, and strip off the stem that runs up the leaf with your other hand. (If the leaves are small and the stems thin, I just cut the stems off close to the bottom of the leaf.) Put the cleaned spinach in a large bowl and cover with cold water. Swish the spinach around in the water to loosen the dirt, then lift the spinach out of the bowl and put it in another bowl. Repeat two or three more times, until there is no dirt at the bottom of the bowl when the leaves are lifted out. Steam until the leaves are wilted but still bright green.

Spinach (1 bunch)..3 to 4 minutes
(4 bunches)..7 to 8 minutes

BASIC RECIPE FOR STEAMED SPINACH

It takes a lot of raw spinach to feed four people because it loses so much volume in the cooking. I count one twelve-ounce bunch per person; four bunches, cleaned and steamed, yield only three and a half cups cooked spinach.

Clean the spinach and wash it well, as above. Then pile it into a large, deep steamer pot with a deep insert and steam just until wilted, stirring halfway through the steaming. Refresh under cold running water and then squeeze the spinach between two hands to remove as much water as possible. In a large frying pan, heat one to two tablespoons unsalted butter or olive oil. Add the spinach and stir over high heat until well coated. Season to taste with salt and pepper and add a squeeze of lemon, if you like.

SPINACH AND MUSHROOM FLANS

Flans d'Épinards aux Champignons

These bright green, woodsy-flavored flans are the ideal accompaniment to the Veal with Spring Carrots on page 242. Manière also suggested serving them with grilled meats, a whole steamed chicken, a stuffed squab, or rack of lamb. They also make an elegant first course, sauced with Chervil Butter Sauce (page 152) or Tarragon Butter Sauce (page 254).

Potato starch, a tasteless starch that looks something like cornstarch, is available in health food stores and some specialty food markets. Manière used it in this recipe to absorb some of the liquid from the vegetables, giving the flans a firmer texture. It's worth trying if potato starch is available, but the flans will hold together without it.

If using a collapsible steamer basket, make sure that the pot you are using allows the basket to expand completely—and take care not to start by setting just one flan on the basket, or it will tilt to one side.

(continued)

Unsalted butter, softened, for buttering the ramekins and foil

2 medium bunches spinach (about 10 ounces each; 4 cups firmly packed leaves), stemmed and well washed (see page 92)

3½ ounces mushrooms, trimmed and halved if large

3 tablespoons crème fraîche or heavy cream

2 large eggs, lightly beaten

1 teaspoon potato starch (optional)

¼ teaspoon salt

⅛ teaspoon freshly ground pepper

Aluminum foil

Four 4-ounce ramekins or 4 Pyrex custard cups

Stackable steamer, steamer pot with insert, pasta cooker, or collapsible steamer basket

 Generously brush the ramekins or custard cups with softened butter.

Put the spinach and mushrooms on the steamer rack, place over simmering water, cover, and steam 10 minutes.

Transfer the mushrooms to the bowl of a food processor or a blender. Refresh the spinach under cold running water and then squeeze it in your hands to get rid of as much liquid as possible. Add the spinach to the mushrooms and process to purée. If you are using a food processor, add the crème fraîche or cream, eggs, potato starch if using, salt, and pepper; process until well mixed. If you are using a blender, purée the vegetables with the cream first, then add the remaining ingredients and blend well.

Divide the mixture among the prepared ramekins or custard cups. Cover each with a small square of buttered aluminum foil, buttered side down, pressing the foil around the rims to seal. Put the flans on the steamer rack, place over boiling water, cover, adjust the heat as necessary, and steam until just set and a knife inserted into the centers comes out clean, about 10 minutes.

Remove the ramekins or custard cups from the steamer and let stand 1 to 2 minutes. Remove the foil, invert the flans onto individual plates, and serve.

SQUASH

Squash can be divided into two groups: thin-skinned summer squashes, such as zucchini, yellow crookneck and straightneck squash, and round green or white pattypans, and hard-skinned winter squash, such as acorn, butternut, spaghetti, and pumpkin.

Summer squashes, mild-flavored to begin with, take on a delicate, sweet, almost buttery flavor in steaming. I steam summer squash until quite soft because it sweetens as it cooks; if you like it barely wilted, steam zucchini five to six minutes, yellow squash four to five minutes. Yellow squash has more and larger seeds than zucchini, and it gets mushy if overcooked.

Serve steamed summer squash with Balsamic Vinaigrette (page 24) or tossed in butter or olive oil, fresh herbs, and garlic, on its own or with other steamed vegetables. Mediterranean flavorings such as thyme, rosemary, basil, garlic, Parmesan cheese, and olive oil are delicious with summer squashes.

Winter squash gets watery and loses flavor when boiled, but

steaming sweetens it and concentrates its flavor. Winter squashes are good in purées and soups, with potatoes added for body (see pages 100–101).

✳ PREPARING SUMMER SQUASH FOR STEAMING

Wash the squash and trim the ends. Then cut into the desired size. If cutting bâtonnets (see page 104), use only the outside, seedless flesh; the seed-filled core gets mushy and won't hold its shape. Steam summer squash until translucent and tender.

Zucchini cut into bâtonnets (no seeds)..6 to 8 minutes

Zucchini cut into ¼-inch-thick rounds ....9 to 10 minutes

Yellow crookneck squash cut into bâtonnets (no seeds)............................5 minutes

Yellow crookneck squash cut into ¼-inch-thick rounds...............................7 to 8 minutes

✳ STEAMING SUMMER SQUASH IN QUANTITY

Allow half a pound of summer squash (one large or two small zucchini or yellow squash) per person. Count on fifteen to twenty minutes when steaming sliced zucchini rounds for four in a nine-and-a-half-inch steamer pot with an insert. Yellow crookneck squash needs less time; count on ten minutes to steam yellow squash rounds for four.

✳ PREPARING WINTER SQUASH FOR STEAMING

Cut small hard-skinned winter squash, such as smaller butternut squash and acorn squash, in half and scrape out the seeds. Steam with the skin on until a knife penetrates with no resistance.

Acorn squash (medium), halved...25 to 30 minutes

Butternut squash (about 3 pounds), halved...35 minutes

Cut pumpkin or other large squash in half. Scrape out the seeds, cut into manageable sections, and cut off the hard skin with a large knife. Cut the flesh into cubes. Steam until the tip of a knife penetrates the squash with no resistance.

Pumpkin, peeled and cut into 1-inch cubes..20 minutes	
Butternut squash, peeled and cut into 1- to 1½-inch cubes.........................12 to 15 minutes	

Stuffed Zucchini

Courgettes Farcies

Manière's inspiration for this recipe must have been a late-summer garden, bursting with zucchini, tomatoes, and basil. Slender hollowed-out zucchini halves are mounded with a gutsy, garlicky bread stuffing, perfumed with fresh basil and olive oil. Manière served the zucchini as a cold first course with *fines herbes* vinaigrette or as a hot main course with a fresh sauce of chopped tomato, full of fresh herbs.

To serve this as a main course for four, double the recipe.

SERVES 4 AS A COLD FIRST COURSE, 2 AS A MAIN COURSE

4 small or 2 large zucchini (about 1 pound total)

BASIL STUFFING

4 ounces salt pork, cut into small cubes,
   or ¼ pound bacon

2 slices white bread, crusts removed

1½ tablespoons olive oil

2 garlic cloves, minced

3 tablespoons chopped parsley

1½ tablespoons chopped fresh basil

⅛ teaspoon freshly ground pepper

1 large egg, lightly beaten

 Wash the zucchini and cut them in half lengthwise. Scoop out the seeds and pulp with a small spoon, leaving a shell about ¼ inch thick; reserve the pulp for the stuffing. If using large zucchini, cut each shell in half crosswise to make 8 "boats."

Make the stuffing: Place the salt pork cubes or bacon strips on the steamer rack, place over simmering water, cover, and steam 7 minutes.

Transfer the salt pork or bacon to the bowl of a food processor and add the reserved zucchini pulp, the bread, oil, garlic, herbs, pepper, and egg. Pulse just to chop. Don't overwork; the filling

Fresh Tomato-Basil Sauce (page 62),
*   warmed, or Basic Vinaigrette (page 26),*
*   made with 1½ teaspoons each*
*   chopped fresh chives, basil, and chervil*

Stackable steamer, steamer pot with
    insert, pasta cooker, or collapsible
    steamer basket

should not be a purée. Spoon the filling into the zucchini boats, mounding it slightly. Put the zucchini on the steamer rack, place over simmering water, cover, and steam 15 minutes.

Serve hot with the tomato–basil sauce or cold with the herb vinaigrette.

SUNCHOKES (Jerusalem Artichokes)

Sunchokes, or Jerusalem artichokes, are not related to artichokes at all—they are the tubers of a variety of sunflower. However, the sweet, nutty flavor of a cooked sunchoke is something like that of a globe artichoke, although the sweetness and texture remind me as much of chestnuts. The pronounced sweetness of the vegetable is less evident raw than cooked, although it fades after a point in the cooking; Manière's steaming time is long enough to allow the deeper, more appealingly nutty taste of the vegetable to come through.

Manière made a low-fat mousse of puréed sunchokes and low-fat cheese, in place of cream, to serve with steak (see page 234). The mousse has an unusual nutty, buttery, slightly sweet taste, something like that of a winter squash. Try it instead of mashed potatoes with roast or steamed chicken, or with fish.

Thinly sliced raw sunchokes add sweetness and crunch to salad.

Manière always peeled sunchokes, but he did so after steaming, because their knobby shape makes them difficult to peel when raw.

✴ **STEAMING SUNCHOKES**

Steam whole unpeeled sunchokes until the point of a knife penetrates easily (at this point, the sunchoke will be soft enough to purée). Then peel with a small knife. Sunchokes needn't be refreshed after steaming.

Whole medium sunchokes..20 to 25 minutes

TOMATOES

Tomatoes come in many colors, shapes, and sizes, some fleshy and good for cooking, some juicy and delicious raw in salads. Tomatoes are best in season, the late summer and early fall. During off-season months, oval plum tomatoes, which are meaty and have fewer seeds than the round variety, give the best flavor for cooking. If fresh plum tomatoes aren't available, use canned in preference to underripe, tasteless winter tomatoes.

TOMATO CONCASSÉ

Manière's recipes use a common French preparation called a tomato concassé, or peeled, seeded, and diced tomatoes. Traditionally, the tomatoes are immersed in boiling water for a minute or so to loosen the skins. Manière steamed the tomatoes instead; the process is both faster and easier, because less water needs to be brought to a boil and you don't need to fish the tomatoes out of boiling water.

To make tomato concassé, core the number of tomatoes called for in the recipe and cut an "x" in the bottom of each one. Put the tomatoes on the steaming rack, place over boiling water, cover, adjust the heat as necessary, and steam two minutes. Refresh under cold running water. Then pull off the tomato skins, using a paring knife. Cut the tomatoes in half through their equator. Use your index finger to scrape out the seeds and the pulpy juices. Roughly chop or dice the tomato flesh.

The juices from seeding tomatoes for concassé can be used to add flavor to stews and sauces (see Smothered Lamb with Eggplant, page 246, and Fresh Tomato-Basil Sauce, page 62). When making a tomato concassé, scrape the seeds and juices into a fine strainer set over a bowl. Then use the back of a spoon to press as much juice as possible through the strainer. Discard the seeds and reserve the juice.

TURNIPS

Not all turnips are round; some of the varieties used in France are cylindrical, like short, thick carrots. Steaming mellows the sharp bite of turnips and sweetens them. Manière often used young spring turnips, steaming them whole or halved to serve as part of a mixed vegetable combination with steamed lamb and poultry (see pages 244 and 190). He also steamed grated spring turnip for salad (see page 99). In America it may be hard to find turnips as small and young as Manière's, but we can steam turnips in wedges or cut them into bâtonnets.

Steamed turnips are delicious as a purée or in a soup (see pages

100–101), either alone or in combination with other winter vegetables such as carrots, potatoes, rutabaga, and celery root. After steaming them in wedges or bâtonnets, I finish them in a frying pan with melted butter, chopped shallots, fresh thyme, salt, and pepper. Sometimes I add a little cream and reduce it to make a sauce.

Buy firm turnips with smooth, unwrinkled skin; old ones are spongy and stay tough even after cooking. If possible, buy turnips with their tops—they are likely to be fresher than packaged turnips, and the greens are peppery and delicious, steamed as for beet or mustard greens on page 80.

✳ PREPARING TURNIPS FOR STEAMING

Peel the turnips and trim the root and stem ends. Cut into wedges or bâtonnets (see page 104) and steam until the tip of a knife penetrates the turnip with just a little resistance. Steamed turnips needn't be refreshed.

Small turnips, quartered	10 to 12 minutes
Turnip bâtonnets	5 to 7 minutes

GRATED TURNIP SALAD RÉMOULADE

Navets Nouveaux en Rémoulade

This is a variation on the traditional French salad of finely julienned raw celery root dressed with a rémoulade sauce, a highly seasoned mayonnaise flavored with capers, anchovy, herbs, and cornichons. Steaming turns the turnips mild, leaving just enough bite to stand up to the salty, spicy mayonnaise.

Cornichons, or gherkins, are a small French pickle, available in some supermarkets and specialty food stores.

(continued)

1 pound small young turnips, peeled and
   coarsely grated

RÉMOULADE SAUCE

1 large egg yolk

1 teaspoon Dijon mustard

¾ cup peanut or vegetable oil

2 teaspoons drained capers, chopped

4 cornichons, chopped

1 tablespoon plus 1 teaspoon chopped
   fresh fines herbes (parsley, chervil,
   chives, and tarragon)

2 anchovy fillets in oil

⅛ teaspoon freshly ground pepper

Salt if necessary

Stackable steamer, steamer pot with
   insert, pasta cooker, or collapsible
   steamer basket

Put the turnips on the steamer rack, place over simmering water, cover, and steam 2 minutes. Drain well on towels and refrigerate until chilled.

Make the rémoulade sauce: Whisk together the egg yolk and mustard in a large bowl. Whisk in the oil, slowly at first and then in a steady stream, until emulsified. Stir in the capers, cornichons, and herbs. Crush the anchovy fillets, either with a fork or in a mortar and pestle, and stir into the sauce. Add the pepper and salt if needed (the anchovies may make the sauce salty enough). Add the turnips and stir to coat with the sauce. Taste for salt and pepper, and serve.

More Basic Vegetable Techniques

The recipes and introduction to this chapter include a number of ways to steam and serve vegetables. Here are others to further expand your repertoire.

✳ VEGETABLE PURÉES

I don't like to make definitive statements about vegetables because they cook so differently depending on season and age, but to the extent I can generalize, I've found that steaming breaks down vegetables less than blanching or stewing. This is often a plus, but it also means that the vegetable (particularly dense root vegetables such as carrots, turnips, and celery root) must be steamed a long time and then worked more than usual to purée. Therefore, if I care, I use a blender rather than a food processor to purée because the blender gives a finer texture. The up side of steaming vegetables for purée is, of course, that fewer nutrients are lost in the cooking and the flavor is exceptionally bright and intense.

One or more vegetables can be puréed to serve as a side dish, with enough hot cream or milk, fresh cheese, stock, or steaming liquid to smooth and thicken the purée, and butter or olive oil added for richness (see the recipe for Celery Root and Potato Purée on page 65 and Manière's low-fat Sunchoke Mousse on page 234). Purée a steamed mealy potato such as Idaho or cooked rice with the vegetable to thicken and add smooth starch; vegetables such as green beans, broccoli, or Brussels sprouts need the added starch because they haven't much of their own. Manière used about half the cleaned weight (the weight of a vegetable after it has been trimmed and peeled, ready to eat) of the vegetables in potato.

BROCCOLI PURÉE

Use one pound (cleaned weight) steamed broccoli florets and half a pound (cleaned weight) steamed Idaho potato. Process the broccoli in a food processor until very finely chopped. Add the potato and process until finely chopped but not quite smooth; potato gets gummy if overprocessed. Add about one cup hot milk, stock, or steaming liquid, or a combination, as needed to smooth the purée, and process briefly to purée. Add half a cup of grated Parmesan cheese, salt and pepper to taste, and a tablespoon of olive oil, if you like, for flavor. (The potato can be replaced by one half to two thirds cup cooked rice.)

✳ SOUPS

We can make a puréed vegetable soup like Manière's Cream of Watercress Soup (page 81) or Cream of Leek and Potato Soup (page 90) by adding milk, cream, stock, or steaming liquid from vegetables, meat, poultry, or fish to puréed vegetables. A very simple low-fat and inexpensive soup can be made by puréeing a mixture of steamed vegetables with a steamed potato, preferably an Idaho, and chicken stock or some of the steaming liquid. It doesn't matter what you use; my last soup was a combination of asparagus, cauliflower, green beans, spinach, kale, carrots, zucchini, and broccoli because those were the vegetables I had on hand. Purée the other vegetables with the stock or water first, and then add the potato and process briefly so the potato will not be gluey. Put the purée in a large saucepan and warm over low heat. Season with fresh herbs or spices, salt, and pepper, and add more stock or water if needed. A little cream, butter, or olive oil adds flavor and gives a velvety texture but is not necessary.

✳ SAUCES

Manière made a cream sauce for lamb with the juices from steamed vegetables (see page 244). It's also possible to make both low-fat and full-fat sauces from puréed vegetables. Some vegetables, such as garlic and onions, can be used to thicken a sauce when steamed and puréed; see page 262 for Manière's Garlic Sauce. He also made a low-fat carrot sauce for smoked haddock with puréed carrot, onion, and yogurt (see page 128).

We can make sauces from other vegetables that are steamed, puréed with steamed potato to thicken, and then thinned slightly with stock or steaming liquid, just as in making soup. Stock adds good flavor without adding fat. I make an unusual, tasty, deep green spinach and kale sauce to serve with lamb: For three cups sauce, enough to serve six generously, steam five cups spinach and one and a half cups sliced kale. Purée with a steamed small baking potato and a sliced shallot that has been cooked in half a tablespoon of butter. Thin with two to three cups of the steaming liquid from the spinach, and add one to two tablespoons olive oil, if you like.

✳ VEGETABLE FLANS

Manière made elegant vegetable flans with puréed steamed celery root and cream (see page 66) and with garlic and cream bound with a bit of potato starch or arrowroot (see page 78). Use the celery root recipe as a model for a carrot, broccoli, cauliflower, turnip, or rutabaga flan, replacing the cleaned weight (see page 101) of celery root with another vegetable.

✳ GRILLED VEGETABLES

Many vegetables are superb grilled. Soft vegetables like zucchini, eggplant, and peppers can be grilled starting from their raw state, but denser vegetables, such as leeks, celery, fennel, asparagus, potatoes, and beans, should be steamed before grilling so that the outside doesn't overcook and char before the inside is tender. Steam the vegetable according to the basic steaming times in the charts throughout the chapter, roll them in olive oil, sprinkle with salt and pepper, and grill about two minutes per side.

✳ STUFFED VEGETABLES

Manière included a few recipes for stuffed, steamed vegetables that I like very much. The stuffings are bound with egg so they hold together, even spooned free-form onto an artichoke bottom. Manière packed zucchini halves with a bread crumb filling seasoned with salt pork or bacon (see page 96), and he rolled wilted cabbage leaves around a sensational, smoky kasha, pork, and beef mixture (see page 236). Another stuffed cabbage recipe (see page 253) flavors the filling with sausage meat. Artichoke bottoms make particularly elegant holders for stuffings; see the recipe on page 33, which hides a rich meat filling between two bottoms. Use any of those stuffings interchangeably with different vegetables. A plate of colorful stuffed red pepper, eggplant, zucchini, and artichoke bottoms makes a spectacular first or main course.

For stuffed artichoke bottoms, steam them until almost soft, about eighteen minutes. Then pile a generous amount of the stuffing on top of each artichoke bottom, shaping it into an even mound with a spoon and your fingers. You'll need one quarter to one third cup stuffing to fill each bottom. Steam the stuffed bottoms twenty minutes.

For stuffed zucchini, hollow out zucchini "boats" with the point of a spoon or a melon baller and chop the pulp, as directed on page 96. (If the seeds are large, remove them before chopping the pulp.) Add the pulp to the chosen stuffing. You'll need about half a cup to three quarters of a cup stuffing for one medium zucchini. Stuff the raw boats as on pages 96–97 and steam fifteen minutes.

For stuffed cabbage, steam whole, large cabbage leaves for two minutes to wilt them and make them flexible (see page 51). Quarter the heart of the cabbage and steam ten minutes. Chop and add to the chosen stuffing; see page 52 for directions on stuffing the leaves. (I think cabbage tastes best stuffed with either of the mixtures on pages 236 and 253. Those stuffings, however, also taste great with other vegetables.)

For stuffed bell peppers, cut off the tops and reserve. Shake the seeds out of the pepper and pull out the ribs with your fingers. Cut a very thin slice off the bottoms if the peppers won't stand upright. Steam the peppers, upside down, for fifteen minutes, or until soft. Then stuff the peppers and steam twenty more minutes. You'll need three quarters of a cup to a cup of stuffing to fill each pepper.

For stuffed eggplant, choose small, fairly straight purple eggplants weighing about six ounces each. Cut off the tops and cut each eggplant in half crosswise. Cut a thin slice off the bottom of each one so the bottom half will stand. Use a melon baller to hollow out the inside of each eggplant "cup," leaving a shell about a quarter inch thick. You'll need a generous half cup of stuffing to fill one six-ounce eggplant, cut into two "cups." Spoon the filling into the eggplant "cups" and steam twenty minutes.

✳ SPECIAL VEGETABLE CUTS

Manière often called for vegetables cut into two special shapes common in French cuisine: thin matchstick pieces called *julienne,* and thick matchstick pieces, called *bâtonnets.* Cut either way, vegetables both cook evenly and look finished and professional on the plate. Vegetables cut into julienne or bâtonnets needn't be peeled, because the peel is cut off in the shaping; for zucchini and yellow squash, the skin is often left on for a pretty presentation.

Vegetable Bâtonnets Typically bâtonnets are cut one and a half inches long by a quarter inch wide. To cut round and cylindrical vegetables such as turnips, carrots, and potatoes into bâtonnets, first cut the vegetable crosswise into one-and-a-half-inch cylindrical sections. Set the cylinders on end and cut off the rounded sides to make rectangles (save the trimmings for a soup or purée; see pages 100–101). Set each rectangle on a long side and slice lengthwise into quarter-inch-thick slices. Then stack the slices and cut them lengthwise into quarter-inch-thick strips.

To cut zucchini or other summer squash into bâtonnets, cut the vegetable crosswise into one-and-a-half-inch cylindrical sections. Then cut off the four sides, discarding the seedy central core. Set the four side pieces on the work surface skin sides up, and cut lengthwise into quarter-inch-thick bâtonnets.

Vegetable Julienne A vegetable julienne strip is typically about an eighth of an inch thick and two to three inches long. For cylindrical vegetables such as turnips, carrots, and potatoes, cut the vegetable into cylinders two to three inches long, depending on how long the julienne is to be. Set the cylinders on end and cut off the rounded sides to make rectangles (save the trimmings for soups or purées; see pages 100–101). Set each rectangle on a long side and cut lengthwise into eighth-inch-thick slices. Stack the slices and cut lengthwise into eighth-inch-thick strips.

To cut celery into julienne, peel the celery deeply and cut it crosswise into sections of the desired length. Then thinly slice it lengthwise.

To cut leeks into julienne, trim off the root end and the green tops (save the greens for stock or soup). Cut the white part crosswise into sections of the desired length. Cut each section in half lengthwise. Separate each cut section into two piles of layers, flatten each pile into a neat stack, and cut it lengthwise into thin strips. Then put the leeks into a bowl, cover with warm water, and wash well.

To cut zucchini or other summer squash into julienne, cut the vegetable crosswise into sections of the desired length. Then cut off the four sides in eighth-inch-thick slices, discarding the seedy central core. Set the side pieces on the work surface and cut lengthwise into eighth-inch-thick strips. The skin gives the julienne a beautiful color.

FISH AND
SHELLFISH

anière obviously loved seafood, and his recipes are superb. In steaming he discovered a way to show off all the subtle variations of flavor and texture possible in the world of fish and shellfish. He convinced me: I went crazy for seafood while working on this chapter. I steamed and ate every fish I could get my hands on. I took myself fishing. I camped out at my local fish store. I chased snapping blue crabs into the steamer. I haven't eaten fish or shellfish any way but steamed for months. I still get up at two o'clock in the morning to wander around the Fulton Fish Market.

Manière observed that home cooks rarely like to cook fish. He recognized that cooking seafood is nerve-wracking for most of us. The flesh is delicate; it can overcook and toughen before you know it. Fish sticks to a grill or frying pan and falls apart in a poaching liquid that is boiling too hard. But this is not so when you steam.

Anyone can steam fish perfectly; the steamer's gentle heat and consistent temperature make it easy. Once in the steamer, the fish is left untouched until done. Steaming is easier than poaching, particularly for whole fish or large pieces of fish. No court bouillon is needed, so there is no danger of burns when taking an unwieldy chunk of fish from boiling-hot liquid. There's no contact with boiling water that can break up the flesh of the fish or hot fat that can toughen it. When fish is steamed, its surface stays fairly dry. A sauce won't be diluted as it can be by the juices oozing from poached fish. The flesh itself stays moist. And fish you have caught yourself doesn't even need messy scaling before steaming. Seafood smells clean while it steams. (Fat is usually the cause of kitchen odors, and steaming uses no fat.)

Steaming is practical for cooking all kinds of shellfish as well. It's fast and doesn't wash the flavor out. Lobster doesn't fill with water as it does when boiled, so there's no boiling-hot liquid cascading down your arm as you crack open the shells. I've always steamed mussels and clams in just a bit of flavored broth, but it makes even more sense to steam shellfish as Manière did, in a steaming compartment *over* the broth rather than *in* it. Mussels and clams are easier to shell because the shells aren't filled with hot broth. The herbs and chopped vegetables stay in the broth where they belong instead of sticking to the shells. Lobster tastes particularly sweet steamed Manière's way, *en papillote* (see page 166). Steamed scallops are ethereal: They cook all the way through without toughening, and they are pure-flavored, sweet, and velvety.

Most fish are moist, tender, and flavorful when steamed. Delicate, flaky, white-fleshed fish such as cod, snapper, and sea bass steam beautifully. Oily fish become surprisingly mild-tasting and buttery-textured. Stronger-flavored fish, such as mackerel and bluefish, will surprise even the cautious because they taste light rather than oily as they do when cooked other ways. Two fish that don't steam well, however, are sturgeon and wild striped bass; the flesh toughens.

Substituting Fish and Shellfish in Manière's Recipes

When buying fish for one of Manière's recipes, the name of the game is substitution. Don't go crazy trying to find a particular fish for any of these recipes. Even if you do find it, it may be somewhat different from its European cousin. There are lots of excellent fish in America. Choose a fish that looks and smells fresh and is good value, and find a recipe that works for it.

Using the Chart of Basic Steaming Times for Fish and Shellfish

Manière's Chart of Basic Steaming Times for Fish and Shellfish makes it easy to substitute fish in his recipes. His original chart listed steaming times for fish available in France; I've added timings for many other fish available to us in America (see page 112). With the chart, you should be able to find an appropriate fish to use for each recipe in this book.

The chart is divided into two categories: lean white-fleshed fish and darker-colored moderately fatty to fatty fish. If you can't find a particular fish called for in one of these recipes, use the chart as a guide to a substitute; choose another fish within the same basic category and adjust the steaming time accordingly. The categories don't mean that the fish are identical, but within the categories, the fish are liable to make reasonable substitutes. So, although swordfish is a lean, white-meated fish, I've included it with tuna in the category of darker-colored, fattier fish because it can be substituted in recipes that call for tuna.

The categories are further divided into "very firm" and "more delicate" textures. These characterizations refer to fillets only. Texture in a given fish varies a lot from fillet to steak to whole fish. Delicate-textured fish falls apart readily when cooked; steam those fillets on a foil tray (see page 163) to make removing them easier.

I've also added suggestions for substitutions in many of the recipes, but don't be limited by them. The pollack (a lean white-fleshed fish in the cod family) called for in the recipe on page 130 is hard to get in most of the United States, although it may be more available on the West Coast. Don't give up on this recipe if you can't find pollack. Cod is a good substitute, but you can also make the dish with another white-fleshed fish and change the steaming time by referring to the chart. Grouper, halibut, tilefish, and mahi-mahi are particularly effective substitutions in this recipe. Fattier fish such as salmon or pompano give a different result, but if you like those fish, you'll like them in the dish.

Use the chart to substitute different shellfish within recipes as well. Manière made his Spiny Lobster Stew with Sweet Red Pepper Sauce (page 156) with a clawless lobster found in warmer waters around the world. It's hard to find spiny lobster in those parts of America where the clawed, or American, lobster is abundant, but the clawed lobster makes a fine substitute. Skate wings may be hard to find, but scallops are probably not, so use them in the recipe for Warm Skate Salad with Red Currants on page 123. Shrimp can be substituted for langoustines in the recipes (see pages 158 and 160) that call for those small members of the lobster family.

✳ CALCULATING STEAMING TIMES FOR WHOLE FISH AND
LARGE CHUNKS

It's easy to calculate the steaming time for any whole fish or large chunk thereof, even fish not listed on the chart, because the time depends on the thickness of the fish. The Canadian rule of ten minutes per inch of thickness holds true except for very small or very large fish. Small white-fleshed fish (one to two pounds) need only eight to nine minutes per inch. Whole fish over five pounds, such as whole salmon, need longer than ten minutes per inch; the timing will depend a lot on the steamer you are using. The fish is done when an instant-read thermometer inserted into the thickest part of the fish reads 140°F. (See page 161 for complete information on steaming whole fish.)

To measure the thickness of a whole fish, lay it on its side on the work surface and measure it at the thickest point (just behind the head).

Steaming with the Lid Ajar Manière made steaming whole fish easier by finishing the steaming time with the lid ajar so that the steamer is open and the heat is reduced. This final, gentler steaming gives more control, allowing the fish to cook through perfectly without overcooking. The open lid permits easy checking on the progress of the steaming at the end of the cooking, when the timing becomes critical. As a general rule, when steaming whole fish, steam the final third or quarter of the time with the lid ajar. You will see examples of whole fish on the chart; I haven't given whole fish times for every kind of fish because the above formula is very reliable.

✳ CALCULATING STEAMING TIMES FOR STEAKS AND FILLETS

There are no hard-and-fast rules for steaming steaks and fillets, so it's important to use the chart. Steaming times vary from variety to variety, although similar types of fish, cut to the same thickness of fillet or steak, steam similarly. If you have a fish that is not on the chart, find a fish with a similar texture (within the same category) and follow its steaming time. Steaks and fillets, with the exception of monkfish fillet, are cooked entirely with the lid on. Monkfish cooks slowly because it is very firm; the timing can best be controlled by treating a monkfish fillet like a whole fish or large chunk.

I've revised Manière's steaming times in the chart to adjust for the differences between the fish available to him and to us and because Americans prefer to cook some fish slightly less than the French do. With the exception of salmon, fish fillets steamed for the times given in the chart will be completely cooked through. For medium-rare fillets, particularly for tuna, reduce the steaming times by a few minutes. Fish steaks continue to cook after they are removed from the steamer because the bone holds the heat. The timings on the chart steam steaks to medium-rare at the bone; I let them finish cooking on the plate. If you like your fish steaks more well done, steam them one minute longer.

✳ STEAMING IN A STACKABLE STEAMER WITH TWO STEAMING COMPARTMENTS

Manière used a two-tiered oval steamer pot for steaming large fillets, such as flounder and skate, and fish and lobsters *en papillote* that are too large to fit in a single layer in a single steaming compartment. If you have a stackable steamer with two steaming compartments, you'll find it useful for many of the recipes in this chapter. Note that food steamed in the top compartment steams somewhat more slowly than food in the lower compartment. If you don't have such a steamer, a large roasting pan with a wire rack or a fish poacher will be large enough for some recipes; others may require two steamer pots.

✳ USING THE STEAMER TO KEEP WHOLE FISH WARM

It's often necessary to let a whole fish stand after cooking, while you finish the sauce. It's also easier to serve a fish that has been allowed to rest five to ten minutes after steaming, because the flesh firms up. Most standard recipes tell you to cover the fish with foil and let stand in a warm place. The steamer works better. After steaming the fish, turn the heat to very low and set the lid ajar; the fish will stay warm without continuing to cook. (We can't use the steamer this way for fillets or steaks; they'll overcook.)

Techniques for Steaming Fish and Shellfish

At the end of this chapter is a compilation of Manière's general instructions for steaming different types of fish and shellfish, with some additional notes from my own experience. There are tips on ways to steam, skin, and serve whole fish; to move fish easily to and from the steamer on a foil tray; and to steam fish in aluminum papillotes. Some of this general information is also included in specific recipes where helpful.

CHART OF BASIC STEAMING TIMES FOR FISH AND SHELLFISH

Below are the major points you need to know to steam whole fish, fillets, steaks, and shellfish. For other useful techniques for preparing seafood, see pages 107–111 and 161–171. Also refer to the general information on steaming and equipment on pages 3–15.

WHOLE FISH
Steam all whole fish weighing from 1½ to 5 pounds for 10 minutes per inch of thickness, regardless of type. Set the lid ajar during the final quarter of the steaming time. Lean, white-fleshed fish weighing less than 1½ pounds need only 8 to 9 minutes per pound. Fish over 5 pounds may need more time; the fish is done when an instant-read thermometer inserted into the thickest part of the fish reads 140°F. I give some whole fish times in the chart for quick reference; I give weights only to show what is available.

FISH FILLETS AND STEAKS
I haven't given weights for fish fillets and steaks because the weight is irrelevant; steaming times are determined by the thickness of the flesh. (For example, both a 1-inch-thick 6-ounce salmon steak and a 1-inch-thick 9-ounce salmon steak take 7 minutes for medium-rare.) Timings are for fillets and steaks steamed in a single layer.

STEAMING FISH NOT ON THE CHART
One of the problems in putting together a chart of this kind is availability and the difference between fish in different parts of the country. You won't find all fish available in the United States on the chart, as some West Coast fish were not available for testing. A great number of those (rockfish, petrale, and rex sole, for example), however, are lean and white-fleshed, falling into the same category as cod and flounder or gray sole.

CATEGORIES
The fish section of the chart is divided into two categories: lean white-fleshed fish and darker-textured moderately fatty or fatty fish. The fish within each category are not identical, but they are liable to make good substitutions for one another. (The timings will permit substitutions in individual recipes; most recipes also list possible substitutes.) The textural indications of "firm" and "delicate" are for fillets only. Exceptions are tuna, which is cut into boneless "loin" steaks, rather than fillets, and blowfish tails, which are sold on the bone. Some fish, such as sea robin and porgy, are rarely sold as fillets.

Some fish, such as wild striped bass and sturgeon, are not included on the chart because they do not steam well.

With the exception of salmon, steaming times are to cook whole fish and fillets through completely. Steaks are cooked to medium-rare at the bone and then finish cooking on the plate.

See page 166 to determine steaming times for fillets and steaks cooked *en papillote*, and for steaming times for "doubled" fillets.

• Lean White-Fleshed Fish •

FISH WITH FIRM-TEXTURED FILLETS

BLOWFISH TAILS:
Whole tails (2 to 2½ ounces, 1 inch thick)..5 minutes

CATFISH:
Fillet (¾ inch thick)..5 minutes

DOVER SOLE:
Fillet (¼ inch thick, folded in half)..5 minutes

MONKFISH:
Fillet (1 inch thick)...10 minutes plus 5 minutes with the lid ajar

ORANGE ROUGHY:

Fillet ($^3/_4$ to 1 inch thick)...8 to 10 minutes

WOLFFISH:

Fillet ($^1/_2$ to $^3/_4$ inch thick)..5 minutes

FISH WITH MORE DELICATE OR FLAKY FILLETS

COD:

Whole fish (4 to 5 pounds; $3^1/_2$ inches thick)...............25 minutes plus 10 minutes with the lid ajar

Steak (1 inch thick)...6 minutes

Fillet (1 inch thick)...6 minutes

Salt cod fillet ($^1/_2$ to $^3/_4$ inch thick)...................................7 to 8 minutes

FLOUNDER, GRAY SOLE:

Whole fish (2 pounds; $1^1/_2$ inches thick)..........................8 minutes plus 5 minutes with the lid ajar

Fillet ($^1/_4$ to $^1/_2$ inch thick, folded in half).........................4 to 6 minutes

GROUPER:

Fillet (1 to $1^1/_2$ inches thick)...10 to 12 minutes

HALIBUT:

Steak (1 inch thick)...6 minutes

Fillet ($1^1/_4$ inches thick)...5 minutes

JOHN DORY:

Fillet ($^1/_2$ inch thick)..5 minutes

MAHI-MAHI:

Fillet (1 inch thick)...8 minutes

OCEAN PERCH:

Fillet ($^1/_2$ inch thick)..5 to 6 minutes

PIKE:

Whole fish or chunk ($2^1/_2$ to 3 inches thick)...................20 minutes plus 5 minutes with the lid ajar

Fillet ($^1/_2$ to $^3/_4$ inch thick)..4 to 6 minutes

PORGY:

Whole fish (1 pound; $1^1/_4$ inches thick)..........................8 minutes plus 5 minutes with the lid ajar

Fillet ($^1/_2$ inch thick)..4 to 5 minutes

SCORPION FISH:

Whole fish ($2^1/_2$ pounds; $2^1/_2$ inches thick).....................20 minutes plus 5 minutes with the lid ajar

SEA BASS:

Whole fish (2 pounds; 2 inches thick)...........................15 minutes plus 5 minutes with the lid ajar

Fillet ($^1/_2$ to $^3/_4$ inch thick)..4 to 5 minutes

SEA ROBIN:

Whole fish ($^3/_4$ to 1 pound; $1^1/_2$ to 2 inches thick).........12 minutes plus 5 minutes with the lid ajar

SKATE:

On the bone (1 pound; about 2 inches thick)....................20 to 25 minutes

Fillet ($^1/_2$ inch thick)..8 minutes

SNAPPER:
Whole fish (2¼ pounds; 3 inches thick)......................20 minutes plus 10 minutes with the lid ajar
Fillet (¾ inch thick)..5 minutes

TILEFISH:
Steak (1 to 1¼ inches thick)...6 to 8 minutes

WEAKFISH:
Fillet (1 inch thick)...8 minutes

WHITING:
Whole fish (5 to 6 ounces; 1½ inches thick)....................8 minutes plus 4 minutes with the lid ajar

• Darker-Colored Moderately Fatty and Fatty Fish •

FISH WITH FIRM-TEXTURED FILLETS

CARP:
Steak (1½ inches thick)..15 minutes

SWORDFISH:
Steak (1 inch thick)...6 minutes

TUNA:
Steak (¾ to 1 inch thick)...3 to 4 minutes for medium-rare
2 minutes for rare

FISH WITH MORE DELICATE FILLETS

ARCTIC CHAR:
Fillet (1 inch thick)..5 minutes

BLUEFISH:
Whole fish (2 pounds; 2 inches thick)...........................15 minutes plus 5 minutes with the lid ajar
Fillet (¾ to 1 inch thick)..7 to 8 minutes

MACKEREL:
Whole fish (10 ounces; 1½ inches thick)......................10 minutes plus 5 minutes with the lid ajar
Fillet (½ to 1 inch thick)..7 to 10 minutes

POMPANO:
Fillet (½ inch thick)...6 minutes
(¾ inch thick)...8 minutes

SALMON:
Whole fish or chunk (3¼ pounds; 3¼ inches thick)....20 minutes plus 10 minutes with the lid ajar
Steak (1¼ to 1½ inches thick).................7 minutes for medium-rare, 8 to 9 minutes for medium
Fillet (1½ inches thick)............................7 minutes for medium-rare, 8 to 9 minutes for medium
Fillet (¾ inch thick)..................................5 minutes for medium-rare, 6 minutes for medium

SALMON TROUT:

    Whole fish (4 to 5 pounds; 3 inches thick)..................20 minutes plus 10 minutes with the lid ajar

SARDINES:

    Whole fish (1 to 2 ounces)..6 minutes plus 3 minutes with the lid ajar

SHAD:

    Whole fish (2½ to 3 pounds; 3 inches thick)..............20 minutes plus 10 minutes with the lid ajar

    Fillet (¾ to 1 inch thick)...7 to 8 minutes

TROUT:

    Whole fish (1 pound; 1½ inches thick).........................10 minutes plus 5 minutes with the lid ajar

• Shellfish •

Manière gave two timings for sea scallops, mussels, cockles, and clams: a timing just to open and a second timing to open and cook through entirely (Total Steaming Time). Sea scallops in the shell weren't available to test. Oysters that are steamed to open cook partially; don't use this technique for oysters to be served raw.

Shrimp size is described in terms of the number of shrimp to the pound (see page 171). Shrimp must be steamed in a single layer.

SEAFOOD	TO OPEN	TOTAL STEAMING TIME
Sea Scallops		4 to 6 minutes
Mussels	2 to 3 minutes	4 minutes
Oysters	3 to 4 minutes	
Cockles	2 to 3 minutes	4 minutes
Soft-Shell Clams	4 minutes	7 to 10 minutes
Hard-Shell Clams	4 minutes	5 to 7 minutes

LOBSTERS (Wrap lobsters *en papillote* [see page 166] before steaming; see page 157 for a recipe):

    1 to 1½ pounds...15 minutes plus 10 minutes with the lid ajar

    1½ to 2 pounds...25 minutes plus 10 minutes with the lid ajar

BLUE CRABS:

    ¾ to 1 pound..5 minutes plus 5 minutes with the lid ajar

SHRIMP:

    Medium to large (16 to 20 per pound)...shelled, 2 minutes

        in the shell, 3 minutes

This section includes recipes using steaks and fillets from various fish. Some of the recipes are quick, while others are very elegant and more time-consuming. Most of the fish should be easy to find in fish stores or supermarkets.

My favorite steamers for steaming fish fillets and steaks are my stackable steamers, steamers with shallow inserts, and collapsible steamer baskets. In these steamers, it's easy to slide a spatula under the cooked fish to remove it. A steamer with a deep insert such as a pasta cooker makes it very difficult to get the fish out of the steamer in one piece. I've often found an oval steamer to be practical for steaming fish.

While it would be reasonable to lead off with Manière's three recipes for sole fillets (pages 118, 121, and 122), since sole is a popular fish and available all over the country, I can't resist beginning with the following recipe for cod steak, as it was my own first experience with steamed fish—and the first time I ever really loved cod. It's quick, easy, and out of this world.

COD STEAKS WITH CAPER-ANCHOVY VINAIGRETTE
Cabillaud Sauce Girondine

This is one of the fastest, cheapest, easiest, and most delicious recipes in the book. Cod doesn't normally get high marks for flavor, but steaming gives it a velvety, melt-in-the-mouth texture and emphasizes its sweetness. Manière perfumed the cod with a fresh, typically French flavor, similar to that of a bouquet garni, by steaming it on a bed of thyme, bay, parsley, and lemon. Be generous with the herbs—the cod should be nestled in a thick, aromatic bed. The sauce is simple, a flavor-packed warm green-and-yellow vinaigrette, tart with sherry vinegar and salty with capers and anchovies. It's delicious with most fish, as well as with cold meats and poultry.

It's not necessary to seed the lemon slices, as they are discarded when the fish is cooked (or you can garnish the plate with them).

8 bay leaves

½ large bunch fresh thyme

Handful of parsley stems (reserve the
leaves for the sauce)

1 lemon, thinly sliced

4 cod steaks (7 to 8 ounces each), about
1 inch thick

Salt and freshly ground pepper

CAPER-ANCHOVY VINAIGRETTE

6 tablespoons unsalted butter

2 tablespoons olive oil

1 teaspoon capers, chopped

2 anchovy fillets, chopped

1 tablespoon chopped fresh chives or
scallion greens

1 tablespoon chopped parsley (see
above)

1 tablespoon sherry vinegar

Freshly ground pepper

Salt if necessary

Stackable steamer, steamer pot with
shallow insert, roasting pan with wire
rack, or collapsible steamer basket

 Make a thick bed of the bay leaves, thyme, and parsley stems on the steamer rack. Top with a layer of the lemon slices. Sprinkle the cod steaks on both sides with salt and pepper. Put the steaks in a single layer on the bed of herbs and lemon. Place the steamer rack over simmering water, cover, and steam 6 minutes.

Meanwhile, make the vinaigrette: Melt the butter in a small saucepan over low heat. Add the oil and then the capers, anchovies, and herbs and stir briskly with a wooden spoon to emulsify. Stir in the vinegar. Add pepper to taste. Taste and add salt if needed. (You probably won't need to add salt because of the anchovies.)

To serve, place the cod on four plates and spoon the sauce over.

✳ **SOLES AND FLOUNDERS**

Manière included three recipes for true Dover sole, a flatfish that is highly regarded in France, and for good reason. It is tasty without being strong-flavored, meaty, and tender. Sole is a mainstay of classic French cuisine.

Go into three different fish stores in this country, however, and ask what is being sold as "sole," and you're likely to get at least three different answers. Sole nomenclature is very confusing here. Gray sole and lemon sole are common to the Northeast, but neither is actually true sole; nor are the West Coast rex and petrale soles. True Dover sole is found only in European waters, and it is in such scarce supply there that very little of it finds its way to America.

What is marketed under the name of sole in the United States is actually one or another of the American flounders, a family of tasty, delicate, mild-flavored flatfish. In my experience, Dover sole is usually sold in whole fish; flounder is sold whole or in fillet. Flounder is a good fish in its own right and versatile enough to be used in most sole recipes. It's useful to note, however, that none of the flounders sold in this country as either sole or flounder is really similar in flavor and texture to a true Dover sole. Flounders have a different flavor, are flakier, and cook much faster than true sole. They have a rounder shape, and their fillets are wider. These differences can be important in substituting flounder for sole in some recipes: Paupiettes (see Sole Fillets Stuffed with Mushrooms, page 122) made with flounder hold their shape less well than with sole. Sole shrinks and tightens as it cooks, encouraging the paupiettes to hold their shape. Flounder stiffens and straightens and consequently needs a toothpick to hold the paupiette together.

You can use gray sole, lemon sole, and fluke, as well as other fillets marketed as flounder, in Manière's recipes that call for Dover sole. Of the flounders, gray sole has very white flesh, soft texture, and substantially milder flavor than other flounders. Fluke has a slightly darker flesh than other flounders, but don't be put off by the color—the flavor is very good.

Manière's sole recipes call for a very small amount of fish by American standards—only about one quarter pound per person—because French meals typically have several courses. Except in the recipe for Sole Fillets Stuffed with Mushrooms, where the weight of fish is critical to the success of the stuffing, I suggest six- to seven-ounce servings of flounder, as a substitute, to reflect the way we eat in America.

Note that when a whole sole is filleted in France, it is filleted in such a way as to give four slender fillets. In America, flounder is usually filleted slightly differently, to yield two wide fillets per fish. Therefore, when Manière calls for four sole fillets, I have substituted two larger flounder fillets.

SOLE STEAMED ON A BED OF CEYLON TEA
Filets de Soles à la Vapeur de Thé

Manière imbued sole with the exotic woody scent of Ceylon tea by steaming the fish on a bed of the leaves.(Loose tea leaves will give more flavor than tea bags.) A rich, warmly colored butter sauce, made with a Ceylon tea–infused vinegar, completes the movement, and a garnish of a sparkling dice of lime cuts the richness of the sauce.

Serve the fish with boiled potatoes or a simple rice pilaf; other vegetables muddy the delicate flavors of fish and sauce. If you have deep plates, spoon all of the sauce onto the plates so that the fish luxuriates in it. If not, spoon some sauce over each fillet and serve the rest in a sauceboat.

SERVES 4 AS A MAIN COURSE

CEYLON TEA BUTTER SAUCE

1 medium shallot, chopped (about 1½ tablespoons)

⅔ cup Ceylon Tea–Infused Vinegar (page 120)

Scant ¼ teaspoon salt

⅛ teaspoon freshly ground pepper, preferably white

3 tablespoons heavy cream

14 tablespoons unsalted butter, cut into pieces

1½ tablespoons loose Ceylon tea (or leaves from 3 to 4 tea bags)

2 Dover sole (see page 117), skinned and filleted (to give 8 fillets), or 4 flounder fillets (6 to 7 ounces each), cut in half lengthwise along the center line of the fillet (see page 165)

Salt

½ tablespoon unsalted butter

2 small limes, peeled, seeded, and cut into small dice

Cheesecloth

Large stackable steamer, stackable steamer with two steaming compartments, or roasting pan with wire rack

 Make the butter sauce: Follow the recipe for Beurre Blanc on page 120, using the tea-infused vinegar instead of the white wine and vinegar. Set aside in a warm place, and cover to keep warm.

Cut a double layer of cheesecloth that it is twice as long as the steamer rack. Lay the cheesecloth on the steamer rack so that half of the cheesecloth covers the rack and the other half falls outside the steamer. Sprinkle the tea over the cheesecloth in the steamer and fold the outer half of the cheesecloth over the tea to enclose it.

Fold each fillet in half, skinned side in. Sprinkle with salt and place in a single layer on the cheesecloth on the steamer rack. Place over simmering water, cover, and steam until tender, 4 to 5 minutes.

Just before the fish is cooked, melt the butter in a frying pan over high heat. Add the lime and sauté just to warm through, about 30 seconds. Remove from the heat.

To serve, divide the fillets among four plates. Sprinkle the lime over the fish and spoon the sauce over.

CEYLON TEA–INFUSED VINEGAR

Vinaigre de Thé

This recipe makes far more vinegar than you will need for the recipe on page 118 but it will keep for several months at least and is delicious in vinaigrette, as in the recipe for Warm Scallop Salad with Lamb's Lettuce (page 149).

MAKES 7 CUPS

7 cups white wine vinegar

8 Ceylon tea bags

Bring the vinegar to a boil in a nonaluminum pot. Add the tea bags, cover, and remove from the heat. Let cool. Store in sealed bottles or jars.

BEURRE BLANC I

This is Manière's master recipe for beurre blanc in the sauce chapter of his original edition. The Ceylon Tea Butter Sauce on page 119 is a variation of this sauce; he uses other variations, prepared using the same method, throughout the book.

MAKES ABOUT 1 CUP

1 medium shallot, chopped (about
   1½ tablespoons)

⅓ cup dry white wine

3 tablespoons cider vinegar

Scant ¼ teaspoon salt

⅛ teaspoon freshly ground pepper,
   preferably white

3 tablespoons heavy cream

14 tablespoons unsalted butter, cut into
   pieces

Combine the shallot, wine, vinegar, salt, and pepper in a nonaluminum saucepan and reduce over medium-high heat until almost dry. Add the cream and reduce by one third. Then, whisking constantly, whisk in the pieces of butter a few at a time, adding more as the butter is emulsified into the sauce, and bring just to a boil. Remove from the heat. Use immediately or keep warm for up to 2 hours in a thermos.

SOLE WITH FRESH TOMATO–BASIL SAUCE

Filets de Soles au Coulis de Basilic

This is a simple fresh recipe for late summer, when basil is plentiful and tomatoes are at their best. Make it with other lean white fish as well as fattier fish such as pompano or bluefish (see the chart on page 112 for steaming times). The fish is steamed on a bed of basil, flavoring it strongly with the pungent, minty taste of the herb. The sauce is a chunky, warm tomato vinaigrette, rich with olive oil and basil and thickened with an egg, which is "poached" in the steamer using Manière's neat, foolproof technique. The egg can be left out, if you prefer—the sauce will be slightly thinner.

SERVES 4 AS A MAIN COURSE

FRESH TOMATO-BASIL SAUCE

3 small or 2 medium tomatoes

2 medium shallots, finely chopped (about
3 tablespoons)

½ cup olive oil

½ teaspoon Dijon mustard

2 teaspoons chopped fresh basil, plus
4 basil leaves, cut into strips with scissors

2 to 3 tablespoons lemon juice (1 lemon)

¼ teaspoon salt

⅛ teaspoon freshly ground pepper

1 large egg, "poached" with ¼ cup
vinegar as directed on page 36

1 teaspoon chopped fresh chervil or
¼ teaspoon chopped fresh tarragon
plus ½ teaspoon chopped parsley

4 large sprigs basil

4 Dover sole (page 117), skinned and
filleted (to yield 16 fillets), or 4 flounder
fillets (6 to 7 ounces each), cut in half
lengthwise along the center line of the
fillet (see page 165)

Salt and freshly ground pepper

Large stackable steamer, stackable
steamer with two steaming compartments, or roasting pan with wire rack

 Make the sauce: Make a tomato concassé with the tomatoes (see page 98).

Warm the shallots gently in the olive oil in a small saucepan over low heat.

In another small saucepan, whisk together the mustard, chopped basil, 2 tablespoons lemon juice, the salt, and pepper. Add the poached egg and the basil strips and whisk well to break up the egg white (there will be bits of the white remaining in the sauce). Place over low heat and whisk in the warm oil-shallot mixture as if making a mayonnaise, slowly at first, until the sauce begins to thicken, and then more quickly, until the sauce is emulsified. Stir in the tomato concassé and the chervil or chopped tarragon mixture. Taste for lemon juice, adding more as necessary. Remove from the heat and cover to keep warm.

Lay the sprigs of basil on the steamer rack(s). Fold the fillets in half, skinned side in. Sprinkle the fillets with salt and pepper and lay them on top of the basil. Place over simmering water, cover, and steam until tender, about 5 minutes.

To serve, place the fillets on four plates and spoon the sauce over.

SOLE FILLETS STUFFED WITH MUSHROOMS
Paupiettes de Soles Farcies aux Champignons

This is an exquisite dish, both in flavor and in appearance. Manière stuffed the pure white sole fillets with a tender, cream-colored mousseline delicately flavored with mushrooms and sauced them with a luminous, light yellow sauce. This is a rich dish, and it's meant to be served as part of a complete French meal, which would normally include a starter, a salad, cheese, and/or a dessert. Therefore, the portions are intentionally small, by American standards—three small stuffed fillets and two stuffed mushrooms for each person.

If you can find the true Dover sole for this recipe, bravo. If not, choose thin fillets of any flounder (see page 117)—thick fillets would be difficult to roll. If you do find Dover sole, it's not likely to be as small as those Manière used—three quarters to one and a quarter pounds is more usual than his half-pound fish. Because the weight is critical only for the stuffing mixture, I suggest buying three whole sole of whatever weight is available to make the twelve fillets, and then four ounces of sole or flounder fillet for the stuffing.

SERVES 4 AS A MAIN COURSE

Three 8-ounce Dover sole (see page 117),
   skinned and filleted (to yield 12 fillets),
   or 3 small flounder fillets (about
   4 ounces each)

8 large mushrooms, trimmed, stems
   removed and reserved

MUSHROOM-SOLE STUFFING

2 tablespoons unsalted butter

2 medium shallots, minced

One 8-ounce Dover sole skinned, filleted
   (see page 165), and cut into small
   pieces, or 1 flounder fillet (about
   4 ounces), cut into small pieces

Reserved mushroom stems (see above)

1 teaspoon Cognac or brandy

6 tablespoons crème fraîche or
   6 tablespoons heavy cream mixed with
   1 teaspoon fresh lemon juice

1 large egg

1 egg white

Scant ½ teaspoon salt

⅛ teaspoon finely ground pepper

 If using flounder, cut each fillet lengthwise into 4 bands for the paupiettes. Using the flat side of a large knife, lightly pound the bands of sole or flounder fillet to flatten slightly.

Make the stuffing: Melt the butter in a nonaluminum saucepan over medium-low heat. Add the shallots, cover, and cook gently, without browning, until translucent, 3 to 5 minutes. Remove from the heat.

Measure 1½ teaspoons of the cooked shallot and put it into the bowl of a food processor, leaving the remaining shallot in the pan for the sauce. Add the fish pieces along with the reserved mushroom stems, the Cognac or brandy, crème fraîche or cream and lemon juice, egg, egg white, salt, and pepper and process until the mixture is finely ground and well mixed. If the stuffing is very loose (as is likely to be the case if your kitchen is very hot), transfer the stuffing to a bowl, set it in an ice bath, and beat with a wooden spoon for a minute, or until stiffened.

To stuff the fish, spoon about 1 tablespoon of the stuffing onto the wider end of one of the fish fillets or bands and then roll up the fillet to enclose the stuffing. If using flounder, use a toothpick to secure the package. Set the paupiette on its end on a plate and repeat with the remaining fish. Use the remaining stuffing to stuff the eight mushroom caps.

A fistful of fresh seaweed, rinsed

VERMOUTH CREAM SAUCE

1 large egg yolk

1 tablespoon fresh lemon juice

½ teaspoon potato starch or arrowroot
   (optional)

Reserved cooked shallots (see
   instructions)

¼ cup dry vermouth, such as Noilly Prat,
   or dry white wine

¼ teaspoon salt

⅛ teaspoon freshly ground pepper

¾ cup crème fraîche or ¾ cup heavy
   cream mixed with 2 teaspoons fresh
   lemon juice

Large stackable steamer with two
   steaming compartments or two
   steamers

Spread the seaweed over the steamer rack and stand the fish fillets on end on the seaweed. Set the filled mushroom caps on the seaweed, place over simmering water, cover, and steam 8 minutes.

Meanwhile, make the sauce: Whisk together the egg yolk, lemon juice, and potato starch or arrowroot, if using, in a small, heatproof bowl.

Gently rewarm the reserved shallots in the saucepan over low heat, then turn up the heat to high, add the vermouth, salt, and pepper, and bring to a boil. Boil until reduced by about one third. Add the crème fraîche or cream and lemon juice and reduce again by about one third. Take the saucepan off the heat and whisk a little of the sauce into the egg yolk mixture to temper it. Then whisk the egg yolk mixture into the sauce, set the sauce over low heat, and whisk constantly until the sauce thickens. Do not boil.

To serve, arrange the paupiettes in the center of a heated platter and place the mushroom caps around them. Pour some of the sauce over the fish and mushrooms, and serve the remaining sauce in a sauceboat on the side.

Low-calorie version: Replace the crème fraîche or cream in the stuffing with the same amount of low-fat *fromage blanc* or a low-fat fresh cheese, such as hoop cheese or low-fat cottage cheese. (If using cottage cheese, purée it until smooth before using.) Replace the crème fraîche or cream in the sauce with ½ cup nonfat yogurt, but do not reduce it—boiling will cause the yogurt to separate. Warm over medium heat and then add the egg yolk mixture as directed above.

Warm skate salad with red currants
Salade de Raie Tiède aux Groseilles

Skate, also occasionally sold as ray, is a common fish in France. It is shaped like a diamond with wide fins and a long tail. The "wings," the pectoral fins, are the edible part. Skate has a sweet taste and a firm, fine-grained, succulent texture. If skate is unavailable, sea scallops are a good substitute; see the variation on page 125. Like scallops, skate is rich. It is traditionally served with an acidic sauce and often garnished with capers. Manière dressed his skate salad with a bright, lemony mustard vinaigrette and sprinkled it with a small dice of lemon and tart fresh red currants. Summer is the season for red currants; during other times of the year, use capers instead.

In France, skate wings are sold on the bone; in America, you may find the wings boned to make wide flat fillets. Manière steamed skate in thick chunks, on the bone and with the skin on. I've steamed it both on and off the bone and prefer it on; the meat stays moist and firm and isn't gelatinous as when poached. Chunks on the bone fall apart less readily when cooked than the delicate fillets, and the skate can be accommodated in a smaller steamer.

If using boneless skate, prepare the dressing and greens first and steam the skate just before serving.

SERVES 4 AS A FIRST COURSE/MAIN COURSE

4 fennel stalks with feathery fronds or
  1 bunch dill
2 pieces skate wing on the bone (about
  1 pound each and 2 inches thick at the
  widest point) or 1 pound boneless
  skate wings
1 medium lemon

LEMON-MUSTARD VINAIGRETTE
1 teaspoon Dijon mustard
¼ teaspoon coarse sea salt
2 tablespoons fresh lemon juice
6 tablespoons olive oil
⅛ teaspoon freshly ground pepper

1 head curly endive (frisée) or 1 small
  head escarole (see page 67) or 3 cups
  packed mesclun (a mix of baby salad
  greens)
¼ cup fresh red currants, stemmed, or
  capers, drained
2 tablespoons chervil leaves or
  1 teaspoon chopped fresh tarragon
  plus 2 teaspoons chopped parsley

Stackable steamer with two steaming
  compartments, roasting pan with wire
  rack, or two steamers

 Spread the fennel or dill over the steamer rack(s). Put the skate wings on top, place over simmering water, cover, and steam about 20 minutes for skate wings on the bone, then set the lid ajar and steam 5 more minutes. For boneless skate wings, steam a total of 6 to 8 minutes. Remove from the heat.

Meanwhile, use a small, sharp knife to cut all of the peel, including the bitter white pith, from the lemon. Cut the flesh into ¼-inch dice, removing the seeds.

Make the vinaigrette: Whisk together the mustard, salt, and lemon juice in a small bowl. Then whisk in the olive oil and finally the pepper.

If using curly endive, pull out the light-colored inner yellow and whitish leaves and rinse them. If using escarole, remove the tough outer green leaves and tear the inner yellow-green leaves into small pieces and rinse them. (Use the darker outer leaves of either lettuce in another salad or in a soup, or steam them as directed on page 68 and serve with lemon juice and olive oil.) Mesclun needs no preparation.

If using skate on the bone, peel off the skin from one side of each piece with a small knife. Slide a small spatula between meat and bone to loosen the meat. Then use the knife or spatula to push the meat off the bone (see illustration on page 125). (The meat will break into pieces.) Cut out and discard any dark flesh. Lift and discard the bone.

To serve, divide the lettuce among four plates. Use a fork to separate the flesh of the skate into "leaves" and arrange them on top of each bed of lettuce. Sprinkle with the lemon dice and currants or capers. Spoon the vinaigrette over and garnish with the chervil or chopped parsley and tarragon. Serve immediately.

Variation: Substitute 1 pound large sea scallops, small white muscles removed (see page 168), for the skate. Proceed as directed on page 124, but prepare the lemon dice, vinaigrette, and greens before you steam the scallops. Put the scallops on the fennel or dill on the steamer rack and steam over simmering water for 4 to 6 minutes. Serve as directed on page 124.

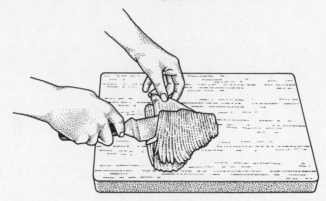

TUNA WITH TOMATOES, GREEN PEPPER, AND GARLIC

Thon à la Luzienne

Manière wrote that tuna, often considered an oily fish, can become dry and stringy, particularly if fried or grilled at too high a heat. Steaming keeps it moist and succulent while rendering much of its fat so that it is rich tasting and satisfying. Manière served this tuna with *riz créole,* a rice pilaf flavored with mushrooms, green peppers, and tomatoes.

Manière cooked the tuna completely to a meaty, dense texture, like well-cooked meat. In America we have become used to eating it rare or medium-rare. If you like your tuna medium-rare, steam it for only three to four minutes.

Manière sauced the tuna with a juicy fresh tomato and bell pepper mixture flavored with the exotic herb liqueur called Izarra, from the Basque region. Izarra is hard to find here, so I substitute Chartreuse or anise-flavored *pastis,* sold under the brand names Pernod or Ricard. (A large bottle of Pernod is expensive, but many liquor stores carry the airline-sized bottles, more than enough for this recipe.) The sauce is gutsy, coarse, and delicious—it begs to be eaten on its own, like a soup, with a spoon. In fact, this sauce is too good to pass up— if you can't find fresh tuna, make the dish with swordfish, mackerel, salmon, pompano, or mahi-mahi. (Use the chart on page 112 for steaming times.) Or serve the sauce with steamed chicken or lamb.

(continued)

TOMATO AND GREEN PEPPER SAUCE

8 small or 4 large tomatoes

¼ cup vegetable oil

1 small onion, chopped

1 medium green bell pepper, cored,
    halved, seeds and ribs removed, and
    cut into thin strips

6 medium cloves garlic, minced

1 tablespoon chopped parsley

1½ tablespoons red or white wine vinegar

1½ tablespoons Izarra or Chartreuse
    liqueur or Pernod

½ teaspoon salt

⅛ teaspoon freshly ground pepper

4 tuna steaks (about 7 ounces each), ¾ to
    1 inch thick

Salt and freshly ground pepper

½ teaspoon dried thyme leaves

1 tablespoon chopped parsley

Large stackable steamer, large steamer pot
    with shallow insert, roasting pan with
    wire rack, or collapsible steamer basket

Make the sauce: Make a tomato concassé with the tomatoes (see page 98).

Heat the oil in a medium saucepan over low heat. Add the onion and pepper and cook 5 minutes, stirring frequently. Add the tomatoes, garlic, parsley, vinegar, Izarra, Chartreuse, or Pernod, salt, and pepper and let simmer, uncovered, over low heat until thickened, about 25 minutes. Taste for salt and pepper.

When the sauce is almost ready, sprinkle the tuna steaks on both sides with salt and pepper and put them in a single layer on the steamer rack. Sprinkle with the thyme. Place over simmering water, cover, and steam 3 to 4 minutes for medium-rare, 8 minutes to cook through completely.

To serve, arrange the tuna on a heated platter and spoon the sauce over. Sprinkle with the chopped parsley.

Mosaic of Saint-Pierre with Saffron
Mosaïque de Saint-Pierre aux Pistils de Safron

Saint-Pierre, or John Dory, is a delicious, meaty, white-fleshed fish from the Mediterranean that is rarely sold in America. It is a ferocious-looking fish with huge head and mouth; round black spots, which are supposed to be the fingerprints of Saint Peter, mark the skin on either side of its flattened body. Saint-Pierre is occasionally imported to America from New Zealand. If you do find it here, have the fish store fillet it, but be sure to take the bones and head home—they have a lot of flavor and will make a rich-tasting stock for a sauce or soup.

If you're lucky enough to find Saint-Pierre, this recipe will make the fish shine. If not, porgy, a moderately firm, white-fleshed fish, or pompano, a firm, darker-fleshed, buttery fish, is an excellent substitute.

In this recipe, Manière played with the flavors of the Mediterranean fish soup bouillabaisse, which commonly uses Saint-Pierre. But what an elegant bouillabaisse he created here: The fish is cut into finger-wide strips, woven together like a cane-backed chair, and set atop a saffron-fragrant mixture of tomato, fennel, and onion. A beurre blanc seamlessly marries the flavors.

SERVES 4 AS A MAIN COURSE

SAFFRON-TOMATO SAUCE

8 small or 4 medium tomatoes

2 tablespoons unsalted butter

1 medium bulb fennel, finely minced

1 small onion, chopped

1 tablespoon minced shallots

⅓ cup dry white wine

1 pinch saffron threads

1 tablespoon small sprigs fresh chervil or
   1 teaspoon chopped fresh tarragon
   plus 2 teaspoons chopped parsley

½ teaspoon salt

⅛ teaspoon freshly ground pepper

BEURRE BLANC II

1½ tablespoons minced shallots

2 tablespoons dry white wine

2 tablespoons cider vinegar

½ teaspoon salt

⅛ teaspoon freshly ground pepper,
   preferably white

1½ tablespoons crème fraîche or heavy
   cream

11 tablespoons unsalted butter

Unsalted butter, softened, for buttering
   the foil

4 Saint-Pierre, porgy, or pompano fillets
   (1¾ pounds total)

Fresh chervil sprigs or tarragon leaves for
   garnish

Aluminum foil

Stackable steamer with two steaming
   compartments, roasting pan with wire
   rack, or two steamers

Make the saffron-tomato sauce: Make a tomato concassé with the tomatoes (see page 98).

Melt the butter in a medium saucepan over medium-low heat. Add the fennel, onion, and shallots and cook 5 minutes, stirring frequently. Add the white wine and saffron and then the tomatoes. If using chervil, cut into bits over the pan with scissors, or add the tarragon and parsley, if using. Add the salt and pepper and simmer over low heat, uncovered, for 30 minutes. Taste for salt and pepper.

While the sauce cooks, make the beurre blanc according to the directions on page 120. Strain it through a fine strainer and set aside in a warm place.

Cut a 24-inch length of aluminum foil, fold it crosswise in half, and cut into four 6-inch squares. Butter them well.

Cut the fish fillets lengthwise into 32 finger-wide strips. Arrange 4 of the fish strips, side by side, on each of the aluminum rectangles. Then, on each foil rectangle, weave 4 more strips of fish into the first 4 to make a latticework pattern (see illustration below). Put the foil squares of fish on the steamer rack, place over simmering water, cover, and steam, Saint-Pierre and porgy for 5 minutes, pompano for 7 to 8 minutes.

To serve, spoon the saffron-tomato sauce onto four plates. Gently slide a fish "mosaic" onto each one. Spoon a little of the butter sauce over the fish and garnish each "mosaic" with two chervil sprigs or with tarragon leaves. Serve the remaining beurre blanc in a heated sauceboat on the side.

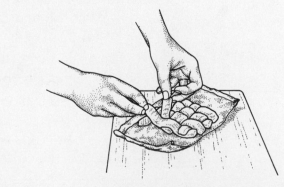

SMOKED HADDOCK WITH SAUERKRAUT

Haddock sur Choucroute

Contrary to popular opinion, Manière said, choucroute doesn't have to be a heavy dish. Steaming can make choucroute low-calorie. And, because this choucroute is made with smoked haddock rather than with pork, there are only two hundred fifty calories—but twenty-five grams of protein—in each serving.

Domestic and imported smoked haddock can be ordered from many specialty food stores that carry smoked fish. If you can't find smoked haddock, smoked cod, which is marketed as sable in the Northeast and black cod on the West Coast, and smoked trout, now sold in many supermarkets, are good substitutes. All three fish are hot-smoked and have a strong smoky flavor; smoked cod and trout are flakier than meaty smoked haddock.

Manière's haddock choucroute has all of the flavor of the traditional dish and almost no fat, and he gave us an easy way to make a rich-flavored, low-fat vegetable sauce: Carrots and onion are steamed along with the sauerkraut, then puréed and thinned with nonfat yogurt. The sauce is both sweet and tart enough to stand up to the rich smokiness of the fish. If calories aren't an issue, replace the yogurt with three quarters of a cup of crème fraîche, or sauce the fish and sauerkraut with Nantais Butter Sauce (page 158) instead.

Manière made this dish with fresh sauerkraut, but it can be made with precooked sauerkraut as well. Fresh sauerkraut, available in some specialty or butcher shops (try an Eastern European butcher), takes about twenty-five minutes to steam. Good-quality precooked sauerkraut comes in jars or plastic packages and just needs to be reheated; longer cooking makes it mushy and tasteless. Steaming makes rinsing the sauerkraut, whether fresh or precooked, unnecessary. (Hebrew National makes a good-quality precooked sauerkraut.)

SERVES 4 AS A MAIN COURSE

1 medium onion, peeled and trimmed but
   root end left intact

3 whole cloves

2 medium carrots, peeled

2 pounds fresh or precooked sauerkraut,
   rinsed

1¼ teaspoons salt

4 cloves garlic, peeled and halved

2 sprigs fresh or dried thyme

2 bay leaves

Small bouquet of parsley (8 to 10 sprigs),
   tied into a bunch with kitchen string

12 juniper berries

 Stick the onion with the cloves. Cut it through the root end into four wedges.

Put the carrots and onion on the steamer rack, place over simmering water, cover, and steam 25 minutes. Remove the carrots and onion from the steamer rack.

Put half of the sauerkraut onto the steamer rack. Sprinkle with 1 teaspoon of the salt. Place the steamed carrots and onion on top, and add the garlic, thyme, bay leaves, and parsley. Sprinkle with the juniper berries and caraway seeds. Cover with the remaining sauerkraut, place over simmering water, cover, and steam 20 minutes.

Uncover and remove the carrots, onion, garlic, and parsley from the sauerkraut, and discard the parsley. Save the vegetables for the

1 teaspoon caraway seeds

1¼ pounds smoked haddock, cut into
   4 equal portions

⅔ cup nonfat yogurt

⅛ teaspoon freshly ground pepper

3 tablespoons chopped fresh chives or
   scallion greens

Large stackable steamer, steamer pot
   with deep insert, pasta cooker, or
   collapsible steamer basket in deep pot

purée. Put the smoked fish on top of the sauerkraut, cover, and steam, haddock or cod for 5 minutes, trout for 3 minutes.

Meanwhile, remove the cloves from the onion. Put the carrot, onion, and garlic into the bowl of a food processor and purée. Add the yogurt, the remaining ¼ teaspoon salt, and the pepper and purée. Taste for seasoning. Stir in the chives or scallions. Let stand in a warm place until you are ready to serve. (The purée may be rewarmed very gently over low heat, but it will break if it simmers.)

To serve, mound the sauerkraut in a serving bowl or on a platter and top with the fish. Serve the hot purée in a sauceboat on the side.

STEAKS, FILLETS, AND SMALL FISH STEAMED *EN PAPILLOTE*

These five recipes are for individual portions of fish steamed in aluminum foil packages called papillotes (see page 166). This is an ingenious way to steam fillets and steaks. It adds flavors to the fish, keeps the flesh moist, and makes its own sauce while the fish cooks. And there are no pots to clean up. Any fillet, steak, or small whole fish can be steamed in this way; see page 167 to adjust times for steaming fish *en papillote*.

Steaming *en papillote* usually results in a lot of flavorful, brothy sauce. This is the place to use sauce spoons, if you're lucky enough to have a set, or soup spoons. Serve bread to sop up the sauce as well. Typically, the papillotes are served unopened. The guests open the packages themselves by cutting a slit in the top with a knife or scissors and then tearing open the foil to breathe in the heady perfume. You may want to ease the contents of the papillotes onto the plates and throw away the aluminum foil wrapper before eating.

You'll need a large steamer to hold papillotes to serve four, because they mustn't overlap. Use a stackable steamer with two steaming compartments, a large roasting pan with a wire rack, or two steamers.

POLLACK WITH FENNEL, TOMATO, AND CREAM

Lieu Jaune au Fenouil

This is an exquisite recipe. Manière used the most ordinary ingredients (and not very many of them) to create a dish that is as subtle and elegantly flavored as if it had been fussed with forever.

Pollack is a lean white fish similar to cod, found in both the Atlantic and Pacific. It may be hard to come by; most West Coast pollack is made into the processed fish product surimi, sold here as imitation crab legs, shrimp, and scallops. If pollack isn't available, use cod—it will be delicious. Or use any other white-fleshed fish steaks or fillets.

SERVES 4 AS A MAIN COURSE

1 medium fennel bulb

2 medium tomatoes or 1 large tomato, peeled (see page 98), cored, thinly sliced, and seeded

4 large mushrooms, thinly sliced

2 medium shallots, minced (about 3 tablespoons)

1½ tablespoons chopped parsley

4 pollack or cod steaks (6 to 8 ounces each), about 1 inch thick

Salt and freshly ground pepper

¼ cup crème fraîche or ¼ cup heavy cream plus 2 teaspoons fresh lemon juice

Aluminum foil

Stackable steamer with two steaming compartments, large roasting pan with wire rack, or two steamers

 Trim the fennel and cut lengthwise in half. Place the halves cut side down on a cutting board and thinly slice through the root end. Put the fennel slices on the steamer rack, place over simmering water, cover, and steam 10 minutes.

To make the papillotes, cut four sheets of aluminum foil about 12 by 30 inches and fold crosswise in half to double. Line the papillotes up on a work surface. Put one quarter of the tomato slices in the center of each papillote. Cover with the fennel and then the mushrooms. Sprinkle with the shallots and parsley. Top each papillote with a pollack or cod steak and sprinkle with salt and a little pepper. Spoon 1 tablespoon of the crème fraîche or cream on top of each steak, and sprinkle over the lemon juice, if using cream. Bring the sides of the foil up to meet over the fish, fold the edges together, and then fold over three times in ¼-inch folds. Fold the open edges over three times in ¼-inch folds to seal.

Put the papillotes on the steamer rack. Place over simmering water, cover, and steam 15 minutes. Set the cover ajar and steam 5 more minutes.

Place the unopened papillotes on four plates and serve.

MONKFISH WITH ZUCCHINI AND GREEN PEPPERCORNS

Lotte aux Courgettes en Papillotes

Monkfish is a sweet, delicate-flavored white fish with a firm, meaty texture, often compared to lobster. It is becoming more and more common in American markets, but if you can't find it, substitute any lean white-fleshed fish (see the chart on page 112) or even an oily fish such as mackerel, pompano, or bluefish.

Monkfish can be tricky to cook: It must be cooked all the way through or it will be tough, but prolonged cooking over high heat can dry it out. Steaming keeps the fish moist, and steaming *en papillote* is added insurance of tender, juicy flesh. The combination of meaty fish, delicately sweet, tender zucchini, and cream is mouth-watering. The peppercorns give the sauce a contrasting hot and crunchy bite.

If you can't find green peppercorns, use the same amount of drained capers. For thinner monkfish fillets, reduce the covered steaming time to fifteen minutes.

SERVES 4 AS A MAIN COURSE

3 small or 2 medium zucchini, sliced into
   thin rounds
1 teaspoon green peppercorns in brine,
   drained and rinsed
1½ pounds monkfish fillet (about 1 inch
   thick), cut into 4 equal portions
Salt
Sweet Hungarian paprika
1 medium clove garlic, minced
1½ tablespoons chopped fresh chives or
   scallion greens
¼ cup crème fraîche or ¼ cup heavy
   cream plus 2 teaspoons fresh lemon
   juice
1 teaspoon fresh thyme leaves or
   ½ teaspoon dried thyme

Aluminum foil
Stackable steamer with two steaming
   compartments, large roasting pan with
   wire rack, or two steamers

 Put the zucchini rounds on the steamer rack, place over simmering water, cover, and steam 5 minutes. Remove from the steamer.

Roughly crush the green peppercorns in a mortar and pestle or roughly chop.

To make the papillotes, cut four pieces of aluminum foil about 9 inches by 12 inches. Lay them side by side on a work surface. Arrange one quarter of the zucchini rounds in the center of each foil rectangle. Cover each with a fillet of monkfish. Sprinkle each fillet with salt, a pinch of paprika, and one quarter of the peppercorns. Then sprinkle with the chopped garlic and chives or scallions. Spoon 1 tablespoon of the crème fraîche or cream over each fillet, and sprinkle over the lemon juice if using cream. Crumble the thyme over the fillets. Bring the sides of the foil up to meet over the fish, fold the edges together, and then fold over three times in ¼-inch folds. Fold the open edges over three times in ¼-inch folds to seal.

Put the papillotes, side by side and overlapping as little as possible, on the steamer rack, place over simmering water, cover, and steam 20 minutes. Then set the lid ajar and steam 5 more minutes. Place the unopened papillotes on four plates and serve.

The next three recipes *en papillote* are for herring and sardines, small, tasty, oily fish that are hard to find fresh in America. Don't despair; mackerel, pompano, and bluefish are more common here, and their luscious meat and rich flavor are equally delicious in these recipes.

Herring is rarely sold fresh in America; most of it is brined, cured, or smoked to make pickled herring, rollmops, kippered herring, and the like. Small herring may be sold as sardines. Sardines may be difficult to find as well; they belong to the herring family, are typically small (one to two ounces), and have rich, dark flesh, like herring.

Small mackerel or small mackerel fillets are a tasty substitute for herring and sardines. When very fresh, mackerel is a wonderful fish: It is flavorful with luxuriously soft, flaky, fat meat. My previous experiences with mackerel had led me to think of it as strong-tasting and oily; in Manière's recipes it emerges mild-tasting and superb.

Pompano is another delicious, oily-fleshed American fish, most of which comes from Florida. Its body is unusually flat, yielding wide, thin fillets. It is one of my favorite fish to steam; it is moist, tender, and succulent, and the flavor is rich without being strong.

Bluefish is an Atlantic fish. Its flesh is soft and somewhat flakier than mackerel. Small bluefish are milder and sweeter than the large fish; buy smaller fish if you have a choice. For those who think they don't like bluefish (I used to be one), try it in one of these recipes: Steamed bluefish is wonderful.

FRESH HERRING WITH MUSTARD AND GREEN PEPPERCORNS

Harengs Frais à la Moutarde et au Poivre Vert

This recipe is typically made with whole small mackerel or with mackerel fillets, but you'll be happy with pompano, bluefish, tuna, salmon, trout, shad, or Arctic char fillet as well. The portion size is small (three to four ounces) because herring is so rich. (Use the chart on page 112 to substitute a different, larger fish or fillet.)

The sauce is mustardy, hot, and creamy, thinned and flavored with the juices from the fish. The fish melts, while the peppercorns pop in your mouth. Serve the fish with steamed unpeeled potatoes (*en robe de champs,* or "in field dress"). If you can't find green peppercorns, use capers.

Manière steamed whole fish with the head on; have the fish store remove the heads if you prefer.

2 tablespoons Dijon mustard

¼ cup crème fraîche or ¼ cup heavy cream mixed with 2 teaspoons fresh lemon juice

1 small jar green peppercorns in brine, drained and rinsed (save the brine for unused peppercorns)

4 small herring (about 6 ounces each), gutted and scaled, 4 small whole mackerel (8 to 10 ounces each), gutted and scaled, or 4 small mackerel fillets (3 to 4 ounces each), about ½ inch thick

Salt

Aluminum foil

Stackable steamer with two steaming compartments, large roasting pan with wire rack, or two steamers

 Whisk together the mustard and crème fraîche or cream and lemon juice in a small bowl.

To make the papillotes, cut four pieces of aluminum foil about 9 inches by 12 inches. Set them on a work surface. Spread a generous ½ tablespoon of the cream mixture in a line down the center of each piece of foil. Then sprinkle 6 peppercorns along each line of cream. Lay one fish or fish fillet, skin side down, on each line of cream and sprinkle with salt. Spread another generous ½ tablespoon of the cream mixture over each fish or fish fillet and sprinkle each with 6 more peppercorns. Bring the sides of the foil up to meet over the fish, fold the edges together, and then fold over three times in ¼-inch folds. Fold the open edges over three times in ¼-inch folds to seal.

Put the papillotes, side by side and overlapping as little as possible, on the steamer rack. Place over simmering water, cover, and steam 10 minutes. If using whole fish, set the lid ajar and steam 3 more minutes for herring, 5 more minutes for whole mackerel.

Place the unopened papillotes on four plates and serve.

HERRING WRAPPED IN CABBAGE LEAVES WITH MINT
Harengs en Feuilles de Chou

This dish is delicious with small whole mackerel or fillets; if you can't find mackerel, substitute bluefish fillet (use the chart on page 112 to adjust the steaming time). The fresh mint will penetrate the flesh of the fillets even more effectively than the flesh of the whole fish.

Manière served the dish with a thick, lemony sauce sweetened with puréed steamed garlic. The sauce recalls a hollandaise, but is much simpler to make because it uses cream instead of butter.

Manière suggested using the leftover head of cabbage from this recipe for another meal of sweet-and-sour cabbage salad with chicken livers. Follow the recipe for Warm Sweet-and-Sour Cabbage Salad (page 54): Steam chicken livers three minutes and cut them on a shallow angle into thin slices, or *escalopes*. Combine the cabbage and livers and serve warm, sprinkled with chopped parsley.

Manière steamed whole fish with the head on; have the fish store remove the heads if you prefer.

S E R V E S   4   A S   A   M A I N   C O U R S E

1 large head cabbage, preferably Savoy

4 small herring (about 6 ounces each), gutted and scaled, 4 small whole mackerel (8 to 10 ounces each), gutted and scaled, or 4 small mackerel fillets (3 to 4 ounces each), about ½ inch thick

Salt and freshly ground pepper

4 large sprigs fresh mint, leaves only, coarsely chopped, or 1 teaspoon dried mint

GARLIC-LEMON SAUCE

4 cloves garlic, peeled

2 large egg yolks

¼ cup plus 2 tablespoons crème fraîche or heavy cream

Juice of 2 medium lemons (6 to 8 tablespoons)

¼ teaspoon salt

⅛ teaspoon freshly ground pepper, preferably white

Aluminum foil

Stackable steamer with two steaming compartments, large roasting pan with wire rack, or two steamers

 Pull off 4 of the large outside leaves from the cabbage head (see page 51); if the head is small, pull off 8 leaves (you will need to use 2 leaves per fish). Pare down the thick center rib of each leaf even with the leaf (see page 52), and rinse the leaves. Put them on the steamer rack, place over simmering water, cover, and steam 2 minutes to soften. Refresh under cold running water and pat dry on paper towels.

To make the papillotes, sprinkle the fish with salt and pepper. Stuff the cavities of the whole fish with the mint, or spread the mint over each fillet. Lay a cabbage leaf—or place 2 small leaves next to each other, overlapping them slightly—on the work surface. Place a whole fish or a fillet across the center of the leaf or leaves and fold the bottom edge up over the fish. Fold over the sides of the leaf or leaves, and then roll the fish over to enclose it in the cabbage. Repeat with the remaining fish.

Cut four 10- by 12-inch pieces of aluminum foil, and place the pieces of foil on the work surface with short sides facing you. Place a fish packet, seam side down, in the center of each piece of foil. Bring the sides of the foil up to meet over the fish, fold the edges together, and then fold over three times in ¼-inch folds. Fold the open edges over three times in ¼-inch folds to seal.

Put the papillotes on the steamer rack so that they overlap as little as possible. Add the garlic cloves to the rack (it's fine to put them on top of the papillotes). Place over simmering water, cover, and steam 12 minutes. Turn off the heat, set the lid ajar, and let the fish stand.

Make the sauce: Place the steamed garlic on a small plate and mash to a purée with a fork. Transfer the purée to a small nonaluminum saucepan, add the egg yolks, crème fraîche or heavy cream, lemon juice, salt, and pepper, and whisk to combine. Put the saucepan over low heat and whisk just until the sauce thickens; do not bring to a simmer. Remove from the heat.

Place the unopened papillote on four plates. Pour the sauce into a warm sauceboat and serve alongside.

SARDINES STEAMED IN SPICY TOMATO AND GARLIC SAUCE

Sardines en Papillotes

Fresh sardines are hard to find, but you can also make this recipe with mackerel, bluefish, or pompano fillets. Manière steamed the fish in a deep red, spicy, garlicky tomato sauce that is almost more of a condiment, reminiscent of Tunisian harissa (see page 248). Flavored with an anise-flavored liqueur called *pastis* (see page 125), this sauce also goes well with lamb or chicken.

Sardines, Manière wrote, have a very refined flavor, but people hesitate to cook them because of their strong "fishy" smell. You won't have this problem with steamed sardines; even oily fish are mild after steaming.

SERVES 4 AS A WARM FIRST COURSE

SPICY TOMATO AND GARLIC SAUCE
6 medium cloves garlic, minced
¾ cup tomato paste
1½ tablespoons chopped parsley
¼ teaspoon fresh thyme leaves or pinch of dried thyme
¼ cup plus 2 tablespoons olive oil
1 teaspoon Pernod or Ricard
⅛ teaspoon cayenne pepper
¾ teaspoon salt

16 fresh sardines (1 to 2 ounces each), scaled and gutted, or 4 mackerel, pompano, or bluefish fillets (about 6 ounces each)

Aluminum foil
Large stackable steamer with two steaming compartments, large roasting pan with wire rack, or two steamers

Make the sauce: Combine all of the sauce ingredients in a blender or food processor. Purée until very smooth.

If using sardines, rinse them quickly and dry them well on paper towels.

To make the papillotes, cut four 12- by 15-inch sheets of aluminum foil for sardines, or 10- by 12-inch sheets for fillets. Place the pieces of foil on a work surface with a long side facing you. Spread a quarter of the sauce down the center of each rectangle. Place 4 sardines, side by side, or 1 fish fillet on top of the sauce on each rectangle. Bring the two long sides up to meet over the fish, fold the edges together, and then fold over three times in ¼-inch folds. Fold the open edges over three times in ¼-inch folds to seal.

Put the papillotes on the steamer rack so that they overlap as little as possible. Place over simmering water and cover. Steam sardines for 8 minutes, then set the lid ajar and steam 7 more minutes; or steam mackerel fillets for 10 minutes, pompano for 8 to 10 minutes, or bluefish for 8 to 10 minutes.

Place the unopened papillotes on four plates and serve.

These six recipes are for whole steamed fish. (See page 161 for basic instructions, Steaming Whole Fish.) Other types of whole fish can be substituted in each recipe, and all but one recipe, the Fisherman's Soup (page 142), can be adapted for fillets and steaks, using the chart on page 112 to determine the timings.

The idea of steaming a whole fish was daunting to me because poaching a whole fish can be tricky. Between making a poaching liquid, getting the fish in and out of it, keeping the liquid at a constant simmer, and guessing at the cooking time, poaching was never much fun. I was relieved to find that, in comparison, steaming a whole fish is simple. There is no poaching liquid, and, because the temperature in the steamer is constant, the timing is absolutely foolproof. With very few exceptions, the steaming time for all whole fish can be reliably determined by measuring the fish at its thickest point (see page 109). I soon realized that steaming a whole fish is as easy as steaming a fillet or steak. The fish must be skinned and boned after steaming, but the results merit the extra fuss: The flesh is uniformly moist and the flavor superb. If you are able to buy whole fish, or large chunks of fish on the bone, do so.

A large stackable steamer or a roasting pan with a wire rack works well for steaming whole smallish fish, such as small snapper, sea bass, pompano, or porgy. For narrowish larger fish, such as cod, salmon trout, bluefish, tilefish, and salmon, a fish poacher placed over two burners, with the rack raised off the floor of the poacher with empty tuna cans (see page 10), works beautifully. A roasting pan with a wire rack will work as well; the advantage of the poacher is that the cooked fish is easily lifted out of the poacher on the poaching rack. Remember that you or the fish store can cut off the head and even the tail of a whole fish to fit it in the steamer.

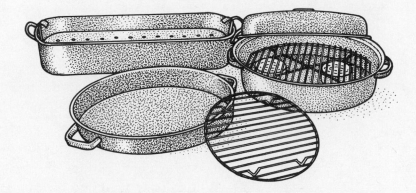

Whole salmon trout steamed on a bed of dill with a warm mayonnaise

Truite Saumonée à la Mayonnaise Chaude

In America, the term *salmon trout* may be used to identify at least a couple of different fish (the French salmon trout is another fish altogether). In the Fulton Fish Market, I have seen both wild freshwater brook trout from Lake Michigan and Norwegian farm-raised steel-head trout marketed as salmon trout. Both are tasty fish, and you can use either in this recipe. The freshwater trout tastes like a cross between a salmon and a trout. The skin is a mottled silver and yellow, and the flesh, which is rich, delicate-flavored, and succulent, ranges from light beige-colored to pink. It's very moist when steamed. The bright silver-skinned steelhead trout looks and tastes very much like a small farm-raised salmon.

Manière called for fish weighing slightly over two pounds; four to five pounds is more usual for salmon trout here. In this recipe you can also substitute a four-pound chunk of a larger salmon cut from the center of the fish, four half-pound to one-pound trout, or a four- to five-pound farm-raised Arctic char (similar in flavor to a salmon but richer and with a finer flake). Arctic char is a delicious fish; I like it steamed even better than salmon.

Manière served the salmon trout with a warm mayonnaise, similar to a hollandaise, made with a vermouth reduction thickened with both oil and melted butter. The sauce is easier to make than a hollandaise because the egg yolks are not whisked over heat. Like a cold mayonnaise, a warm mayonnaise is firm, not frothy.

(continued)

Bunch of fresh dill or stalks from 1 large
    fennel bulb
One 4- to 5-pound salmon trout, gutted
    and scaled

WARM MAYONNAISE
¼ cup wine vinegar
3 tablespoons dry vermouth, such as
    Noilly Prat
4 tablespoons unsalted butter
1 teaspoon Dijon mustard, thinned with
    2 teaspoons water
3 large egg yolks
½ cup olive oil
½ teaspoon salt
⅛ teaspoon freshly ground pepper

Aluminum foil
Fish poacher with raised rack (see page
    10) plus stackable steamer or steamer
    pot with shallow insert for the sauce

 Use half of the dill or fennel stalks to make a bed for the trout on a foil tray (see page 163) on the steamer rack. Place the trout on the herbs and cover with the remaining dill or fennel stalks. Place the rack over simmering water, cover, and steam for 20 minutes. Then set the lid ajar and steam for 10 minutes longer. (If you are not ready to serve the fish immediately, let it stand in the poacher over very low heat with the lid ajar; it will hold for 30 minutes.)

Meanwhile, make the mayonnaise: Combine the vinegar and vermouth in a medium nonaluminum saucepan and reduce by half over high heat. Meanwhile, melt the butter.

Whisk the mustard into the vinegar-vermouth reduction. Take the saucepan off the heat and whisk in the egg yolks. Then gradually whisk in the melted butter in a thin, steady stream. Return the saucepan to medium heat and whisk in the oil in a thin stream. Whisk in the salt and pepper.

Just before serving, put the pan of sauce on the steamer rack over briskly simmering water and whisk until the mayonnaise thickens. (Or, if you let the mayonnaise stand near the steamer while the fish is steaming, the heat from the steamer should be enough to thicken the mayonnaise.)

When the fish is cooked, grasp opposing corners of the foil tray and lift the fish onto a cutting board. Skin it and remove the meat from the bones (see page 163). Divide the fish among the serving plates. Pour the mayonnaise into a very hot sauceboat and serve it on the side.

PIKE WITH MINT AND THYME AND A MUSCADET BUTTER SAUCE

Brochetons Beurre Nantais

Pike is a freshwater fish with lean, firm white flesh. Typically freshwater fish have a milder flavor than ocean fish but can have an earthy or even muddy taste. There are many recipes from Angers in the Loire Valley for pike with a white butter sauce, a tart, silky sauce flavored with vinegar and shallots. The sauce brightens the grassy flavor of the pike but it is also delicious in combination with any of the lean white-fleshed ocean fish listed in the chart on page 112. Manière's sauce uses Muscadet, a dry white wine from the region of Nantes, in Brittany.

Manière steamed small whole pike (*brochetons*) on a bed of wild mint and thyme. Such small pike may be hard to find, but don't worry: Manière's recipe yields five-ounce portions, ample for a first course; you'll be happier with two two-pound or one three-pound pike as a main course. If using fillets, use five-ounce fillets for a first course, six- to eight-ounce fillets for a main course.

SERVES 4 AS A FIRST COURSE/MAIN COURSE

Small bunch of fresh thyme or
  1 tablespoon dried thyme
4 large sprigs fresh mint or 1 tablespoon
  dried mint
2 small pike (1¼ to 1½ pounds each) or
  two 2-pound or one 3-pound pike,
  gutted, or 4 pike fillets (5 to 8 ounces;
  see headnote)
Salt and freshly ground pepper

MUSCADET BUTTER SAUCE I
1 medium shallot, chopped
  (about 1½ tablespoons)
⅔ cup Muscadet or other dry white wine
¼ teaspoon salt
⅛ teaspoon freshly ground pepper,
  preferably white
3 tablespoons crème fraîche or heavy
  cream
14 tablespoons unsalted butter

Aluminum foil, if steaming whole fish
Cheesecloth, if using dried herbs
Large stackable steamer, fish poacher
  with rack, roasting pan with wire rack,
  or two steamers

 Make a bed of the fresh herbs on a foil tray (see page 163), if using whole fish, or directly on the steamer rack, if using fillets. If using dried herbs, line the steamer with cheesecloth as described on page 161; the cheesecloth can be used in lieu of the foil tray. Sprinkle the cavity of the whole fish with salt and pepper, or season the fillets, and set on the bed of herbs. Place over simmering water, cover, and steam according to the times in the chart on page 112.

Meanwhile, make the sauce, following the directions for Beurre Blanc on page 120. Strain the sauce through a fine strainer and cover to keep warm.

When the fish is cooked, grasp opposing corners of the foil tray or the ends of the cheesecloth, if steaming a whole fish, and lift the fish onto a cutting board. Skin the fish and remove the meat from the bones (see page 163). Place the boned fish or the fillets on a serving platter and serve the sauce in a warm sauceboat on the side.

WHOLE STEAMED SHAD WITH SORREL

Alose à l'Oseille

Perhaps it's because spring seemed very long in coming after a hard, snowy winter, but it will be quite some time before I forget my first taste of early spring shad prepared in this way. The fish is stuffed with sorrel and sauced with a tart sorrel butter sauce. The dish is admittedly rich, but what a delight to eat: Shad is a tasty fish in its own right, but the alchemy of the fish and sorrel is perfection.

Shad, a member of the herring family, is a gleaming bright silver–scaled fish. Steamed, the white flesh is soft, moist, flaky, and rich without being strong-flavored. The only draw-back to the shad is that it is full of tiny bones: In addition to the back and rib bones of the main skeleton, there are two extra rows of "floating" bones in each fillet. In France, shad is sold whole; in the United States, it's sold as boned fillets.

Shad and sorrel are both spring events. We start to see shad from warm areas such as Georgia during late February or early March, depending on the weather. It moves north-ward during the season—shad are fished in the Hudson River from late March until the middle of May—and lasts into May or even June.

Garden, or French, sorrel is a very tart herb with shield-shaped leaves that is easily culti-vated in a garden. The French traditionally cook whole shad with sorrel because the acidity of sorrel is supposed to soften the little bones in the fish. In America, we don't have to worry about the bones, but we can still enjoy the irresistible combination of tart, lemony sorrel and rich fish. If you can't get shad, serve the sauce with salmon or salmon trout.

Sorrel must be cut into thin julienne strips with a knife or kitchen scissors or it will be stringy. Always use stainless steel pots and utensils; other metals will blacken sorrel and ruin the flavor. (It's all right to use an aluminum foil tray in this recipe, because the foil is not in contact with the sorrel.)

Use a neutral-flavored white bread made without fat in the stuffing (Manière probably used baguettes, made with just flour, water, yeast, and salt).

It's easiest to steam the fish in a large stackable steamer or in a fish poacher with the rack raised on empty tuna cans (see page 10). You can use a roasting pan with a wire rack, but since it's hard to steam the sorrel on a rack, I would steam it in another pot.

SERVES 4 AS A FIRST COURSE/MAIN COURSE

SORREL STUFFING

¾ pound sorrel leaves

3 tablespoons crème fraîche or

   3 tablespoons heavy cream mixed with

     1 to 2 teaspoons fresh lemon juice

1 cup fresh bread crumbs

 Make the stuffing: Stem the sorrel as you would spinach (see page 92). Wash it and dry it well. To shred it, stack and roll several leaves together at a time, hold them in one hand, and slice them across into shreds. Spread the sorrel on the steamer rack, place over simmering water, cover, and steam 1 minute. Stir with a stainless steel fork,

½ teaspoon salt

¼ teaspoon freshly ground pepper

2 boneless shad fillets with skin
(about ¾ pound each)

Salt and freshly ground pepper

SORREL BUTTER SAUCE

1½ tablespoons chopped shallots

⅓ cup white wine

½ teaspoon salt

⅛ teaspoon freshly ground pepper

3 tablespoons crème fraîche or
3 tablespoons heavy cream mixed with
1 to 2 teaspoons fresh lemon juice

14 tablespoons unsalted butter, cut into
pieces

3 tablespoons reserved steamed sorrel
(see instructions)

Aluminum foil

Large stackable steamer, fish poacher
with raised rack (see page 10), or
roasting pan with wire rack plus
another steamer pot for the sorrel

and steam 1 minute longer, or until the sorrel has completely wilted.

Measure 3 tablespoons of the sorrel and set it aside for the sauce. Transfer the remaining sorrel to a bowl. Add the crème fraîche or cream and lemon juice, the bread crumbs, salt, and pepper and stir gently to mix. Taste for seasoning.

Lay 1 shad fillet, skin side down, on a foil tray (see page 163) on the work surface. Sprinkle with salt and pepper. Spread the sorrel stuffing over the fillet. Lay the second fillet, skin side up, on top. Place the fish in its foil tray on the steamer rack, place over simmering water, cover, and steam 15 minutes. Set the lid ajar and steam 5 minutes longer.

Meanwhile, make the sauce: Put the shallots, wine, salt, and pepper in a medium nonaluminum saucepan and reduce over medium-high heat until syrupy. Add the crème fraîche or cream and lemon juice and bring to a boil. Whisking constantly, whisk in the pieces of butter a few at a time, adding more as the butter is emulsified into the sauce, and bring to a boil. Remove from the heat and stir in the reserved sorrel.

When the fish is cooked, grasp opposing corners of the foil tray and lift the fish onto a cutting board. Use a fork to remove the skin from the top fillet. Cut the fillets crosswise into 4 portions. Place the shad on four plates. Pour the sauce into a warm sauceboat and serve it on the side.

KIPPERS WITH LEMON BUTTER

Kippers au Beurre Citronné

Golden-colored kippers are herring that have been boned and split down the back but not separated into two fillets, then brined and cold-smoked. They are available in specialty food stores and even in some supermarkets. Although they have been smoked, kippers must be cooked briefly before eating. They are often sold frozen; defrost them in the refrigerator before steaming. Kippers have a pleasantly strong smoky taste that is delicious with just a squeeze of lemon; Manière's Lemon Butter is lighter on the butter than a beurre blanc and delivers a strong lemon kick. Try it on steamed broccoli, asparagus, cauliflower, or artichokes as well.

(continued)

4 kippers (about ½ pound each)

LEMON BUTTER
7 tablespoons unsalted butter
2 to 3 tablespoons fresh lemon juice
⅛ teaspoon salt
⅛ teaspoon freshly ground pepper

Large stackable steamer, stackable steamer with two steaming compartments, large roasting pan with wire rack, or two steamers

 Put the kippers on the steamer rack, place over simmering water, cover, and steam until warmed through, 6 to 8 minutes.

Meanwhile, make the lemon butter: Melt the butter. (Manière simply put the butter in a bowl and placed it on the flat lid of his steamer.) Whisk in 2 tablespoons lemon juice, the salt, and pepper. Taste for lemon juice, adding more as necessary.

Remove the kippers from the steamer and scrape off the skins with a knife. Place the kippers on four plates and serve with the lemon butter in a warm sauceboat on the side, accompanied by steamed potatoes (see page 89) or sauerkraut. (Good-quality precooked sauerkraut will take 8 to 10 minutes to warm in a steamer.)

FISHERMAN'S SOUP

Bouillinade de Pêcheurs

Manière wrote that this is a soup to be made with the catch of the day after a day of fishing with friends; it's even simple enough to be made on the boat. Manière didn't specify a type or exact quantity of fish; he used whatever he caught that day. The yield and flavor of the soup are determined by the size of the catch and of the steamer pot. Use this recipe as a guide and adjust the quantities of potatoes and seasonings according to the size of the fish.

The soup is almost as good with fish you buy at the store. Make it with whatever whole fish or large chunks of fish are available, using the chart on page 112 to determine the steaming time. (Quick-cooking steaks and fillets won't work: The fish must steam long enough to flavor the broth below.) The first time I tested this recipe I used a whole cod; the soup couldn't have been better, and cod is readily available and inexpensive. You can substitute any white fish such as snapper, sea bass, or porgy, or a small monkfish tail or a chunk of a larger monkfish, or use a combination of fish.

The broth is marvelously simple, flavored with olive oil, thyme, garlic, and strands of reddish saffron. Manière used seawater, but water salted with coarse sea salt can be substituted.

I like to make the soup salty to mimic the saltiness of sea water; start with 1½ teaspoons and add more if you like.

If you don't have a steamer large enough to accommodate a whole fish, try a roasting pan; you may need to cut the fish in half.

SERVES 6 AS A MAIN COURSE

2 quarts seawater or 2 quarts water mixed with 1½ to 2 teaspoons coarse sea salt, to taste

6 small boiling potatoes (3 to 4 ounces each), peeled and cut into ¼-inch slices

6 medium cloves garlic, crushed and peeled

1 medium bay leaf

3 to 4 sprigs thyme or ¼ teaspoon dried thyme

5 to 6 parsley sprigs

Pinch of saffron threads

¼ teaspoon freshly ground pepper

⅔ cup olive oil

1 cod (4 to 5 pounds), gutted but not scaled (see page 162), or your catch of the day

Toasted bread, for serving

Aluminum foil

Large stackable steamer, roasting pan with wire rack, or fish poacher with rack

 Put the seawater or fresh water and salt into the steamer pot. Add the potatoes, garlic, bay leaf, thyme, parsley, saffron, pepper, and olive oil. Bring to a boil, reduce the heat, and simmer, uncovered, for 10 minutes.

Put the fish on a foil tray (see page 163) on the steamer rack and place over the simmering broth. Cover and steam for 30 minutes, then set the lid ajar and steam for 5 minutes longer. (Or use the chart on page 112 to determine the steaming time for your catch.)

To serve, grasp opposing corners of the foil tray and lift the fish onto a cutting board. Skin the fish and remove the meat from the bones (see page 163). Cut the fish into pieces and put them in warm bowls. Arrange the potatoes on top of the fish. Ladle the broth over, discarding the bay leaf, thyme, and parsley. Serve with the toast.

Salt cod aïoli
Aïoli de Morue

Aïoli is both a thick, garlicky, olive-oil mayonnaise and a grand Provençal feast of various fresh Mediterranean fish as well as salt cod, sea snails, vegetables, hard-cooked egg, and sometimes chicken or meat served with fragrant bowls of the garlicky sauce. The fish and vegetables are traditionally poached, but steaming is better: It's easier and less messy, while holding on to the flavors.

Although this dish can be made very simply with just fresh vegetables and fresh cod, Manière's *grande aïoli* calls for salt cod, sea snails (*bulots*), which rarely come to our markets here, and two Mediterranean fish that are difficult to find in America. The first, *grondin,* or gurnard, is a fantastic-looking fish with a bony armored head and winglike fins belonging to the family of scorpion fish. The second, *dorade,* or what we call red bream, does not actually belong to the bream family at all. One type of gurnard, the sea robin, is plentiful in the Atlantic, but fishermen usually throw it back as trash fish. That's too bad, as its flesh is meaty and has an earthy, rather than sweet, flavor that is delicious with aïoli. In America we can use whole fish such as scorpion fish, porgy, snapper, sea bass, or cod; or cod, tilefish, or monkfish steaks or fillets.

Sea snails, or whelks, are traditional in aïoli, and I have included Manière's method for poaching them in a note in case you can find them. Many cooks in Provence use land snails, available in cans in specialty and fish stores.

Salt cod is cod fillet that has been salted and dried. It must be desalted and rehydrated for twenty-four hours before steaming, so you'll need to start the recipe a day ahead if using it. Steamed salt cod has a firm texture and a salty, concentrated, rich flavor that is fabulous with aïoli. Dehydrated salt cod will last for months in the freezer if well wrapped.

Aïoli is traditionally made with a potato or soaked bread rather than the egg yolk that is the base of a classic mayonnaise. Manière, however, called for an egg yolk, but he suggested adding a mashed steamed potato as well. The potato makes the mayonnaise very thick and gives it a gutsy, starchy texture.

In testing this recipe, I learned Manière's method of steaming rather than boiling hard-cooked eggs. I'm quite enamored of this trick: The eggs never crack, and thirteen minutes is always perfect. Steaming hard-cooked eggs is easier than boiling, and absolutely foolproof.

SERVES 6 AS A MAIN COURSE

¾ to 1 pound boned salt cod or fresh cod fillet

 If using salt cod, put it on a wire rack set in a shallow bowl or baking dish so the fish is raised above the bottom of the bowl where the salt will collect. Add cold water to cover the cod and let soak for 24 hours, changing the water five or six times.

AÏOLI

1 small waxy potato (optional), scrubbed

1 small head garlic

2 large egg yolks

1 cup olive oil

Salt and freshly ground pepper

1 pound whelks (see Note) or one
    4-ounce can snails (optional)

4 medium carrots, peeled

2 medium zucchini

3 medium turnips, peeled

1 medium fennel bulb, trimmed

6 small waxy potatoes, scrubbed

3 small sweet potatoes (optional),
    scrubbed

½ medium head cauliflower, trimmed and
    cored

¼ pound haricots verts or green beans,
    ends trimmed

6 large eggs

3 pounds whole fish or 2 pounds steaks or
    1½ pounds fillets (see suggestions in
    headnote)

Stackable steamer with two steaming
    compartments or roasting pan with
    wire rack plus steamer pot with insert
    or collapsible steamer basket

Make the aïoli: If using the potato, put it on the steamer rack over simmering water, cover, and steam 20 to 25 minutes, until tender. Let cool, and then peel.

Meanwhile, peel the garlic. Mash it to a paste in a mortar and pestle or chop it very fine.

Put the garlic in a bowl, add the potato, if using, and mash with a fork (or with the pestle) to a paste. Whisk in the egg yolks and then gradually whisk in the oil, slowly at first and then in a steady stream until emulsified. Season to taste with salt and pepper. Refrigerate.

If using whelks, see Note; if using canned snails, drain and rinse under cold running water until the snails smell fresh.

Cut the carrots in half lengthwise, then cut in half crosswise and quarter each half lengthwise. Cut the zucchini in half lengthwise. Then cut each half in half crosswise, and cut each piece lengthwise into three bâtonnets. Cut the turnips into sixths or eighths, depending on size. Cut the fennel bulb into eighths through the root end.

Steam the vegetables and eggs in one steamer: Layer the potatoes, sweet potatoes, if using, turnips, cauliflower, carrots, fennel, zucchini, and then the beans on the steamer rack. Place over simmering water, cover, and steam 10 minutes. Add the eggs and steam 13 more minutes.

Meanwhile, in a second steamer pot, or in the second compartment of a stackable steamer, steam the fresh fish, including the fresh cod, if using, according to the times given in the chart on page 112. Remove the fish from the steamer; set aside. Drain the salt cod, if using, place on the steamer rack, cover, and steam until cooked through and tender, 7 to 8 minutes. If using canned snails, add them to the steamer for the last 3 minutes.

To serve, peel the eggs. Skin the fish and remove the meat from the bones (see page 163). Arrange the fresh fish, salt cod, whelks or snails, and vegetables on a large serving platter. Scrape the aïoli into a serving bowl and serve alongside.

Note: To cook whelks, combine 2 cups dry white wine, 2 quarts water, 16 peppercorns, 1 bay leaf, and 2 teaspoons sea salt in a large pot. Bring to a boil, then reduce the heat, add the whelks, and simmer, uncovered, for 1 hour to 1 hour and 15 minutes. Remove from the court bouillon with a slotted spoon.

Manière was so passionate about shellfish that he had saltwater tanks installed in his Paris restaurant, Dodin Bouffant, to hold them live. This passion is evident in his recipes for scallops, mussels, cockles, oysters, and lobsters, as well as for langoustines, small members of the lobster family also called Dublin Bay prawns. Each recipe is a little gem; the food is often simple but each dish is very special.

Manière believed that steaming is a particularly good way to cook crustaceans such as lobster, crabs, and langoustines because it intensifies their sweet taste of the sea. He also recommended steaming crustaceans whenever possible on a bed of seaweed to reinforce this flavor.

I would go even further: I haven't found a single type of shellfish that doesn't benefit from steaming. Crustaceans and mollusks such as clams and mussels retain their flavor better and take in less water when they are steamed rather than boiled—so there is less of the boiling juice that usually streams down your arms after cracking a lobster claw. Manière steamed lobster *en papillote,* as in the recipe on page 157; the result is lobster meat that is remarkably sweeter than that steamed the conventional way.

Manière used the steamer to open live mollusks such as mussels, scallops, clams, and oysters easily without using a shucking knife. This technique can't be used for shellfish that are to be served raw, but it's a very useful trick for soups or dishes cooked with oysters or clams served in the shell (see Oysters in the Shell with Spinach and Curry, page 155).

We can substitute different shellfish in these recipes as easily as we substitute fish in the other recipes in this chapter. Manière used spiny lobster, difficult to find in many parts of America, and langoustines, very difficult to buy fresh here, in several recipes (pages 156, 158, and 160). Clawed lobsters (see page 170) can be substituted for the spiny variety, and shrimp can be used instead of langoustines. I give suggestions for substitutions in the recipes where appropriate.

SCALLOPS WITH A MUSCADET BUTTER SAUCE

Coquilles Saint-Jacques à la Vapeur

The gentle acidity of a white butter sauce is a good match for the sweet, creamy flesh of scallops. Manière used a Muscadet wine for the sauce, a white wine that is traditionally paired with shellfish because of its acidity. The seaweed Manière called for is the variety that is commonly used to line oyster shipping crates. Your fish store should be able to get some for you.

SERVES 4 AS A FIRST COURSE/MAIN COURSE

MUSCADET BUTTER SAUCE II

1 medium shallot, chopped (about 1½
    tablespoons)

⅔ cup Muscadet or other dry white wine

¼ teaspoon salt

⅛ teaspoon freshly ground pepper,
    preferably white

3 tablespoons crème fraîche or heavy
    cream

11 tablespoons unsalted butter

A large fistful of seaweed, rinsed, or 6 bay
    leaves

16 sea scallops, with their coral, if
    possible, small muscles removed (see
    page 168)

Salt and freshly ground pepper

Stackable steamer, steamer pot with
    shallow insert, or collapsible steamer
    basket

Make the butter sauce, following the directions for Beurre Blanc on page 120. Set aside in a warm place, and cover to keep warm.

Make a bed of seaweed on the steamer rack or lay the bay leaves over the rack. Sprinkle the scallops with salt and pepper and put them on the seaweed or bay leaves. Place over simmering water, cover, and steam until the scallops are just cooked through, 4 to 6 minutes, depending on their size.

Divide the scallops among individual plates and spoon the sauce over.

Sea scallops in champagne sauce with mussels and shrimp

Coquilles Saint-Jacques en Coquilles

Ever practical, Manière used all parts of the scallop in this recipe: The shells became elegant containers in which to steam and serve the scallops, and he used the "beards" of the scallops to flavor the sauce. It's entirely possible to make this recipe with shucked scallops as well. Use the small white muscle on the sides of the scallops in place of the beard in the sauce. Specialty cookware and some hardware stores sell scallop shells; or the scallops may be steamed in scallop-shaped porcelain molds, on small heatproof plates, or in ramekins.

Manière used seaweed as a base on which to steam the scallops. The gnarled seaweed helps to hold the shells upright. Check with your fish store for seaweed; if it is unavailable, the shells will stand fine on their own. A large stackable steamer or a stackable steamer with two steaming compartments, like Manière's, is ideal for this recipe because the scallop shells are large. A roasting pan with a wire rack will work, but you'll need a second steamer as well to steam the mussels.

SERVES 4 AS A FIRST COURSE

1 cup Champagne or other sparkling dry white wine, or more as necessary

8 cultivated mussels, cleaned (see page 169)

8 sea scallops in the shell or 8 large shucked scallops (about ½ pound)

CHAMPAGNE SAUCE

2 tablespoons unsalted butter

1 teaspoon chopped shallot

Reserved mussel steaming liquid (see instructions)

1 large egg yolk

½ teaspoon potato starch or arrowroot

1½ tablespoons crème fraîche or heavy cream

1 fresh (about ½ ounce) or jarred (¾-ounce jar) black truffle (optional), trimmed and cut into thin match sticks (julienne)

 Put the Champagne or wine in the steamer pot and bring to a boil over high heat. Lay the mussels in a single layer on the steamer rack, place in the steamer pot, cover, and steam until the mussels open, about 4 minutes. Remove the mussels from the steamer. Strain the steaming liquid into a bowl and set aside. Shell the mussels and reserve the meat.

If using scallops in the shells, open them in the steamer, in several batches if necessary, and clean them as directed on page 168; reserve the frilly "beard." (Reserve the four most attractive shells, with their tops.) Cut off and discard the round black sacks on the "beards," wash the "beards," and set them aside. Wash the scallops and pull off and discard the small opaque white muscle on the side of each one.

Wash and dry the reserved scallop shells.

If using shucked scallops, pull off the small translucent muscle on the side of each scallop, and set them aside.

If the scallops are very large, slice them in half crosswise.

Make the sauce: Melt the butter in a medium saucepan over medium-low heat. Add the shallot, cover, and cook until translucent, 2 to 3 minutes. Add the reserved scallop "beards" or muscles

8 small to medium (26/35 count) shrimp
(about ¼ pound), shelled and deveined

⅛ teaspoon salt

⅛ teaspoon freshly ground pepper,
preferably white

A large fistful of seaweed, rinsed
(optional)

Aluminum foil

4 scallop shells or small heatproof plates
or ramekins

Large stackable steamer, stackable
steamer with two steaming
compartments, or roasting pan with
wire rack plus another steamer pot
for the mussels

and cook, stirring constantly, until they stiffen, 2 to 3 minutes. Measure the reserved mussel steaming liquid and, if necessary, add more Champagne or wine to equal ¾ cup. Pour it into the saucepan and simmer very gently over low heat for 15 minutes, or until reduced to about ⅓ cup.

Meanwhile, whisk together the egg yolk, starch or arrowroot, and crème fraîche or cream.

Strain the reduced Champagne into another medium saucepan and bring it to a boil. Remove from the heat and whisk a little of the Champagne into the egg yolk mixture to temper the yolks. Then whisk the tempered mixture into the Champagne. Add the scallops, mussels, the truffle, if using, and the shrimp and gently stir to coat with the sauce. Stir in the salt and pepper.

Divide the seafood and the sauce among the scallop shells, plates, or ramekins. Cover the shells with their tops if you have them, or cover the shells, plates, or ramekins with foil, pressing it around the edges to seal.

Spread the seaweed, if using, over the steamer rack. Set the filled shells on the rack, place over simmering water, cover, and steam 5 minutes.

Serve the seafood in the shells (with their tops) or on the plates or in the ramekins.

WARM SCALLOP SALAD WITH LAMB'S LETTUCE AND TEA-INFUSED VINEGAR

Salade de Mâche et de Saint-Jacques au Vinaigre de Thé

Mâche, or lamb's lettuce, has dark green, tender leaves that I like to think are shaped like little lamb's tongues. The leaves are attached in small bouquets at the root end, which is trimmed if necessary and rinsed but left intact to hold the bouquets together. Lamb's lettuce must be washed very well because it grows in sandy soil. Its taste is delicate but distinctively earthy. There is really no flavor substitute; if it is unavailable, use watercress or a buttery lettuce such as Boston or Bibb.

Manière combined lamb's lettuce with silky steamed scallops and a vinaigrette flavored with tea-infused vinegar. The flavors and textures of the salad are warm, soft, and subtle, and the vinaigrette adds an earthy, woodsy note that is picked up perfectly by the truffle—if you want to splurge.

8 large sea scallops (about ½ pound)
3 cups loosely packed lamb's lettuce
    (mâche), trimmed watercress, or Bibb
    or Boston lettuce, well rinsed and dried

CEYLON TEA VINAIGRETTE
1½ tablespoons Ceylon Tea–Infused
    Vinegar (page 120)
3 tablespoons vegetable oil
1½ tablespoons olive oil
¼ teaspoon salt
⅛ teaspoon freshly ground pepper

1 tablespoon snipped fresh chervil or
    ½ teaspoon chopped fresh tarragon
    plus 1 teaspoon chopped parsley
1 fresh (about ½ ounce) or jarred
    (¾-ounce jar) black truffle (optional),
    trimmed and thinly sliced

Stackable steamer, steamer pot with
    insert, or collapsible steamer basket

Put the scallops in a single layer on the steamer rack, set over simmering water, cover, and steam 2 minutes just to firm the flesh.

Cut the scallops crosswise into thin slices, and put them in a serving bowl. Add the lettuce, then add the vinegar and oils and sprinkle with the salt and pepper. Mix well. Sprinkle with the chervil or the chopped tarragon and parsley. If you have one, add the truffle, and serve.

COCKLE SALAD WITH RADISHES, TOMATO, AND ALMONDS

Salade de Coques aux Radis Roses

Cockles are beautiful green-and-blue-tinged mollusks that look like tiny clams. We get them mainly from New Zealand. They are absolutely delicious, fresh-tasting and both salty and sweet; they taste exactly the way the sea smells. There are different varieties of cockles in different parts of the world: The French *coques* have prickly spines and are gritty; the cockles we get from New Zealand have no spines and are very clean. It is a rare treat to simply steam them and then gobble them up on the spot.

For those with the patience to wait, Manière's cockle salad combines a variety of seemingly disparate elements that set each other off quite magically: The cockles are sweet and salty, the almonds are rich, the radishes are crunchy and slightly peppery, and the tomato is fresh-tasting and a bit acid. Manière marries these ingredients with a light mayonnaise sharply flavored with sherry vinegar.

....

S E R V E S   4   A S   A   C O L D   F I R S T   C O U R S E

....

4 large or 8 small radishes, trimmed,
    washed, and sliced into thin rounds

1 medium tomato

1 to 1¼ pounds cockles, well washed

⅓ cup whole almonds (unblanched or
    blanched)

SHERRY VINEGAR MAYONNAISE

1 large egg yolk

1 teaspoon Dijon mustard

1½ tablespoons sherry vinegar

¼ teaspoon salt

⅛ teaspoon freshly ground pepper

⅔ cup vegetable oil

1½ tablespoons chopped fresh chives or
    scallion greens

1½ tablespoons snipped fresh chervil or
    1 teaspoon chopped fresh tarragon
    plus 2 teaspoons chopped parsley

Large stackable steamer, steamer pot
    with insert, pasta cooker, or
    collapsible steamer basket

 Put the radishes and the tomato on the steamer rack, place over simmering water, cover, and steam 2 minutes. Remove from the steamer and set the radishes aside. Refresh the tomato under cold running water and make a tomato concassé (see page 98).

Put the cockles on the steamer rack. If using unblanched almonds, put them on the rack next to the cockles. Place over simmering water, cover, and steam until the cockles open, about 4 minutes.

Remove the cockles and set aside to cool slightly. Wrap the almonds in a towel and rub them against one another to loosen the skins, then pop them out of their skins.

Make the mayonnaise: Whisk together the egg yolk and mustard in a medium bowl. Whisk in the vinegar, salt, and pepper. Then whisk in the oil, slowly at first and then in a steady stream until emulsified.

Shell the cockles and rinse the meat if it seems sandy.

To assemble the salad, put the cockles, radishes, tomato concassé, almonds, and chives or scallions in a large bowl. Pour the mayonnaise over and toss to coat. Spoon into a serving bowl and garnish with the chervil or the tarragon and parsley.

FISH MOUSSE WITH MUSSELS
Flan de Moules

This is a heavenly dish. The mousse is smooth and tender and airy with egg. Whole mussels give it texture, and their sweet flavor delicately perfumes the mousse. (Make sure the fish fillets or scallops, the cream, and the eggs are cold when you prepare the mousse to prevent it from breaking.) The mousse reheats very successfully; you can make it up to twelve hours before serving and then steam it for ten minutes to heat through. You can also prepare the mousse base four to five hours ahead, fill the mold(s), and then refrigerate until you are ready to steam the mousse.

If pike or whiting is hard to find, sea scallops work very well as a substitute.

SERVES 4 AS A WARM FIRST COURSE

Unsalted butter, softened, for buttering the ramekins and foil

12 small cultivated mussels, cleaned (see page 169)

2 tablespoons unsalted butter

1 shallot, finely chopped (about 1½ tablespoons)

⅓ cup dry white wine

1 teaspoon potato starch or arrowroot

7 ounces skinless whiting or pike fillet or sea scallops, small muscles removed (see page 168)

⅓ cup heavy cream

3 large eggs, lightly beaten

¼ teaspoon salt

⅛ teaspoon freshly ground pepper, preferably white

CHERVIL BUTTER SAUCE

¼ cup crème fraîche or heavy cream

¼ teaspoon salt

⅛ teaspoon freshly ground pepper, preferably white

6 tablespoons unsalted butter

 Coat the ramekins, custard cups, or soufflé dish with softened butter; set aside.

Lay the mussels in a single layer on the steamer rack, place over boiling water, cover, and steam until the mussels open, about 4 minutes. Shell the mussels and put the meat into a bowl.

Melt the butter in a small saucepan over medium-low heat. Add the shallot and cook until translucent, 2 to 3 minutes. Add the wine, turn up the heat to high, and reduce the liquid by half. Remove from the heat and whisk in the potato starch or arrowroot. Set aside to cool.

Put the whiting, pike, or scallops in the bowl of a food processor and purée until very smooth. The fish must be uniformly puréed, with no large pieces, to prevent the mousse from breaking. Add the cream through the feed tube and purée until very smooth. Add the beaten eggs along with the cooled shallot reduction. Process until very smooth and the texture of thick cream. Add the salt and pepper.

Divide the mixture among the individual ramekins or custard cups using a quarter-cup measure, or pour the mixture into the soufflé dish. Press the mussels into the mousse with your finger so that they are entirely concealed.

Cover the container(s) with buttered aluminum foil, buttered side down, and press around the edges to seal. Set the mousse(s) on the steamer rack, place over simmering water, cover, and steam, the large mousse for 20 minutes, small for 12 minutes.

1 tablespoon fresh lemon juice, or more
    to taste
3 tablespoons fresh chervil leaves or
    1 tablespoon chopped fresh tarragon
    plus 1 tablespoon chopped parsley

Aluminum foil
Four 6-ounce ramekins or Pyrex custard
    cups or a 1½-quart soufflé dish
Stackable steamer, steamer pot with
    insert, or roasting pan with wire rack

Then set the lid ajar and steam the large mousse for 10 more minutes, small for 5 more minutes.

Meanwhile, make the butter sauce: Bring the crème fraîche or cream to a boil in a small saucepan over medium-high heat, whisking constantly. Add the salt and pepper. Then, still whisking constantly, whisk in the butter a few pieces at a time, adding more as the butter is emulsified into the sauce, and bring to a boil. Add 1 tablespoon lemon juice and the chervil or tarragon and parsley. Taste for lemon juice and add more as necessary. Remove from the heat and cover to keep warm.

To serve individual mousses, turn the mousses out onto four plates and spoon a shallow pool of sauce around each. Serve the remaining sauce in a warm sauceboat on the side. Or turn the large mousse out onto a serving plate and serve the sauce in a sauceboat on the side.

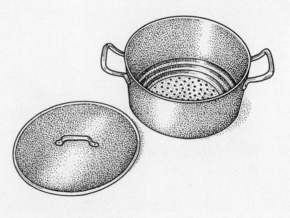

CURRIED MUSSEL SOUP

Crème de Moules "Billy Bye"

Manière said that the name of this creamed mussel soup may also be spelled "bilibi." Some say it was named by Barthe, the chef at Maxim's, for a regular customer named Billy who adored mussels. Another story is that Billy is the name of an American soldier who participated in the liberation of Normandy, and that this soup was served to him at a good-bye dinner given by a hotel keeper at Salanelles after the liberation. Which story is true? Manière didn't have the answer, but he recommended the soup.

Manière puréed some of the mussels to add flavor and body to the soup; the potato starch or arrowroot further binds the soup but is not essential. Use crème fraîche in this recipe if you can; its acidity rounds out the big flavor of the mussels and curry.

(continued)

CROÛTONS (OPTIONAL)

4 slices white bread

2 tablespoons unsalted butter

4 tablespoons unsalted butter

2 tablespoons chopped shallots

1 cup dry white wine

3 cups water

24 small cultivated mussels, cleaned (see
    page 169)

1½ tablespoons curry powder

½ cup crème fraîche or ½ cup heavy
    cream plus 1 to 2 teaspoons fresh
    lemon juice

4 large egg yolks

1 rounded teaspoon potato starch or
    arrowroot

¾ teaspoon salt

⅛ teaspoon freshly ground pepper

1½ tablespoons snipped fresh chervil,
    chopped, or 1 teaspoon chopped fresh
    tarragon plus 2 teaspoons chopped
    parsley

Large stackable steamer, stackable
    steamer with two steaming
    compartments, large steamer pot with
    insert, or collapsible steamer basket

 Make the croûtons, if using, according to the directions on page 82.

Melt the butter in the steamer pot over low heat. Add the shallots, cover, and cook until translucent, 2 to 3 minutes. Add the wine and water and bring to a boil. Lay the mussels in a single layer on the steamer rack (use two steamer compartments, if necessary, or steam them in two batches), set over the boiling liquid, cover, and adjust the heat as necessary. Steam until the mussels open, about 4 minutes. Shell the mussels and reserve the steaming liquid.

Put 12 of the mussels into a soup tureen and set aside.

Put the remaining mussels in the bowl of a food processor, add the curry, and process to purée. Transfer the purée to a large saucepan. Strain the reserved cooking liquid through a fine strainer into the saucepan. Whisk well to mix. Bring the mixture to a boil, reduce the heat, and simmer gently for 5 minutes.

Meanwhile, whisk together the crème fraîche or the cream and 1 teaspoon of the lemon juice, the egg yolks, and potato starch or arrowroot in a small bowl.

Whisk a little of the simmering liquid into the egg yolks to temper them, and then pour the egg mixture back into the saucepan, whisking constantly. Warm gently but do not boil. Season with the salt and pepper. Taste for lemon juice, if using heavy cream.

Pour the soup into the soup tureen. Sprinkle with the chervil or the tarragon and parsley and serve with the croûtons, if using.

OYSTERS IN THE SHELL WITH SPINACH AND CURRY

Huitres à la . . . Coque

This type of dish is traditionally prepared by opening raw oysters with an oyster knife, poaching the oysters, and then returning them to the shells with the sauce. Shucking oysters can be difficult and requires a certain amount of skill. Manière sidestepped the shucking by simply steaming the oysters for a few minutes—long enough to open them but not long enough to cook them completely.

He probably used a large, flat oyster, to give him a broad base for the spinach, but our "cupped-shell" oysters work perfectly well. They are steamed on a bed of seaweed to keep them level. Check with your fish store for seaweed; if it isn't available, use the stems of the spinach for the same purpose. This is a low-fat dish, made with yogurt rather than cream.

SERVES 4 AS A WARM FIRST COURSE

12 oysters

1 medium bunch spinach

¼ teaspoon salt

1 tablespoon unsalted butter, at room temperature (optional)

1 large egg

⅔ cup low-fat yogurt

1 teaspoon curry powder

⅛ teaspoon freshly ground pepper

A fistful of seaweed, rinsed, or stems from the spinach

Stackable steamer with two steaming compartments or roasting pan with wire rack plus another steamer for the spinach

 Open the oysters in a single layer in the steamer, as directed on page 170. Run a knife underneath each oyster to cut the muscle that attaches it to the shell. Remove the oysters and set aside. Wash both the top and bottom shells.

Stem the spinach and wash it well in several changes of water to remove all of the sand; reserve the spinach stems if you do not have seaweed. Put the leaves on the steamer rack, place over boiling water, cover, adjust the heat as necessary, and steam 4 minutes. (If you have a stackable steamer with two steaming compartments, you can cook the spinach at the same time as the oysters.)

Rinse the spinach in the basket under cold running water and press it between your hands to squeeze out as much liquid as possible. Roughly chop the spinach and put it in a bowl. Stir in the salt and the butter, if using.

Divide the spinach mixture among the reserved cupped bottom oyster shells. Place an oyster on top of each spinach bed.

To make the sauce, lightly beat the egg in a small bowl. Whisk in the yogurt, curry, and pepper. Spoon the sauce over the oysters, filling each shell. Cover the oysters with the top shells.

Spread the seaweed or reserved spinach stems over the steamer rack and carefully set the oysters on top. Place over simmering water, cover, and steam 5 minutes.

Serve immediately.

SPINY LOBSTER STEW WITH SWEET RED PEPPER SAUCE

Étuvée de Langouste à la Crème de Poivrons Doux

The ingredients in this recipe reflect the warm southern home of France's spiny lobster (see page 170), but the recipe works equally well with clawed lobster. The cream sauce is flavored with sweet red pepper and Banyuls, a red dessert wine made in the eastern Pyrenees. (A sweet port, such as a tawny, makes a fine substitute.) It is rich, subtly spicy, and, except for peeling the peppers, very easy to put together.

Manière called this dish a stew. Technically, this isn't correct because the lobster is steamed separately, but the sauce has the mysterious, hard-to-define taste of ingredients that have cooked together for a long time and gently married.

SERVES 4 AS A MAIN COURSE

RED PEPPER CREAM SAUCE

2 red bell peppers

2 small carrots, peeled and cut into ¼-inch-thick bâtonnets (see page 104)

1 stalk celery (or 1 small celery root), peeled and cut into ¼-inch-thick bâtonnets (see page 104)

2 tablespoons unsalted butter

1½ tablespoons chopped shallots

¼ teaspoon salt

⅛ teaspoon freshly ground pepper

½ cup plus 3 tablespoons Banyuls or port wine

2 cups crème fraîche or heavy cream

1 teaspoon potato starch or arrowroot

2 large egg yolks

1 tablespoon fresh lemon juice, or more to taste

2 large lobsters (about 2 pounds each)

Large fistful of seaweed, rinsed (optional)

1½ tablespoons chopped fresh chives or scallion greens

Put the bell peppers on the steamer rack, place over simmering water, cover, and steam 10 minutes. Add the carrots and celery to the steamer, cover, and steam 5 to 7 minutes, until tender. Remove the vegetables from the steamer and set aside.

Cut two sheets of heavy-duty aluminum foil about two and a half times the length of the lobsters. Put half of the seaweed in the center of each piece of foil. Fold the tails of the lobsters underneath themselves and put them on the seaweed beds. Bring the sides of the foil up to meet over the lobsters. Fold the edges together and fold over three times in ¼-inch folds. Then fold the open edges over three times in ¼-inch folds to seal.

Put the lobster papillotes on the steamer rack, place over boiling water, cover, adjust the heat as necessary, and steam 25 minutes. Then set the lid ajar and steam 10 more minutes.

Meanwhile, make the sauce: Cut the steamed peppers in half through the stem ends, cut out the stems and ribs, and remove the seeds. Peel the peppers, using a small knife and your fingers. Put the peppers in the bowl of a food processor and purée until very smooth.

Melt the butter in a medium saucepan over medium-low heat. Add the shallots, cover, and cook until translucent, 2 to 3 minutes. Add the salt and pepper and the ½ cup wine and bring to a boil. Add the red pepper purée, bring back to a boil, and add the

Heavy-duty aluminum foil

Large stackable steamer, stackable
  steamer with two steamer
  compartments, or large roasting pan
  with wire rack plus a second steamer
  for the vegetables

crème fraîche or cream. Bring to a boil, reduce the heat, and simmer for 5 minutes. Keep warm.

When the lobsters are cooked, take them out of their foil packages and clean them as directed on page 170 for serving out of the shell. Scrape out the tomalley and coral, if any, with a small spoon and reserve in a small bowl.

To finish the sauce, add the potato starch or arrowroot, egg yolks, lemon juice, and the remaining 3 tablespoons wine to the lobster tomalley and coral. Whisk a little of the warm sauce into the egg yolk mixture to temper it, and then pour it into the saucepan, whisking constantly. Whisk over medium heat until the sauce just comes to a boil. If using heavy cream, taste for lemon juice and add more if the sauce tastes bland. Add the carrots and celery and heat through.

To serve, arrange the lobster pieces on a deep oval serving plate. Pour the sauce over and sprinkle with the chives or scallion greens.

LOBSTER STEAMED ON A BED OF SEAWEED

Homard aux Algues

Lobster steamed as Manière did, *en papillote,* is much sweeter than ordinary steamed lobster. A purist, he preferred to eat lobster dressed simply with a drizzle of excellent olive oil. But for a special occasion, he sauced it with a beurre nantais, a white butter sauce made with Muscadet wine and flavored with tarragon. A simple white butter sauce is well suited to shellfish, and the anise taste of the tarragon in this one highlights the sweet ocean flavor of the lobster.

If you are steaming four small lobsters, you'll need a large stackable steamer with two steaming compartments, a large roasting pan, or two steamers.

(continued)

4 small lobsters (1¼ pounds each) or
2 large lobsters (about 2 pounds each)

A fistful of seaweed for each lobster,
rinsed

NANTAIS BUTTER SAUCE

1 medium shallot, chopped
(about 1½ tablespoons)

3 tablespoons chopped fresh tarragon

⅔ cup Muscadet or other dry white wine

⅛ teaspoon salt

⅛ teaspoon freshly ground pepper,
preferably white

3 tablespoons heavy cream

14 tablespoons unsalted butter

Heavy-duty aluminum foil

Large stackable steamer with two
steaming compartments, large
roasting pan with wire rack, or
two steamers

 For each lobster, cut a sheet of heavy-duty aluminum foil, about two and a half times the length of the lobster. Divide half the seaweed among the pieces of foil, placing it in the center of each piece. Fold the tails of the lobsters underneath themselves and put them on the seaweed beds. Cover the lobsters with the remaining seaweed. Bring the sides of the foil up to meet over the lobsters, fold the edges together, and fold over three times in ¼-inch folds. Then fold the open edges over three times in ¼-inch folds to seal.

Put the lobsters in a single layer on the steamer rack, place over simmering water, cover, and steam, smaller lobsters for 15 minutes, larger ones for 25 minutes. Then set the lid ajar and steam 10 minutes more.

Meanwhile, make the butter sauce, following the directions for Beurre Blanc on page 120. Use half of the tarragon in the reduction and stir the remainder into the sauce at the end.

To serve, take the lobsters out of the foil packages and clean them as directed on page 170 for serving in the shell. Divide the seaweed among four plates and place 2 lobster halves, if using small lobsters, or half of each large lobster on the seaweed. Serve the sauce in a warm sauceboat on the side.

LANGOUSTINES WITH BELGIAN ENDIVE AND LIME

Langoustines aux Endives et Citron Vert

Langoustines are small lobsterlike shellfish found in various parts of the world (see page 171). They're rarely available fresh in America, although you sometimes can buy them frozen. I give Manière's instructions for steaming them fresh in case you do come upon them. Shrimp is a good substitute, as is lobster; I've included instructions for using shrimp in the recipe. To substitute lobster, steam two one-and-a-half- to two-pound lobsters (according to the chart on page 112), then shell them. Cut the tails crosswise into quarter-inch-thick rounds and serve half a tail and one claw per person.

Manière served the langoustines with steamed Belgian endive and a lime-flavored butter sauce. Steaming sweetens the bitterness of the endive, and the sharp lime sets off the flavor of both endive and seafood.

S E R V E S   4   A S   A   W A R M   F I R S T   C O U R S E / M A I N   C O U R S E

1 lime

4¼ pounds (about 24) langoustines for a main course or 3 pounds (about 20) for a first course; or 2 pounds medium to large shrimp (16/20 count) for a main course or about 1 pound for a first course, peeled and deveined

4 medium Belgian endive, trimmed, rinsed, and cut crosswise in ¼-inch-thick strips

LIME BUTTER SAUCE

1½ tablespoons chopped shallots

Reserved lime juice (see instructions)

⅓ cup dry white wine

¼ teaspoon salt

⅛ teaspoon freshly ground pepper, preferably white

3 tablespoons crème fraîche or 3 tablespoons heavy cream mixed with 1 teaspoon fresh lemon juice

14 tablespoons unsalted butter

3 tablespoons unsalted butter

16 snipped sprigs fresh chervil or ½ teaspoon chopped fresh tarragon plus 1 teaspoon chopped parsley

Aluminum foil

Large stackable steamer with two steaming compartments or roasting pan with wire rack if using langoustines; large stackable steamer with one or two steamer compartments, steamer pot with insert, or collapsible steamer basket if using shrimp

 Using a paring knife or a vegetable peeler, peel off the lime zest in strips, avoiding the bitter white pith. Cut the zest into fine julienne strips. Halve the lime and squeeze the juice for the sauce. Set aside.

If using langoustines, put them on the steamer rack, place over simmering water, cover, and steam 4 minutes. Then set the lid ajar and steam 4 more minutes. Remove from the steamer.

Put the endive on the steamer rack. Put the lime zest on a little square of aluminum foil and place it on the rack. Place over simmering water, cover, and steam 6 minutes. (If you are using a stackable steamer with two steaming compartments, steam the endive and lime zest along with the langoustines.)

Make the butter sauce, following the directions for Beurre Blanc on page 120, adding the lime juice to the shallots with the wine. Remove from the heat and cover to keep warm.

If using langoustines, twist off and discard the heads and bodies; peel the tails. Keep them warm in the steamer over low heat.

If using shrimp, put them on the steamer rack in a single layer, place over simmering water, cover, and steam until just cooked through, about 2 minutes.

Melt the butter in a medium frying pan over medium-high heat. Add the endive and sauté 1 to 2 minutes.

To serve, divide the endive among four plates, placing it in the center. Arrange the langoustines or shrimp on top. Spoon the sauce over the shellfish and endive, and sprinkle with the lime zest and herbs.

LANGOUSTINES WITH SPRING VEGETABLES AND SAFFRON

Langoustines aux Petites Légumes

Langoustines are not generally available in America, but shrimp are a good substitute in this recipe. And although Manière used sole, he suggested substituting almost any fish fillet. Lean white-fleshed fish fillets work best; use the chart on page 112 to determine the steaming time.

SERVES 4 AS A MAIN COURSE

8 pearl onions or 8 medium scallions, roots and green parts trimmed

2 medium carrots, peeled and cut into ¼-inch-thick bâtonnets (see page 104)

1 medium turnip, peeled and cut into ¼-inch-thick bâtonnets (see page 104)

¼ pound haricots verts or green beans, ends trimmed and halved lengthwise

1 cup fresh or frozen peas

Salt and freshly ground pepper

¼ cup crème fraîche or heavy cream

16 langoustines (see page 171) or 16 medium to large (16/20 count) shrimp, peeled and deveined

1 whole Dover sole (see page 117), filleted, or 1 pound flounder or other lean white fish fillet, cut into 4 pieces

SAFFRON-VERMOUTH SAUCE

3 tablespoons dry vermouth, such as Noilly Prat

Small pinch of saffron threads

3 tablespoons crème fraîche or 3 tablespoons heavy cream mixed with 1 teaspoon fresh lemon juice

4 tablespoons unsalted butter, cut into pieces

¼ teaspoon salt

⅛ teaspoon freshly ground pepper

Put the onions, if using, on the steamer rack, place over simmering water, cover, and steam 5 minutes. Peel.

Cut a 12- by 28-inch piece of aluminum foil. Put all the vegetables, including the onions or scallions, in the center of the rectangle and sprinkle with ¼ teaspoon salt and ⅛ teaspoon pepper. Spoon or pour the crème fraîche or heavy cream over. Bring the sides of the foil up over the vegetables, fold the edges together, and fold over three times in ¼-inch folds. Then fold the open edges over three times in ¼-inch folds to seal. (Wrap the vegetables somewhat loosely to allow for steam building up inside the foil package; if the vegetables are packed too tightly, they won't cook.) Put the foil package on the steamer rack (make sure it doesn't completely cover the steamer holes), place over simmering water, cover, and steam 30 minutes. Remove the foil package from the steamer.

If using langoustines, put them in a single layer on the two steamer racks, place over simmering water, cover, and steam 4 minutes. Set the lid ajar and steam 4 more minutes. Take the langoustines out of the steamer and set aside.

Sprinkle the fish fillets with salt and pepper and put them on the steamer rack in a single layer. Cover and steam according to the time given in the chart on page 112. If using shrimp, scatter them in a single layer around the fish, if there's room, and steam for the final 2 minutes. (Or steam them separately.) Then turn off the heat, set the lid ajar, and let stand while you make the sauce.

Open one corner of the vegetable papillote and pour the liquid into a small saucepan. Add the vermouth and saffron and bring to

12 snipped sprigs fresh chervil or
    ½ teaspoon chopped fresh tarragon
    plus 1 teaspoon chopped parsley

Aluminum foil
Large stackable steamer with two
    steaming compartments if using
    langoustines; large stackable steamer
    or large steamer pot with shallow
    insert if steaming shrimp

a boil. Add the crème fraîche or heavy cream and lemon juice and bring to a boil. Lower the heat to medium high and reduce the liquid by one third. Then, whisking constantly, whisk in the pieces of butter a few at a time, adding more as the butter is emulsified into the sauce, and bring just to a boil. Add the salt and pepper and taste for seasoning.

To serve, place a fish fillet in the center of each plate. Scatter the vegetables around and spoon the sauce over the fish and vegetables. Place the langoustines, in their shells, or the shrimp around the fish and sprinkle each serving with the chervil or chopped tarragon and parsley.

Basic Techniques for Steaming Fish and Shellfish

Manière wrote for readers who had a wide choice of seafood to buy. Many Americans have more limited resources. But all of his recipes can be adapted to the fillets or steaks and shellfish available, using the chart on page 112. The general information I've included in this section will give you more practical ways to cook whatever seafood is available to you.

✳ STEAMING ON A FLAVORFUL BED
Manière steamed whole fish, fillets, steaks, and shellfish on beds of aromatic herbs, vegetables, or seaweed to add flavor (see page 116). Don't be stingy with the herbs or vegetables; the fish must sit on a substantial bed to pick up the flavor. A lot of strong-flavored herbs added to the steaming water will also flavor the fish, but a bed is more effective.

If fresh herbs are not available, dried herbs will work as well. Manière's recipe for Sole Steamed on a Bed of Ceylon Tea (page 118) gives us a way to steam fish on a bed of tea leaves. Use the same system for dried herbs: Cut a double layer of cheesecloth that is twice as long as the steamer rack. Lay the cheesecloth on the steamer rack so that half of the cheesecloth covers the rack and the other half falls outside the steamer. Sprinkle the dried herb over the cheesecloth and fold the outer half of the cheesecloth over the herb so the herb is enclosed and will not touch the fish. Put the fish on the cheesecloth-covered rack and steam as usual.

✳ STEAMING WHOLE FISH
If you can buy whole fish, do so. Fish steamed on the bone is richer-tasting and moister than fillets or steaks. This is particularly

true for small flatfish, such as a flounder. The delicate flesh dries out easily when cooked in fillets; cooked on the bone, flounder is moist and doesn't fall apart. A steamed whole cod, with no sauce at all, is one of the most delicious things I have ever tasted. If you have a fish poacher or a large covered roasting pan with a wire rack, steaming whole fish is effortless. You'll have the added pleasure of discovering fish cheeks, tasty little nuggets hidden in the head of the fish.

Choosing a Steamer for a Whole Fish When I'm cooking fish for several people, I often steam a whole large fish because it tastes fabulous and is easier to prepare than several fillets or steaks. A whole fish under four to five pounds fits easily into a large roasting pan with a wire rack or into a fish poacher (see page 10). A larger fish requires some ingenuity. The largest fish I've steamed is an eight-and-a-half-pound salmon, three inches thick at its widest, to serve twelve people. With the head and tail cut off, the fish fit perfectly into my twenty-three-inch fish poacher. However, because the fish covered the rack so completely that the steam couldn't rise freely, the thick part of the fish wasn't cooked through even after an hour of steaming. I removed the cooked tail meat to allow the steam to penetrate, and the rest of the fish finished cooking very quickly. Despite the long steaming, the salmon was moist and delicious (but dinner was late).

If you are steaming such a large fish, make sure you have a pan that is big enough to allow a lot of room around the fish to let the steam move freely. Or cut the fish in half and steam it in two steamers.

To test for doneness, Manière advised pushing a skewer into the fish up to the bone. The fish is perfectly cooked when the skewer meets no resistance and feels hot to the touch. You can also use the ten minutes per inch rule for whole fish (see page 109) or test with an instant-read thermometer; the fish is cooked when the thermometer reads 140°F. (The fish continues to cook out of the steamer.) Pick up the fish on its foil tray (see page 163) and put it on a cutting board. Let the fish stand five minutes; it will firm up so that it is easier to serve.

✳ SCALING FISH

Manière recommended against scaling very fresh fish because scaling damages the pristine flesh so that it softens during cooking. So if you have caught the fish yourself, you might want to try steaming it unscaled. If you are buying fish in a fish store or supermarket, the fish most likely has been scaled already. Don't worry about it; chances are only a perfectionist like Manière could tell the difference between the cooked flesh of a scaled and an unscaled fish.

✳ STEAMING ON A FOIL TRAY

It is easier to move a large fish if it is put on a foil tray made from a triple layer of aluminum foil: Cut a piece of foil three times the length of the fish and fold it over to make a triple layer the length of the fish. Make a bed of seaweed or aromatic herbs on the foil for flavor (see page 161). Lay the fish on the foil and sprinkle the cavity with salt and pepper. With the fish on the foil tray, pick it up by grabbing opposing corners of the foil and transfer it to the steamer.

✳ SKINNING AND FILLETING A COOKED ROUNDFISH

A cooked roundfish, such as salmon, snapper, trout, or cod, is skinned by making a shallow cut through the skin with the point of a knife all along the top of the backbone from the head to the tail (A). Make a shallow cut through the skin behind the head, starting at the backbone and angling down to the belly, cutting just behind the fin that lies behind the head (B). Cut the skin above the tail. Pull up the corner of skin formed by the two cuts at the head and use the tip of the knife to push the skin gently down toward the tail (C). The skin will pull neatly away from the flesh, taking any scales with it. Pick up the fish (on the foil tray) and tip it over the sink to drain the juices. Then carefully turn it over onto a serving plate, and skin the other side of the fish.

There is a line of short, fine bones that stand up all along the top of the fish; use the tip of the knife to push them out (D).

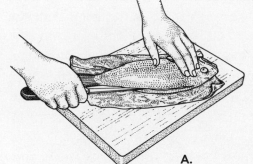

A.

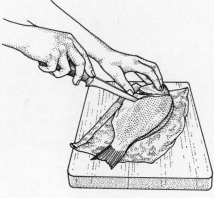

B.

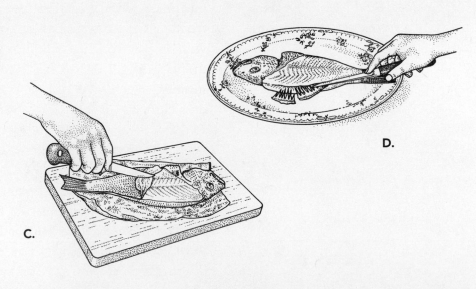

C.

D.

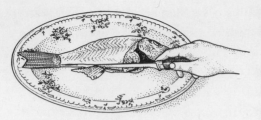

E.

There are more bones along the bottom of the belly that attach other fins; push these bones out as well (E). Now push off the bony gill area on both fillets (F).

The fish can be served at the table on the bone. Or, it can be boned in the kitchen to make table service easier. I use a knife and a short spatula to bone the fish; some cooks use a large fork and spoon or two large spoons. Loosen the meat behind the head and then at the tail with the knife. Cut down the dark center line of the top fillet to the bone, splitting the fillet lengthwise in two. With the spatula, carefully push each half of the top fillet to the side and off the bone (G). (If the meat doesn't slide off easily, run the knife between the flesh and bone to loosen it.)

To remove the backbone and head, gently pull up the backbone at the tail and carefully dislodge the bottom fillet. Continue to lift the bone, dislodging the flesh, until it comes free from the bottom fillet and can be removed in one piece along with the head (H).

Use a spatula, two large spoons, or a large spoon and fork to put both sides of the top fillet (in sections if the fish is large) back on top of the bottom fillet. The fish is boned and ready to serve.

F.

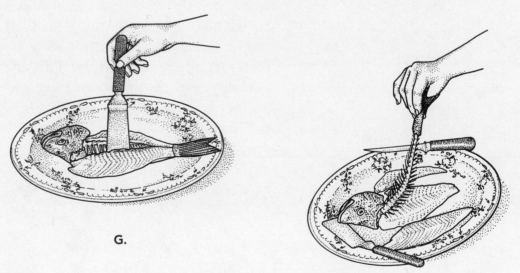

G.

H.

✳ **SKINNING AND FILLETING A COOKED FLATFISH**

A flatfish such as flounder is skinned and filleted slightly differently from a roundfish. I always ask my fish store to cut the head off flounder so that the fish fits easily into my steamer. The cooked fish is easier to skin and fillet without the head. Every cook has his or her own way of filleting a cooked fish; I use a knife and short spatula, as for roundfish (above).

To skin a flatfish after steaming, make a shallow cut through the skin above the tail. Then pull up a corner of the skin at the head end and push the skin gently down toward the tail with the knife, just as for a roundfish. Pick up the fish (on the foil tray) and carefully turn it over onto a serving plate. Skin the other side of the fish in the same way.

Use the tip of the knife to push out the short, fine bones that run along the outside edges of the fish (see illustration above). Cut down the center line of the top fillet to the bone, splitting the fillet in two lengthwise. Then push the fillets off the bone with the spatula, and pull the bone off the bottom fillet just as you would for a roundfish.

✷ STEAMING FILLETS, STEAKS, AND LARGE CHUNKS OF FISH

For fillets, steaks, and large chunks of fish, use a stackable steamer, a collapsible steamer basket, or a steamer with a shallow insert—it's very difficult to remove delicate fish from a deep steamer pot, such as a pasta cooker. Put the fish in a single layer on the steamer tray and steam according to the timings in the chart on page 112. (Make a foil tray as described on page 163 for large chunks of fish and delicate fillets; foil keeps the fish from sticking to the steaming tray.)

Steaming large fillets for four people in a single layer requires a large steamer, but fillets can be steamed in a small steamer by folding the fillets in half, overlapping the fillets, or stacking two fillets on top of another. All of these methods also help keep the fillets moist.

Traditionally, the tail ends of skinned sole and flounder fillets are folded under the fillet before cooking. This keeps the thin end from overcooking, and the delicate fillet falls apart less readily when moved. (Do this with small scrod fillets as well.) Small, unskinned fillets of delicate roundfish such as snapper, bass, or porgy will not fold easily; arrange them in the steamer so that the fat end of one fillet overlaps the tail end of the fillet next to it. The

steaming time will be the same as for fillets in a single layer.

Thin (half to three quarters of an inch thick) six- to eight-ounce fillets of fish such as snapper, sea bass, bluefish, mackerel, and cod, and the tail-end fillets of salmon, can be steamed by doubling them: Lay one fillet skin side down on the work surface. Lay a lettuce or cabbage leaf over the fillet to keep the two fillets from sticking together. Set the second fillet, skin side up, on top of the leaf (see illustration at left). Steam the fillets according to the timings in the chart on page 112, allowing about one minute less than twice the steaming time for a single fillet.

* STEAMING FISH *EN PAPILLOTE*

To steam fish *en papillote* means to enclose the fish in a package (traditionally made with parchment paper; Manière used aluminum foil), seal it well, and steam it in the package. The fish gives off juices as it cooks and steams in them. A tablespoon of liquid added to the package at the start will flavor the fish and make a sauce at the same time. Wine and cream are the usual choice in France, but flavored oils, citrus juices, or Asian condiments such as soy sauce, rice wine vinegar, and sesame oil are delicious, with the addition of cilantro, lemon grass, ginger, and scallions. Traditional Western flavorings such as chopped fresh herbs, finely chopped shallots, garlic, or leeks, and mushrooms or tomatoes complement wine or cream. Manière usually added a garnish of steamed vegetables to his papillotes along with the liquid so that each package would be practically a meal in itself (see page 131).

Steaming *en papillote* is a little more work at the outset, but it is my first choice for steaming fish fillets and steaks. Whatever flavor is lost in cooking the fish off the bone is made up for by the flavorings in the foil packages. And steaming *en papillote* keeps delicate fish moist. The possibilities for combinations of fish, vegetables, and sauce are endless, and the procedure is easy, quick, and almost foolproof. It is a terrific way to use up leftover vegetables. The result is fancy enough for entertaining but easy enough for a weeknight dinner.

Cut pieces of aluminum foil large enough to enclose each piece of fish and set them out on a work surface. If using a vegetable, cut it into bite-sized pieces, or smaller, and steam if necessary until cooked through. For summer squash or zucchini, cabbage, leek, celery, fennel, endive, potatoes, carrots, or other root vegetables, see the charts throughout the vegetable chapter for steaming times. Mushrooms, tomatoes, quick cooking greens such as watercress or spinach, and finely julienned vegetables such as carrots, leeks, and snow peas don't need to be steamed first. Place the vegetables in the center of the pieces of foil. Set the fillets or steaks on top of the vegetables and sprinkle with salt and pepper and chopped herbs or aromatics. Add about a tablespoon of liquid to each papillote. Bring the sides of the foil up to meet over the fish (A), fold the edges together, and fold over three times in quarter-inch folds. Then fold the open edges over three times in quarter-inch folds to seal (B).

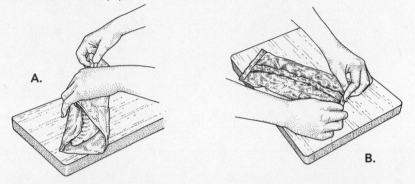

To steam the papillotes check the chart on page 112 for the steaming times; a fillet steamed *en papillote,* with a tablespoon of liquid, takes about one minute longer than the basic time noted in the chart. A fillet steamed on a substantial bed of vegetables takes twice the basic time. (Fillets and steaks with very short steaming times, such as flounder and tuna, generally take one to two minutes longer than twice that time.)

A fish steak steamed *en papillote* with a tablespoon of liquid takes twice the basic time noted in the chart. A steak steamed on a bed of vegetables takes about one to two minutes less than three times the basic time.

Monkfish has its own rules: A one-inch-thick fillet steamed *en papillote* on a bed of vegetables takes twenty minutes covered plus five minutes with the lid ajar; a thinner fillet takes a few minutes less.

Add one to two minutes to the steaming times for all fish if your vegetables have been refrigerated.

The papillotes may be opened in the kitchen with scissors. Manière served them to his guests still sealed. It's fun to open the papillotes at the table (give everyone scissors or a knife to do so) so that each guest is enveloped in the fragrant steam from the just-opened package.

✳ USING STEAMING LIQUID FOR SOUP

After steaming fillets, steaks, or whole fish, you can use the steaming liquid, flavored with juices from the fish, as a base for fish soup. (See page 142 for a soup made this way.) Or, if you steam fish often, you may want to reduce the steaming liquid to use as a base for sauces. The steaming liquid from any fish can be used, though whole fish give more flavor to the broth than fillets or steaks. Flavor the broth with herbs, spices, and vegetables, and thicken with a little butter or olive oil, or cornstarch or arrowroot dissolved in a little cold water or broth.

✳ STEAMING SHELLFISH

Sea Scallops In France, scallops are sold alive in the shell, as mussels, clams, and oysters are here. Typically the scallops are large and thick. Occasionally fish markets here sell scallops in the shell, but they are usually shucked and cleaned at sea to slow spoilage. The French love to eat the coral—the crescent-shaped brown, pink, or orange roe. In America, some scallops are sold with the coral, but usually it is removed when the scallop is shucked. If you see scallops with the coral, try them.

In France, live scallops are traditionally shucked with a knife, like oysters. Manière devised an easy alternative to shucking: Wash the shells and scrub them with a brush to get rid of all the grit. Put the scallops in a single layer on the steamer rack, curved shells down, and steam for two to three minutes, just until they open. Carefully run a knife between the meat and the top shell to cut the scallop from the shell. Pull up and twist off the top shell. Then scrape underneath the scallop to detach it from the bottom shell. Clean the scallop by holding it in one hand and pulling off everything but the white meaty scallops and the coral. Wash the scallops with their corals, and pull off and throw away the small opaque white muscle on the side of each one. (Even shucked scallops come with this fibrous muscle attached.)

The frilly black- or beige-rimmed membrane attached to the scallop is called the "beard" (*barbe*) in France. Manière added them to sauces for flavor. (See Sea Scallops in Champagne Sauce with Mussels and Shrimp, page 148.) The beards must be cleaned of the round black sacks attached to them; cut them off with a knife. If you buy shucked scallops, you can use the small white muscle on the side of the scallop in sauces in place of the beards.

If you are lucky enough to get live scallops in the shell, don't throw the shells out. Scrape them clean and then boil them in a large pot with water to cover until they no longer have any smell. Use the cleaned shells as containers for cooked seafood (see the Scallops in Champagne Sauce recipe).

Some scallops are treated with phosphate chemical dips that act as a preservative, whiten the flesh of the scallop, and cause it to absorb water. Dips also give the scallop an unpleasant, often soapy taste, and, because they deodorize the scallop, they make it hard for the consumer to determine freshness. The law requires that chemically treated scallops be marked as such on the containers in which they are sold (the containers must also be marked "25 percent water added"). Theoretically this law informs and protects the consumer, but in fact, since the consumer isn't likely ever to see the original container, he or she must depend on the integrity of the fish seller, who is not legally required to say anything. You may be able to recognize treated scallops because they look whiter and wetter than "dry" scallops, which are a pearly, off-white color and slightly sticky to the touch, but it is difficult to tell without a trained eye.

Mussels Mussels vary somewhat in flavor and appearance depending on variety, place of origin, and whether they are wild or cultivated. I'm very fond of mussels from Prince Edward Island, cultivated on ropes suspended from rafts, because they are free of silt and barnacles and are smaller and have a milder flavor than wild mussels. Our small cultivated mussels most closely resemble the sweet little cultivated mussels called *moules de bouchot* that Manière used. The beautiful green-shelled mussels imported from New Zealand have very large shells. The meat can be larger than that of smaller shelled varieties, but this is not always the case.

Make sure mussels are alive before steaming them. Any open shells are suspect. Gently press the open halves of the shells together: If the mussel is alive, it will close tightly. If it doesn't close, throw the mussel away. Throw away any mussels with broken shells and any that are very heavy; they are carrying an impossible amount of silt that will ruin your broth. When in doubt, don't cook it; mussels are cheap.

It's best not to soak mussels; their delicate flavor washes away in water. Wash them under cold running water. For wild mussels, scrub the shells with a stiff plastic brush or scouring pad. Don't use a metal pad; bits of metal may get inside the shells. Scrape off any barnacles with a small knife that you don't care too much about. Just before steaming, pull off the hairy beards, if any, that stick out of the mussel shells. Do this at the last minute; the mussels weaken quickly after the beards are removed. Cultivated mussels usually just need to be rinsed because the shells are very clean. The beards have often been clipped to remove them without damaging the animal.

Oysters Manière probably used the famous flat-shelled Belon oyster from Brittany for his steamed oyster recipes. In the United States, you are more likely to find a cup-shelled variety, from our

Atlantic or Pacific coastal waters, although a small number of flat, or so-called Belon, oysters are also farmed on both coasts. Cup-shelled oysters work perfectly well in Manière's recipes. Like mussels, oysters must be alive when you buy them, with tightly closed shells.

For oysters to be served cooked, Manière opened the shells just as he opened live scallops: Put the oysters in a single layer on the steamer rack and steam them according to the time given in the chart on page 112 to open.

Remove the oysters from the steamer. Carefully run the blade of a small knife along the underside of the flat top shell to cut the muscle that attaches the oyster to the shell. Pull off the top shell. Then run the knife underneath the oyster to free it from the bottom shell. This is not recommended as a method for opening oysters to be eaten raw; the steaming cooks the meat somewhat.

Lobsters Manière used two kinds of lobsters in his recipes: the clawed European *homard* that very closely resembles our clawed lobster found in the Atlantic Ocean off North America, and the spiny lobster, or *langouste,* found in warmer waters around the world, which looks like a large-tailed lobster without claws. The two lobsters can be substituted for each other in Manière's recipes.

The greenish tomalley, or liver, of the lobster and the coral, or roe, bright pink or red in a cooked lobster, are often used to flavor and thicken sauces, as in Manière's Red Pepper Cream Sauce on page 156. The roe is found only on female lobsters. It's very easy to tell the difference between a male and a female: Turn the lobster on its back and look for the tiny pair of claws at the top of the underside of the tail. On a female, these claws are slender and feathery; on a male, they are thicker, stiff, and bony.

Manière steamed lobster *en papillote,* which gives an exceptionally sweet-meated lobster. When positioning the live lobster on the foil, fold the tail underneath itself and set the lobster on the foil; with the tail folded this way, the lobster stays very still.

To serve a steamed lobster in its shell, first use a large knife to cut it in half down the center. Remove the contents of the head, leaving the greenish tomalley and the pink roe, which are good to eat, and crack the claws in two or three places with a large knife or a nutcracker.

To shell a lobster for serving, twist off the head. Pull out the tomalley and coral, to use in a sauce if you like. Cut down through the underside of the tail shell with kitchen scissors; pull apart the two sides of the tail shell and pull the tail meat out in one piece. Crack the claws with the back of the knife or a nutcracker and pull the meat out. Cut along the length of the "arms" with kitchen scissors and pull out the meat. Cut the tail into quarter-inch to half-inch rounds; leave the claws whole.

Langoustines Manière also steamed a small member of the lobster family variously called a langoustine, Dublin Bay prawn, Norway lobster, or the Italian *scampo,* depending on where the lobster is found. Fresh langoustines are tough to find in America outside of the occasional restaurant kitchen, but you may find them frozen; some are imported from New Zealand. Langoustines weigh two to three ounces. The edible part of the animal, the tail, is about four inches long. You can substitute medium to large (16/20 count) shrimp (see below) in most recipes.

Shrimp Manière rarely steamed shrimp in his book, but they're easy to get in America and steaming is an excellent way to cook them. Shrimp is also a good substitute for langoustine.

Most shrimp sold in America are farm-raised and almost always have been frozen. Shrimp are often sold thawed in retail stores and marketed as "fresh-frozen," which simply means they were fresh once. While the quality varies enormously, frozen shrimp can be very good, often better than fresh shrimp that have been poorly handled. The quality further depends on where the shrimp come from. Buy shrimp in the shell or shelled; the shell doesn't seem to add flavor to the shrimp in steaming.

Shrimp are usually sold as small, medium, large, or jumbo, but as the sizes aren't regulated, they're meaningless. The only reliable way to talk about shrimp size is to use the language of the industry, where shrimp are graded by number to the pound: A commonly available, truly "medium" shrimp is a 16/20, meaning there are sixteen to twenty shrimp of these size per pound. Most retail stores don't describe shrimp this way; ask a counterperson the number per pound.

Shrimp must be steamed in a single layer or they cook unevenly. You can pack a lot of shrimp into one layer by snuggling them right up next to one another; even touching, they'll cook perfectly.

Sauces for Steamed Seafood

The recipes in this chapter give many suggested combinations of seafood and sauces. Beyond this, Manière wrote that he liked to eat whole steamed fish drizzled simply with very good quality olive oil or fresh lemon juice, or sauced with a plain beurre blanc (see page 120) or one flavored with herbs (see page 189), Fresh

Tomato–Basil Sauce (page 121), or with a ragout of vegetables, steamed alongside the fish and moistened with a beurre blanc.

Many of the sauces in this chapter are delicious on almost any type of fish, whether steamed as whole fish, fillets, or steaks, and on shellfish. The Caper-Anchovy Vinaigrette, for example, that moistens the cod on page 117 is a salty, gleaming, warm vinaigrette that can make almost any fish sparkle, including fattier fish than cod. Serve it with scallops and lobster as well. (It's also delicious with steamed beef.) Below is a list of sauces for easy reference.

✳ VINAIGRETTE SAUCES
Caper-Anchovy Vinaigrette (page 117)
Ceylon Tea Vinaigrette (page 150)
Lemon-Mustard Vinaigrette (page 124)

✳ MAYONNAISES
Aïoli (page 145)
Sherry Vinegar Mayonnaise (page 151)
Warm Mayonnaise (page 138)

✳ TOMATO SAUCES
Fresh Tomato-Basil Sauce (page 121)
Saffron-Tomato Sauce (page 127)
Spicy Tomato and Garlic Sauce (page 135)
Tomato and Green Pepper Sauce (page 126)

✳ BUTTER SAUCES
Beurre Blanc (pages 120, 127, and 189)
Ceylon Tea Butter Sauce (page 119)
Chervil Butter Sauce (page 152)
Garlic-Lemon Sauce (page 134)
Lemon Butter (page 142)
Lime Butter Sauce (page 159)
Muscadet Butter Sauce (pages 139 and 147)
Nantais Butter Sauce (page 158)
Saffron-Vermouth Sauce (page 160)
Sorrel Butter Sauce (page 141)
Tarragon Butter Sauce (page 254)

✳ CREAM SAUCES
Red Pepper Cream Sauce (page 156)
Vermouth Cream Sauce (page 123)

POULTRY

anière opened his poultry chapter with the story of a poached truffled chicken, the *raison d'être* for his book. As Manière tells the story, he was visiting a friend, the chef Lucien Vanel, at Vanel's mother's inn at Lacapelle-Marival, near Cahors. One morning, Manière helped Vanel's mother, Mémée, an excellent cook in her own right, prepare a truffled *poularde en vessie*, from an ancient recipe in which the fattened chicken is stuffed with truffles, tied up in a pig's bladder, and carefully poached for two and a half hours. As Manière attended the long, slow, closely watched poaching, he remembered a recipe for Steamed Truffled Bresse *Poularde* that he had recently come across in *La Table au Pays de Brillat-Savarin*, written in 1892 by the lawyer and gastronome Lucien Tendret. Here is a translation of that recipe:

STEAMED TRUFFLED BRESSE *POULARDE*

•

Take a good-quality Bresse poularde *with pure white fat, a fine, silky skin, and black or grey feet. Clean the bird, pull out and render the excess fat. Salt the cavity.*

Take one or two pounds of round, delicate-skinned black truffles. Peel them and dice them about the size of a hazelnut. Combine the truffles with the chopped liver of the poularde *and sauté this mixture in the melted fat. Add one half a Bordeaux glass full of Cognac, and salt and pepper. Spoon this mixture into the cavity of the* poularde *and wrap the* poularde *in a clean cloth. Let the* poularde *stand to give the truffles time to suffuse the skin of the bird with their aroma.*

Put a three-legged steel trivet, measuring ten centimeters [about four inches] high in the bottom of an earthen pot, or "pot-au-feu." Pour in six glasses of beef broth and two glasses of dry white wine. Rub the skin of the poularde *with lemon and put it on the trivet; the* poularde *must not touch the liquid. Salt the bird. Cover the "pot-au-feu" and seal the lid with a length of cloth coated with bread dough. Steam the* poularde *one hour and thirty minutes.*

When the poularde *is cooked, make a roux. Moisten it with a few soup spoons of cream and finish it with some of the steaming liquid. Add salt and pepper and bind the sauce with two egg yolks mixed with a little cream or milk and serve with the* poularde.

Fat-fleshed birds have better flavor steamed than poached in consommé.

It was hard for Manière to believe that steaming could improve upon Mémée's delicious poached chicken. Nonetheless, the last line of Tendret's recipe haunted him, and he tried the recipe when he returned to Paris. He followed the instructions to the letter except that he used a *couscousière* (see page 247) in place of Tendret's pot-au-feu and trivet to steam the bird. The results amazed him: The flavor of the truffles was even more pronounced and the flesh moister in the steamed chicken than in Mémée's. The steamed chicken took an hour less to cook than Mémée's and required no attention except to check the level of the steaming liquid. Really interested now, Manière tried the recipe again and determined this time that the bouillon used to steam the bird added no flavor. Each experiment with steaming gave him new information and, eventually, the material for this book.

In America, we're partial to crisp-skinned birds. (I've often suspected that our love of chicken is merely an excuse to eat the skin; we like chicken roasted, grilled, and broiled, but almost never boiled.) The French are different. They love a braised or poached chicken and may even remove the skin; Mémée's and Tendret's meltingly tender, intoxicatingly truffled chickens, sauced to perfection, are about everything *but* the skin. Nowadays, many Americans don't want to eat skin at all because it contains most of the fat. Steaming makes this easy; while the skin sticks to the flesh of a raw bird, it pulls off effortlessly after steaming. And if you're saucing the bird, the sauce clings better if the skin has been removed.

A steamed chicken will never be mistaken for roasted; each has its own advantages. Steamed chicken is a different mood. The silky-skinned flesh is soft and inviting. The flavors are seductively simple, pure and blessedly uncomplicated. The moist smell is gentle, comforting, and benevolent. If I could afford to fill the cavity of my steaming chicken with truffles I would be in heaven, but I'm generally very satisfied with thyme and bay leaf.

Not every fowl is a chicken. Manière's recipes embrace as well luscious Cornish game hens, rich-meated duck, goose, and squab, fat-breasted capon, and tender guinea hen (a farm-raised bird that tastes like a chicken but with more flavor). You'll find rabbit in this chapter as well because lean white rabbit meat is similar to poultry in its mild taste and delicate texture and may be substituted for chicken in some of the recipes. Manière's recipes for less common poultry can also be made with chicken.

A standard three-and-one-half-pound chicken is firm, moist, and flavorful; since steaming, I've come to enjoy breast meat because it isn't dry. Steaming works for all sizes and cuts of chicken, sold whole and in pieces, under different names depending on age: Broilers and fryers are nine to twelve weeks old, roasters are three to five months. Tiny Cornish game hens, a hybrid breed of chicken butchered at four to six weeks, are even more delicate and tender than ordinary chickens because of their age. Capon, a large neutered male chicken, tastes like a chicken but has an exceptionally full, fat, fine-textured breast.

Steaming has some special advantages for red-meated duck, goose, and squab. It is a superb way to cook duck and goose, which have a thick layer of fat under the skin. Steaming renders this fat very efficiently without drying or toughening the meat; the skin, broiled or browned after steaming in a hot oven, covers the juicy flesh with a thin, crisp shell. Although duck legs cut off the carcass and steamed separately are sometimes tough, steamed still attached to the leg half of the carcass, as described on page 217, they melt in the mouth like confit. Rewarming homemade or store-bought duck confit in the steamer rids it of much of the excess fat while keeping it moist. Steaming keeps four- to five-week-old squabs from tasting gamy, even cooked well done.

Steaming, easier and faster than poaching, keeps all of these birds moist and intensifies their essential flavors. Remember when steaming chicken that while a three-and-a-half- to four-pound bird is large enough to serve four people if your guests like both white and dark meat, you'll need two chickens if everyone likes only white meat. Leftovers are a bonus. Cold steamed poultry is terrific; the flesh relaxes as it rests so that it is firm, moist, and particularly tender.

Using the Chart of Basic Steaming Times for Poultry

The chart on page 182 gives steaming times for many types of poultry and for rabbit. Manière's original listing included whole birds only; with the exception of duck, poultry is most tender and moist when steamed whole. I have added timings for chicken parts because they taste good, steam quickly, and brown better than whole chickens. (When steaming a quartered chicken, steam the breast quarters a few minutes less than the legs, as indicated in the chart, so that the breast meat doesn't overcook.)

The times in the chart let us substitute chicken parts for whole chicken as well as different types of poultry within Manière's recipes. I give suggestions for substitutions in the recipes where appropriate. Use the chart to put together a meal of steamed chicken with a sauce, as simple or elegant as you like, made from the steaming liquid (see page 208), reduced and served as a simple broth, or thickened with reduced cream or with puréed steamed vegetables (see page 101). (A steamed whole chicken flavors the broth better than parts because it cooks longer.) Chicken "au Blanc," on page 186, is a recipe for chicken and vegetables served with a rich cream sauce made with the steaming liquid.

The times in the steaming chart are broken into three columns: steaming time with the lid closed, steaming time with the lid ajar, and an optional browning time in the oven or broiler. Steaming with the lid partially ajar lowers the temperature of the steam chamber, allowing the bird to finish steaming at a gentler temperature, keeping the flesh moist. Manière used this two-step method for several but not all of the birds.

Browning in the Oven or Broiler

Although Manière was convinced that steaming was a healthier way than roasting to cook poultry and meats, he was aware that his readers might object to losing the golden brown, crisp skin of a roasted bird. So he devised a system to combine the advantages of steaming with those of roasting: After steaming the poultry, brush the skin with a light coating of oil, chicken fat, or butter. Set it in a roasting pan or baking dish and brown it in a 500°F oven for the amount of time shown in the chart. (For whole poultry, eliminate the steaming time with the lid ajar and shorten the basic steaming time by the number of minutes needed for browning.) Oddly enough, Manière's recipes rarely call for browning the skin. (The recipe for Stuffed Guinea Hen on a Bed of Parslied Cabbage, page 194, is the exception.)

Manière's browning times were probably calculated using a professional oven—my oven took significantly longer to brown poultry than his chart allowed. Therefore, except for whole goose, I can't recommend browning in home ovens. The added time in the hot oven undermines the benefits of steaming, particularly for chickens and turkey—the flesh dries out. The skin colors but doesn't get crisp enough to make it worth subjecting the bird, juicy and moist from the steamer, to the rigors of dry heat. Goose works in the oven because the steamed skin is fatty enough to brown well, even in the oven. It does get crisp, and the meat doesn't dry out. (To brown a whole goose in the oven, follow the steaming times exactly as in the chart, and add the browning time indicated in the last column.)

✳ USING THE BROILER

Since my broiler browns poultry reasonably quickly and evenly, I use it rather than the oven for browning. Chicken parts and butterflied poultry are good candidates for the broiler, although the flesh of chicken dries out a bit more than I like. Duck and goose parts brown exceptionally well, and the flesh stays moist. If you do brown chicken parts or butterflied chicken under the broiler, cut out the steaming time with the lid ajar and shorten the basic steaming time by the number of minutes given in the column for browning. If browning goose and duck parts, follow the steaming times in the chart, and simply add the browning time. Be careful when using the broiler; the heat is powerful and overcooks food quickly.

Unfortunately, you can't brown a whole bird in most broilers. If you must have a browned skin on the steamed bird, use your oven with the temperature set to broil for maximum heat and follow the timings in the chart. With the exceptions of duck and goose, as noted above, I don't often brown steamed poultry in the oven or under the broiler. Steaming offers a different, softer way to eat chicken. When I want crisp skin, I roast; when I want something luscious, tender, and yielding, I steam.

Testing for Doneness

The standard way to test doneness in a well-done bird is to pierce the thigh with a skewer: If the juices run clear, the poultry is done; if the juices are pink, it needs more time. An instant-read thermometer inserted into the thigh of the bird makes timing poultry easy, particularly if you are concerned about salmonella. Use the thermometer when steaming meat as well.

Salmonella in poultry and eggs was not a concern in France when Manière wrote his book, but it must be considered in American poultry recipes, particularly those that use a stuffing. The salmonella bacteria in poultry is killed if held at 160°F for at least fifteen seconds. Therefore, the timings in the chart for chicken, Cornish game hens, turkey, capon, and guinea hens are calculated to cook the birds to an internal temperature of at least 160°F. At this temperature the legs are cooked through and tender and the breast is still moist. Since squab, quail, and duck breasts are typically cooked to medium-rare in France, the timings on the chart are for medium-rare; if you are concerned about salmonella, cook them to 160°F. The internal temperature of properly steamed goose and duck legs is higher than 160°F, because they must steam for such a long time.

Stuffed poultry should reach a higher internal temperature than unstuffed, because the stuffing, a nasty medium for the growth of salmonella, must be cooked to 165°F to be safe. For the stuffing to get that hot, the bird must reach an internal temperature of at least 180°F, which means it is overcooked. Therefore, I have adapted those recipes that use a bread or rice stuffing to steam the stuffing separately, wrapped in aluminum foil, so that the bird stays moist but meat and stuffing are safe to eat.

As an added protection against salmonella bacteria, all of the times in the chart are calculated for poultry that comes directly from the refrigerator; room-temperature poultry will steam much more quickly.

Using the Steamer to Keep Poultry Warm

It's often necessary to let poultry stand after cooking, while you finish a sauce or reduce the steaming liquid. Most standard recipes tell you to cover the poultry with foil and let stand in a warm place. The steamer works better: After steaming the poultry, turn the heat to very low and set the lid ajar; the poultry will stay warm without continuing to cook.

If a recipe calls for letting the poultry stand while you reduce the steaming liquid, you can still use the steamer to keep it warm. If you have a stackable steamer, it's easy; remove the covered steaming compartment to a plate. The food will stay warm while you reduce the steaming liquid. If you are using another kind of steamer, you may need to add a step: Bring another pot of water to a boil while the poultry is steaming. Then, when the poultry is cooked, pour the steaming liquid into a large pot and reduce. Pour the boiling water into the steamer pot and let the poultry sit in the steamer over very low heat, with the lid ajar, until you are ready for it.

Additional Techniques for Steaming Poultry

At the end of this chapter, I give several basic techniques for steaming poultry, drawn from Manière's recipes and my own experience. There are instructions for trussing, steaming whole birds and parts, carving, boning, and making stocks, as well as special instructions for steaming turkey, duck, and rabbit. Don't be put off by this "technical" information; much of it is refinement. Steaming doesn't have to be a lot of work. Poultry doesn't have to be trussed, wishbones needn't be removed, and a butcher can do any boning needed.

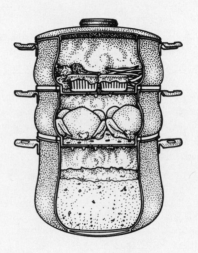

Below is a brief listing of things you need to know to steam poultry. Descriptions of other relevant techniques, such as trussing and carving, can be found on pages 205–221. Also see the general information on steaming and equipment on pages 3–15.

TIMING

Manière included this chart primarily for quick reference. For more complete information about timings and thermometer temperatures, check the specific recipes.

Times are for poultry taken directly from the refrigerator, not at room temperature.

For health reasons, chicken, Cornish game hen, capon, turkey, and guinea hen are steamed to an internal temperature of at least 160°F (see page 179). Duck breast, squab, and quail are steamed to medium-rare. An instant-read thermometer makes timing poultry easy; insert the thermometer into the thigh meat.

TIMING COLUMNS

The timings in the chart are divided into three columns: steaming with the lid closed, steaming with the lid ajar, and an optional browning time in the oven or broiler (see page 178).
Optional Browning: The steaming times alone are adequate to cook the birds. When browning (except for duck parts and whole goose), cut out any steaming time with the lid ajar and shorten the steaming time with the lid closed by the time needed to brown. For duck parts and goose, steam exactly as long as indicated in the chart, adding the browning time to the steaming time.

STEAMING LIQUID

For long-cooking poultry, the steaming liquid may need to be replenished during steaming. The rate of evaporation depends on the size and shape of the steamer and the type of poultry. (Chicken gives off so much juice that it is rarely necessary to add water to the steamer.) Have a kettle of water on hand and check the level of the steaming liquid frequently, adding boiling water if necessary.

Pay special attention when steaming fatty duck and goose; the birds render a tremendous amount of fat, so while it may look like there's plenty of steaming liquid in the pot, it may be mostly fat. If you are using a roasting pan with a wire rack, you'll certainly need to skim the fat at least once during steaming to make room for more water.

WHOLE POULTRY

Steam whole birds trussed or not, as you like. After steaming, turn the heat to low, set the lid ajar, and let the bird rest for 10 minutes to allow the juices to re-distribute; the poultry will not continue to cook.

For crisp skin, brown whole poultry in the oven as directed on page 178.

POULTRY PARTS

For crisp skin, brown poultry parts under the broiler as directed on page 179.

See page 213 to determine steaming times for boneless skinless breasts steamed *en papillote*.

DUCK

The chart gives a steaming time for whole steamed duck, but I recommend cutting the duck apart (see page 214) and steaming the parts separately. Duck breasts are steamed to medium-rare. Legs are steamed longer, until tender.

Brown duck parts under the broiler as directed on page 179.

RABBIT

Rabbit, like duck, is best steamed in parts, as described on page 219.

BUTTERFLIED POULTRY

Butterflying is a technique in which the backbone of the bird is removed and the breastbone cracked or removed entirely so the bird lies flat. Butterflying is practical for grilling. A butterflied bird steams no better than a whole bird, but it browns more evenly under the broiler or on a grill after steaming.

	MINUTES WITH THE LID CLOSED	MINUTES WITH THE LID AJAR	(OPTIONAL) MINUTES TO BROWN IN OVEN (OR BROILER)
CHICKEN (3 TO 3¼ POUNDS UNLESS OTHERWISE NOTED)			
Whole chicken	50 to 55	5	12
Whole chicken, butterflied	50 to 55	5	10 (broiler)
Whole chicken (4 pounds)	55	5	12
Half-chicken	35	5	5 to 6 (broiler)
Leg quarters	35 to 40	5	5 to 6 (broiler)
Breast quarters	25 to 30		5 to 6 (broiler)
Thighs	20 to 25		5 to 6 (broiler)
Drumsticks	20		5 to 6 (broiler)
Boneless skinless breasts			
(6 to 8 ounces)	15 to 17		
(5 ounces)	14		
(3 to 4 ounces)	8 to 10		
Chicken Liver	2 to 3		
CORNISH GAME HENS (1¼ TO 1½ POUNDS)			
Whole hen	30		5
Whole hen, butterflied	30		5 (broiler)
Half-hen	20		5 (broiler)
CAPON			
Whole bird (7 to 8 pounds)	75	15	15
TURKEY			
Whole bird (9½ to 10 pounds)	80	15	
Breast (4½ pounds)	20		
GUINEA HEN			
Whole bird (2½ pounds)	40		8
DUCK (5 POUNDS)			
Whole duck	60	15	10
Breast on the bone	15		5 (broiler)
Boneless breasts (8 ounces)	7		2 to 3 (broiler)
Legs on the carcass	55		8 to 10 (broiler)
Confit (leg)	15		2 to 3
GOOSE			
Whole bird (9½ pounds)	1½ hours	1 hour	15 to 20
(10½ pounds)	1¾ hours	1 hour	15 to 20
SQUAB (1 POUND)			
Whole bird	10	5	
Whole bird, boned	10	5	
QUAIL (5 TO 6 OUNCES)			
Whole bird	7		
Whole bird, boned	5		
RABBIT (3 POUNDS)			
Saddle	15		
Legs	45		

CHICKEN QUARTERS STEAMED ON A BED OF LIME FLOWERS

Poulet à la Vapeur de Tilleul

The flowers of the lime tree, or *tilleul* in French, have a pungent, very sweet smell. The dried flowers are easy to find in markets in France and are used for tea infusions. In America, you may be able to find dried flowers loose in specialty shops that sell herbs, spices, and teas. They are also available in tea bags sold either as lime flowers or tilleul. (The German company Pompadour sells lime flower infusions in tea bags.) I have found small packages of leaves and stems in stores in Spanish neighborhoods from the company Badia, in Florida. If you can't find either, use fresh mint or another herb, or substitute another infusion, such as chamomile.

The lime flowers suffuse the chicken with their scent, making an elaborate sauce unnecessary; steamed zucchini bâtonnets served with the chicken and sauced with a few tablespoons of cream are enough. The zucchini is sweet and delicious on its own, even without the cream, or you can substitute nonfat yogurt instead: Warm it in the sauté pan as you would the cream, whisking to loosen it, but do not boil, or it will break.

This is an elegant way to use chicken quarters, practical because they are quick to steam. Boneless skinless chicken breasts, whole chicken, Cornish game hen, guinea hen, or rabbit parts may be used in place of the chicken quarters. (Use the chart on page 182 to determine the timings.)

SERVES 4 AS A MAIN COURSE

A large fistful of dried lime flowers, or leaves and flowers, or 3 tea bags lime flower tea (see headnote)

1 chicken (about 3½ pounds), quartered

Salt and freshly ground pepper

ZUCCHINI WITH CREAM AND FRESH HERBS

3 medium zucchini, cut into ¼-inch-thick bâtonnets (see page 104) or sliced into ¼-inch-thick rounds

3 tablespoons crème fraîche or 3 tablespoons heavy cream mixed with ½ teaspoon fresh lemon juice

⅛ teaspoon salt

⅛ teaspoon freshly ground pepper

 If using lime flowers or flowers and leaves, put half of them on the steamer rack. (If using a roasting pan with a wire rack, line the rack with a layer of cheesecloth to keep the flowers from falling through.) If using tea bags, cut a double layer of cheesecloth twice the size of the steamer rack. Dampen the cheesecloth and lay it on the steamer rack so that half of the cheesecloth covers the rack and the other half falls outside the steamer. Open the tea bags and pour the tea over the cheesecloth on the rack. Fold the other half of the cheesecloth over the tea.

Sprinkle the chicken quarters with salt and pepper and put them in a single layer on the steamer rack. If using dried flowers or flowers and leaves, sprinkle the remainder over the chicken. Place over simmering water, cover, and steam 30 minutes. Remove the breasts, cover, and set aside in a warm place. Steam

1½ tablespoons snipped fresh chervil sprigs or ½ teaspoon chopped fresh tarragon plus 1 teaspoon chopped parsley

Cheesecloth, if using a roasting pan and/or tea bags

Stackable steamer with two steaming compartments, large stackable steamer, or roasting pan with wire rack plus another steamer for the zucchini

the legs 5 more minutes, then set the lid ajar and steam until the juices run clear when the thigh is pierced with a skewer, about 5 more minutes.

Meanwhile, put the zucchini on the steamer rack, place over simmering water, cover, and steam until tender, about 6 minutes for bâtonnets, 9 to 10 minutes for slices.

Brush any flowers or leaves off the chicken quarters. If desired, brown the skin (see page 178) or remove it. Put the crème fraîche or cream and lemon juice in a frying pan, add the salt and pepper, and bring to a boil. Add the zucchini and herbs, and toss or stir gently to coat the zucchini with the cream. Adjust the seasoning if necessary.

Serve the chicken with the zucchini.

CHICKEN WITH FRESH GINGER AND SCALLIONS

Poulet au Pot Dit "Îlot"

I pulled this Chinese-style recipe from Manière's chapter on foods from around the world. The dish requires a mold with a "chimney" in the center, such as a ring mold, a kugelhopf mold, or a Bundt pan. The chicken cooks "à l'étouffée," smothered in the juices from the meat and bones, flavored with scallion and ginger.

This is a terrific and very simple way to cook chicken. It's particularly good for the white meat, which stays tender and very juicy. The refreshingly simple broth is delicious because it is so concentrated.

(continued)

1 chicken (3 to 3¼ pounds)

2 scallions, trimmed and cut into ¼-inch
   slices

3 slices unpeeled fresh ginger, about
   ⅛ inch thick

1 teaspoon salt

¼ cup Chinese rice wine, dry sherry,
   Cognac, sake, or dry white wine

¼ cup water

Aluminum foil

8- to 9-inch ring mold, kugelhopf mold,
   or Bundt pan

Large stackable steamer, steamer pot
   with insert, roasting pan with wire
   rack, or large collapsible steamer

 Have the butcher cut the chicken into 2- to 3-inch pieces, or do it yourself with kitchen scissors (see page 210).

Put the chicken pieces in the mold. Scatter the scallions and ginger over the chicken. Sprinkle with the salt. Pour in the wine and water. Cover the mold with aluminum foil and press around the edges to seal. Put the mold on the steamer rack, cover, place over simmering water, and steam 1 hour. Serve the chicken directly from the mold.

CHICKEN "AU BLANC"

Poulet "au Blanc"

Manière culled Poulet "au Blanc"—a dish of braised chicken bathed in a rich white sauce made with the strained braising liquid, thickened with cream and egg and garnished with mushrooms—from the repertoire of classic French cuisine. But Manière's steamed chicken has more flavor than the usual braised chicken; the juices drip into and enrich the stock below. Ask the butcher for a veal knuckle bone and have him quarter it; the gelatin in the bone will give the stock richness and body without added fat.

Manière's version of this dish betters the classic in another way: The traditional recipe uses vegetables solely to give flavor to the braising liquid; the vegetables are strained out of the stock when they have done their work. Manière steamed additional vegetables with the chicken and served them alongside.

About 3 quarts water

1 chicken (3¼ to 3½ pounds)

Salt and freshly ground pepper

2 medium leeks

1 medium onion

2 whole cloves

3 medium carrots, peeled and halved
  lengthwise

1 veal knuckle bone, sawed into 4 pieces
  by the butcher (optional)

2 medium turnips, peeled and cut into 4
  to 6 wedges

7 ounces mushrooms, trimmed and sliced

"AU BLANC" SAUCE

4 tablespoons unsalted butter

1½ tablespoons finely chopped shallots
  (about 1 shallot)

½ cup dry vermouth, such as Noilly Prat,
  or dry white wine

2 cups chicken stock (see instructions)

3 large egg yolks

½ cup crème fraîche or heavy cream

1 teaspoon potato starch or arrowroot

1 to 2 tablespoons fresh lemon juice

1 teaspoon salt

¼ teaspoon freshly ground pepper,
  preferably white

Kitchen twine

Large stackable steamer with two
  compartments or roasting pan with
  wire rack raised off the floor of the
  pot to the height of two stacked tuna
  cans (see page 9)

 Put 3 quarts of water in the steamer pot (or as much as the pot will hold without the water touching the steamer rack). Bring to a boil.

Meanwhile, remove the giblets from the chicken. Cut out the wishbone and cut off the wing tips at the first joint (see page 206). Reserve the wing tips. Sprinkle the cavity of the chicken with salt and pepper and truss the bird with kitchen twine (see page 207).

Cut off the green parts of the leeks and reserve them. Cut the leeks in half lengthwise and rinse well. Stick the onion with the cloves and cut the onion in half through the root end if necessary so that it will fit underneath the steamer rack.

When the water boils, add 1 carrot, the leek greens, onion, and chicken neck and wing tips to the pot. Add the veal bone, if using. Add ½ teaspoon salt and ⅛ teaspoon pepper. Boil gently for 5 minutes. Then skim the stock with a ladle or a skimmer, and reduce the heat to a brisk simmer.

Put the trussed chicken on the steamer rack. Sprinkle it with salt and pepper. Place over the simmering stock, cover, and steam 25 minutes. Add the remaining carrots, the leeks, turnips, and mushrooms to the steamer rack, or put them in a second steamer compartment, cover, and steam until the juices run clear when the thigh of the chicken is pierced with a skewer, about 30 more minutes. Check the level of the stock occasionally, and add more water if necessary. Keep the chicken and vegetables warm in the steamer over low heat with the lid ajar while you make the sauce.

Melt the butter in a large saucepan over medium-low heat. Add the chopped shallots and cook, stirring often, until translucent, 3 to 5 minutes. Add the vermouth or wine, raise the heat to high, and bring to a boil. Boil until reduced by one half. Ladle out 2 cups of stock from the steamer pot and add to the saucepan. (Strain and save the remaining stock for another use.)

Put the egg yolks, crème fraîche or cream, potato starch or arrowroot, and 1 tablespoon lemon juice in a small bowl. Whisk until smooth. Whisk a little of the hot vermouth-stock mixture into the egg mixture and then gradually add this mixture to the saucepan, whisking constantly. Return just to a boil and immediately remove from the heat. Add the salt and pepper. Taste for lemon juice and add more if the sauce tastes bland. Strain the sauce through a fine strainer.

Cut the chicken into serving pieces (see page 208) and remove the skin if you like. Put the chicken on a heated platter and arrange all of the steamed vegetables except the mushrooms around the chicken. Scatter the mushrooms over the chicken, spoon the sauce over, and serve.

CHICKEN STEAMED WITH VEGETABLES AND TARRAGON

Poularde à la Vapeur de Légumes

For this recipe and the one that follows, Manière used a specially raised and fattened hen called a *poularde,* an especially rich and fine-tasting chicken, weighing a little over four pounds. The best known are raised in the region of Bresse, near Lyon. They are free-range, fed exclusively on corn and milk products, and slaughtered at sixteen weeks. *Poulardes* are tagged and numbered, and they are very expensive. Only one million *poulardes de Bresse* are raised per year, as against twelve to fifteen million regular chickens throughout France.

A large free-range chicken or a capon makes a fine substitute for the *poularde.* Cut the carrots and turnips into slightly larger pieces (quarters and eighths) and steam the capon according to the time given in the chart on page 182. If you happen to have any leftovers, they will be delicious: Cold steamed chicken remains very moist. (Use the leftover carcass to make chicken broth.)

Manière steamed the chicken on a bed of vegetables with sprigs of tarragon, wrapped in foil, or *en papillote.* The foil holds in all the juices so that they are suffused with the flavor of the vegetables and the herb. The undiluted juices are so flavorful that they are sauce enough, with no added fat necessary.

SERVES 4 AS A MAIN COURSE

1 chicken (4 to 4¼ pounds), preferably free-range

Salt and freshly ground pepper

2 medium leeks, white parts only, cut into ½-inch slices and well rinsed

3 medium carrots, peeled and cut into ¼- by 2-inch bâtonnets (see page 104)

2 medium turnips, peeled and cut into ¼- by 2-inch bâtonnets (see page 104)

4 medium stalks celery, peeled and cut into ¼- by 2-inch bâtonnets (see page 104)

2 sprigs fresh tarragon

Remove the giblets from the chicken. Cut out the wishbone and cut off the wing tips at the first joint (see page 206). Sprinkle the inside of the chicken with salt and pepper. Cut a 12- by 48-inch piece of aluminum foil and fold it crosswise in half.

Lay the foil on a work surface with a long side facing you. Make a bed of the vegetables in the center of the foil. Lay the tarragon sprigs on top and put the chicken on top of them. Bring the sides of the foil up to meet over the chicken. Fold the edges together and fold over three times in ¼-inch folds. Fold the open edges over three times in ¼-inch folds to seal.

Put the papillote on the steamer rack, place over simmering water,

Aluminum foil
Large or oval stackable steamer or
   roasting pan with wire rack

cover, and steam 1 hour. Set the lid ajar and steam 5 more minutes.

Put the papillote on a platter and bring it to the table to open. Slit the top of the package with a knife or scissors. Cut the chicken into serving pieces (see page 208), remove the skin, if desired, and serve.

CHICKEN WITH RICE STUFFING AND SPRING VEGETABLES

Poularde Farcie aux Petits Légumes

This elegant, colorful dish is party food. Manière used a succulent *poularde* (see page 188), not available in America, but a large chicken or a capon will substitute well. Although there are a lot of steps in the recipe, some can be done ahead. You can steam the vegetable medley up to twelve hours before cooking the chicken; refresh the vegetables as directed in the recipe, and refrigerate them. Then sauté them in the butter, as in the recipe, just before serving. The sauce can be made ahead and held for several hours in a thermos.

More often than not, I make the chicken with the stuffing and serve it with just the juices that collect on the plate as the chicken rests.

Manière's stuffing is deliciously rich with butter, but it can be made with half the amount. Although Manière steamed the *poularde* with the stuffing in the cavity, health concerns (see page 179) make it more practical to cook the stuffing separately and serve it on the side. Manière used an egg to bind the stuffing, but it's not necessary if the stuffing is cooked separately.

SERVES 4 AS A MAIN COURSE

SPRING VEGETABLE MEDLEY

1 pound fava beans, shelled and skinned
   (see page 42)

1 bunch spring onions or scallions,
   trimmed of all but 2 inches of greens,
   or 8 small to medium pearl onions,
   peeled (see page 84)

5 ounces baby carrots, scrubbed, or
   3 medium carrots, peeled and cut into
   ¼- by 2-inch bâtonnets (see page 104)

4 baby turnips, scrubbed, or 1 medium
   turnip, trimmed, peeled, and cut into
   ¼- by 2-inch bâtonnets (see page 104)

⅔ pound fresh peas, shelled
   (about 1 cup), or 1 cup frozen peas

Put the fava beans, onions or scallions, carrots, and turnips on the steamer rack. Place over simmering water, cover, and steam 5 minutes. Add the fresh peas, if using, and steam 7 minutes. Add the asparagus tips and steam 3 minutes longer. Alternatively, if using frozen peas, steam the favas, onions, carrots, and turnips for 12 minutes, then add the peas and asparagus and steam 3 minutes. Refresh the vegetables under cold running water, drain well, and set aside.

Remove the giblets from the chicken or capon, cut out the wishbone, and cut off or secure the wing tips (see page 206). Trim the fat and veins from the center of the liver and cut it into small pieces. Set aside. (Save the neck, heart, and gizzard for stock, as described on page 220.)

(continued)

1 bunch medium asparagus, tips only
   (see Note)

1 chicken (about 4 pounds), preferably
   free-range, or 1 capon (7 to 8 pounds)
Salt and freshly ground pepper

RICE STUFFING
4 tablespoons unsalted butter
1 small carrot, peeled and cut into ¼-inch dice
2 ounces green beans (a small handful),
   ends trimmed and cut into ¼-inch pieces
⅓ pound fresh peas, shelled (about
   ½ cup), or ½ cup frozen peas
Generous ½ cup long-grain white rice
Reserved chicken or capon liver (see
   instructions)
1 cup chicken stock or water
½ teaspoon salt
⅛ teaspoon freshly ground pepper

HERBED BEURRE BLANC
1 shallot, finely chopped (about
   1½ tablespoons)
⅓ cup dry white wine
3 tablespoons cider vinegar
3 tablespoons snipped fresh chervil sprigs
   or 1 teaspoon chopped fresh tarragon
   plus 2 teaspoons chopped parsley
Scant ¼ teaspoon salt
⅛ teaspoon freshly ground pepper,
   preferably white
3 tablespoons heavy cream
16 tablespoons (½ pound) unsalted butter

4 tablespoons unsalted butter
1 teaspoon sugar
½ teaspoon each chopped fresh tarragon
   and chervil or 1 teaspoon chopped
   fresh tarragon

Kitchen twine
Aluminum foil
Large or oval stackable steamer, large steamer
   pot with insert, or roasting pan with wire
   rack plus another steamer for the vegetables

Sprinkle the cavity of the chicken or capon with salt and pepper and truss with kitchen twine (see page 207), or cross and tie the legs together. Put the bird on the steamer rack, place over simmering water, cover, and steam until the juices run clear when the thigh is pierced with a skewer, 55 minutes for chicken, 75 minutes for capon. Then set the lid ajar and steam chicken for 5 more minutes, capon for 15 more minutes.

Meanwhile, make the stuffing: Melt the butter in a medium frying pan over medium-low heat. Add the carrot, beans, and peas, cover, and cook until softened, about 5 minutes. Add the rice and the reserved liver and stir well to coat the rice. Add the chicken stock or water and bring to a boil. Reduce the heat, cover, and simmer until the rice is tender, 18 to 20 minutes. Stir in the salt and pepper. Remove from the heat and set aside, covered, in a warm place.

While the rice is cooking, make the beurre blanc, following the directions on page 120. Use half of the herbs in the wine and vinegar reduction and stir the rest into the sauce at the end. Set aside in a warm place.

When the chicken or capon is cooked, take it out of the steamer and put it on a plate. Cover with aluminum foil and let it rest in a warm place while you sauté the vegetable medley.

Melt the butter in a frying pan over medium heat. Add the steamed vegetables, sprinkle with the sugar and herbs, and toss the vegetables until the sugar is melted and the vegetables are warmed through and coated with the butter.

To serve, spoon the stuffing into a serving bowl. Remove the kitchen twine from the chicken or capon, cut the bird into serving pieces (see page 208), and remove the skin, if desired. Arrange the chicken or capon and the vegetable medley on a serving platter. Pour the sauce into a warm sauceboat and serve on the side.

Note: Save the asparagus stalks for another dish: Make a soup by steaming the stalks and then puréeing with chicken stock and cooked rice to thicken. Or cut the stalks into 2-inch pieces, steam as directed on page 37, and serve with Chicken with Garlic-Parsley Butter and Onion-Raisin Jam, page 192.

CORNISH GAME HENS WITH FRESH HERBS

Coquelets à l'Estragon

Coquelets are small young chickens that weigh one and a quarter to one and a half pounds; our Rock Cornish game hens are about the same size. Cornish game hens steam beautifully—the breasts stay moist and tender while the legs cook through completely. Manière sauced these delicate little birds with a cream sauce, made in minutes, flavored with whole tarragon leaves. Tarragon is much appreciated in France, particularly with poultry, but the sauce is luscious with other fresh herbs as well; try chopped parsley, chives, thyme, rosemary, oregano, or basil. (Use about one tablespoon of the stronger herbs, such as thyme, rosemary, and oregano.) The sauce is also delicious with a quartered chicken, chicken breasts, or a whole chicken, guinea hen, or rabbit.

S E R V E S   4   A S   A   M A I N   C O U R S E

2 Cornish game hens (1¼ to 1½ pounds each)

1 small bunch fresh tarragon or other fresh herb (see above), leaves removed and reserved for sauce, stems reserved

Salt and freshly ground pepper

HERBED CREAM SAUCE

2 large egg yolks

½ cup crème fraîche or ½ cup heavy cream mixed with 1 teaspoon fresh lemon juice

¼ cup loosely packed fresh tarragon leaves, 2 tablespoons chopped fresh parsley, chives, or basil, or 1 tablespoon chopped fresh thyme, rosemary, oregano, or other strong herbs (see headnote)

¼ teaspoon salt

⅛ teaspoon freshly ground pepper

Stackable steamer with two steaming compartments, large roasting pan with wire rack, or large collapsible steamer basket

Split the game hens in two with a large knife or poultry shears as directed on page 210.

Make a bed of the reserved herb stems on the steamer rack. Sprinkle the game hens with salt and pepper and put the four halves, skin side down, on the herb bed. Place over simmering water, cover, and steam 20 minutes.

Meanwhile, make the sauce: Put the egg yolks in a small bowl. Put the crème fraîche or cream and lemon juice in a small saucepan, add the herbs, salt, and pepper, and bring to a boil, whisking constantly. Whisk a little of the hot cream into the egg yolks to temper them, and then, off the heat, whisk the egg yolk mixture into the cream. Return the saucepan to low heat and cook, whisking constantly, until the sauce thickens slightly; do not boil. Taste for salt and pepper. (See Note.)

When the game hens are cooked, remove the skin if you like. To serve, put the hens on a platter and pour the sauce over.

Note: To make the sauce in a food processor, bring the seasoned cream and herb mixture to a boil in a saucepan. Put the egg yolks in the bowl of the food processor. With the machine running, add the hot cream. The sauce will thicken immediately and needn't be returned to the heat.

CHICKEN WITH GARLIC-PARSLEY BUTTER AND ONION-RAISIN JAM

Escargots de Poulet à la Confiture d'Oignons et de Raisins

Manière's inspiration for this dish was the traditional Burgundian recipe for snails with garlic-parsley butter. He boned chicken legs, butterflied the breast pieces, and stuffed them all with a garlic-parsley butter flavored with ham and thickened slightly with bread crumbs. As the chicken steams, the flesh is drenched with the butter; the melting butter mixes with the chicken juices to make a mouthwatering sauce. (If the quantity of butter seems a bit *too* mouthwatering, it can be cut by one half to two thirds.)

The Onion-Raisin Jam is a chunky, tomato-y, sweet-and-sour contrast to the buttery sauce. This jam can be served with other steamed poultry, with lamb, or with an assertive fish, such as mackerel, salmon, or bluefish, in place of a sauce. I don't have the patience to peel the grapes Manière used in the jam so I use raisins, his second choice.

Although this recipe doesn't require a stock, Manière took the opportunity to make a stock underneath the steaming chicken, using the chicken carcass and vegetables. He suggested straining it and adding tapioca or vermicelli to make a first-course soup for another meal.

SERVES 4 AS A MAIN COURSE

1 chicken (about 3½ pounds)

CHICKEN STOCK

1 small onion, peeled

3 whole cloves

Reserved chicken carcass (see
  instructions), cut into pieces with a
  cleaver or kitchen scissors, with neck,
  wing tips, leg bones, and gizzard

1 large carrot, peeled

1 medium turnip, peeled

1 stalk celery, trimmed

¼ teaspoon salt

⅛ teaspoon freshly ground pepper

2 quarts cold water

GARLIC-PARSLEY BUTTER STUFFING

12 tablespoons unsalted butter, at room
  temperature

 Have the butcher cut up and bone the chicken to make two butterflied boneless breast pieces, with the wing bones still attached, and two whole boneless legs; or do it yourself as directed on page 211. Leave the skin as intact as possible. Save the carcass, wing tips, and leg bones, as well as the neck and gizzard, for the stock.

Make the stock: Stick the onion with the cloves. Put all the ingredients into the steamer pot and bring to a boil over high heat. Skim the stock with a skimmer or ladle, then reduce the heat and simmer while you make the stuffing.

Melt 1½ tablespoons of the butter in a medium saucepan over medium-low heat. Add the shallots and cook until translucent, 3 to 5 minutes. Scrape the mixture into a bowl. Add the ham, garlic, parsley, bread crumbs, salt, pepper, and the remaining 10½ tablespoons butter and mash together with your hands to make a paste.

Cut four 12-inch squares of aluminum foil.

To stuff the chicken, lay the chicken pieces skin down on the work surface with a short side of each leg facing you and the

1½ tablespoons chopped shallots

⅓ pound boiled ham, finely chopped

4 medium cloves garlic, finely chopped or
    mashed in a mortar and pestle

1½ tablespoons chopped parsley

¼ cup fresh bread crumbs

¼ teaspoon salt

⅛ teaspoon freshly ground pepper

ONION-RAISIN JAM

¼ pound white Muscat grapes or ¼ cup
    raisins

2 tablespoons unsalted butter

12 ounces pearl onions, peeled (see
    page 84)

1½ tablespoons sugar

1½ tablespoons red or white wine vinegar

⅓ cup dry white wine

3 tablespoons tomato paste

¼ teaspoon salt

⅛ teaspoon freshly ground pepper

Sprig of fresh thyme or ⅛ teaspoon dried
    thyme

Aluminum foil

Large stackable steamer with one or two
    compartments, roasting pan with wire
    rack, or two steamers

wider ends of the breasts, with the wing bones, facing away from you. Open out the butterflied breasts. Divide the stuffing among the four pieces of chicken: Put the stuffing on the bottom halves of the legs and on one side of each butterflied breast. Fold the top halves of the legs over the stuffing. Fold the other sides of the breasts over the stuffing.

Put a stuffed chicken piece in the center of each piece of foil. Bring the sides of the foil up to meet over the chicken. Fold the edges together and fold over three times in ¼-inch folds. Fold the open edges over three times in ¼-inch folds to seal. (Make note of which papillotes hold the thighs.) Put the papillotes in a single layer on the steamer rack, place over the simmering stock, cover, and steam 35 minutes. Take the breasts out of the steamer and steam the thighs 5 more minutes.

Meanwhile, make the jam: If using raisins, put them in a small bowl with warm water to cover and let soak to soften. (Or steam 2 minutes.)

Melt 1 tablespoon of the butter in a medium saucepan over medium-high heat. Add the onions and brown lightly in the butter, about 5 minutes. Sprinkle with the sugar and cook, stirring often, until golden brown, 2 to 3 minutes. Add the vinegar and cook until reduced to a glaze. Add the wine and tomato paste and stir well. Add the salt, pepper, and thyme, cover, reduce the heat, and simmer gently until the onions are tender, about 20 minutes. Remove from the heat.

If using grapes, while the onions are simmering, peel them with a small knife, cut them in half, and take out the seeds. Melt the remaining 1 tablespoon butter in a frying pan over low heat. Add the grapes or raisins and stir to coat with the butter.

Scrape the cooked onion mixture into the frying pan with the grapes or raisins and stir to mix.

To serve, put the chicken papillotes on plates and pass the onion-raisin jam in a bowl on the side.

To finish the stock, simmer, uncovered, adding water as necessary, until it has flavor and has cooked for about 2 hours. Strain and reserve for a soup or a sauce.

Stuffed Guinea Hen on a Bed of Parslied Cabbage

Pintade Farcie sur Chou Croquant

A guinea hen is a farm-raised bird that tastes like a very flavorful chicken. It has a slightly darker flesh than a chicken, but the flavor isn't gamy. Guinea hen steams beautifully; the legs are tender and the breast is juicy. They are available at some butchers and through D'Artagnan (see page 299). A whole chicken, chicken parts, or two Cornish game hens can be substituted for the guinea hen.

In this dish, the hen is stuffed with a low-fat cheese and bread crumb stuffing, crunchy with pine nuts, and nestled on a bed of sweet, creamy parslied cabbage. Because of health concerns, however, I've adapted the recipe to steam the stuffing separately (see page 179). Manière used Savoy cabbage, the thin and crinkly-leaved light green variety that has a subtler flavor than smooth-leaved green cabbage. If you can find Savoy, it makes a particularly pretty dish, but you'll be just as happy with the more readily available green cabbage.

Just before serving, the hen is roasted in the oven on its bed of cabbage to brown the skin. The juices from the hen imbue the cabbage with flavor and combine with the cream to make a luxurious sauce.

SERVES 4 AS A MAIN COURSE

1 guinea hen (about 2½ pounds) or
   1 chicken (3 to 3½ pounds)

CHEESE AND PINE NUT STUFFING
Reserved liver and gizzard (see
   instructions)
½ cup fromage blanc or ½ cup low-fat
   cottage cheese, puréed in the blender
1 large egg
¼ teaspoon salt
⅛ teaspoon freshly ground pepper
1 clove garlic, minced
¼ cup fresh bread crumbs
1½ tablespoons chopped parsley
¼ cup pine nuts

Salt and freshly ground pepper
1 small head cabbage, preferably Savoy

Remove the giblets from the guinea hen or chicken, cut out the wishbone, and cut off or secure the wing tips (see page 206). Reserve the liver and gizzard for the stuffing. (Save the neck for stock, as described on page 220.)

Make the stuffing: Put the reserved liver and gizzard on the steamer rack. (Put them on a square of aluminum foil if using a roasting pan with a wire rack.) Place over simmering water, cover, and steam 6 minutes.

Roughly chop the liver and gizzard and put them in a medium bowl. Add the cheese and stir well. Lightly beat the egg with the salt and pepper and stir into the cheese mixture. Add the garlic, bread crumbs, parsley, and pine nuts. Taste for salt and pepper. Wrap the stuffing in a rectangle of aluminum foil and fold the edges together to seal.

Sprinkle the cavity of the bird with salt and pepper. Truss with kitchen twine (see page 207) or cross and tie the legs together. Put the bird on the steamer rack, place over simmering water, cover,

½ cup crème fraîche or ½ cup heavy
   cream mixed with 1 teaspoon fresh
   lemon juice
1½ tablespoons chopped shallots
1½ tablespoons chopped parsley

Kitchen twine
Aluminum foil
Large or oval stackable steamer with one
   or two steaming compartments, large
   steamer pot with insert, roasting pan
   with wire rack, or two steamers

and steam, guinea hen for 25 minutes, chicken for 40 minutes. Lift the bird out of the steamer and put it on a plate.

Meanwhile, pull off any discolored or old leaves from the cabbage. Quarter the cabbage through the core. Cut out the core and cut each quarter lengthwise into ½-inch-thick slices. (Use a serrated knife and a sawing motion to cut through the cabbage easily.) There should be about 10 cups sliced cabbage.

Make a bed of the cabbage on the steamer rack, put the bird on top, and steam until the juices run clear when the thigh of the bird is pierced with a skewer and the cabbage is wilted but still has a bite, about 15 more minutes. If the steamer is large enough or two-tiered, add the foil-wrapped package of stuffing to the steamer and steam with the bird during this final 15 minutes. If not, steam the stuffing in a separate steamer for 15 minutes. Keep warm.

Preheat the oven to 500°F.

Transfer the bird to a plate, cover with foil, and set aside in a warm place. Remove the cabbage and set aside.

To finish the cabbage, pour off the steaming liquid from the pot. Add the crème fraîche or cream and lemon juice to the pot and bring to a boil. Add the cabbage, shallots, parsley, ¼ teaspoon salt, and ⅛ teaspoon pepper and stir to coat the cabbage with the cream.

Make a bed of the creamed cabbage on a metal serving platter, or in a baking dish or shallow casserole. Put the guinea hen or chicken on top. Roast 8 minutes to brown the skin.

To serve, spoon the stuffing into a serving bowl. Remove the kitchen twine and cut the bird into serving pieces (see page 208). Arrange the pieces on the bed of cabbage and serve.

Warm salad of guinea hen with wild mushrooms

Salade de Pintade "Soir d'Été"

This salad is made with frisée, also called curly endive in America, a crisp and mildly bitter chicory popular in France (see page 67). The leaves are long and slender and edged with jagged, lacy "teeth"—similar in shape to escarole leaves but spikier. Frisée has a milder and more delicate flavor than escarole. It has a white-yellow heart and green outer leaves. The darker leaves are stronger-tasting and tougher than the heart; Manière used only the heart for his salads. If frisée is difficult to find, substitute escarole, using only the light-colored inner leaves, or Belgian endive.

Manière used cèpes in this recipe—wonderful, large, meaty mushrooms that are rarely available fresh in America—and showed us an interesting way to cook mushrooms without fat: They are sautéed in a dry nonstick pan so that their flavor is concentrated. They taste of the essence of mushroom. If you can't find cèpes, also known as porcini, or other wild mushrooms, don't worry; this technique will get the most out of the flavor of even standard white mushrooms. Or use other more exotic cultivated mushrooms such as shiitake, oyster, or cremini, which have a darker, wilder flavor than white mushrooms.

If you can't find guinea hen, available at specialty butchers and from D'Artagnan (see page 299), chicken, rabbit, and duck all make delicious substitutes. The salad is a particularly good way to use boneless, skinless duck breasts. Or use leftover steamed poultry, warmed a few minutes in the steamer.

SERVES 4 AS A MAIN COURSE

1 guinea hen (about 2½ pounds)
    or 1 chicken (3 to 3¼ pounds)
1¼ pounds cèpes or other wild
    mushrooms, such as chanterelle or
    black trumpet, or shiitake, oyster,
    cremini, or white mushrooms, cleaned
    and thinly sliced
1 head frisée or escarole or 4 medium
    Belgian endive

SHERRY VINEGAR VINAIGRETTE
3 tablespoons sherry vinegar
1 teaspoon Dijon mustard
¼ teaspoon salt

Remove the giblets from the guinea hen or chicken, cut out the wishbone, and cut off or secure the wing tips (see page 206). (Save the liver to use in a salad, as on page 54; save the neck, heart, and gizzard for stock, as described on page 220.)

Put the hen or chicken on the steamer rack, place over simmering water, cover, and steam, guinea hen for 40 minutes, chicken for 55 minutes. Then turn the heat to low and set the lid ajar to keep the bird warm while you prepare the rest of the salad.

Heat a large nonstick frying pan over high heat until very hot. Add the mushrooms and cook, stirring, until the juices have evaporated and the mushrooms are lightly browned, 2 to 3 minutes. (Don't crowd the pan; you may need to cook the mushrooms in two batches.) Set the mushrooms aside.

⅛ teaspoon freshly ground pepper

½ cup olive oil

1½ tablespoons snipped fresh chervil
sprigs or 2 teaspoons chopped fresh
tarragon plus 2 teaspoons chopped
parsley

Large or oval stackable steamer, large
steamer pot with insert, or roasting
pan with wire rack

Wash and dry the greens, using only the inner white-yellow heart of the frisée or escarole. If using Belgian endive, pull off any browned leaves and trim the ends. Starting from the bottom end, cut each endive into ¼-inch-thick rounds, and leave the top 1½ inches whole.

Make the vinaigrette, following the directions for the Basic Vinaigrette on page 26.

To assemble the salad, cut the breasts and legs off the carcass (see page 211). Cut the breast meat on an angle into large, thin slices. Cut the meat off the legs in thin slices.

Make a bed of greens on each serving plate and scatter the mushrooms over the greens. Arrange slices of breast and leg on each plate. Drizzle the vinaigrette over the salads and garnish with the chervil or chopped tarragon and parsley.

Red wine–steamed duckling with pears

Canette à la Vapeur de Vin

Manière made this dish with a *canette,* a young, tender duck that is quite small (less than four pounds). Manière fed four people with one duck; French courses are typically smaller than ours in America, and the sauce is rich. The duck is steamed whole to *rosée,* or medium-rare; Manière felt that duck cooked past that point lost something in flavor and texture. The ducks that are available in this country (mostly Long Island ducks) generally run about five pounds. They can't be steamed whole to medium-rare because the leg would be too tough to eat. And if the duck is steamed until the legs are cooked through and tender, the breast is cooked far past the succulent pink that Manière was aiming for.

The best way to steam Long Island duck is to remove boneless breast pieces and to cook them and the legs separately. The breast takes just a few minutes to steam to rare or medium-rare. The legs take almost an hour. The breast emerges tender, pink, and juicy, while the legs are as moist and succulent as if they had been cooked as confit.

(continued)

Red wine has enough body to flavor steamed duck. It turns light-colored foods like the pears a beautiful shade of pink with a delectable wine flavor. If all the wine doesn't fit under the steamer rack, start with as much as possible and add more as it evaporates. If it evaporates too fast (the rate depends on the steamer), bring as much wine as needed from the third bottle to a boil, then add it to the steamer. Steaming will render a great deal of fat into the wine so the level of the steaming liquid is deceptive—skim the fat at least once during the steaming and don't let the level get too low, or the wine will scorch.

Ducks are often sold frozen. A five-pound duck takes about two days to defrost in the refrigerator.

1 Long Island duck (about 5 pounds)

4 tablespoons unsalted butter, plus 10 tablespoons cold unsalted butter, cut into pieces

1½ tablespoons chopped shallots

2 to 3 bottles young, tannic red wine such as Côtes-du-Rhône or Bordeaux

Salt and freshly ground pepper

4 medium (about ½ pound each) Anjou or Bartlett pears

Juice of ½ lemon

3 tablespoons crème fraîche or 3 tablespoons heavy cream mixed with ½ teaspoon fresh lemon juice

Large or oval stackable steamer or roasting pan with wire rack raised off the floor of the pot to the height of two stacked tuna cans (see page 9)

 Separate the breast from the legs of the duck as directed on page 215. Leave the breast halves in one piece on the bone, or, if you prefer, bone them as directed on page 214. Leave the legs on the carcass.

Melt the 4 tablespoons butter in the bottom of the steamer pot over medium-low heat. Add the shallots, cover, and cook gently, stirring often, until translucent, 3 to 5 minutes. Add 2 bottles of wine and bring to a brisk simmer.

Sprinkle the duck legs with salt and pepper and put the carcass, back side down, on the steamer rack. Place over the simmering wine, cover, and steam until the legs are tender, about 55 minutes.

Meanwhile, peel the pears and cut in half. Use a knife or a melon baller to cut out the cores. Keep the pears in a bowl of cold water with the lemon juice to keep them from discoloring.

When the legs are cooked, transfer them to a large plate. Put the pears on the steamer rack, cover, and steam 5 to 10 minutes, depending on ripeness. Add to the plate with the duck legs and cover with aluminum foil to keep warm. Add the duck breasts to the steamer and steam, skin side down, 15 minutes if on the bone or about 7 minutes if boneless. Add to the plate and cover to keep warm.

Preheat the broiler.

To make the sauce, strain the steaming liquid through a fine strainer into a small saucepan. There will be a great deal of fat on the surface of the wine: Skim it off with a ladle, or use a degreasing cup. Boil the wine over high heat until reduced to ½ cup. Add the crème fraîche or heavy cream and lemon juice and reduce by half. Reduce the heat to low. Whisk the 10 tablespoons cold butter into the wine, a few pieces at a time, adding more as the butter is emulsified into the sauce. Bring just to a boil. Whisk in pepper and taste for salt; the sauce may not need any. Keep warm.

Cut the legs off the carcass (see page 216). Remove the skin, if desired.

To serve, cut the legs and the breasts into serving pieces. Put them on a serving platter and arrange the pears around. Pour the sauce into a warm sauceboat and serve on the side.

Duck breasts with black currants and pears
Magrets aux Grains de Cassis

A magret is the breast of a fattened moulard duck, thick and meaty and served rare or medium-rare, like steak. Moulards, raised in southwestern France, are force-fed to produce the fattened liver sold as foie gras. They are large ducks, typically seven to eight pounds; each half-breast weighs one pound. The legs of moulards are traditionally made into confit (see page 201).

Real magrets are hard to find in America, although they can be ordered through D'Artagnan (see page 299). But the breasts of Long Island ducks are meaty and delicious and an excellent substitute in this recipe; whole boneless breasts weighing three quarters of a pound to a pound are sold at many butcher shops, usually frozen. To my surprise, steaming is a perfect and practically foolproof way to cook boneless duck breast. The steamed meat is tender and juicy with consistent color and texture throughout—the outside of the meat doesn't get tough from high-temperature dry heat. Even if you don't plan to eat the skin (most of the fat in a duck is in the skin, which is easily removed), steam the breast with the skin on to protect the meat. Then pull off the skin, using a knife where the skin adheres to the meat, before serving.

Manière glazed the duck breasts with an exquisite deep-red black currant sauce that tastes much harder to make than it is. Black currants are common in France, but much less so in America. I substitute fresh cranberries or dried cherries, with a little crème de cassis—black currant liqueur—or sirop de cassis, a thick, nonalcoholic, sweetened cassis-flavored syrup, to give the right flavor. Although the recipe calls for only one tablespoon of crème or sirop de cassis, the remainder of the bottle will keep; use a splash in white wine to make the traditional Burgundian kir, or make a kir royale, with Champagne, or serve it over ice cream or with fresh berries.

If you like duck breasts try them also with Green Peppercorn Sauce (page 232).

(continued)

4 boneless duck breast halves
  (about ½ pound each)
Salt and freshly ground pepper
4 medium ripe pears, such as Anjou or
  Bartlett

BLACK CURRANT SAUCE
6 tablespoons cold unsalted butter
1½ tablespoons minced shallots
¼ cup fresh black currants or chopped
  fresh cranberries or 3 tablespoons
  dried cherries
1 teaspoon sugar, if using currants or
  cranberries
1 tablespoon crème de cassis or sirop de
  cassis, if using cranberries or cherries
3 tablespoons Armagnac or brandy
⅔ cup red wine
½ cup beef stock or ½ Knorr beef
  bouillon cube
⅛ teaspoon salt
⅛ teaspoon freshly ground pepper
½ teaspoon potato starch or arrowroot,
  dissolved in 1 tablespoon cold water

Large or oval stackable steamer with one
  or two steaming compartments,
  roasting pan with wire rack, or large
  collapsible steamer basket

 Score the skin of the duck breasts using a small sharp knife. Sprinkle the breasts with salt and pepper.

Peel the pears and cut in half. Use a knife or a melon baller to cut out the cores. Keep the pears in a bowl of cold water with the lemon juice to keep them from discoloring.

Put the duck breasts, skin side down, on the steamer rack, place over simmering water, cover, and steam to medium-rare, 7 to 9 minutes. Remove from the steamer. Put the pears on the steamer rack, cover, and steam 5 to 10 minutes, depending on ripeness.

Meanwhile, make the sauce: Melt 1 tablespoon of the butter in a large frying pan or large wide saucepan over medium-low heat. Add the shallots, cover, and cook until translucent, 3 to 5 minutes. Add the duck breasts, skin side down. Add the black currants, if using, and sprinkle with sugar, or add the cranberries, cassis, and sugar; if using cherries, add them and the cassis, omitting the sugar. Add the Armagnac or brandy and carefully light with a match to flame. When the flames die down, pour in the wine. Add the bouillon cube, if using. Bring to a boil. Take the duck out of the pan and set aside in a warm place.

If using stock, add it to the pan and boil until reduced by half. Season the sauce with the salt and pepper. Whisk in the dissolved potato starch or arrowroot mixture, reduce the heat, and simmer for 3 minutes over low heat. Cut the remaining 5 tablespoons butter into small pieces and whisk them into the sauce, a few pieces at a time, adding more as the butter is emulsified into the sauce, and bring just to a boil. Immediately remove from the heat.

To serve, remove the skin, if desired, and cut the breast pieces on an angle into thin slices, keeping the slices together. Place a sliced breast in the center of each plate. Spoon the sauce over the meat and arrange the pears around.

DUCK CONFIT WITH FRESH FAVA BEANS

Confit de Canard aux Fèves Nouvelles

Duck confit refers to duck legs (or, occasionally, breasts), that have been salted and then simmered slowly in duck fat until meltingly tender. They are cooled and preserved in the fat for at least several weeks. This is a traditional way to preserve fall-slaughtered meats through the winter, and the time in the fat also helps develop flavor in the confit. Duck leg confit is available in some supermarkets or butcher shops and from D'Artagnan (see page 299).

Confit is traditionally reheated in the oven before serving to remove excess fat, heat it through, and crisp the skin. Steaming is a terrific way to reheat confit: It renders much of the fat and gently warms the meat without drying. Then you can crisp the skin a few minutes under the broiler.

Manière's presentation for confit is not traditional. It's steamed on a bed of fava beans and then stewed with the beans in a little water with shallots and mint. The confit is not browned, but simply served on the bed of light green beans, which are creamy-textured, rich with duck fat, and brightened with fresh mint. If you prefer, you can brown the confit under the broiler after steaming (see page 179).

You'll need a large steamer for four legs of confit. A roasting pan will work, or if you have a steamer with two compartments, you can steam two legs in each.

SERVES 4 AS A MAIN COURSE

---

1 pound (about 3 cups) shelled fresh fava beans (3 to 4 pounds in the shell), skinned (see page 42)

4 legs or 2 whole breasts duck confit (see above)

2 tablespoons unsalted butter

1 teaspoon chopped shallot

4 fresh mint leaves, cut into thin strips with scissors, plus 4 whole leaves

⅛ teaspoon salt

⅛ teaspoon freshly ground pepper

½ cup boiling water

Cheesecloth, if using a roasting pan
Large or oval stackable steamer with one or two steaming compartments, roasting pan with wire rack, or collapsible steamer basket

Make a bed of the fava beans on the steamer rack. (If using a wire rack in a roasting pan, lay a piece of cheesecloth over the rack to keep the fava beans from falling through.) Put the confit on top of the beans in a single layer, place over simmering water, cover, and steam 12 minutes. Remove from the heat.

Melt the butter in a large frying pan over medium heat. Add the shallot, fava beans, confit, mint leaf strips, salt, and pepper. Add the boiling water and bring to a boil. Reduce the heat, cover, and simmer gently 8 minutes.

To serve, put the confit on a serving plate. Spoon the beans around the confit and garnish with the whole mint leaves.

SMOTHERED GOOSE
WITH GINGER AND ONIONS
Oie à l'Étuvée

This is a Chinese recipe for goose steamed with a stuffing of chopped onion and fresh ginger, enriched with bits of goose liver and gizzard. Goose has a wonderful rich, deep, meaty flavor that is well balanced in this recipe by the refreshing bite of the ginger and the sweetness of the long-cooked onion.

Geese are very fatty. The fat is delicious, so it's worth spending the time to render it, as in this recipe. It can be used for sautéed potatoes, in a warm vinaigrette for lentils or beans, in soup, or for confit (see page 217).

Manière sewed the cavity closed after stuffing rather than trussing the bird; an untrussed goose renders fat best. (The recipe will work even without sewing the cavity closed.) He didn't brown the skin after steaming, serving it soft and moist, or "smothered." I like to brown the skin because, the underlying fat layer having melted away, it gets wonderfully crisp under the broiler. The skin also pulls off easily after steaming, if you like.

Geese are available at butcher shops, from D'Artagnan (see page 299), and in some supermarkets. They run anywhere from eight to twelve pounds but are most often in the ten- to twelve-pound range. In supermarkets they are usually sold frozen; allow three to four days to defrost in the refrigerator.

Manière served this goose with short-grain rice and soy sauce spiked with a hot pepper. Blue Rose and Kokuho Rose are two good brands of domestic short-grain rice available in stores that sell Asian foods; use two cups of raw rice for four people. To make a quick, spicy soy sauce, just add a chopped fresh chile, such as jalapeño, hot red pepper flakes, or Tabasco sauce to the soy sauce to taste.

SERVES 6 TO 8 AS A MAIN COURSE

---

1 goose (10 to 11 pounds)

3 medium onions, chopped (about 3 cups)

One 2-inch piece fresh ginger, peeled and grated or very finely chopped, or ½ teaspoon powdered ginger

Salt and freshly ground pepper

⅓ cup dry white wine

Kitchen twine and trussing needle

Large roasting pan with wire rack

 Remove the neck, liver, heart, and gizzard from the goose, and cut out the wishbone (see page 206). Chop the liver and the gizzard. (Save the neck and heart to make stock, as described on page 220.)

Put the liver, gizzard, onion, and ginger in a medium bowl. Add ½ teaspoon salt, ⅛ teaspoon pepper, and the wine and set aside to marinate for 1 hour.

Meanwhile, to render the goose fat, pull out the excess fat from the cavity and put it into a large saucepan with ¼ cup water. Set over low heat and render it as directed on page 216. Transfer to a container and let cool.

Prick the skin of the goose all over with a fork, particularly around the legs, where there are substantial fatty deposits. Spoon the marinated stuffing into the cavity of the goose. Loosely sew the large opening of the cavity closed with a trussing needle and kitchen twine, if you like.

Place the goose, breast up, on the steamer rack and sprinkle generously with salt and pepper. Place over simmering water, cover, and steam 1 hour and 45 minutes. Then set the lid ajar and steam until very tender, about 1 hour longer. The goose will render an enormous amount of fat during steaming, which will collect in a layer on top of the water in the steamer pot. Remove the rendered fat twice during the steaming time: Take the goose out of the steamer with two large forks and set it on a platter. Remove the steamer rack. Using a ladle or a bulb baster, skim the fat into a bowl; reserve the fat. Add boiling water to the steamer, replace the goose on the rack, and continue steaming.

When the goose is cooked, take it out of the steamer with two large forks. Cut the twine at the opening of the cavity and spoon the stuffing into a bowl. Cut the breast meat off the goose in large, thin slices with a long sharp knife or cut each breast half off the bone in one piece (see page 209) and then slice them. Set the goose on one side and cut off the leg, as for a chicken (see page 208). Cut off the other leg. Cut the legs in half at the joint (see page 209).

To serve, put the goose on a platter and spoon the stuffing over the pieces. Serve with rice and soy sauce spiked with a chopped fresh chile, dried red pepper flakes, or Tabasco.

To reserve the goose fat, skim the fat from the steaming liquid and add it to the bowl with the reserved skimmed fat. Let cool, then cover and refrigerate until chilled. The chilled fat will float to the top of the bowl and harden in a white layer; scrape it off with a spoon and add it to the container with the rendered fat.

SQUAB STUFFED WITH SPINACH AND STEAMED IN LETTUCE

Pigeons Farcis

A squab is a farm-raised pigeon less than four weeks old. The meat is dark, rich-flavored, and tender. The breast meat is served medium-rare. Steamed squab is milder-tasting than roasted or grilled squab. Even fully cooked, steamed squab isn't gamy.

In this recipe, the squab are stuffed with a rich, salty, spinach stuffing flavored with lean salted but unsmoked pork belly, often called salt pork. Use lean salt pork if you can find it, or substitute bacon—it gives the stuffing a smoky flavor that tastes delicious with the squab and is less salty than salt pork.

Manière made this dish with either whole squab or squab from which the breast, rib, and backbone were removed, leaving a boneless casing for the stuffing. His instructions for boning are on page 218, or you can buy boned squabs from D'Artagnan (see page 299). If you like the breast meat medium-rare rather than medium, bone the squab; the breastbone acts as a heat conductor and cooks the meat rather quickly.

The lettuce wrapping has the practical job of holding the juices in the squab—and of dressing up the pale steamed skin of the birds. The lettuce is in turn steeped in the juices, flavoring the leaves with a luscious, rich, meaty flavor.

SERVES 4 AS A MAIN COURSE

4 squab (about 1 pound each), with gizzards and livers if possible

SPINACH STUFFING

6 ounces salted unsmoked lean pork belly (salt pork) or bacon, cut into small cubes

Reserved gizzards and livers from the squab, if any

6 ounces spinach, well washed and large stems removed (4 cups tightly packed leaves; see page 92)

1 medium shallot, finely chopped (about 1½ tablespoons)

1½ tablespoons chopped parsley

½ cup fresh bread crumbs

1 large egg

Bone the squab as directed on page 218, or leave the bones in, as you prefer.

Make the stuffing: Put the pork or bacon on the steamer rack with the gizzards, if you have them, and the spinach leaves. Place over simmering water, cover, and steam 5 minutes. Add the livers, if you have them, and steam 3 more minutes.

Let the spinach cool and then squeeze out as much liquid as possible. Roughly chop the spinach, pork or bacon, and gizzards and livers, if using, and place in a medium bowl. Add the shallot, parsley, bread crumbs, egg, crème fraîche or cream and lemon juice, salt, pepper, and tarragon. Mix well. Taste for seasoning.

Put the lettuce leaves on the steamer rack, place over simmering water, cover, and steam 3 minutes, or until wilted. Remove from the steamer and set aside.

Spoon the stuffing into the cavities of the squab. Arrange 4 lettuce leaves on the work surface so that they overlap in the center to form a square. Lay a stuffed squab, on its back, across the center

3 tablespoons crème fraîche or
    3 tablespoons heavy cream mixed
    with ½ teaspoon fresh lemon juice
¼ teaspoon salt
⅛ teaspoon freshly ground pepper
1 teaspoon chopped fresh tarragon

16 large leaves Boston lettuce

Large stackable steamer or steamer pot
    with insert, or roasting pan with wire
    rack plus another steamer for the
    spinach and pork belly or bacon

of the leaves. Fold the bottom of the lettuce square up over the bird. Fold over the two sides, and roll the bird over to enclose it in the lettuce. Wrap the remaining squab in the same way.

Put the wrapped squab, seam side down, in a single layer on the steamer rack. Place over simmering water, cover, and steam 15 minutes. Then set the lid ajar and steam 5 more minutes.

Transfer the wrapped squab to dinner plates and serve.

Basic Techniques for Steaming Poultry

The basic techniques outlined in this section tell you how to prepare chicken and other poultry for steaming whole and in parts. After years of using a knife to cut poultry, I'm now sold on poultry shears or kitchen scissors. Scissors are less dangerous than knives. A good pair of scissors (I use seven-inch Fiskars with curved serrated blades) cuts through cooked poultry like a dream and can even handle a thigh or drumstick bone on an uncooked average-sized chicken much more easily than any knife short of a cleaver. They are also very useful for tricky operations like taking a wing off the breast at the joint.

✳ STEAMING WHOLE POULTRY

Preparing the Poultry for Steaming Chickens, capons, guinea hens, geese, and turkeys all are prepared similarly for steaming whole. Duck is treated separately on page 213. Small birds such as Cornish game hens, squab, and quail need no special preparation apart from removing the giblets, if there are any. They are rarely trussed, and, as they are usually served whole or cut in half, they are not carved as a larger bird might be.

Start by pulling out the giblets and any excess fat from the cavity of the bird. With the exception of the liver, the giblets may be used to make a poultry stock (see page 220). The liver is too strong to be used in stock; steam it for a warm salad, as on page 54. Rinse the bird under cold water and pat it dry.

To cut out the wishbone, lay the bird on its back on a cutting board with the legs facing away from you. Lift up the skin at the neck end and feel with your fingers for the wishbone. The top "handle" of the wishbone attaches to the breastbone and the two "arms" curve out and down to attach on either side of the neck. Scrape down the arms of the wishbone with a knife until the bone is exposed. Cut around and behind the arms (A) and handle to free them from the flesh. Hook your index and middle fingers behind the two arms and pull down sharply to pull the wishbone out (B).

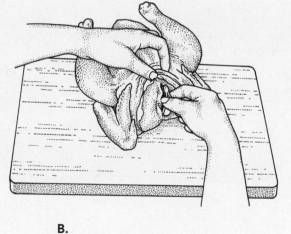

A.

B.

C.

Fold the wings back on themselves so that the wing tips are securely tucked behind the wings (C). Occasionally, when making a stock with the steaming liquid, as on page 220, Manière cut off the last two sections of wing to use in the stock, leaving the meaty first joint attached to the breast.

Sprinkle the cavity of the bird with salt and pepper. Stuffing the cavity with aromatic herbs or vegetables adds flavor to the bird as it steams. I don't recommend steaming a bird stuffed with a carbo-hydrate stuffing because of salmonella concerns (see page 179), but any of Manière's stuffings can be wrapped and steamed sepa-rately as in the recipe on page 194.

Trussing Except for turkey and goose, Manière usually trussed larger, whole poultry for steaming; he sewed the cavities of turkey and goose closed. Trussing gives birds a plump, compact shape that makes them look appetizing, and it holds in the stuffing if there is one. (A trussed bird takes a bit longer to steam, however, particu-larly the legs, so, unless you are presenting the bird whole at the table, you may choose not to truss.) There are many ways to truss. Since Manière assumed that the reader had a favorite way and didn't give specific instructions, I offer one easy method below. However, it is often enough to simply cross the drumsticks and tie them.

To truss the bird, set it on its back on a cutting board with the legs toward you. Cut a piece of kitchen twine that measures about double the circumference of the bird. Center the twine under the top of the back, just below the wing joints. Bring both ends of the twine up over the joints and then around and under the wings (A). Bring the two ends along the sides of the bird, between the legs and body. Cross the ends of the twine underneath the pointed end of the breast (B). Cross the drumsticks over one another and bring the ends of the twine up to cross over the top (C). Set the bird on its neck end and push the crossed legs toward the breast (D). Bring the ends of the twine around the tail and cross them underneath (E) and then back over the drumsticks. Set the bird on its back and knot the twine securely (F).

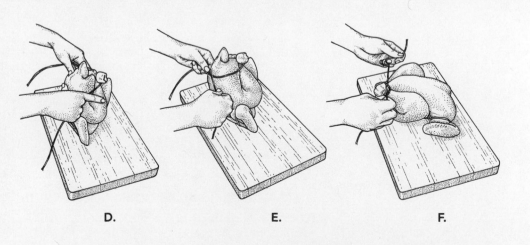

A.

B.

C.

D.

E.

F.

Steaming Breast Down Sprinkle whole birds all over with salt and pepper and place breast down on the steamer rack. Steam according to the times given in the chart on page 182. The bird is done when the juices run clear if a skewer is inserted into the meatiest part of the thigh or when an instant-read thermometer inserted into the thigh registers 160°F to 165°F.

Making Use of Essential Juices A shallow bowl or deep plate (I use an aluminum pie plate) placed on the steaming rack under the bird as it steams will collect the intensely flavored juices. A fresh herb on the plate adds flavor and depth. These juices are an invaluable bonus to the cook. Serve them with the bird as a light, low-fat sauce, rich with the essential taste of the poultry. Or refrigerate them to use another time in soups, stews, or sauces. Oriental and Italian dishes, which rarely use stocks, often call for a small amount of these flavorful *sucrés,* or "sugars," as the juices are called in French. At the very least, the juices will turn a simple rice pilaf into a much more special dish. To keep condensation from the lid from falling into the juices and diluting them as the bird steams, place a damp towel under the lid.

Letting the Bird Rest in the Steamer After the bird is cooked, if you are not browning it, turn the heat down very low and let the bird stand in the steamer with the lid ajar for ten minutes before carving to let the juices redistribute through the meat. Or, brown the bird in the oven (see page 178) and then let stand in the steamer ten minutes before carving.

Carving a Whole Steamed Bird into Serving Pieces If you're cutting up a chicken or capon in the kitchen, it's easiest to do it with kitchen scissors unless you're very handy with a knife. If you're cutting the bird up at the table, use a sharp knife and a cutting board, and be sure to give yourself a bowl for the carcass. (Save the carcass for making stock, as on page 220, for the next time you steam a bird.)

CUTTING THE LEGS OFF THE CARCASS WITH A KNIFE Start by cutting the trussing twine and remove it. Then put the bird on its back with the legs to your right. Take hold of the leg closest to you with your hand or a fork and pull it gently away from the body. Cut through the skin that holds the leg to the body, along the top of the thigh. Bend the leg away from the body and then back on itself to break the hip joint (A).Gently pull the leg off the carcass with the fork (B). Do the same with the other leg. Set the legs

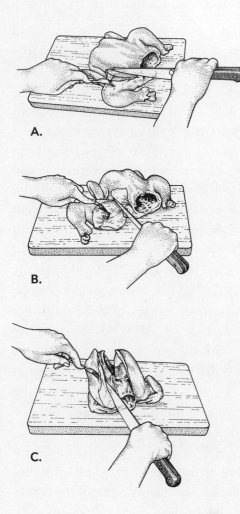

A.

B.

C.

skin side down and find the line of fat that runs along the joint between the thigh and drumstick. Cut along that line to cut the legs in half at the joint.

REMOVING THE BREAST MEAT WITH A KNIFE For chickens and guinea hens, cut the breast off in two whole pieces. Set the bird on its back with the cavity facing away from you. Cut along the left side of the breastbone down to the ribs. Cut through the wing joint so that the wing stays attached to the breast. Then, pulling the meat away from the carcass with a fork, cut and pull the breast half off the ribs in one piece (C). Rotate the bird and cut the other breast piece off the carcass in the same way. Cut both pieces in half on an angle.

For larger birds with large breasts, such as turkey, capon, and goose, it makes the most sense to carve the breast into thin slices. (For a turkey or goose, it may be easier to cut each breast half off the breast bone in one piece and then slice the meat.) Use a long, slender sharp knife and cut thin slices parallel to the rib cage.

Cutting Cooked Poultry into Serving Pieces with Kitchen Scissors To cut a cooked chicken, guinea hen, or capon into serving pieces with kitchen scissors, cut down the center of the backbone from the tail to the neck. Then cut down the center of the breastbone to cut the bird in two. Take one half of the bird and cut through the skin over the top of the thigh that holds the leg to the body. Starting underneath the point of the breast, cut diagonally, above the thigh, through the ribs and then through the backbone to cut the leg off the breast. Cut the leg in half between the drumstick and thigh. Do the same with the other half of the bird. Cut the breasts in half on an angle.

Removing the Skin Since almost all of the fat in poultry is in the skin or the layer of fat underneath it, you may want to remove the skin. This is easiest to do after the bird is steamed and while still hot. (Don't remove the skin before steaming—it keeps the flesh moist.) It makes no difference whether you remove the skin before or after cutting a steamed bird into serving pieces. Scrape off any fat underneath the skin with a small knife.

✴ STEAMING POULTRY PARTS

Chicken parts are practical and steam well. The breast meat always cooks faster than the legs; when the parts are steamed separately, the timing can be adjusted so that breast and legs cook perfectly. Legs steamed still attached to a bit of the backbone are juicier and more tender than chicken thighs and drumsticks.

Cut poultry into halves, quarters, or smaller pieces with a boning knife or poultry shears, as below. Cornish game hens cook quickly and are juicy and delicious when steamed in halves, as in the recipe on page 191.

Salmonella can be passed from raw poultry to other foods if uncontaminated food comes in contact with knives or cutting boards used to prepare contaminated poultry. After cutting up raw poultry, wash your knives and cutting boards in a weak bleach solution, and wash your hands well with soap before touching other food. Never put cooked food on an unwashed cutting board used to prepare raw poultry.

To steam poultry parts, sprinkle them with salt and pepper and put them skin down in a single layer on the steamer rack. (Steaming skin down keeps the juices in.) If steaming chicken breasts, the thin end of one may be tucked under the fat end of the breast next to it to keep the thinner end from drying out. This won't change the timing. Steam according to the times given in the chart on page 182.

Brown the skin under the broiler if you like (see page 179), or pull off the skin.

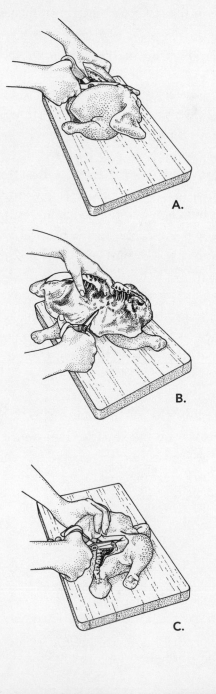

Cutting Raw Poultry into Halves and Quarters To cut a chicken, guinea hen, capon, or Cornish game hen in half with poultry shears, cut all the way down the center of the backbone (A). Open the chicken and cut down the center of the breastbone to split the bird in half (B).

To cut the bird in half with a large knife, stand it on its tail end on a cutting board with the back facing you. Cut down one side of the backbone. Then cut down the other side, and remove the backbone. Lay the bird on its breast on the board and press on the breastbone to flatten. Cut the bird in half through the breastbone.

To cut the halves into quarters with scissors or a knife, pull each leg away from the body and cut through the skin above the thigh. Starting under the pointed tip of the breast, cut diagonally through the ribs to the backbone to separate the leg from the breast (C).

Cutting Poultry into Small Pieces The recipe for Chicken with Fresh Ginger and Scallions on page 185 calls for a chicken cut into smaller pieces. This is easy to do with poultry shears. Cut the chicken into quarters as above. Cut the first two sections of each wing off, leaving the meaty sections attached to the breasts. Put each leg skin down on the cutting board, find the line of fat that runs between the thigh and drumstick, and cut along the line to cut the leg in two at the joint. Cut each thigh and drumstick in half again. Cut each breast half into three or four pieces.

Boning Chicken Breasts and Legs In Manière's recipe for Chicken with Garlic-Parsley Butter and Onion-Raisin Jam on page 192, the chicken is cut into two boneless butterflied breast halves and two boneless legs for stuffing. Use a boning knife to do this. First cut out the wishbone (see page 206). Then cut the last two sections of wing off the meaty top section.

CUTTING THE LEGS AND BREASTS OFF THE CARCASS Pull one leg away from the body and cut the skin over the top of the thigh. Set the chicken on its side and bend the leg back on itself to break the hip joint (A). Starting at the tail end of the thigh, cut the thigh off the bone (B). Pay special attention to the small nugget of meat, called the oyster, that lies in an indentation in the bone at the top of the thigh; when you pass the hip joint, stop cutting and just pull the leg off the bone; the oyster should pull right out (C). Do the same to remove the other leg.

Put the chicken on the cutting board with the neck away from you. Make a shallow cut down the left side of the whole length of the breastbone. Angling the blade into the bone so as to waste as little flesh as possible, continue cutting down to the ribs, holding the knife flush to the bone. Cut through the wing joint. Pull the breast meat away from the carcass with your left hand, and then cut and pull the breast off the ribs (D). Turn the chicken around and cut off the second breast half. (Save the carcass and wing tips for stock, as on page 220.)

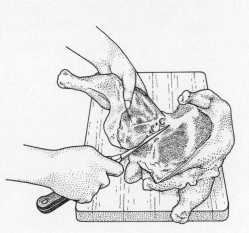

A.

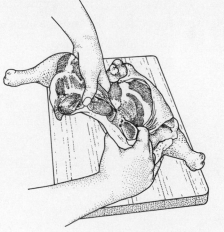

B.

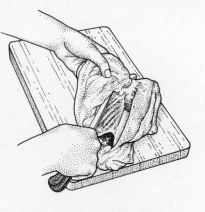

C.

D.

BONING THE LEGS Lay a leg, skin side down, on the cutting board. Feel for the thigh and drumstick bones with your fingers. Put the point of the knife at the exposed end of the drumstick bone. Cut straight down the line of the bone, feeling for the bone with the knife, to the joint between the drumstick and thigh. The bone is now exposed. Do the same with the thigh bone. Carefully cut along either side of the bones and underneath, cutting and scraping the meat off the bones (E). Cut around the hip joint to free it from the flesh (F). Cut the skin around the bottom of the drumstick. Finally, cut around the center joint between thigh and drumstick (G) and remove the bone in one piece. Bone the other leg the same way.

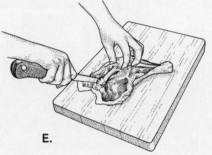

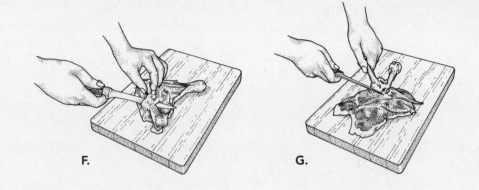

E.   F.   G.

BUTTERFLYING THE BREAST HALVES Put a breast half, skin side down, on the cutting board so that the wing tip is on top. Starting at the thick wing side of the breast, and holding the knife parallel to the cutting board, cut along the length of the whole side of the breast, slitting it from the wing to the tip of the breast (H). Cut under the wing joint and then, still holding the knife parallel to the cutting board, cut through the center of the breast to within about half an inch of the other side so that you can open the breast up like a book (I). Butterfly the other breast half in the same way.

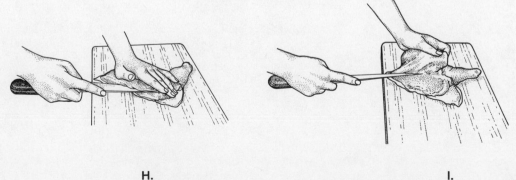

H.   I.

✳ STEAMING CHICKEN BREASTS EN PAPILLOTE

Manière's use of foil-wrapped papillotes is such an easy, practical, and delicious way to steam fish fillets that it made sense to borrow the idea for boneless, skinless chicken breasts. The preparation is exactly the same as for fish (see page 166). Steaming in foil has similar advantages for chicken breasts; it keeps them moist and adds flavor. Follow the directions on page 166 to make the foil packages. A twelve-inch square of aluminum foil is large enough to hold one chicken breast and a reasonable amount of vegetables for one serving.

A breast steamed in foil with just a tablespoon of liquid will take the same amount of time as a skinless breast steamed without foil wrapping (see the chart on page 182). With a bed of vegetables, the breast will take one and a half times the basic steaming time in the chart. Chicken breasts can be substituted for fish fillets and steaks in any of the recipes on pages 130–135; use the poultry chart to determine the timing.

✳ DUCK

Manière steamed whole duck as well as just the boneless breasts. His small French ducks were tender enough to steam whole to a juicy medium-rare, but our larger Long Island ducks don't steam the same (see page 197), so I steam them in parts. Further, I find that when the legs are cut off the carcass they are sometimes tough even after long steaming. I like to steam the legs as a unit, still attached to the carcass—they are exceptionally tender that way. The breast meat tastes pretty much the same steamed on or off the bone. (For those who do want to steam duck whole—so that both breast and legs are steamed to medium—the timing is given on the chart on page 182.)

It's fairly easy to find whole duck, either at a butcher or supermarket; it's relatively hard to find boneless breasts. Therefore, when I want to steam duck, I buy the whole bird and cut it up myself with a knife or kitchen scissors: I cut off the breast, in boneless pieces or on the bone, and steam it to serve with the Black Currant Sauce on page 200 or the Green Peppercorn Sauce on page 232, or as a substitute for guinea hen in the Warm Salad of Guinea Hen with Wild Mushrooms on page 196. The next night, I steam the legs on the carcass to serve as steamed "confit" on page 217, or with Cabbage with Cream and Shallots on page 53. I get two meals out of one duck because I'm cooking for only two; if you're cooking for four, serve breast and legs with either sauce or the cabbage, above.

Preparing Duck for Steaming Pull out the giblets and the loose fat in the cavity of the duck. With the exception of the liver, the giblets can be used to make stock. You can steam the liver until rare (three to four minutes) for a salad, as on page 54. Cut off the extra skin at the neck, and save the fat and skin for rendering, as directed on page 216.

CUTTING OUT THE WISHBONE Cut out the wishbone as directed on page 206. The wishbone on a duck is harder to pull out than on a chicken; you may need to cut around the ends of the "arms" to free them from the carcass.

REMOVING BONELESS BREAST HALVES FROM THE CARCASS To cut boneless breast halves off a whole duck, first cut off the wings. It's easiest to do this with poultry shears, but a knife will work fine. Turn the duck on its breast and wiggle the wings to find the joints that attach the wings to the duck. Cut through the joints and remove the wings (A). Turn the duck over and set it on a cutting board so that the neck faces you. Make a shallow cut down the left side of the whole length of the breastbone with a knife. Then continue cutting down to the ribs, pressing the blade of the knife flat against the bone. Follow the angle of the breastbone and pull the meat away from the bone with your left hand as you go. Cut the meat away from the ribs, continuing to pull the meat away from the carcass. When you come to the white fat under the breast meat, cut through the fat and skin underneath to cut the breast half off the carcass (B). Be careful not to cut into the legs or the skin of the legs. Turn the duck around and cut off the second breast half.

A.

B.

PREPARING THE LEGS FOR STEAMING Now use poultry shears or a knife to separate the leg half of the carcass from the breastbone: With the legs facing you, cut diagonally through the ribs on both sides of the duck, following the line of the top of the legs, all the way to the backbone (C). Turn the duck so that the legs are to the right, upend it on its neck end, and, holding the breastbone in your left hand and the leg end of the carcass in your right, snap the backbone back on itself to break it in half above the legs (D). Trim the skin around the tail and legs and save it for rendering as on page 216. Chop the breast half of the carcass into pieces to use for stock (see page 217).

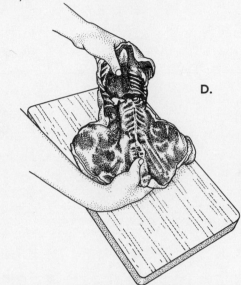

C.

D.

PREPARING A WHOLE BREAST TO BE STEAMED ON THE CARCASS The quickest and easiest way to prepare the breast for steaming is simply to separate it from the leg half of the carcass as above, with poultry shears or a knife. The breast is then steamed on the bone.

Steaming Duck Parts Prick the skin of the legs all over with a fork; lightly score the skin of the breast with a small sharp knife to let it render as much fat during steaming as possible. Sprinkle all over with salt and pepper. Steam the parts skin down, according to the timings in the chart on page 182. Let duck breasts, boneless or on the bone, rest about five minutes before carving to allow the juices to redistribute. Duck parts can be held in the steamer over very low heat with the lid ajar for about ten minutes without overcooking.

Browning or Removing the Skin The skin may be browned to a delicious, crackling crispness as described on page 178 or removed entirely after the duck is steamed; most of the fat in a duck is in the skin or in a layer of fat underneath the skin. It's easier to remove the skin from a duck when it is cooked than raw, and easiest while still warm. It's not possible to simply pull the breast skin off the meat; you'll need a knife to do the job.

If browning the skin of the legs, cut them first off the carcass (see below). Brown the breasts under the broiler rather than in the oven; the broiler browns faster and is less likely to overcook them.

Carving Steamed Duck for Serving Cut the legs off the carcass as for a chicken on page 211: Lay the carcass on a cutting board, skin down, with the drumsticks facing you. Pull the left leg away from the carcass with your left hand, and cut down to the hip joint, pushing the carcass away from the leg with the knife. Bend the leg back on itself to break the hip joint. Cut the leg away from the body completely, taking care to catch the "oyster," the nugget of meat that sits in a cupped indentation of bone at the top of the thigh, just underneath the ribs. Do the same with the other leg. Or, cut the legs off the carcass with poultry shears, as for a chicken, and cut the legs in half at the joint (see page 209).

To carve a breast steamed on the bone, cut the meat off the carcass on the diagonal in large thin pieces, following the angle of the ribs. Boneless breasts can be sliced in the same way or simply cut into thin slices or in half on the diagonal.

Rendering Duck Fat Duck fat has a wonderful, rich flavor that makes just about everything taste delicious. In the winter, potatoes sautéed in duck fat or a warm potato salad dressed with red wine vinegar and duck fat are divine. Use the fat in warm vinaigrettes for salads of bitter chicory or escarole or for bean or lentil salads, or add to stews or rice dishes or soups for flavor. Duck fat lasts for several months in the refrigerator in a covered container, so it makes sense to render the fat every time you steam a duck and just keep adding it to the container. Goose fat (see Smothered Goose with Ginger and Onions, page 202) is rendered in exactly the same way.

To render the fat, cut it and any reserved skin into small pieces and put them into a large saucepan. (A large pan will contain the spattering of the fat as it renders.) Add a quarter cup of water, set over low heat, and simmer, uncovered, until the fat is clear; the fat will sputter at first as the water evaporates. Do not let the fat brown, or it will take on an acrid flavor. When the fat is clear, let it cool, then strain it into a clean container, cover, and refrigerate.

Steamed Duck Leg "Confit" Duck legs steamed on the carcass and then broiled to brown the skin are so meltingly tender, their flavor so rich, and the contrast between succulent meat and shatteringly crisp skin so marked that the legs are reminiscent of confit. True confit was devised as a means of preserving duck through the winter in an age without refrigeration. For confit, the duck is first salted overnight, then poached in fat and stored covered in the same fat. Nowadays confit making could be considered an anachronism, but we still make it because it tastes so good. Steamed duck legs give us something close to the rich taste and luscious softness of confit without the salt and the fat—and they make a delicious winter meal.

To prepare steamed duck legs for two, you'll need to buy a whole duck; take the opportunity to make use of every part of the bird. Cut off the boneless breasts (see page 214), wrap them well, and refrigerate or freeze them to serve them in a salad or with a sauce. Render the duck fat as directed on page 216 to use with sautéed potatoes, in vinaigrettes, or in soups. Prepare the duck legs for steaming on the carcass (see page 215); save the gizzard and liver for a first-course salad to serve before the legs.

To steam the legs, you'll need a large stackable steamer with one or two steaming compartments or a roasting pan with a wire rack that is lifted off the floor of the pan with empty cans or wadded-up aluminum foil so there is adequate room under the rack for the stock.

Make a stock while you steam the duck legs: Cut the breast half of the carcass into pieces with a cleaver or kitchen scissors. Put it, along with the neck, heart, a bay leaf, about ten peppercorns, and water to cover in the steamer pot. Bring to a boil and skim well.

To steam the legs, prick all over with a fork and sprinkle with salt and pepper. Put the legs on a bed of fresh or dried thyme on the steamer rack with the gizzard, and steam over the stock. When the legs are cooked, remove them from the steamer. Skim the stock well, let it cool, and then store covered, in the refrigerator, to use in a soup, stew, sauce, or pasta or rice dish.

To serve the legs, cut them off the carcass (see page 216) and brown them (see page 178). Then steam the duck liver for three minutes for medium-rare, thinly slice it and the gizzard, and serve in a warm first-course salad of bitter chicory or escarole. Follow the salad with the browned duck legs, accompanied by sliced potatoes and apples sautéed in duck fat or by lentils cooked in red wine and duck fat. Alternatively, remove the duck meat from the bone, shred it, and serve it in a main-course salad with the liver and gizzard.

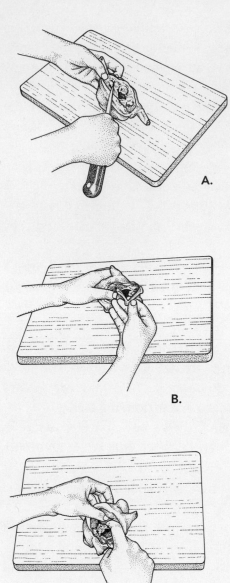

A.

✳ BONING A SQUAB WHOLE

To bone a squab whole, first cut off the neck and wing tips. Then cut out the wishbone as directed for a chicken on page 206. Turn the squab so that the legs are to the right. Press down sharply on the breastbone with the heel of your hand to break the bone. If you don't hear the bone crack, reach into the cavity through the tail end with the middle and index fingers of your right hand. Put your thumb on top of the breastbone and bend the breast back on itself to break the bone. Feel for the joints on either side that attach the wings to the carcass and cut through them (A). With your index and middle fingers, pull out the two V-shaped bones that connect each wing joint to the breastbone (B). Slide your finger between meat and breastbone to loosen the bone (C) and pull out the loose broken pieces of breastbone. Feel inside the cavity and pull off the remaining pieces of breastbone and the ribs.

To remove the backbone, use your thumb to push the thigh bones out of the hip sockets on both legs. Bend the backbone back on itself to break it in half. Pull the top half of the backbone off the flesh and out through the neck opening (D). (It will tear off the flesh easily.) Turn the squab almost inside out and cut through the hip joints (E). Cut and pull the remaining half of the backbone down through the wide opening of the cavity and gently tear and cut it off the skin. Use a knife to scrape the skin off the backbone at the tail end of the bird so as not to damage the skin. The backbone will come free in one piece with a lot of little bones attached; feel inside the cavity with your fingers for any remaining small bones and pull them out. The cavity of the squab is now boned.

B.

C.

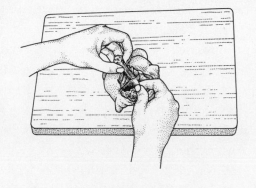

D.

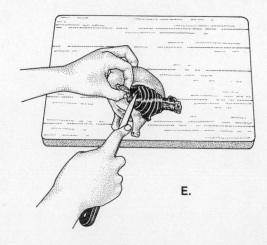

E.

There are no recipes for turkey or rabbit in this book, but you can steam them using the timings in the chart on page 182.

Turkey The chart on page 182 lists times for a whole small turkey and a turkey breast on the bone. While turkey legs steamed on the whole bird are moist and wonderful, steamed turkey drumsticks are tough and I have omitted them from the chart. Don't rely on pop-up timers sold in whole turkeys; they are calibrated to pop at just under 180°F, by which point the breast is dry as sawdust. Pull out the pop-up timer before cooking.

Rabbit I haven't included Manière's recipe for rabbit here, but rabbit can be steamed in pieces, according to the times given in the chart on page 182. Serve it with Herbed Cream Sauce (page 191), Spring Vegetable Medley and Herbed Beurre Blanc (pages 188–189), Sorrel Butter Sauce (page 141), or Cabbage with Cream and Shallots (page 53). If you like, brush the steamed rabbit parts with a little fat and brown them quickly on a grill or in a sautée pan. Be careful not to overbrown the loin; it's small and lean and dries out over high heat.

Rabbit is sold frozen, cut into parts, in many supermarkets, or it can be ordered fresh from D'Artagnan (see page 299). Like duck, rabbit is best steamed in parts, because the legs take three times as long to cook as the loin, the center section of the rabbit that lies just above the legs. If you buy a rabbit whole, cut it into parts (two legs and the loin): Lay the rabbit on its back on a cutting board.

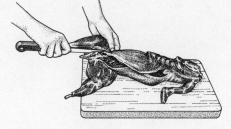

A.

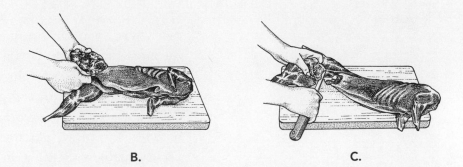

B.   C.

First cut off the legs: Cutting along the fat line where the meaty top of the leg joins the belly flap, cut down to the hip bone (A) and follow it all the way down the inside of the thigh. Break the hip joint (B), just as on a chicken. Then, starting at the top of the leg and holding the knife flat against the hip bone, cut and pull the leg off the body (C). Do the same to cut off the other leg.

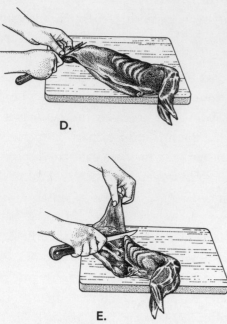

D.

Then, starting at the top of each, cut underneath both hip bones (D) to free them and pull them off the backbone. Cut and break off the exposed backbone at a joint.

To cut up the rest of the rabbit, cut through the thin skin of the belly flap down to the bottom bone of the rib cage (E). Then, holding the knife flat against that rib bone, cut all the way to the backbone (F). Do the same on the other side. Now turn the rabbit over and break the backbone (G) where the rib cage meets the loin. Trim off the belly flaps. Cut off the arms and split the ribs down the center and down the backbone; use them and the other bones for stock.

E.

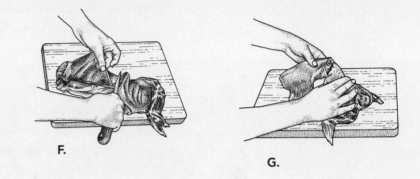

F.

G.

Making Stock as Poultry Steams

The steaming liquid from poultry, like that from steamed meats, is an incredibly useful by-product. With no extra work or additional ingredients, we end up with a broth that can be reduced for quick sauces, soups, rice dishes, and pasta sauces. (Depending on how much water is in the steamer, the liquid may need to be reduced for more flavor; taste it as it reduces and stop when it really has some taste.) When steaming a whole chicken, I usually put the wing tips, neck, heart, and gizzard in the steaming water, to add flavor and to cook the gizzard at the same time; fifty to fifty-five minutes is just the right amount of time to poach the gizzard to velvety softness. Any fat in the liquid coagulates on top after refrigeration and can simply be scraped off with a spoon. (I don't usually find the time to make stocks, so I love having this bonus of steaming liquid in my refrigerator at all times: Suddenly it's possible to make a risotto at the last minute. A simple soup takes ten minutes.) The steaming liquid can also be reused to steam other poultry or meat to give it even more flavor.

With just a little extra work, the flavor of the steaming liquid can be boosted by adding bones, herbs, and vegetables to the water. In the recipe for Poulet "au Blanc" (page 186), Manière did just that, making a rich-tasting bouillon under the steaming chicken to be used as a base for a sauce. Use chicken necks and backs purchased at the supermarket or leftover bones or a carcass from any type of steamed poultry (bones can be frozen until you're ready to use them) to make a stock when steaming a whole chicken. The stock won't greatly flavor the chicken, but the chicken juices will double the flavor of the stock.

When making a stock in this way, use a steamer pot fitted with a rack raised far enough off the floor of the pan (see page 9) to allow room for the bones. I use a large deep stackable steamer or a deep roasting pan and raise the rack with empty cans or crumpled aluminum foil. Chop carcasses, wings, or backs into pieces with a cleaver or cut them with kitchen shears. Put them into the pot with the desired vegetables and herbs (see the recipe on page 186) and cover with water. Bring the water to a boil and then skim it carefully to remove the foam, fat, and bits of coagulated protein that rise to the surface. The French use either a ladle or a special tool called an *écumoire,* or skimmer, for skimming. A skimmer is like a perforated spoon with a flat perforated disk in place of the bowl of the spoon. A skimmer catches the foam and impurities while allowing the liquid to drain through the holes.

After skimming, reduce the heat so that the stock simmers. Add the steaming rack and the bird and steam the bird until cooked. Strain the stock through a fine strainer into a bowl.

If you are not using the stock immediately, set the bowl, uncovered, in a larger bowl of ice and water and chill. (Quick cooling prevents stock from spoiling; warm stock is a good breeding ground for bacteria.) When the stock is cool, cover and refrigerate for up to two to three days, or freeze in a well-sealed container for up to six months. Stock freezes beautifully and can be thawed in a microwave or in a saucepan over low heat. Any fat in the stock will rise to the top and congeal when the stock is chilled and can be easily scraped off with a spoon.

MEATS

anière was sure his readers would be skeptical about steamed meat and pointed out that people imagine wrongly that it tastes bland, like boiled meat. One of my early experiences with steamed meat was the Smothered Lamb with Eggplant on page 246, a steamed lamb stew. The results floored me. The lamb was as flavorful as any I had ever eaten; it wasn't dry or stringy, nor did it fall apart as stewed meat can. The cubes were succulent, springy nuggets of pure lamb essence, and after an hour and a half of steaming, the meat was still pink in the center. The fragrant, winey steaming liquid was clear-tasting and light. The eggplant was mild without a trace of bitterness. The kitchen smelled divine.

As with all steamed foods, steaming concentrates the essential, rich flavors of meats. Expensive cuts such as rack or leg of lamb or filet mignon are always tender; prepared Manière's way, steamed and then browned to acquire a light crust, they are superbly flavorful and juicy with a rich, mouthwatering red color all the way through. Just as successful are the cheaper stewing cuts, such as pork shoulder, beef chuck, and beef shin. These long-cooking cartilaginous cuts hold their hearty flavor as well as their shape but melt in your mouth.

Understanding his readers' hesitation to stray from traditional ways of cooking meat, Manière tempted them with some eye-opening and unusual recipes as well as with his versions of standard French favorites. For example, he gave us an extraordinary recipe for a salted leg of lamb marinated in red wine (see page 243), reminiscent of cured beef or ham but with a sturdy winey taste and the distinctive flavor of lamb. His hot beef "terrine" (see page 232), suffused with the flavors of a Provençal daube, uses the steamer to cook the meat so gently that it "meditates," rather than simmers. His traditional dishes, such as Veal Blanquette (page

240) and Couscous (page 247), are vivid improvements on old favorites.

For those who like variety meats as much as the French do, Manière's recipes show these meats at their best. Even those who have never been fans may change their minds. Steaming is a perfect way to cook these powerfully flavored meats; it softens any acrid flavors, particularly in liver and kidneys, leaving them still potent but much mellowed. Even cooked through, steamed liver is mild and delicious.

Steaming respects the delicate flesh of variety meats so they don't toughen. Manière's steamed Calves' Liver with a Ragout of Cucumber, Spring Onions, and Mint (page 260), in which a one-pound piece of calves' liver is wrapped in a lacy veil of caul fat and steamed to an unctuous medium-rare, is so mild-flavored and tender that it recalls foie gras. The Madeira-flavored Sweetbread Mousse on page 258 is superb; the smooth texture of the sweetbreads makes a mousse that takes minutes to put together but has a buttery texture and rich, elegant flavor. Steamed beef tongue (see page 257) is delectable and soft as butter.

Cold steamed meats are particularly good. Much of the fat is rendered during steaming, so there is less solid fat left on the meat, and it is lean, tender, and flavorful. Serve leftover cold beef chuck, pork shoulder, or beef tongue with mustard, pickles, and coarse salt, or with one of Manière's cold sauces, such as Caper-Anchovy Vinaigrette (page 117), Aïoli (page 145), or Fresh Tomato-Basil Sauce (page 62).

Using the Chart of Basic Steaming Times for Meats

The chart on page 228 gives steaming times for the cuts of meat Manière used in his recipes, as well as some flavorful cheaper cuts, such as beef shin and chuck, that I added because they are so good steamed.

Steaming times for large pieces of meat vary depending on the shape of the meat. An instant-read thermometer makes judging doneness easier: Meat is rare at 120°F, medium-rare at 130°F to 140°F, and medium at 145°F to 150°F. Remember that meat continues to cook for a time after leaving the steamer, and the internal temperature rises by five to ten degrees. Timing is less critical in steaming than in roasting. Even if the meat is a bit less pink than you would like, it will still be tender and succulent and the flavor excellent. Let the meat rest ten minutes in the steamer with the lid ajar over very low heat to allow the juices to redistribute; the meat won't be overcooked.

Cheaper, long-cooking cuts such as shoulder and shank must be cooked until the cartilage and connective tissue break down into gelatin. Judge their exact doneness by touch and taste; both the flesh and connective tissue should be very tender.

Browning

The second column of the chart gives an optional time for browning the meat, in the oven for large cuts or in a sauté pan for steaks. Manière's system for browning meats is the same as for poultry; again, I prefer the broiler to the oven where possible. The broiler browns more quickly than the oven; the meat is subjected to high, dry heat for only a short time. Roast beef is often too large to brown under the broiler and it doesn't brown enough in the oven to make it worth the drying effect of the heat; I don't brown it at all. Pork butt may not fit under the broiler, but it is fat enough to brown well if you can get the oven very hot, and it won't easily dry out or overcook. Turn the oven to broil and let it preheat for at least ten minutes.

Rack of lamb and boneless and bone-in leg of lamb brown beautifully under the broiler. Here we really get the best of both worlds. Steaming gives the meat superb texture and flavor, while the broiler gives it a thin tasty crust of caramelization without drying it out. Turn leg of lamb at least once during the browning to get even color. Rack of lamb need only be browned on the meat side. Brown center-cut pork loin only on the meaty side, under the broiler. Be careful when using the broiler—don't overcook the meat.

Using the Steamer to Keep Meat Warm

It's often necessary to let meat stand after cooking, while you finish a sauce or reduce the steaming liquid, or simply to allow the juices to redistribute through the flesh. (During cooking, the juices flee to the center of the meat. If the meat is cut into right after cooking, the center is pink while the outside is gray; after resting ten minutes, however, the meat is uniformly pink.) Most standard recipes tell you to cover the meat with foil and let stand in a warm place. The steamer works better. After steaming the meat, turn the heat to very low and set the lid ajar; the meat will stay warm without continuing to cook. If the meat is browned under the broiler, you can still let it rest afterward in the steamer; the steam will soften the crust only slightly.

If a recipe calls for letting the meat stand while you reduce the steaming liquid, you can still use the steamer to keep it warm, just as for poultry; see page 180.

Using American Cuts of Meat, and Other Technical Tips

American cuts of meat are different from French cuts. At the end of this chapter (see pages 263–268), there is information about French and American cuts of meat, what cuts to buy, how to substitute different cuts in Manière's recipes, and the best cuts to steam. On page 268, there are tips on using the steaming liquid from steamed meats and on making stocks and steamed "stews" pulled from Manière's recipes.

CHART OF BASIC STEAMING TIMES FOR MEATS

Below is a brief listing of what you need to know to steam meat. For information on cuts of meat, see pages 263–268. Also see the general information on steaming and equipment on pages 3–15.

TIMING
Manière included this chart primarily for quick reference. For more complete information about timings and thermometer temperatures, check the individual recipes. (Or see Using American Cuts of Meat, above.)

Times are for meats taken directly from the refrigerator, not at room temperature.

Trichinae, the parasites that cause trichinosis, are killed at 138°F. Steam pork to at least 140°F, or even 145°F to 150°F, to be safe.

TESTING FOR DONENESS
For large pieces of meat, the steaming time varies depending on the shape of the roast. Use an instant-read thermometer to adjust for shape differences. Meat is rare at 120°F, medium-rare at 130°F to 140°F, and medium at 145°F to 150°F. The internal temperature of meats rises by 5 to 10 degrees after leaving the steamer.

For long-cooked meats, cooked past well-done, judge doneness by texture and taste; both the flesh and connective tissue should be very tender.

TIMING COLUMNS
The timings in the chart are divided into two columns: steaming time and an optional browning time in the oven, under the broiler, or in a sauté pan.

To brown in the oven or under the broiler, shorten the steaming time by the number of minutes in the browning column so as not to overcook the meat. For filet mignon and veal steaks, browned in a sauté pan, just add the browning time to the steaming time (the meat shouldn't cook further in the pan).

LETTING MEATS REST
After steaming, turn the heat to low, set the lid ajar, and let the meat rest 10 minutes to allow the juices to redistribute through the meat. The low heat will not cook the meat further.

STEAMING LIQUID
For long-cooking meats, the steaming liquid usually needs to be replenished during steaming. The rate of evaporation depends on the size and shape of the steamer and the type of meat. Have a kettle of hot water on hand and check the level of the water frequently, adding boiling water as necessary.

	STEAMING TIME	MINUTES TO BROWN
BEEF		
Chuck (4$^1/_2$ to 5 pounds)	2$^1/_2$ to 2$^3/_4$ hours	
(2$^1/_2$ pounds)	2 to 2$^1/_4$ hours	
Filet mignon steak (1$^1/_4$ to 1$^1/_2$ inches thick)		
Rare	5 minutes	2 (sauté pan)
Medium-rare	8 minutes	2
Medium	10 minutes	2
Sirloin steak (1$^3/_4$ pounds, 1$^1/_4$ inches thick)		
Blue	5 minutes	
Rare	8 minutes	
Medium-rare	9 to 10 minutes	
Shin (1$^1/_4$ pounds, 1$^1/_2$ inches thick)	2 to 2$^1/_4$ hours	
LAMB		
Boned and tied leg (6$^1/_2$ pounds)		
Medium-rare	1 hour and 10 minutes	8 to 10 (broiler)
Shank end from 9- to 10-pound leg, with bone (3$^1/_2$ pounds)		
Medium-rare	45 to 50 minutes	8 to 10 (broiler)
Boned and tied shank end of leg (3 pounds)	35 minutes	8 to 10 (broiler)
Rack (2$^1/_4$ to 3$^1/_4$ pounds, trimmed)		
Medium-rare	20 minutes	5 to 8 (broiler)
PORK		
Center-cut loin (4 ribs: 3$^1/_4$ to 3$^1/_2$ pounds)	1 hour	5 to 10 (broiler)
Boston butt (6 pounds without bone)	2$^3/_4$ to 3 hours	5 to 10
Tenderloin (1$^1/_2$ pounds)	20 minutes	
VEAL		
Rib chop (1$^1/_4$ inches thick)	8 minutes	2 (sauté pan)
Loin chop (1 inch thick)	7 minutes	2
Fillet (*grenadin*, see page 239; $^3/_4$ inch thick)	6 minutes	
Top sirloin (2 pounds)	45 to 50 minutes	
CALVES' LIVER		
Whole piece (1 pound)		
Medium-rare	18 minutes	
BEEF TONGUE		
Whole (4 pounds)	3 hours	
VEAL KIDNEYS		
Whole (10 ounces)	7 to 8 minutes	
	(plus 10 minutes with lid ajar)	

Chopped beef tournedos "tartare"

Tournedos Hachés Tartare

This recipe is a lively, playful twist on both steak tartare—lean, raw, chopped beef seasoned with capers, onion, egg, and parsley—and beef *tournedos*—thick round steaks cut from the fillet of beef. Manière mixed lean ground beef with the usual ingredients of a steak tartare, formed it into a roll, and cut thick steaks like tournedos. The tournedos are steamed to medium-rare, then quickly browned on both sides. They are easy, different, and wonderful.

Manière wrapped the beef in a thin strip of pork fatback to keep it juicy. Bacon works as well and adds its smoky, salty taste to the beef. If using fatback, ask your butcher to cut it thin on the slicing machine. The fatback and bacon are delicious but can be removed before serving. Without them, the dish is fairly low in fat. Manière's recipe uses one and a half tablespoons of oil in the meat mixture and one and a half more to brown the tournedos after steaming; for a leaner dish, brown them without the fat in a nonstick pan.

Manière made this with sirloin; you can also use the top round, a cheap, very lean cut. While its leanness makes top round tough and dry in some preparations, in this recipe it's terrific because the meat is first ground, which tenderizes it, and then steamed, which keeps it moist.

SERVES 4 AS A MAIN COURSE

1¼ pounds boneless sirloin, trimmed and
  ground

3 tablespoons finely chopped onion

1 teaspoon chopped shallot

1½ tablespoons chopped parsley

1½ tablespoons capers, chopped

1 large egg yolk

1 teaspoon Dijon mustard

8 drops Tabasco sauce, or to taste

Put the meat in a medium bowl and add the onion, shallot, parsley, capers, egg yolk, mustard, Tabasco, 1½ tablespoons of the oil, the salt, and pepper. Stir with a fork until well mixed.

Transfer the meat mixture to a cutting board and shape into a fat 6-inch-long roll. If using fatback, lay the meat across the fatback and bring the ends up over the roll, overlapping them slightly to cover the meat. Tie the roll with kitchen twine at 1-inch intervals to secure the fat. If using bacon, lay the slices ver-

3 tablespoons peanut or vegetable oil

½ teaspoon salt

¼ teaspoon freshly ground pepper

One 6- by 12-inch thin slice of pork fatback (or 2 to 3 smaller pieces to make a rectangle of that size) or 6 slices bacon

Kitchen twine

Aluminum foil

Large stackable steamer, steamer pot with insert, roasting pan with wire rack, or collapsible steamer basket

tically side by side, overlapping them slightly, on the work surface to make a rectangle. Lay the meat across the center and bring the ends of each slice of bacon up over the roll, overlapping them to cover the meat. Tie a piece of twine around each slice of bacon. Using a sharp knife, and being careful to compress the roll as little as possible, cut the roll into four 1½-inch-thick slices, or tournedos.

Cut four doubled squares of aluminum foil slightly larger than the tournedos. Put each tournedo on a square of foil, and set them on the steamer rack. Place over simmering water, cover, and steam, 8 minutes for medium-rare, 11 minutes for medium. Then set the lid ajar and steam 5 more minutes.

Heat the remaining 1½ tablespoons oil in a large frying pan over medium-high heat. Add the tournedos and brown 1 minute on each side.

Cut off the string and remove the fatback or bacon, if you like. Put the tournedos on plates and serve immediately.

FILET MIGNON WITH GREEN PEPPERCORNS

Filet de Boeuf au Poivre Vert

In his version of classic *steak au poivre,* Manière used green peppercorns—soft, underripe peppercorns preserved in brine—and tender filet mignon. Steaming keeps this lean cut of beef juicy and brilliantly red. This sauce is also excellent with steamed duck breast.

(continued)

Four 6-ounce filet mignon steaks, about
    1¼ to 1½ inches thick
Salt and freshly ground pepper
1½ tablespoons chopped shallots

GREEN PEPPERCORN SAUCE
1½ tablespoons green peppercorns
    packed in brine, drained and rinsed
½ cup Armagnac or brandy
6 tablespoons crème fraîche or
    6 tablespoons heavy cream mixed
    with 1 teaspoon fresh lemon juice
¼ teaspoon salt
⅛ teaspoon freshly ground pepper

Large or oval stackable steamer, steamer
    pot with insert, roasting pan with wire
    rack, or collapsible steamer basket

Sprinkle the steaks on both sides with salt and pepper and place in a single layer on the steamer rack. Sprinkle the chopped shallots over the steaks. Place over simmering water, cover, and steam, 5 minutes for rare, 8 minutes for medium-rare, or 10 minutes for medium. Remove from the steamer.

Heat a large nonstick frying pan over medium-high heat. Add the steaks and brown 1 minute on each side. Add the peppercorns, then add the Armagnac or brandy and carefully light with a match to flame. Shake the pan over the heat until the flame dies. Add the crème fraîche or cream and lemon juice and bring to a boil. Remove the meat to a heated platter.

Let the sauce boil, stirring with a wooden spoon, until slightly thickened and reduced to about ½ cup. Stir in the salt and pepper.

Pour any juices that have collected on the plate of meat into the sauce, then pour the sauce over the meat and serve.

Hot beef "terrine" with olives, anchovies, and white wine
Terrine Chaude de Boeuf à la Façon des Mariniers du Rhône

A *terrine* is both a traditional covered earthenware cooking dish and the food cooked in it—usually some variation on a pâté. Manière's beef terrine is actually an elegant Provençal *daube,* or stew, prepared in the style of the bargemen on the Rhône River, the great river of the region of Provence that feeds into the Mediterranean. Manière made the stew rather extravagantly with New York strip steak, a flavorful and tender cut, sliced into thin strips and marinated in white wine, orange zest, and herbs. Then the meat stews slowly in the terrine mold with the marinade, olives, anchovies, and a delicate dice of vegetables in the steamer. The Mediterranean ingredients come together to make a hearty but perfectly balanced mixture of flavors. Because of the slow steaming, the meat is moist but tender enough to be cut with a spoon. Manière served steamed potatoes with the meat to soak up the sauce.

Depending on the size of your mold, an oval steamer or roasting pan works well for this recipe. If, however, you are using a Pyrex loaf pan with "handles" at either end, the handles can be used to suspend the pan over a nine- to nine-and-a-half-inch pot so that a rack or insert isn't necessary. (Cover both the loaf pan and steamer pot with aluminum foil to steam.)

The meat must marinate overnight, so start this a day before it is to be served. As with all stews, any leftovers are even better the next day.

SERVES 4 AS A MAIN COURSE

MARINADE

1½ cups dry white wine, preferably
    Côtes-du-Rhône

1 strip orange zest, preferably dried

3 sprigs fresh thyme or ½ teaspoon
    dried thyme

2 bay leaves

2 whole cloves

1¼ pounds New York strip steak, trimmed
    and cut into 8 thin slices

1 teaspoon potato starch or arrowroot

3 tablespoons tomato paste

3 tablespoons olive oil

½ cup chopped onions

¾ cup chopped peeled carrots

3 tablespoons chopped shallots

¼ cup Niçoise olives, pitted (see Note)
    and chopped

4 anchovy fillets, chopped

3 tablespoons chopped garlic

3 tablespoons chopped parsley

¾ teaspoon freshly ground pepper

Salt if needed

1 to 1¼ pounds small whole new
    potatoes or halved larger potatoes

Aluminum foil

6-cup terrine mold, 7½-inch soufflé dish,
    or 8-inch Pyrex loaf pan

Large stackable steamer with one or two
    steaming compartments, large
    steamer pot with insert, roasting pan
    with wire rack, or deep 9- to 9½-inch
    pot if using Pyrex pan

 Put all of the marinade ingredients in a medium saucepan and bring to a boil. Lay 2 of the slices of steak side by side in the bottom of the terrine mold, soufflé dish, or loaf pan. Pour one quarter of the marinade over. Use 2 more steak slices to make a second layer and pour another quarter of the marinade over. Repeat with the remaining steak and marinade. Add any orange zest, thyme, bay leaves, or cloves remaining in the pan to the meat, cover, and refrigerate overnight.

Stir the potato starch or arrowroot into the tomato paste.

Heat the oil in a large nonreactive saucepan over medium-low heat. Add the onions, carrots, and shallots, and cook, stirring often, until softened, about 8 minutes. Remove the steak from the marinade and set it aside. Strain the marinade through a fine strainer into the saucepan and bring to a boil. Add the olives, anchovies, garlic, parsley, pepper, and the tomato paste mixture. Taste for salt and add if necessary. Bring to a simmer and let simmer 15 minutes.

To assemble the terrine, spread about one fifth of the vegetable mixture with the juices over the bottom of the terrine mold, soufflé dish, or loaf pan. Lay 2 of the steak slices over the vegetables. Spread with another fifth of the vegetables and then two more slices of steak. Continue layering in this fashion, finishing with the vegetable mixture.

Cover the terrine with a square of aluminum foil, pressing around the rim to seal. Place on the steamer rack over simmering water, cover, and steam 1½ hours. Thirty minutes before the meat is done, add the potatoes to the rack (or put them in a second steaming compartment or in another steamer), and steam 30 minutes.

To serve, arrange the steak and potatoes on dinner plates. Spoon the sauce over the steak and serve.

Note: To pit olives, wrap them in a towel and roll a rolling pin over the towel. Remove the pits.

Sirloin steak with sunchoke mousse

Pavé de Rumsteak à la Mousse de Topinambours

Although the idea of steaming steak is unusual, it makes a lot of sense for this low-calorie dish of lean sirloin steak, particularly so for Manière, who was using French beef, not nearly so tender as ours. Sirloin is exceptionally flavorful but it needs careful cooking to keep it from drying and toughening; steaming keeps it succulent and rosy without adding any fat. Manière advised cooking the steak blue, rare, or medium-rare; the French prefer their steaks this way, but undercooking also offers the advantage of assuring a tender dish. Any leftovers are sublime in cold salads or sandwiches.

Steaming brings alive the warm flavors of the dried Mediterranean herb mixture known as *herbes de Provence*, sprinkled on the steaks. The mixture varies but typically includes thyme, rosemary, bay, basil, summer savory, and, sometimes, lavender and marjoram. *Herbes de Provence* are sold in specialty food stores and in the spice section of many supermarkets, or you can make a mixture yourself with equal parts of these dried herbs.

Manière served the steak with a mousse made from puréed steamed sunchokes, low in fat because it's enriched with low-fat cheese instead of cream. Steamed sunchokes make a magnificent buttery, ivory-colored purée, silky smooth, nutty, and pleasantly sweet, like a delicious winter squash. This low-fat recipe is superb, but if you like, you can replace the cheese with a quarter cup of crème fraîche (or the same amount of heavy cream mixed with half a teaspoon of fresh lemon juice) and two to three tablespoons of butter. Serve this mousse with fish and poultry dishes as well.

Manière made the mousse up to an hour before the steak and then reheated it, in its serving bowl, in a second steaming compartment, while the steak steamed. If you don't have a steamer with two steaming compartments, reheat the mousse in another steamer or in a saucepan over low heat.

Try this recipe with a thick tuna steak, steamed to medium-rare.

S E R V E S   4   A S   A   M A I N   C O U R S E

SUNCHOKE MOUSSE

1¾ pounds sunchokes (Jerusalem artichokes)

⅔ cup fromage blanc or ⅔ cup low-fat cottage cheese, puréed

½ teaspoon salt

⅛ teaspoon freshly ground pepper

One 1¾-pound boneless sirloin steak, about 1¼ to 1½ inches thick

Make the mousse: Put the sunchokes on the steamer rack, place over simmering water, cover, and steam until tender, about 25 minutes. Remove from the steamer, let cool slightly, and then peel with a paring knife. Put the sunchokes into the bowl of a food processor, add the *fromage blanc* or cottage cheese, salt, and pepper and purée until smooth. Transfer to a bowl to keep warm in the steamer (see headnote), or transfer to a saucepan and set aside.

Season the steak on both sides with salt and pepper. Put the steak on the steamer rack and sprinkle with the *herbes de Provence*.

Salt and freshly ground pepper

½ teaspoon dried herbes de Provence (see headnote)

Large or oval stackable steamer, roasting pan with wire rack, or large collapsible steamer basket with removable center post

Place over simmering water, cover, and steam, 5 minutes for blue; 8 minutes, or until the internal temperature of the steak registers 120°F, for rare; 9 to 10 minutes, or until the temperature registers 130°F, for medium-rare. Reduce the heat to low, set the lid ajar, and let the steak rest 5 minutes in the steamer.

Meanwhile, reheat the mousse if necessary.

To serve, cut the steak across the grain into thin slices. Serve with the mousse.

SKEWERED BEEF

Brochettes de Boeuf

Manière's two-step method of steaming and then browning beef cubes on a grill or in a sauté pan makes the beef more tender than if it were simply grilled or sautéed. It also allows us to taste the meat rather than the smoky flavor of the grill. The meat is cooked with very little fat. If you don't have an outdoor grill, a cast-iron grill pan heated on a stovetop burner works well. These pans are inexpensive and easy to use, and they give the beef a surprisingly true grilled flavor. The grill or the pan must be quite hot so as to sear the beef quickly without overcooking it.

Manière served this dish with Celery Root and Potato Purée (page 65).

SERVES 4 AS A MAIN COURSE

1¼ pounds beef sirloin tip or top round, cut into 1- to 1¼-inch cubes

1½ tablespoons Armagnac or brandy

3 tablespoons peanut or vegetable oil

Salt and freshly ground pepper

Metal or bamboo skewers small enough to fit into the steamer

Large stackable steamer (preferably oval) or roasting pan with wire rack

 Put the beef cubes in a bowl, add the Armagnac or brandy and the oil, and stir to coat. Cover and let marinate 2 hours in a cool place.

Heat the grill, if using.

Drain the meat and thread it onto skewers, leaving a little space between the cubes to allow the steam to penetrate. Sprinkle the skewered meat all over with salt and pepper. Put the skewers in a single layer on the steamer tray (you may need to do this in more than one batch). Place over simmering water, cover, and steam, 2 minutes for rare, 3 minutes for medium-rare, or 4 minutes for medium.

(continued)

Meanwhile, if using a pan to brown the meat, heat a large non-stick frying pan or a grill pan over medium-high heat.

Place the skewered beef on the grill or add it to the grill pan or frying pan and brown on all sides, no more than 1½ to 2 minutes in all.

Remove the meat from the skewers and transfer to dinner plates. Serve with the purée, if you like.

STUFFED CABBAGE WITH KASHA
Paupiettes de Choux à la Kacha

This is a Russian dish that appeared in Manière's chapter on foods from around the world. Individual leaves of cabbage are rolled around a kasha stuffing and served with a tart yogurt sauce. Kasha—roasted hulled and crushed buckwheat kernels, or groats; buckwheat is a plant native to Russia—has a distinctive, intensely nutty flavor. It comes in coarse, medium, or fine grind.

I was never a great fan of kasha before I tasted this; now I make the kasha often, without meat, as a side dish. Manière flavored it with ground beef and pork, but it can be made just as well with leftover cooked meats or with ground turkey or chicken. It is cooked with stock—this is a good place to use steaming liquid saved from steaming beef, veal, pork, or chicken—but I often just use water. The stuffing is versatile: Use it to stuff other vegetables, such as zucchini, peppers, or artichoke bottoms (see page 103), or serve it with poultry.

S E R V E S   4   A S   A   M A I N   C O U R S E

KASHA STUFFING
4 tablespoons unsalted butter
3 tablespoons chopped onion
¼ pound ground beef
¼ pound ground pork
¾ teaspoon salt
⅛ teaspoon freshly ground pepper
¾ cup medium-grind kasha
1 cup beef or chicken stock or water

 Make the stuffing: Melt the butter in a medium heavy-bottomed saucepan over medium-low heat. Add the onion, ground meats, salt, and pepper, stirring to break up the meats. Cover and cook 5 minutes, stirring often. Add the kasha and the stock or water, cover, and cook 15 minutes over very low heat. Remove from the heat and let stand, covered, for 5 minutes.

Meanwhile, put the cabbage on the steamer rack, place over briskly simmering water, cover, and steam 2 minutes to loosen the

1 large head cabbage, preferably Savoy,
   damaged or wilted leaves removed
   and cored
1 large egg, lightly beaten

YOGURT-LEMON SAUCE
½ cup crème fraîche or heavy cream
½ teaspoon salt
¼ teaspoon freshly ground pepper
⅓ cup plain yogurt
1½ to 2½ tablespoons fresh lemon juice

Large stackable steamer with one or two
   steaming compartments or roasting
   pan with wire rack

outside leaves. Remove from the steamer and gently pull off the large outside leaves without ripping them; you will need at least 12 or up to 16 leaves. If it becomes difficult to remove the leaves as you reach the center of the head, return the head to the steamer for another 2 minutes.

Pare down the thick center rib of each cabbage leaf even with the flat leaf as directed on page 52. Cut the remainder of the cabbage into quarters through the core end. Wash the leaves and quarters. Put the cabbage on the steamer rack, place over simmering water, cover, and steam 5 minutes. Remove the cabbage from the steamer and set the whole leaves aside. Finely chop the cabbage quarters.

When the kasha is cooked, stir in the chopped cabbage and the egg. Taste for seasoning.

To stuff the leaves, lay 4 leaves on the work surface, the outsides of the leaves down. Mound ¼ cup to ⅓ cup of the stuffing in the center of each leaf. Fold up the bottom edge of each one over the stuffing, fold over the sides, and roll the cabbage and stuffing over to enclose the stuffing. Repeat with the remaining stuffing and leaves.

Place the stuffed cabbage leaves in a single layer on the steamer rack, place over simmering water, cover, and steam 45 minutes.

Just before the cabbage is cooked, make the sauce: Bring the crème fraîche or cream to a boil in a small saucepan. Stir in the salt and pepper and remove from the heat. Whisk in the yogurt and lemon juice to taste (add the larger amount if using heavy cream).

To serve, put the stuffed cabbage leaves on a heated platter and pour the sauce over.

VEAL CHOPS WITH CIDER AND APPLES

Côtes de Veau au Cidre

A well-known recipe from Normandy sauces veal with Calvados, or apple brandy, and cream. Manière made his version with hard apple cider, a bubbly, low-alcohol drink made by fermenting apple cider. If you can't find hard cider, a combination of apple cider or juice, wine, and brandy works well. (Hard cider is not sweet, so standard apple cider or juice makes a sauce much sweeter than Manière intended.) You can also make your own hard cider with the unpasteurized apple cider sold at specialty food stores or cider mills in the fall: Uncap the cider and let it sit at room temperature for several hours or overnight, until the cider foams and you can taste the fermentation. Keep close watch on it: It may take several hours to begin fermenting, but once it starts, it will turn quickly. Reclose the cider and refrigerate until you're ready to use it.

The hint of sweetness in the sauce makes it a good choice for steamed pork tenderloin as well as veal (see the chart on page 228 for steaming times).

SERVES 4 AS A MAIN COURSE

3 cups hard cider or 1¼ cups apple cider or juice mixed with 1¼ cups dry white wine and ¼ cup brandy

4 veal rib chops, about 1¼ inches thick

Salt and freshly ground pepper

5 small (2½-inch) apples, such as McIntosh or Golden Delicious, peeled, halved, and seeded, or 3 larger apples, such as Granny Smith or Golden Delicious, peeled, quartered, and seeded

Pour the cider or apple juice mixture into the steamer pot or roasting pan and bring to a brisk simmer. Sprinkle the chops on both sides with salt and pepper and put them in a single layer on the steamer rack. Arrange the apples around the veal or put them in a second steamer compartment or steamer. Place the steamer rack over the simmering cider, cover, and steam until the chops are just cooked through and the apples are tender, about 8 minutes. Remove two apple halves or quarters from the steamer and set aside for the sauce. Keep the veal and remaining apples warm in the steamer (see page 227) while you make the sauce.

Measure the cider in the steamer and pour it into a small saucepan. If you have more than ¾ cup, simmer it until reduced to

SAUCE NORMANDE

¾ cup reserved reduced hard cider
   (see instructions)

2 large egg yolks

½ teaspoon potato starch or arrowroot

6 tablespoons crème fraîche or
   6 tablespoons heavy cream mixed
   with 1½ teaspoons fresh lemon juice

¼ teaspoon salt

⅛ teaspoon freshly ground pepper

1 teaspoon chopped parsley

Large stackable steamer with two
   steaming compartments or roasting
   pan with wire rack plus another
   steamer, if necessary

¾ cup. Add the reserved apple halves or quarters and mash with a fork. Bring the mixture to a boil.

Meanwhile, in a small bowl, whisk the egg yolks with the potato starch or arrowroot and the crème fraîche or cream and lemon juice. Whisk in the salt and pepper.

Whisk some of the hot cider into the egg yolk mixture to temper it. Then pour it into the saucepan, whisking constantly. Bring just to a boil, whisking constantly, and remove from the heat. Stir in the parsley.

To serve, arrange the chops in the center of a heated platter and set the apples, cut sides down if using halves, around them. Spoon some of the sauce over the chops and apples. Pour the rest of the sauce into a warm sauceboat and serve on the side.

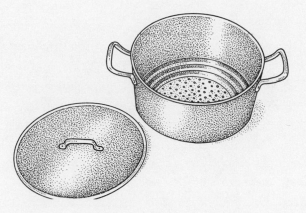

Fillet of veal with red pepper and paprika cream sauce

Grenadins de Veau Sauce Paprika

Veal *grenadins* are thick slices cut from the boneless tenderloin, a lean and very tender part of the animal. (You can also use sliced, boneless veal loin—not quite as tender, but still tasty.) The sauce combines the richness of cream with the sweet bitterness of red bell pepper; the flecks of green parsley against the red-orange sauce are gorgeous. The sauce is also superb on veal chops, pork, chicken, and fish.

(continued)

RED PEPPER AND PAPRIKA CREAM SAUCE

1 medium red bell pepper, cored, halved,
   and seeds and ribs removed

4 tablespoons unsalted butter

1 medium shallot, minced (about
   1½ tablespoons)

1½ tablespoons brandy

½ cup crème fraîche or ½ cup heavy
   cream plus 1 teaspoon fresh lemon
   juice

¼ teaspoon salt

⅛ teaspoon freshly ground pepper

Pinch of cayenne pepper

1½ tablespoons tomato paste

4 boneless veal loin chops or 4 slices
   veal tenderloin (about 7 ounces each),
   about ¾ inch thick

Salt and freshly ground pepper

1 tablespoon chopped parsley

Stackable steamer or roasting pan with
   wire rack

 Make the sauce: Put the red pepper halves on the steamer rack, place over simmering water, cover, and steam 15 minutes.

Peel the skin from the pepper with a small knife or your fingers. Purée the pepper in a food processor or blender; set aside.

Melt the butter in a medium saucepan over medium-low heat. Add the minced shallot and cook, stirring occasionally, until translucent, 2 to 3 minutes. Add the brandy and carefully light it with a match to flame. When the flames die, add the crème fraîche or cream, salt, pepper, and cayenne. Bring to a boil. Whisk in the tomato paste, the red pepper purée, and the lemon juice if using heavy cream. Reduce the heat and simmer 2 to 3 minutes. Remove from the heat.

Sprinkle the veal on both sides with salt and pepper and put it in a single layer on the steamer rack. Place over simmering water, cover, and steam until barely pink in the center, about 6 minutes.

Just before serving, bring the sauce back to a simmer.

To serve, put the veal on a platter or individual plates and spoon the sauce over. Sprinkle with the chopped parsley.

VEAL BLANQUETTE

Blanquette de Veau

Veal blanquette is a creamy white veal stew made with sweet little pearl onions and mushrooms brightened with lemon juice. Manière's blanquette is made with cubed veal shoulder, a cheap and tasty cut. Traditionally the veal is poached and, if not carefully tended, it becomes dry and stringy. The steamed veal cubes stay moist with no fuss.

Manière made a stock underneath the steaming veal to serve as a base for the sauce. Add water as needed during steaming, but add as little as possible so as not to dilute the flavor of the stock. Serve the blanquette with white rice.

VEAL STOCK

1 medium onion, peeled

3 whole cloves

2 small carrots or 1 medium carrot,
    peeled

½ stalk celery

4 cloves garlic, peeled

⅔ cup dry white wine

3 to 4 cups water

2 large sprigs fresh or dried thyme or
    1 tablespoon dried thyme

2 bay leaves

4 large sprigs parsley

1¾ to 2 pounds trimmed veal shoulder,
    cut into 1½- to 2-inch cubes

Salt and freshly ground pepper

12 pearl onions, peeled (see page 84)

8 medium mushrooms, trimmed and
    quartered

SAUCE

3 large egg yolks

1 teaspoon potato starch or arrowroot

6 tablespoons crème fraîche or
    6 tablespoons heavy cream

Juice of ½ lemon (about 1½ tablespoons,
    or 2 tablespoons if using heavy cream),
    or more as needed

1 teaspoon salt

¼ teaspoon freshly ground pepper

Pinch of freshly grated nutmeg

2 cups Veal Stock (see instructions)

Cheesecloth, if using dried thyme

Large stackable steamer or deep
    steamer pot with insert

Make the stock: Stick the onion with the cloves. Put the onion, carrot(s), celery, garlic, and white wine in the steamer pot. Add water to cover the vegetables by about an inch and bring to a brisk simmer.

Spread the thyme, bay leaves, and parsley over the steamer rack; if using dried thyme, enclose the herb between two layers of cheesecloth as directed on page 161. Put the veal cubes on top and sprinkle with salt and pepper. Place over the simmering stock, cover, and steam 40 minutes.

Add the pearl onions and steam 10 more minutes. Add the mushrooms and steam 20 more minutes. Lower the heat, set the lid ajar, and let the meat rest while you make the sauce.

Whisk together the egg yolks, potato starch or arrowroot, crème fraîche or cream, lemon juice, salt, pepper, and nutmeg in a medium saucepan. Ladle out 2 cups veal stock from the steamer and strain it through a fine strainer into a bowl. Gradually add the hot liquid to the egg yolk–cream mixture, whisking constantly. Place the saucepan over low heat and whisk constantly until the sauce just comes to a boil. Taste for seasoning and lemon juice, adding more if needed.

To serve, put the meat, onions, and mushrooms in a deep serving plate and pour the sauce over. Serve with rice.

TOP SIRLOIN OF VEAL WITH SPRING CARROTS, PARSLEY, AND GARLIC

Quasi de Veau aux Carottes Nouvelles

The *quasi* is a muscle cut from the leg of the veal; in America, the muscle is called the top sirloin. According to my French butcher, it is the most tender piece of meat on the animal. It's very lean and consequently dries out easily; steaming helps keep it moist. In this recipe, the meat is steamed with baby carrots and finished with a mixture of garlic and parsley called a *persillade*. If you can't find baby carrots, buy peeled and trimmed two-inch carrots, sold in one-pound packages and labeled "mini" or "baby" carrots.

Before serving, the veal and carrots are browned in the oven. Because the veal has no fat on it, it glazes rather than browns; be sure the oven is really hot (turn it to broil), and don't leave the veal in the oven for longer than ten minutes, or the meat will dry out.

Manière served the veal with Spinach and Mushroom Flans (page 93). If you don't have time to make the flans, steam extra carrots (at least a pound in all).

(If using a roasting pan with a wire rack, use another steamer to steam the carrots.)

SERVES 4 AS A MAIN COURSE

2 pounds top sirloin of veal, rolled and
 tied
¾ pound baby carrots, peeled, or dwarf
 carrots (see page 55)
Salt

PERSILLADE
1 clove garlic, minced
1½ tablespoons chopped parsley

Freshly ground pepper
1½ tablespoons unsalted butter, melted

Large stackable steamer or steamer pot
 with insert or roasting pan with wire
 rack plus another steamer for the
 carrots

 Put the veal on the steamer rack and arrange the carrots around it. Or put the carrots on the rack of a second steamer. Sprinkle the veal and carrots with salt. Place over simmering water, cover, and steam for 10 to 15 minutes, until the carrots are tender. Take the carrots out of the steamer, cover, and set aside in a warm place. Continue steaming the veal until an instant-read thermometer inserted in the thickest part of the roast reads 135°F, 30 to 35 minutes longer.

Meanwhile, preheat the oven to broil.

Make the persillade: Chop the garlic and parsley together. Set aside.

When the veal is cooked, put it in a roasting pan and scatter the carrots around it. Sprinkle the veal with pepper and pour the butter over the veal and carrots. Roast 8 to 10 minutes, until glazed.

Transfer the veal and carrots to a platter. Sprinkle the persillade over the carrots.

To serve, cut the meat into thin slices. Serve with the carrots and with Spinach and Mushroom Flans, if desired.

LEG OF LAMB CURED IN RED WINE

Jambon d'Agneau à la Bourguignonne

This recipe is very special. The lamb is marinated in red wine, salted overnight, and then steamed over the wine. The taste of the lamb recalls a ham but with a more unusual flavor; it's salty, lean but succulent, winy, and meaty. The lamb is traditionally served cold, so it makes a terrific dish for a summer party. Try it with a lentil salad, dressed with a vinaigrette. Although Manière served the lamb cold, I couldn't resist trying it hot; it's delicious reheated in the steamer and served with sautéed potatoes.

The leg needs to be started four days (or five; see instructions) before you plan to serve it. Manière recommended starting it at about seven o'clock the evening of the first day; it marinates forty-eight hours, then stands in salt overnight. Don't salt the leg for more than twelve to fourteen hours, or it will be too salty.

A dome-lidded enameled roasting pan works well for marinating, salting, and finally steaming the lamb.

SERVES 10 TO 12 AS A COLD MAIN COURSE/FIRST COURSE

1 small bone-in leg of lamb (see page 265), trimmed (7 to 8 pounds trimmed weight)

3 bottles young strong-flavored red wine, such as a Côtes-du Rhône, Cahors, or Bordeaux

1 medium onion, peeled and sliced

1 large carrot, peeled and sliced

6 garlic cloves, crushed and peeled

4 small sprigs fresh thyme or 1 teaspoon dried thyme

2 bay leaves

12 parsley stems

2 whole cloves

12 black peppercorns

1 cup coarse sea salt

Large, deep oval dome-lidded roasting pan with wire rack

Put the lamb in the roasting pan or another non-reactive pan just large enough to hold it. Pour over the wine and add the onion, carrot, garlic, thyme, bay leaves, parsley, cloves, and peppercorns. Cover and let marinate in the refrigerator 48 hours.

On the third day, remove the lamb from the pan and transfer the marinade to a bowl. Pat the leg dry with paper towels, wipe out the pan, and return the lamb to it. Sprinkle about half the salt over the meat, turn the leg, and sprinkle with the remaining salt. Cover and let stand overnight in the refrigerator. Cover the marinade and refrigerate.

The morning of the fourth day, remove the leg from the pan and rinse off the salt. Pour the marinade into the roasting pan and bring to a brisk simmer.

Put the leg on the steamer rack, place over the simmering marinade, cover, and steam 1 hour and 15 minutes. Set the lid ajar and continue steaming 30 more minutes. Remove from the steamer and let cool 2 hours. Then refrigerate for at least 6 to 8 hours (or overnight) before serving.

Cut the leg into thin slices as you would a ham and serve cold.

RACK OF LAMB WITH SPRING VEGETABLES
Carré d'Agneau Printanier

I was skeptical about this recipe: steamed rack of lamb? And when a friend helping in the kitchen prepared the rack for me, trimming off every shred of fat, I wondered, could it possibly taste good? It did. Rack of lamb is always a tender, choice cut, but Manière's is more tender and juicy than most; the color is gorgeous, the flavor excellent. A few minutes under the broiler gives the crisp browned crust we expect.

A rack of lamb consists of eight small chops. Manière served four diners with a single rack, but in America a rack is generally only enough for two hungry people or two adults and a child; we need two racks to serve four. As it takes too many pots to steam two racks and all the vegetables at the same time for four, I prefer to make this recipe for two, steaming one rack. Therefore, I cut Manière's vegetable quantities in half. If you want to feed four people, steam two racks in two steamer pots, and serve them with a potato gratin made in the oven and a green vegetable such as asparagus, broccoli, or green beans that can be steamed in minutes in one of the pots while both racks rest in the other.

Manière's oval two-tiered steamer pot allowed him to steam the lamb and the foil-wrapped vegetables in separate compartments at the same time. You'd need a very large, round stackable steamer to do this (I've never seen an oval stackable steamer like Manière's in America), so I have modified the recipe to steam them in two steamers.

Have the butcher trim the thick top layer of fat and meat off the rack and ask him to french, or clean, the rib bones, or not, as you choose (see page 264). Also ask him to cut off the chine bone so it's easy to cut the rack into chops after steaming.

SERVES 2 AS A MAIN COURSE

VEGETABLES

2 medium artichokes

1 lemon, halved (for the artichokes)

2 ounces (small handful) haricots verts or green beans, ends trimmed

¼ pound medium asparagus, 3-inch tips only

 Trim the artichokes to make artichoke bottoms (see page 29), cut each one into 4 wedges, and place in lemon water until ready to steam. Gather the haricots verts or green beans into a bundle and tie with kitchen twine; do the same with the asparagus tips.

Cut a 12- by 40-inch piece of aluminum foil and fold it in half lengthwise. Lay it on a work surface with a long side facing you.

4 small young carrots or 2 medium
   carrots, peeled and cut into 2-inch-
   long bâtonnets (see page 104)
2 small young turnips, peeled and
   quartered, or 1 medium turnip, peeled
   and cut into bâtonnets (see page 104)
¼ medium head cauliflower, cut into
   florets
4 spring onions or scallions, trimmed
   of all but 2 inches of greens
½ cup fresh or frozen peas
1½ tablespoons unsalted butter
¼ teaspoon salt
⅛ teaspoon freshly ground pepper

4 large sprigs fresh or dried thyme or
   1 tablespoon dried thyme
1 large sprig fresh rosemary or
   1 tablespoon dried rosemary
1 rack of lamb, trimmed, frenched if
   desired (see headnote), and chine
   bone removed (2¼ to 3¼ pounds
   after trimming)
Salt and freshly ground pepper

VEGETABLE CREAM SAUCE
Reserved juices from steamed
   vegetables (see instructions)
1 clove garlic, chopped
1½ tablespoons chopped parsley
½ cup crème fraîche or ½ cup heavy
   cream mixed with 1 teaspoon fresh
   lemon juice
¼ teaspoon salt
⅛ teaspoon freshly ground pepper

Aluminum foil
Cheesecloth, if using dried herbs
Kitchen twine
Large roasting pan with wire rack or
   large stackable steamer, or steamer
   pot with insert plus pasta cooker or
   collapsible steamer basket with
   removable center post for the
   vegetables

Arrange the carrots, turnips, cauliflower, onions or scallions, artichoke hearts, and peas in the center and dot with the butter.
Sprinkle with the salt and pepper. Bring the sides of the foil up to
meet over the vegetables, fold the edges together, and then fold
over three times in ¼-inch folds. Fold the open edges over three
times in ¼-inch folds to seal. Put the foil package on the steamer
rack, place over simmering water, cover, and steam 30 minutes.
Remove from the steamer.

Meanwhile, make a bed of the fresh thyme and rosemary on
the second steamer rack. If using dried herbs, enclose them
between layers of cheesecloth as described on page 161. Sprinkle
the rack all over with salt and pepper and lay it, fat side up, on the
bed of herbs. Put the asparagus on one side of the lamb and the
beans on the other. Place over simmering water, cover, and steam
until medium-rare (130°F to 140°F), 20 to 25 minutes. (If you are
browning the meat under the broiler, steam until rare—about
120°F—15 to 20 minutes.)

Preheat the broiler if you are browning the lamb.

When the lamb is cooked, reduce the heat under the steamer to
very low, set the lid ajar, and let the lamb rest for 5 to 10 minutes.
Or, if you like, brown the lamb, meat side up, for 5 minutes under
the broiler, then return to the steamer rack set over very low heat,
set the lid ajar, and let rest.

Meanwhile, make the sauce: Cut off one corner of the foil
package and pour the juice from the vegetables into a small
saucepan. Set the vegetables aside in the foil to stay warm. Add
the garlic, parsley, crème fraîche or cream and lemon juice, salt,
and pepper to the juices and bring to a boil, whisking. Taste for
salt and pepper. Keep warm over low heat.

Transfer the lamb to a cutting board, meaty side up, and cut
between the ribs to cut into chops. Remove the string from the
beans and asparagus. Put the chops in the center of a platter and
arrange the vegetables around them. Pour the sauce into a heated
sauceboat and serve on the side.

SMOTHERED LAMB WITH EGGPLANT

Étuvée d'Agneau aux Aubergines

This was one of the first of Manière's meat recipes that I tried; it convinced me that his idea of steaming meat isn't crazy: It really works. This is a steamed version of a lamb stew. The lamb, vegetables, and herbs are steamed above a white wine–tomato broth, which is reduced to serve as a light, fragrant sauce. The meat is tender, clear-flavored, and not a bit stringy. Each element of the stew stands on its own; the individual flavors are not at all muddied.

Manière used lamb shoulder cubes, which may be difficult to find in America, but cubed leg of lamb or cut-up shoulder steaks also work well.

The stew can be as fat-free as you like; reduce the broth as in the recipe, skimming the fat that rises to the surface. Or, if you have the time to make it ahead, refrigerate the broth separately from the meat and vegetables. When chilled, the fat rises and firms on the surface of the broth and is easily removed with a spoon. Leg of lamb is less fatty than the shoulder.

SERVES 4 AS A MAIN COURSE

4 medium tomatoes, peeled (see page 98), or 6 canned plum tomatoes, drained

⅔ cup dry white wine

2 to 4 cups water

1½ pounds trimmed lamb shoulder or leg, cut into 1½-inch cubes, or 2 to 2½ pounds lamb shoulder steaks, with bone, cut into 3 or 4 pieces each

1 teaspoon salt

¼ teaspoon freshly ground pepper

2 small onions, peeled and cut into quarters, or 1 medium onion, peeled and cut into eighths

½ teaspoon chopped fresh thyme or ¼ teaspoon dried thyme

2 bay leaves

6 cloves garlic, peeled and thinly sliced

2 medium eggplants (about ¾ pound each), seeded and cut into 1- to 1½-inch cubes

¼ cup plus 1 tablespoon chopped parsley

Large stackable steamer, deep steamer pot with insert, or pasta cooker

 Cut the tomatoes in half through the equator and use your fingers to scrape the seeds and juices into a fine strainer set over a bowl. Discard the seeds and pour the juices into the bottom of the steamer pot. Add the wine to the pot along with 2 to 4 cups water, depending on the amount of space underneath the steamer rack. Bring to a brisk simmer.

Place the lamb cubes on the steamer rack, sprinkle with ½ teaspoon salt and ⅛ teaspoon pepper, and place over the simmering wine mixture. Put the onion(s) on top of the meat and sprinkle with the thyme and bay leaves. Scatter the garlic over, then the eggplant, and sprinkle with the remaining salt and pepper. Sprinkle ¼ cup parsley over all, and place the tomatoes on top. Cover and steam until the lamb is tender, 1¼ to 1½ hours. Check the level of the steaming liquid frequently, adding boiling water as necessary.

Transfer the lamb and vegetables to a deep serving platter and cover to keep warm.

Measure the steaming liquid; there should be about 1½ cups. If necessary, boil until reduced to 1½ cups. Skim off the fat and taste for salt and pepper. Pour half the sauce over the meat and the rest into a heated sauceboat. Sprinkle the meat with the remaining 1 tablespoon parsley and serve with the sauceboat on the side.

Couscous with Lamb and Chicken

Couscous

Couscous is both a North African stew and the tiny steamed pasta with which it is served. The grain used for the pasta is not always the same; often, as in this recipe, it is made from semolina (the ground kernels of a particularly hard variety of wheat) mixed with water, but it can also be made with barley or millet. Traditionally, the stew is made in a *couscousière,* a deep pot topped with a perforated steamer insert; the pasta steams over the fragrant stew simmering beneath it. Manière steamed both the pasta and the stew, making a light, clean-flavored broth underneath the steaming meats and vegetables.

His two-tiered steamer was large enough to steam both the stew and the grain in separate compartments at the same time. I found that I needed a large stackable steamer with two steaming compartments just to make the stew, and another steamer for the grain. (A large roasting pan with a wire rack is also large enough to steam the stew; but steam the chick peas separately because they'll fall through the rack.) The easiest way to do this is to steam the stew several hours or a day ahead. Then rewarm it in a steamer or in the broth in a deep pot while you steam the couscous in another steamer.

You can also use this recipe as a model to make a fish couscous, using small whole lean white-fleshed fish such as red snapper, porgy, or sea bass or fish fillets or steaks of cod, halibut, tilefish, or monkfish. (Use the chart on page 112 to determine the steaming times for the fish.)

Keep an eye on the level of the steaming liquid as the stew cooks and add more as needed; you'll need about twelve cups of broth to serve with the stew.

If you haven't the patience to trim raw artichoke bottoms, steam the artichokes separately, whole, as directed on page 29, then simply pull off the leaves (use them for Artichoke Mayonnaise on page 31) and scoop the inedible choke out of the bottoms.

SERVES 6 TO 8 AS A MAIN COURSE

4 medium carrots, peeled, halved
    lengthwise and then crosswise

6 small turnips, peeled and halved, or
    4 medium turnips, peeled and
    quartered

4 stalks celery, cut into 3-inch bâtonnets
    (see page 104)

4 medium tomatoes, cored and quartered

4 cloves garlic, coarsely chopped

12 sprigs parsley

4 sprigs fresh or dried thyme

To make the broth, put half a carrot and half a turnip in the steamer pot. Add half the celery, the tomatoes, garlic, parsley, thyme, bay leaves, the 1 teaspoon harissa, and ¼ teaspoon each salt and pepper. Add 3 quarts water, or as much as will fit under the steamer rack, and bring to a brisk simmer.

Put the lamb on the steamer rack and sprinkle with salt and pepper. Scatter the coriander over the lamb, place over the simmering water, cover, and steam 45 minutes.

Meanwhile, if you have a stackable steamer with two steaming compartments, steam the couscous with the salt in a second com-

2 small bay leaves

1 teaspoon harissa, plus extra for serving
   (see Note)

Salt and freshly ground pepper

3 quarts water, approximately

2¼ pounds lamb neck or lamb shoulder
   chops with bone or 1¾ pounds
   boneless leg of lamb, cut into 2-inch
   chunks

2 small handfuls fresh coriander leaves

COUSCOUS

2 pounds couscous

2 teaspoons salt

8 tablespoons unsalted butter, cut
   into bits

4 medium artichokes

1 lemon, halved (for the artichokes)

1 chicken (about 3½ pounds), cut
   into 8 pieces (see page 210)

1 large red bell pepper, cored, halved,
   seeds and ribs removed, and cut into
   ¾-inch-wide strips

2 medium zucchini, halved lengthwise
   and cut into 2-inch chunks

1 medium eggplant, peeled and cut into
   1½-inch cubes, or 3 Chinese eggplants,
   unpeeled, halved lengthwise and cut
   into 2-inch chunks

1 cup cooked chick peas

8 merguez sausages (see Note)

Cheesecloth

Large stackable steamer with two
   compartments, two large steamer
   pots with inserts, or large roasting pan
   with wire rack plus another steamer
   for the couscous (see page 249)

partment as directed on page 249 for 30 minutes, stirring the grain with a fork every 10 minutes. Or steam it in a second steamer. Transfer it to a baking dish or jelly-roll pan and add the butter as on page 249.

While the lamb steams, trim the artichokes to artichoke bottoms, as directed on page 29. Cut each bottom in half and place in lemon water until ready to steam.

When the lamb has steamed 45 minutes, put the chicken pieces on top of the lamb and add the bell pepper, zucchini, and eggplant, along with the remaining carrots, turnips, and celery. (Use a second compartment, if you have one.) Sprinkle with salt and pepper, cover, and steam 40 more minutes. Add the chick peas and steam 5 more minutes. Rewarm the couscous in a second steamer for 15 minutes.

Meanwhile, heat a large frying pan over medium-high heat. Prick the sausages all over and add them to the pan. Sauté until cooked through and browned, 5 to 8 minutes. Drain on paper towels.

Strain the steaming liquid and measure it; you need 12 cups. If there is more, reduce it over high heat.

To serve, spoon the couscous onto a large serving platter. Rake it quickly with a fork to make sure there are no lumps. Arrange the lamb, chicken, and vegetables on another platter. Pour the strained broth into a soup tureen or large bowl. Put some harissa in a small serving bowl and serve alongside. Let each guest serve himself a plate of couscous, topped with meats and vegetables and some of the broth poured over to moisten the grain.

Note: Harissa is a spicy paste made with chile peppers, garlic, oil, and sometimes coriander. It is sold in small cans or tubes in specialty stores.

Merguez is a thin, spicy sausage made with either lamb or beef (but never pork). Use kielbasa if you can't find merguez.

STEAMED COUSCOUS

Couscous

Packaged couscous is almost always "instant" or "precooked," so that it simply needs to be steeped for a short time in a measured quantity of water to rehydrate it. Steeped in this way, however, couscous is heavy and gummy. Steaming takes a little longer, but the results merit the effort. Steamed couscous is wonderfully light, dry, and fluffy, with each grain separate from the others.

Some cookbooks call for steaming couscous uncovered so that condensation from the steam doesn't fall back on the grain and make it gummy—but then it must be removed from the steamer midway through the steaming and moistened with water. Manière steamed couscous covered, under a layer of cheesecloth, protecting it from condensation and enabling him to eliminate the intermediate step of moistening.

You'll need a large steamer pot—at least 10 inches in diameter and larger if possible—so that the couscous isn't piled so deeply that it doesn't steam.

SERVES 4 AS A SIDE DISH

1 pound couscous

1 teaspoon salt

4 tablespoons unsalted butter, cut into
   bits, at room temperature

Cheesecloth

Large stackable steamer, steamer pot
   with insert, roasting pan with wire
   rack, or large collapsible steamer
   basket with removable center post

 Put the couscous in a fine strainer and rinse under cold running water, stirring with your hand to wet all the grains. Cut a piece of cheesecloth large enough so that when doubled it will cover the bottom of the steamer rack and generously overhang the sides. Dampen the cloth and center it over the steamer rack. Turn the couscous onto the steamer rack and sprinkle with the salt. Fold the overhanging edges of cheesecloth over to cover the couscous.

Place over simmering water, cover, and steam 10 minutes. Uncover the steamer and stir the couscous with a fork to break up the clumps. Be sure to reach the sides and bottom of the couscous. Cover the couscous with the cheesecloth and then the lid and steam 10 more minutes. Stir again, cover, and steam a final 10 minutes.

Transfer the couscous to a large baking dish or a jelly-roll pan. Stir in the butter with a fork. Spread the grain out in the dish or pan to cool. Then rub the couscous between the palms of your hands to separate the grains. Cover with a cloth until ready to use.

Skewered Lamb with Couscous, Chick Peas, and Raisins

Brochettes d'Agneau au Cumin

Manière marinated cubed lamb in cumin, vinegar, and paprika and steamed it over fresh thyme and coriander sprigs, then browned the skewered lamb cubes on a grill. If you don't have an outside grill, use a cast-iron grill pan. Manière used no oil in the marinade and the bare minimum to brown the meat. (To use the smallest amount of oil possible, brush it on the lamb with a pastry brush.)

The lamb is served with couscous, steamed and bejeweled with chick peas and raisins. Steam the couscous while the lamb marinates and then rewarm it just before serving.

⅓ cup red or white wine vinegar

⅔ cup water

1 rounded teaspoon cumin seeds

1½ tablespoons sweet Hungarian paprika

Bunch of fresh coriander or 20 coriander
  seeds, crushed in a mortar and pestle
  or with the bottom of a heavy saucepan

1 small bunch fresh thyme or 1 teaspoon
  dried thyme

1 pound trimmed boneless lamb shoulder
  or leg, cut into 1- to 1¼-inch cubes

COUSCOUS

1 pound couscous

1 teaspoon salt

1 cup cooked chick peas

¼ cup raisins

3 tablespoons unsalted butter, cut into
  bits

Salt and freshly ground pepper

About 2 tablespoons olive oil

Combine the vinegar, water, cumin, and paprika in a large bowl. If using coriander seeds and/or dried thyme, add it now. Add the lamb cubes and stir to coat them with the marinade. Let marinate 1 hour in a cool place.

While the lamb marinates, steam the couscous with the salt on a cheesecloth-lined rack as directed on page 249. Transfer it to a bowl. Add the chick peas. Put the raisins on the cheesecloth-lined rack, place over simmering water, cover, and steam 5 minutes to warm through. Add the raisins to the couscous along with the butter and stir well. Set aside in a warm place. Remove the cheesecloth from the rack but save it to rewarm the couscous.

Heat a grill, a cast-iron grill pan, or the broiler.

Drain the lamb cubes and thread them onto skewers, leaving a bit of space between each cube to allow the steam to penetrate. Sprinkle the lamb all over with salt and pepper. Make a bed of the fresh coriander and/or thyme, if using, on the steamer rack. Put the lamb skewers on the rack. Place over simmering water, cover, and steam until the lamb just firms up, about 3 minutes for medium-rare, 4 minutes for medium. Remove from the steamer and set aside.

Line the steamer rack again with the cheesecloth, add the couscous mixture, and place over simmering water. Cover with the cheesecloth and the lid and steam about 5 minutes, to rewarm.

Meanwhile, pour the oil onto a plate and roll the skewered lamb in it (or use a brush). Put the lamb skewers on the grill or

Cheesecloth

Metal or bamboo skewers small enough to fit into the roasting pan

Roasting pan with wire rack plus another steamer for the couscous (see page 249)

grill pan, or under the broiler, and brown on all sides, turning, about 2 minutes. Do not overcook.

Put the skewers on plates and serve with the couscous.

PORK

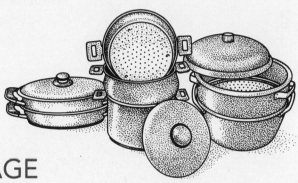

PORK WITH GARLIC AND SAGE
Échine de Porc à la Sauge

The *échine* is a cut of pork that includes part of the neck and shoulder of the animal. There's no exact equivalent in America, but fresh Boston butt, cut from the shoulder, is a delicious substitute; it's a succulent piece of meat that becomes very tender with long steaming and melts in your mouth. It's more commonly sold smoked than fresh; make sure you're buying fresh. Because the flavor and texture of the meat is so luscious, it needs no sauce. The pork is browned in the oven and served with creamy stuffed potatoes gratinéed with cheese.

Sage is a traditional flavoring for pork in both France and America, but other pungent herbs such as rosemary, thyme, marjoram, or oregano are also excellent with pork.

Manière's *échine* served only four, but a six-pound Boston butt serves twelve generously. Steam the pork for a large party, or prepare it for fewer guests and then reheat the leftovers in the steamer or use in hot sandwiches or soup.

(continued)

1 fresh Boston butt (about 6 pounds),
    trimmed, boned, and tied
4 medium garlic cloves, cut into slivers
4 large sprigs fresh sage or 2 tablespoons
    powdered sage
Salt and freshly ground pepper

Twice-Cooked Potatoes (page 91)

Cheesecloth, if using powdered sage
Large stackable steamer, steamer pot
    with insert, or roasting pan with wire
    rack

Using a small sharp knife, make slits in the pork and slide a garlic sliver into each. Lay the fresh sage on the steamer rack; or, if using powdered sage, enclose it between two layers of cheesecloth as directed on page 161.

Sprinkle the pork all over with salt and pepper and put it on top of the sage. Place over simmering water, cover, and steam 2½ hours. Then set the lid ajar and steam 30 more minutes, or until tender.

Meanwhile, make the potatoes.

Preheat the broiler, or turn the oven to broil to get it as hot as possible.

Put the pork under the broiler or in the oven and broil or roast until browned, 5 to 10 minutes. (You can brown the potatoes along with the pork.)

Put the pork in the center of a large platter. Arrange the potatoes around the pork and serve hot.

PORK WITH WHOLE-GRAIN MUSTARD

Côtes de Porc aux Graines de Moutarde

Manière made this dish with pork chops cut from the loin. American pork is leaner than French pork and the loin can be dry, so I prefer to make the recipe with a whole pork tenderloin. The tenderloin is also lean, but when steamed it is more tender and juicier than the loin. For the sauce, the vermouth and cream are flavored and thickened with crunchy whole-grain mustard.

4 large fresh sage leaves or 1 tablespoon
    powdered sage
1 pork tenderloin (about 1¼ pounds)
Salt and freshly ground pepper

Make a bed of the fresh sage leaves on the steamer rack. If using powdered sage, enclose it between two layers of cheesecloth as directed on page 161. Sprinkle the pork all over with salt and pepper and put it on top

MUSTARD SAUCE

1½ tablespoons unsalted butter

1 teaspoon chopped shallot

3 tablespoons dry vermouth, such as
Noilly Prat

½ cup crème fraîche or ½ cup heavy
cream mixed with 1 teaspoon fresh
lemon juice

⅛ teaspoon freshly ground pepper

2 teaspoons whole-grain Dijon mustard

Salt, if needed

Cheesecloth, if using powdered sage

Large stackable steamer or roasting pan
with wire rack

of the sage. Place over simmering water, cover, and steam until an instant-read thermometer inserted into the thickest part of the pork registers 150°F, about 20 minutes. Let the meat rest in the steamer over low heat, with the lid ajar, for 5 to 10 minutes.

Cut the pork on an angle into 1-inch-thick slices.

Make the sauce: Melt the butter in a large frying pan over medium-low heat. Add the shallot and cook until translucent, 2 to 3 minutes. Add the vermouth and crème fraîche or cream and lemon juice to the pan and stir to combine. Add the pork slices in a single layer and stir to coat with the sauce. Add the pepper and bring to a simmer. Simmer until the sauce has reduced slightly and thickened.

Remove the pork to a serving platter. Stir the mustard into the sauce and taste for seasoning; depending on the saltiness of the mustard, the sauce may not need salt. Pour the sauce over the meat and serve immediately.

"GREEN CHICKEN" (STUFFED CABBAGE)
Chou Farci ou Poule Vert

....

Cabbage with pork is peasant food. Regional recipes of southwestern France combine the two to make hearty and delicious soups called *potées* and *garbures*. Some recipes replace some of the meat in the soup with cabbage leaves stuffed with a bread crumb–pork mixture. Each of these little stuffed cabbage rolls is called a *poule vert*, or "green chicken." Manière's Green Chicken is larger (a bigger hen) and more elegant: Cabbage leaves are layered with a pork sausage stuffing, then carefully drawn up to re-form the cabbage head. Typically, stuffed cabbage made in this way is braised and simply sauced with the braising liquid; Manière's cabbage glistens with a tarragon butter sauce.

Manière wrapped the cabbage in a thin piece of pork fat to keep it moist and hold it together during steaming. Ask your butcher to cut the fatback very thin on the slicing machine; the fat is delicious to eat, or it can be removed before serving. If you can't get fatback, sliced bacon will keep the cabbage moist and give it a rich, smoky, salty flavor.

Watch the level of water in the steamer carefully as the cabbage cooks, and add more as needed.

For a less rich sauce, steam the cabbage over chicken broth or over steaming liquid saved from steaming a chicken (see page 220). Then, when the cabbage is cooked, reduce the broth until flavorful and spoon over the slices of cabbage.

(continued)

PORK STUFFING

1 large head cabbage, preferably Savoy
(see page 50)

¼ pound fatback or bacon, cut into
¼-inch dice

3 large eggs, lightly beaten

2 medium cloves garlic, mashed in a
mortar to a paste or very finely
chopped

1 pound sausage meat (see Note)

3 tablespoons crème fraîche or
3 tablespoons heavy cream mixed
with ½ teaspoon fresh lemon juice

1½ cups fresh bread crumbs

3 tablespoons chopped parsley

⅛ teaspoon freshly ground pepper

Salt, if needed

Thin sheet pork fatback, about 3 by 24
inches (or 2 to 3 pieces to make up a
rectangle of that size) or 4 slices bacon

3 medium carrots, peeled, halved
lengthwise, and cut into 2-inch lengths

6 small or 3 medium turnips, peeled and
cut into quarters if small or eighths if
medium

6 small or 3 medium leeks, trimmed,
halved lengthwise, and well washed

TARRAGON BUTTER SAUCE

¼ cup crème fraîche or heavy cream

¼ teaspoon salt

⅛ teaspoon freshly ground pepper,
preferably white

6 tablespoons unsalted butter, cut into
pieces

Juice of ½ lemon (about 2 tablespoons),
or to taste

1½ tablespoons snipped fresh tarragon
leaves

 Make the stuffing: Pull off any damaged leaves from the outside of the head of cabbage and cut out the core. Put the cabbage and fatback or bacon on the steamer rack, place over simmering water, cover, and steam 10 minutes. Put the fatback in a bowl and set aside.

Gently pull off the large outer leaves of the cabbage without ripping them; you need 17 whole leaves. If it becomes difficult to remove the leaves as you get into the center of the head, return the head to the steamer for another 2 minutes to loosen them. Then pare down the thick center rib of each leaf even with the leaf, as directed on page 52.

Cut the remaining center part of the cabbage into quarters through the core end and finely chop it. Add it to the fatback.

Add the eggs, garlic, sausage, crème fraîche or cream and lemon juice, bread crumbs, parsley, and pepper. Mix well. Steam a small ball of the stuffing and taste for seasoning. Add salt, if needed.

To stuff the cabbage, if using fatback, cut four 24-inch lengths of kitchen twine. If using bacon, cut a double layer of cheesecloth about 24 inches square, moisten it with cold water, and set it on the work surface. Lay the 4 largest cabbage leaves on the work surface, or on top of the cheesecloth, the outer sides down, overlapping them by 1 to 2 inches in the center (like the petals of a flower). Spread one quarter of the stuffing over the center 5 inches of the leaves. Lay 4 more leaves over the stuffing, overlapping them in the center as before. Spread with one third of the remaining stuffing. Overlap 3 more leaves to cover the stuffing, and spread half of the remaining stuffing over. Repeat with 3 more cabbage leaves and the rest of the stuffing. Cover with the remaining 3 leaves.

To re-form the cabbage head, fold the leaves up and over the center to cover the stuffing. If using fatback, wrap the fat around the re-formed head and tie the head: Center one piece of twine under the cabbage and bring the ends up over the top and tie them. Give the cabbage a quarter turn and tie it again. Give the cabbage an eighth of a turn and tie the third string around. Then give it another quarter turn and tie it.

If using cheesecloth, lay 2 pieces of bacon over the top of the cabbage head, and lay the other 2 slices over them to form a cross. Bring up the four sides of the cheesecloth to enclose the cabbage and tie at the top with twine.

1½ tablespoons snipped fresh chervil
leaves or 1 teaspoon snipped fresh
tarragon leaves plus 2 teaspoons
snipped parsley leaves

Kitchen twine

Cheesecloth, if using bacon

Large stackable steamer with one or two
steaming compartments or roasting
pan with wire rack

Put the cabbage on the steamer rack, place over simmering water, cover, and steam 30 minutes.

Add the vegetables to the steamer rack, or to a second steaming compartment placed over the cabbage, and steam 40 more minutes.

About 10 minutes before the cabbage is cooked, make the sauce: Bring the crème fraîche or cream to a boil in a small saucepan. Add the salt and pepper. Whisk in the butter a piece at a time, adding more as it is emulsified into the sauce, and bring the sauce to a boil. Remove from the heat and whisk in the lemon juice and herbs. Taste, and add more lemon juice if necessary.

To serve, untie the cabbage. Remove the cheesecloth and bacon, if using, or remove the fatback, if desired. Place the cabbage in the center of a serving platter and arrange the vegetables around it. Pour the sauce into a heated sauceboat and serve on the side. Cut the cabbage into wedges with a serrated knife.

Note: The stuffing can be made with a commercial sausage, which is likely to be flavored with some combination of herbs and spices. Or make your own, using a mixture of two thirds of a pound of ground lean pork mixed with one third of a pound of ground pork fat. I add a chopped small onion; minced garlic or shallots or herbs such as thyme and parsley also taste good with the cabbage. Season the sausage with half a teaspoon of salt and a quarter teaspoon of pepper.

CHOUCROUTE

Formidable Choucroute Garnie

Like the stuffed cabbage on page 253, choucroute garnie is a satisfyingly hearty regional French dish of pork and cabbage. Here the region is Alsace, an area of France that borders Germany, in which country choucroute is called *sauerkraut*. Choucroute can be a very rich plate, with lots of delicious pork fat and sausage. Manière's is lighter but no less tasty; a great deal of the fat is rendered during the steaming. This is a surprisingly quick dish to put together. Everything is already cooked; the steaming is only to rewarm the ingredients and marry the flavors.

The French have a great wealth of cured and smoked cuts of pork as well as a variety of different pork sausages. We can't find all of those Manière used, but we have enough to make a marvelous choucroute. We can use a piece of smoked pork loin and smoked shoulder butt instead of the smoked pork shank and shoulder or *échine* (see page 251) in Manière's recipe. If you can't find the smoked loin, you'll be very happy with two more pounds of smoked shoulder butt, a wonderfully succulent, tender piece of pork.

This dish can be made with fresh or prepared sauerkraut, available jarred or in plastic bags in supermarkets or specialty food stores. (Hebrew National makes a very good quality prepared sauerkraut.) Serve choucroute with lots of Dijon mustard.

SERVES 8 AS A MAIN COURSE

1 medium carrot, peeled and thinly sliced

1 stalk celery

1 large sprig fresh or dried thyme or
½ teaspoon dried thyme

2 bay leaves

1 small bunch parsley, tied in a bundle
with kitchen twine

4 pounds fresh or precooked sauerkraut,
drained

1½ tablespoons juniper berries

1 teaspoon caraway seeds

1 teaspoon black peppercorns

1 medium onion

6 whole cloves

1 smoked pork shoulder butt (about
2 pounds), sliced ¾ to 1 inch thick

¾ pound lean slab bacon

8 small waxy potatoes (no more than
1½ inches in diameter), peeled, or
4 medium potatoes, peeled and cut
in half

2 pounds smoked pork loin, cut into
chops (or into 1-inch-thick pieces if
boneless), or additional smoked
shoulder butt, cut into slices as above

8 hot dogs, preferably kosher

2 pounds ham, cut into 4 slices

Dijon mustard, for serving

Kitchen twine

Large stackable steamer, steamer pot
with insert, or pasta cooker

Put the carrot, celery, thyme sprig, if using, bay leaves, and parsley on the steamer rack. Cover with half of the sauerkraut. Sprinkle with the dried thyme, if using, and with half of the juniper berries, caraway seeds, and peppercorns. Stick the onion with the cloves and put it in the center of the bed of sauerkraut. Add the smoked pork shoulder butt. Cover with the rest of the sauerkraut and sprinkle with the rest of the juniper berries, caraway seeds, and peppercorns. Put the bacon on top and surround with the potatoes. Place over simmering water, cover, and steam 10 minutes.

Add the smoked pork loin, if using, and steam 10 more minutes. Add the hot dogs and ham and steam 5 more minutes.

To serve, remove all of the meat from the steamer. Cut the bacon into ¼-inch-thick slices. Discard the onion, parsley, and thyme sprig, if using. Mound the sauerkraut in the center of an oval serving platter and arrange the pork butt, bacon, and pork loin around it. Lean 2 ham slices against each long side of the mound of sauerkraut, and place 2 hot dogs in between each slice of ham. Arrange a "bouquet" of potatoes at each end of the platter. Serve with lots of Dijon mustard.

BEEF TONGUE WITH PARSLEY SAUCE

Langues de Porc (ou d'Agneau) Sauce Persil

Manière made this dish with either lamb or pork tongue, both of which are smaller than a beef tongue and take only fifty minutes to steam. But lamb and pork tongue are hard to find in America, so I've adapted the recipe for beef tongue. Although it takes much longer to steam, it is worth the time; it's velvety and soft as butter with a rich beef flavor. You may need to order fresh beef tongue from the butcher; smoked tongue is more usual.

Beef tongue is delicious hot but can also be served cold as a first course or in a salad or sandwich. The steaming liquid has a strong meaty flavor, good in bean or lentil soup.

Start this recipe the day before you plan to serve it.

SERVES 6 TO 8 AS A MAIN COURSE/FIRST COURSE

1 fresh beef tongue (about 4 pounds) or
    4 lamb or pork tongues
¼ cup sugar
¼ cup coarse sea salt
Bunch of flat-leaf parsley, rinsed and
    tough stems removed

PARSLEY SAUCE
Reserved bunch of flat-leaf parsley (see
    instructions)
1 large egg yolk
1½ tablespoons strong Dijon mustard
1½ tablespoons wine vinegar
⅛ teaspoon salt
⅛ teaspoon freshly ground pepper
½ cup peanut or vegetable oil

Parsley sprigs, for garnish

 Place the tongue(s) in a large bowl, cover with ice water, and refrigerate for 3 hours.

Rinse the tongue(s) and pat dry with paper towels. Combine the sugar and salt. Put the tongue(s) in a baking dish or on a large plate and pat the salt mixture all over it (them). Cover with a cloth or plastic wrap and refrigerate overnight.

The next day, make a bed of the parsley on the steamer rack. Rinse the tongue(s) and place on top of the parsley. Place over simmering water, cover, and steam, beef tongue for 1 hour, lamb or pork tongues for 50 minutes. Remove the parsley and set aside for the sauce. If using beef tongue, return the tongue to the steamer and continue steaming until very tender and soft when touched, about 2 hours longer.

Peel the tongue(s) with a small knife; the skin will pull off easily. Return the tongue(s) to the steamer rack and place the steamer over low heat with the lid ajar to keep the tongue(s) warm while you make the sauce.

Purée the steamed parsley in a food processor. Add the egg

Large stackable steamer, steamer pot
with insert, roasting pan with wire
rack, or collapsible steamer basket
with removable center post

yolk, mustard, vinegar, salt, and pepper and process until smooth.
With the motor running, add the oil in a thin stream and process
until emulsified.

Thinly slice the tongue(s) and place on a platter or on individual plates. Garnish with parsley sprigs. Scrape the sauce into a
sauceboat and serve on the side.

SWEETBREAD MOUSSE
WITH HAM, MADEIRA, AND TRUFFLES
Parfait de Ris d'Agneau ou de Veau

When I first began working on this book, I spoke to a woman in Paris, Madame Lepaute,
who had known Manière. She told me something of the man and his work and raved about
this recipe in particular; she told me that she had made it several times, that it was foolproof
and her favorite in his book. Reading the recipe, it was hard to imagine the result. But on
her recommendation I tried it, and it is excellent. Sweetbreads are less exotic to the French
than to Americans, so the recipe may seem less unusual to a French cook. To me, it is pure
magic that sweetbreads can become this luscious thing, suffused with the intoxicating
flavors of truffles and Madeira, with a rich, buttery texture that can only be compared to
foie gras.

This is terrific party food, because it's made ahead. It can be unmolded, sliced, and served
on individual plates, or placed on a buffet table in the mold. Set it out with toasted small
slices of bread and a small knife.

Start this recipe the day before you plan to serve it. It keeps for up to three days in the
refrigerator, covered with aluminum foil.

Jarred black truffles in juice are available in specialty food stores. A three-quarter-ounce
jar holds two to three truffles. I used all of the juice for this recipe and stored the remaining
truffles in Madeira for the next time I made this dish.

....
SERVES 8 AS A COLD FIRST COURSE
....

1 pound veal or lamb sweetbreads
Salt and freshly ground pepper
¼ cup plus 2 tablespoons Madeira
1 jarred black truffle, with its juice
   (see headnote)

To clean the sweetbreads of blood and impurities,
put them in a bowl in the sink, place a rack on top,
and let cold water run over them for 1 hour. Or, put
the sweetbreads in a bowl with cold water to cover and refrigerate
1 hour, changing the water twice during that time.

One ¼-ounce package powdered gelatin

¼ cup crème fraîche or heavy cream

¼ pound boiled ham, cut into ¼-inch
  cubes

Hot toasted slices of egg-rich bread, such
  as brioche, for serving

Aluminum foil

6-cup terrine mold, 8-inch Pyrex loaf pan,
  or 1½-quart soufflé dish

Large stackable steamer, steamer pot
  with insert, or roasting pan with wire
  rack

Drain the sweetbreads and put them on the steamer rack. Place over simmering water, cover, and steam 5 minutes to firm them. Remove them from the steamer and peel off the thin, transparent skin and the white ducts and fat.

Cut a piece of aluminum foil 12 inches by 42 inches and fold it crosswise in half to double it. Put the sweetbreads in the center of the rectangle and sprinkle with salt and pepper. Fold up the edges of the foil to form a shallow container and pour over 3 tablespoons of the Madeira. Bring the two long sides of the foil up to meet over the sweetbreads, fold the edges together, and then fold over three times in ¼-inch folds. Fold the open edges over three times in ¼-inch folds to seal. Put the foil package on the steamer rack, place over simmering water, cover, and steam 15 minutes.

Meanwhile, roughly chop the truffle; reserve the juice.

When the sweetbreads are cooked, open the package and transfer the sweetbreads and their juices to the bowl of a food processor. Process to purée. Add the gelatin and the remaining 3 tablespoons Madeira, the crème fraîche or cream, ¼ teaspoon salt, and ⅛ teaspoon pepper, plus the chopped truffle and its juice, and purée until very smooth. Add the cubes of ham and pulse once or twice to mix. Pour the mixture into the terrine mold, loaf pan, or soufflé dish, cover with plastic wrap or aluminum foil, and refrigerate overnight.

To serve, run the blade of a thin knife around the edges of the mold. Plunge the bottom of the mold into a bowl of very hot water for 10 to 20 seconds to loosen the mousse. Then turn the mousse out onto a plate. Cut into thin slices and serve with hot toast slices.

CALVES' LIVER WITH ONIONS, PARSLEY, AND VINEGAR

Foie d'Agneau aux Oignons

The original version of this recipe uses lambs' liver, which is not available in America, but calves' liver is superb in this quick and easy sweet-and-sour dish.

The liver is steamed to medium, but even if you normally like liver pink, you won't find this too cooked. Steaming gets rid of any acrid flavor and gives the meat a soft, mellow taste.

(continued)

PERSILLADE

2 medium cloves garlic, peeled

3 tablespoons chopped parsley

4 slices calves' liver, ¼ to ½ inch thick
    (each about 4 ounces), cut crosswise
    into ½-inch-wide strips

2 medium onions, peeled and sliced into
    thin rounds

1 tablespoon unsalted butter

1½ tablespoons peanut or vegetable oil

Salt and freshly ground pepper

3 tablespoons red or white wine vinegar

Large stackable steamer, steamer pot
    with insert, or collapsible steamer
    basket

Chop the garlic and the parsley to make the persillade.

Put the liver and onions on the steamer rack, place over simmering water, cover, and steam 5 minutes. Set the lid ajar and steam 5 more minutes. Remove from the heat.

Melt the butter with the oil in a large frying pan over high heat. Add the liver and onions, sprinkle with salt and pepper, and cook, stirring often, until lightly browned, 3 to 4 minutes. Add the persillade and vinegar and heat, scraping up the browned bits on the bottom of the pan to deglaze.

Divide the liver among four plates and serve hot.

CALVES' LIVER WITH A RAGOUT OF CUCUMBER, SPRING ONIONS, AND MINT

Foie de Veau au Ragoût de Concombres et aux Oignons Nouveaux à la Menthe

This is an unusual recipe—try it. Manière wrapped a one-pound chunk of calves' liver in caul fat, the lacy membrane that lines a pork stomach, and steamed it medium-rare. The liver emerges rosy, moist, mild-flavored, and velvety-smooth. It is served with a pale-green-and-ivory-colored stew of cucumbers and spring onions, sweetened with apple.

Ask your butcher for caul fat, a beautiful, pure white, soft, lacy web of fat interwoven with crystal-clear transparent membrane. It's forgiving and easy to work with. It can be gently pulled into whatever shape is needed. It clings like plastic wrap, so it can be pieced to cover a hole and doesn't need to be tied. During steaming, it melts into the meat, moistening it and leaving a beautiful, slightly raised design on the liver. Manière removed the caul fat before serving, but it is edible and may be left on. Since caul fat may be hard to find, the liver can alternatively be wrapped in cheesecloth that has been dunked in melted butter; the butter both flavors the liver and keeps it moist during steaming. Any leftover liver can be used for another meal.

1 small bunch fresh mint

¼ pound caul fat or 4 tablespoons unsalted butter

1 pound trimmed calves' liver, in one piece, cut from the thick end of the liver

25 small spring onions or scallions, trimmed of all but 1 inch of green

1 small Golden Delicious, McIntosh, or Cortland apple, peeled, quartered, and cored

1 European hothouse cucumber or 2 American cucumbers, peeled, halved, seeded (see page 71), and cut into ⅜-inch slices

½ cup crème fraîche or ½ cup heavy cream mixed with 1 to 1½ teaspoons fresh lemon juice

¼ teaspoon salt

⅛ teaspoon freshly ground pepper

Cheesecloth, if caul fat is not available

Kitchen twine, if using cheesecloth

Large stackable steamer with one or two compartments, large steamer pot with insert, or roasting pan with wire rack plus another steamer for the vegetables

 Stem the mint and chop enough leaves to make 3 tablespoons. Save the stems.

If using caul fat, rinse under cold running water and pat dry with paper towels. If using cheesecloth, cut a doubled square piece large enough to wrap the liver; melt the butter in a small saucepan over low heat and dunk the cheesecloth in it. Spread the caul fat or cheesecloth out on the work surface. Shape the caul fat, if using, into a rectangle, positioning it with a short end facing you. Set the liver at the bottom edge of the rectangle of caul fat and fold the bottom edge over the liver. Then fold over the sides and roll the liver up. If using cheesecloth, place the reserved mint branches in the center of the cheesecloth and the liver on top. Bring the four corners of the cloth up over the liver to enclose it, and tie the cloth at the top.

If using caul fat, make a bed of the reserved mint branches on one side of the steamer rack and put the wrapped liver on the branches. Or put the cheesecloth-wrapped liver on one side of the steamer rack. Place over simmering water, cover, and steam 6 minutes.

Place the spring onions or scallions, apple, and cucumber(s) on the other side of the rack. (Or steam in a second steamer, if using a roasting pan for the liver.) Cover and steam about 10 more minutes, or until the liver registers about 130°F on an instant-read thermometer inserted into the thickest part.

When the liver is cooked, transfer the onions and cucumbers to a small saucepan; set aside. Put the apple in the bowl of a food processor or blender (a blender gives a smoother purée). Set the lid of the steamer ajar, turn the heat down to low, and let the liver rest 10 minutes.

Meanwhile, purée the apple until as smooth as possible. Add the crème fraîche or cream and lemon juice, salt, and pepper and process until smooth. Pour into the saucepan with the steamed vegetables. Add the chopped mint. Place over medium heat and warm gently until hot; do not boil.

To serve, pull the caul fat off the liver, if you like, or remove the cheesecloth and mint branches. Cut the liver into thin slices and put them on a serving platter. Spoon the vegetables and sauce around and serve immediately.

VEAL KIDNEYS WITH SWEET GARLIC SAUCE

Rognons de Veau à la Crème d'Ail Doux

The French love veal kidneys. They often cook them with Madeira, a sweet wine somewhat like port that balances the powerful flavor of the kidneys. Here Manière created the same balance by saucing the kidneys with a purée of garlic steamed until sweet and mild and bound with cream. The sauce is delicate enough to be served with chicken or fish.

Like calves' liver, veal kidneys have a potent flavor that sometimes verges on the acrid. Steaming gets rid of any sharpness, leaving the kidneys mild-tasting. Steaming also prevents toughening.

Manière held the kidneys flat during steaming by threading two skewers through each one on a diagonal to cross in the centers. Flat kidneys are easier to slice. Make sure your skewers are short enough to fit in the steamer; you can use bamboo skewers, broken to the length needed.

Serve the kidneys with white rice.

S E R V E S   4   A S   A   M A I N   C O U R S E

2 veal kidneys (about 10 ounces each)

SWEET GARLIC SAUCE

3 medium heads garlic (about ½ pound total)

Salt

⅛ teaspoon freshly ground pepper, preferably white

6 tablespoons crème fraîche or
   6 tablespoons heavy cream mixed
   with 2 teaspoons fresh lemon juice

1½ tablespoons chopped parsley

4 short metal or bamboo skewers

Large stackable steamer with two compartments or roasting pan with wire rack

 Peel off the thin transparent skin that covers the kidneys. Trim off all the white fat and ducts in the center of the inner sides of the kidneys with a small knife. Push a skewer diagonally through one of the kidneys, then push a second skewer through on the opposite diagonal to cross the first in the center. Repeat with the second kidney.

Peel the garlic cloves and remove any white or green sprouts in the center (see page 78). Put the garlic on the steamer rack, place over simmering water, cover, and steam 10 minutes. Set the kidneys on top of the garlic, inner sides down, and sprinkle heavily with salt. Cover and steam until the kidneys are medium-rare, 7 to 8 minutes.

Transfer the garlic to the bowl of a food processor or a food mill set over a bowl. Turn the kidneys over on the steamer rack, set the lid ajar, and let the kidneys rest for 10 minutes (this step will get rid of any acrid flavor).

To make the sauce, purée the garlic. Add ½ teaspoon salt, the pepper, and the crème fraîche or cream and lemon juice and process or stir until blended. The sauce should be slightly thicker than heavy cream; add a little water if it is too thick.

To serve, remove the skewers from the kidneys. Cut the kidneys crosswise into thin slices, keeping the slices together. Place the sliced kidneys on a serving plate, spoon the sauce over, and sprinkle with the parsley. Serve with rice.

Using American Cuts of Meat for Steaming

The French cut meat differently from the way we do in America. As a rule, French butchers cut the meat into separate muscles rather than cutting across groups of muscles, as American butchers do. The meat itself is different in France as well—the lambs are much smaller, the pork is fattier, and the beef not nearly as tender. Some cuts of meat common in France are difficult to buy here. In the recipes and in the chart on page 228, I have substituted comparable American cuts where necessary and adjusted the steaming times accordingly. Your butcher may be able to special-order less common cuts of meat and variety meats, and even in supermarkets, butchers will cut meats to order if you have a special request.

✳ BEEF

Manière included very few recipes for beef, because it's less important in the French diet than in ours. The French enjoy other meats, particularly lamb and pork, more often than beef. French beef is leaner than ours, so it may be tougher and less flavorful.

In addition to the cuts of beef listed by Manière in his chart, I have included several other cheaper cuts that we like to cook in America. Steamed chuck is very moist with a strong, rich beef flavor; I steam it with vegetables, slice it, and use the reduced steaming liquid to moisten meat and vegetables for a lean pot roast. (Rump roast is drier than chuck and doesn't steam as well.) Beef shin is stout-flavored, meaty, and delicious steamed, and you get the added bonus of the beef marrow in each slice; have your butcher saw the shin across the bone like osso buco, into 1½-inch-thick slices. Serve it hot or cold with Manière's Caper-Anchovy Vinaigrette (page 117) or with a risotto made with the steaming liquid from the beef and other steaming liquid added to make up the necessary amount.

✳ LAMB

Shoulder Manière used lamb shoulder cubes for his Smothered Lamb with Eggplant (page 246) and Skewered Lamb (page 250). Cubed boneless lamb shoulder is hard to find in America and expensive. Some butchers don't sell lamb shoulder at all, others sell it cut into chops sold as either blade chops or arm chops, depending on whether the chops are cut across the triangular-shaped blade bone or the round arm bone. Shoulder chops have some bone and a fair amount of fat. (Supermarkets almost always carry lamb shoulder chops.)

If using shoulder chops in a recipe that calls for boneless shoulder, trim as much fat as possible and cut the chops into pieces, leaving the bone or not as you like. Cubed boneless leg of lamb makes a fine substitute for shoulder and has a milder flavor. Lamb neck (see below) is also an excellent substitute. When substituting a cut of lamb with bone, such as neck or shoulder chops, in one of Manière's recipes that calls for a boneless cut, such as shoulder, buy one and a third times as much meat as called for to make up for the bone.

Neck Lamb neck is an exceptionally flavorful but bony cut of meat used as stew meat in France. (See the Couscous recipe on page 247.) If neck is available, do buy it, because it has a gutsy lamb flavor and succulent texture. If not, substitute shoulder or leg.

Rack Rack of lamb steamed and then browned under the broiler is absolutely incredible. I served it to a friend who had looked at me politely crosswise when I told him what I was doing. He ate his crosswise looks along with the lamb.

Manière trimmed and frenched the rack, cutting off the top layer of fatty meat to expose the bones just above the eye (the round, meaty part) of the rack. I often like to leave a thin layer of this fatty meat on the rack because I like the fat and I like to gnaw on the bones—and you do lose a lot of meat by frenching. Whether or not you french the bones, the rack stays a bit more fatty than if roasted; I cut off some of the cooked fat that I would normally eat on a roasted rack. Ask the butcher to cut off the chine bone so that it's easy to cut the rack into chops.

While Manière served four with one rack, for us, one rack traditionally serves two people. If you want to serve four, you'll need two racks and a steamer pot for each (or at least a stackable steamer with two steaming compartments). This is very doable, but you'll want to prepare at least one of the accompanying vegetables in the oven (see page 244).

Oddly enough, both a two-and-a-quarter-pound rack and a three-and-a-quarter-pound rack take about twenty to twenty-five minutes to steam medium-rare, or fifteen to twenty minutes steaming time plus five to eight minutes under the broiler to brown. Use an instant-read thermometer if you like, steaming the lamb to 130°F to 140°F for medium-rare, or to about 120°F if you're going to brown it.

Legs Bone-in legs of French lambs typically weigh about five to six pounds. An American leg may weigh as little as six to seven pounds but is more likely to weigh closer to ten. (Part of this size difference is due to the different ways French and American butchers trim lamb legs. French butchers sell what is called a "shortened leg," which stops short of the meat around the aitch-bone at the top end of the leg.)

It's difficult to fit a large bone-in leg into even a large steamer; a seven-pound leg just fits into my large enameled roasting pan. But butcher shops and supermarkets cut legs in half and sell both the butt-half and the shank-half. I like the shank-half because it has an attractive shape, it's easier to carve than the butt-half, and I get the shank with it, one of my favorite parts of the animal. (I don't steam lamb shank on its own, because it doesn't get as tender as I'd like.) I give timings for a bone-in and boneless shank-half of leg in the chart on page 228. The shank-half is slightly smaller than the butt-half and will feed four, with leftovers.

If steaming a shank-half of leg on the bone, remember that the meat close to the bone will be far less cooked than the meat away from the bone. The timing in the chart is to steam the meat medium-rare, but the first several slices from the outside of the leg will be well-done, with the meat progressively less cooked as you cut toward the bone. (One way to get around this is to slice half-slices of the leg: Hold the knife at the shank end of the leg, on top of the bone and parallel to the work surface. Cut along the bone, from the shank end in toward the center. Then cut thin slices straight down to the bone. Each slice will have some well-done meat and some pink meat. When you have finished with the top side of the leg, turn it over and slice the bottom side.) If using an instant-read thermometer, take the leg out of the steamer at about 135°F for medium-rare; if browning under the broiler, take the leg out of the steamer at 120°F and brown according to the times in the chart on page 228.

I prefer to steam boneless leg; a boned and tied leg of lamb is not only easy to carve, it steams more evenly and fits more easily into a steamer than a bone-in leg. Ask your butcher to bone out the leg from the inside (like a tunnel), leaving the center section of the leg, between the shank bone and the aitchbone, whole. Slices from a cooked leg boned in this way won't fall apart. The timings in the chart are calculated to steam a leg, before browning, just to 110°F; eight to ten minutes under the broiler or in a very hot oven finishes cooking the lamb medium-rare. If the leg is not to be browned, it should be steamed to 120°F to 125°F; it continues to cook as it rests.

✳ PORK

In his recipe for Pork with Garlic and Sage (page 251), Manière used a cut of pork called an *échine,* which isn't available in America. The *échine* includes part of the neck and shoulder of the animal; it's tender and fattier than the loin. I substitute fresh Boston butt, cut from the shoulder, which takes much longer to cook than the *échine* but is wonderfully succulent and tasty; pork shoulder has never tasted better to me than when steamed.

Manière steamed pork loin as well as chops. Because American pork is bred leaner than French pork, the chops toughen when steamed; I substitute pork tenderloin, a long, slender piece of meat that is both lean and very tender. A tenderloin weighs three quarters of a pound to a pound. I like steaming pork loin less than the shoulder because, depending on the animal, it may be dry; if you do steam it, don't cook it over 150°F to 155°F.

Manière's recipe for Stuffed Cabbage (page 253) calls for pork sausage. Some very good quality pork sausages are available in supermarkets and at butcher shops, but their seasoning gives them the wrong flavor for a French stuffing. Choose a neutral-flavored pork sausage or make your own: Use two thirds lean ground pork and one third ground pork fat. Minced onion, garlic, and herbs can be added as you like.

Trichinae, the parasites that cause trichinosis, are killed at 138°F. There hasn't been an outbreak of trichinosis here for years, so it's not nearly as worrisome as it once was. Nevertheless, pork should be cooked to at least 140°F, or even to 145°F to 150°F, to be safe.

✳ VEAL

There are two different types of veal in America: milk-fed veal, from three- to four-month-old calves raised on milk or a milk substitute, and grass-fed veal, from calves that have fed on solid food. Milk-fed veal is lighter colored than grass-fed veal and has a lighter flavor. Grass-fed veal can be younger and smaller than milk-fed. Traditionally, European veal is milk-fed. A good quality grass-fed veal like that available from Summerfield Farms in Virginia, where the animals aren't penned (see page 299), is delicate-flavored and tasty.

✳ VARIETY MEATS

The French love variety meats and have markets that sell nothing but these meats. Manière devoted an entire section to offal, pointing out that his research suggested that steaming leaches out hormones and pesticides that can be stored in the organs of animals. We don't have the variety of offal in America that was available to Manière, so I have made substitutions where possible. Manière's recipe for steamed tongue (see page 257) was written for pork or lamb tongue, both of which, although available in some ethnic butcher shops, are hardly standard fare in America; fortunately, beef tongue is easy to find and a delicious substitute. The recipe for Sweetbread Mousse with Ham, Madeira, and Truffles (page 258) was written for lamb or veal sweetbreads, the thymus glands of the animal. I used veal sweetbreads, which can be special ordered if your butcher doesn't carry them. Manière's recipe for Calves' Liver with Onions, Parsley, and Vinegar (page 259) was written for lambs' liver but it is terrific with our more readily available calves' liver.

Other Special Techniques

✳ USING THE STEAMING LIQUID

Any steamed food gives some flavor to the liquid simmering below it, but the broths made from steaming beef and veal are particularly potent and versatile. (Depending on the amount of water used to steam, the broth may need to be reduced.) Veal flavors the liquid less powerfully than beef. Lamb and pork broths can add flavor to soups, particularly bean and lentil soups. Fragrant beef broth can be used to moisten a pot roast or a stew. A friend who often steams meat now talks gleefully about how satisfied he feels when he has a couple of containers of beef steaming liquid in the refrigerator, produced with no extra effort and reduced until they jelled, just waiting for an opportunity to turn a mundane meal into something much more special.

Intensifying the Flavors of the Liquid You can tailor the taste of the broth by adding bones, vegetables, herbs, and wine to the liquid under the steaming meat (see Veal Stock on page 241). Ask your butcher for bones (when you buy a boned leg of lamb, for instance, have him give you the bones) and have him crack them—or save the bones from meat you have steamed. (Carcasses from steamed chickens add a lot of flavor to steaming liquid and can be frozen until you're ready to use them.)

Typically, broths are flavored with vegetables such as carrot, onion, celery, mushrooms, or turnips, and herbs such as thyme, bay leaf, and parsley, but use whatever you like. Lamb and beef make a very robust-flavored steaming liquid on their own; you may want to add wine, herbs, or vegetables for a specific flavor, but bones aren't essential. Veal broth needs the extra boost from bones. If you have steaming liquid saved from another meal, use it instead of or in addition to water to steam meat for the next meal; the broth gets stronger and richer each time it's used.

✳ MAKING STEAMED "STEWS"

In this chapter, Manière included a few recipes for stew-type dishes, in which chunks of meat are steamed over water that is beefed up with vegetables, herbs, and sometimes bones or wine to give flavor. After the meat is cooked, the broth is reduced, sometimes thickened, and then seasoned and spooned over the meat to be eaten as a sauce. (See Smothered Lamb with Eggplant, page 246; Veal Blanquette, page 240; and Couscous with Lamb and Chicken, page 247.) This system is a good one; the meat stays firm and moist and flavors the broth underneath without giving up its essence.

Use the recipe for Smothered Lamb with Eggplant as a model for making a steamed "stew." Or steam a larger whole piece of meat, such as beef chuck, and serve it sliced with the broth, like a *pot-au-feu,* or pot roast. Use a long-cooking cut of meat such as lamb shoulder or leg, beef chuck or shin, veal shoulder, or Boston butt of pork. Trim the fat from shoulder and leg cuts and cut them into large cubes, or leave beef chuck in a large chunk. Cut beef shin across the bone into one-and-a-half-inch- to two-inch-thick slices. (See the chart on page 228 for steaming times.) Vegetables may be cooked along with the meat for the whole length of the steaming time, as in the Smothered Lamb, or added along the way and steamed just long enough to cook them through, as in the Veal Blanquette.

For the broth, add bones, vegetables, and herbs as described in Intensifying the Flavors of the Liquid on page 267. Veal and chicken broths are neutral and can be used for any meat. Use beef broth for steamed beef and lamb stews.

Either a stackable steamer or a pasta cooker works well for these stews, because the steamer pots of both are deep. Check the level of the steaming liquid a few times during steaming and add more water as necessary. When the meat is cooked, taste and reduce the broth or not, as you like. (A *pot-au-feu*-type meal of steamed chuck or shin and vegetables is served with an unbound broth.) To defat the broth after steaming, strain it into a bowl, refrigerate it until the fat congeals on top, and scrape the fat off the top with a spoon.

You can use this technique with chicken, whole or in parts, as well. (See the chart on page 182 for steaming times.)

DESSERTS

This is a slender chapter because Manière limited himself to desserts that really benefit from steaming; many desserts, as he pointed out, particularly those using doughs, require an oven. In any case, the steamer fits well with the French liking for fruits and lighter finishes to a large meal. The recipes here are for fresh fruit desserts, simple egg-based custards like Crème Caramel (page 277), and steamed puddings and charlottes, such as Semolina Pudding with Plum Compote (page 288) and Apple Charlotte (page 290). The recipes are modest by Manière standards and almost all are quick and easy to make. Manière also included basic instructions for caramel and crème Chantilly, two important mainstays of French dessert making; I've added a recipe for homemade crème fraîche and information about vanilla beans and extract.

Cooking Fresh Fruit in the Steamer

In a world where everyone wants something sweet at the end of the meal but is watching his or her weight or cholesterol, it's a pleasure to have the option of serving a silken piece of steamed fruit for dessert. Steamed apples, pears, bananas, and pineapples are quick and easy for the cook, sweetly satisfying and fat-free for the guest. The fruit can be served hot, at room temperature, or cold, eaten plain or gussied up with a sauce.

Steaming is a particularly good alternative to poaching for apples, pears, and pineapples. It's faster than poaching because there's no poaching liquid to make, and the flavor of steamed fruit is truer to its natural flavor. (You're better off poaching underripe or tasteless fruit, however; the poaching liquid will sweeten the fruit in a way that steaming will not.) Steaming is a good way to cook apples, which tend to fall apart in a simmering poaching liquid. Because the fruit isn't moved during steaming, even soft, ripe pears stay intact during cooking. (Most pears get soft as they ripen; the exception is Bosc pears, which are firm even when ripe.)

Using the Chart of Basic Steaming Times for Fresh Fruits

The chart on pages 275–276 gives steaming times for some common types of apples, pears, and grapes, and for bananas steamed as is or *en papillote* (wrapped in aluminum foil). There is a simple recipe for steamed pineapple on page 274.

Steamed Apples and Pears

Serve steamed apples and pears at room temperature or chilled; their sweetness and fruit flavor intensify as they cool. Eat them plain or with a dollop of cream, crème fraîche, sour cream, ice cream, or mascarpone cheese. Or sauce them with chocolate sauce, Caramel Sauce (page 296), Rum Crème Anglaise (page 281), or a berry sauce.

Fruit Sauces

A steamed perfectly ripe whole apple or pear standing in a brilliant pool of puréed raspberry sauce makes a satisfying low-fat end to a meal. Fruit sauces can be made with fresh or frozen fruit, cooked or uncooked. The easiest sauce is one made with fresh berries such as raspberries or strawberries, puréed, strained through a fine sieve, and sweetened with sugar or honey accented with a little lemon or lime juice. (Citrus juice brings out fruit flavor; lime does something magical for raspberries.) I make blueberry sauce with fresh or frozen blueberries cooked in a small covered saucepan with sugar, spices, and a strip of lemon zest until the berries are soft; I press the sauce through a fine strainer with the back of a large spoon to remove the skins. Make a fresh apricot sauce by steaming halved, pitted apricots for five to ten minutes, until soft, and then pressing them through a fine strainer to purée. Sweeten with sugar to taste and fresh lemon or lime juice.

Out of season, frozen berries make a very good sauce, immeasurably better than one made from tasteless unripe fresh fruit. Although the fruit can be cooked in a saucepan, the flavor is fresher if the fruit is steamed: Steam still-frozen strawberries or raspberries until thawed and softened (five to ten minutes). Press the fruit through a fine strainer with the back of a large spoon and stir in sugar and lemon or lime juice to taste. These purées often need to be thinned: Add just enough steaming liquid to the sugar to dissolve it and stir the sweetened liquid into the purée until it reaches the right consistency. A one-and-a-quarter pound bag of frozen strawberries yields about one cup of sauce.

Fruit sauced with two sauces of contrasting colors makes a really gorgeous and impressive plate. Try crème anglaise and a blueberry sauce for apples; use strawberry and blueberry, or one of the fruit sauces with crème anglaise, for pears.

Saucing Steamed Apples with the Steaming Liquid

You can make a different kind of sauce for steamed apples with the reduced steaming liquid. Add the cores and skin to the water to add pectin and flavor. When the apples are cooked, remove them from the steamer and reduce the steaming liquid until slightly thickened, flavorful, and sweet. (For four apples, reduce the liquid to about one and a quarter cups.) Strain through a fine strainer, pressing on the skins and cores with the back of a large spoon to extract as much flavor as possible. The liquid is quite sweet and needs only a squeeze of lemon juice or a tablespoon of butter to finish it.

A steaming liquid can be reused several times before it is reduced for sauce; the more fruit steamed over the liquid, the more flavor it takes on. Refrigerate the liquid between uses. Also add a whole spice, such as a cinnamon stick or clove, or a strip of lemon or orange zest to the steaming liquid, if you like.

Macerating Steamed Fruit

Manière macerated ripe peaches variously in wine, lemon juice, and strawberry purée, thus flavoring both peaches and macerating liquid to create an alchemy that is much more interesting than either of the two elements tasted separately. In the same way, steamed pears and apples can be macerated in wine (with spices, if you like) or another alcohol sweetened with sugar, honey, or some of the reduced steaming liquid. The fruit has a chance to develop its own flavor as it steams, before being macerated; the macerating liquid perfumes the fruit without masking its true essence. Cooked fruit also absorbs a macerating liquid more rapidly than raw fruit. Serve the macerated fruit cool or chilled.

Steamed Grapes, Pineapple, and Banana

Steaming transforms grapes and pineapple in an extraordinary way; their raw bite is replaced by an unctuous, warm, exotic sweetness that fills the mouth. It's as if the fruit makes its own sauce as you chew it. Steamed ripe pineapple is an unforgettable way to end a meal and takes only a few minutes to prepare (see below). Warm steamed grapes add a sweet note to a warm first-course salad made with fish, duck, or chicken.

Peeled bananas, cut in half lengthwise and steamed *en papillote* with butter, sugar, and perhaps an alcohol such as brandy or rum, are delicious. Made without the alcohol, this is a dessert a child could love; flambéed, it's a dessert to serve at a dinner party. Peeled bananas can also be steamed on their own (see the chart on pages 275–276 for times), cut lengthwise in half, and served in a pool of Rum Crème Anglaise (page 281), chocolate sauce, or Caramel Sauce (page 296). Unlike apples and pears, bananas, grapes, and pineapple have the most flavor hot or warm.

BARBARA'S WARM STEAMED PINEAPPLE

You'll need a large steamer pot with two inserts or a roasting pan with a wire rack.

Cut off the top and bottom of a ripe four- to five-pound pineapple with a large knife. Leave the skin on. Cut the pineapple in half lengthwise. Then cut each half lengthwise into quarters to give eight long pineapple wedges. Holding the knife parallel to the skin, cut between the skin and the flesh of each wedge to remove the flesh in one piece. Slice each wedge crosswise into half-inch-thick pieces and replace the pieces on the skin.

Put each wedge on a small piece of doubled aluminum foil. Pick up each piece of foil by two opposing corners and place on the steamer rack. Place over simmering water, cover, and steam two minutes. Pick up the foil pieces, again by two opposing corners, to remove the wedges from the steamer. Place two wedges on each of four plates and serve hot or warm, as is or with Caramel Sauce (page 296), vanilla ice cream, or an exotic-flavored sorbet such as passion fruit or mango.

Apples and pears should be peeled and cored; leave the stem ends of the pears intact. It's easiest to core whole and halved apples and pears with a melon baller; or use a small knife. If preparing a number of apples or pears, hold them in a bowl of lemon water (as for artichokes, page 29) to keep them from turning brown.

Steam whole pears and apples standing up. Steam halved apples and pears rounded sides up so that condensed steam doesn't collect in the hollow where the core has been removed. Use a spatula to remove the fruit from the steamer.

Steam whole and halved apples and pears in a single layer. A 9½-inch vegetable steamer or collapsible steamer basket opened to maximum capacity is large enough to steam four whole apples or four whole pears. Use a roasting pan with a wire rack to steam the same number of apples or pears cut in half. It's easier to remove delicate steamed fruit from a shallow pan than from a deep one.

Eaten raw, each variety of apple and pear has a unique taste (a combination of sweet and tart) and texture; the same is true of the steamed fruit.

APPLES

Whole apples are more likely to fall apart than halved apples because the steaming time is longer. (Whole apples expand almost as if blown up and then settle down again during steaming.) Golden Delicious and Rome Beauties are the sweetest of the apples I steamed, and both stay fairly intact in the cooking; the outside layer of the Golden Delicious gets a puffy, cottony look but settles and tightens as the apple cools. Golden Delicious have the best flavor of all the apples I steamed, with a good balance of tart and sweet and almost caramel overtones; they turn a bright yellow color in steaming. (The French almost always use Golden Delicious in cooking because they taste good and don't fall apart.)

Granny Smiths are less sweet and have a tart bite; they don't fall apart in steaming. McIntosh and Cortland apples are less sweet than Goldens and not as tart as Grannys; they fall apart readily if overcooked.

Serve steamed apples room temperature or chilled.

PEARS

With the exception of Bosc pears, which are hard even when ripe and sweet, the steaming time for pears varies depending more on the ripeness of the pear than on its variety; a very ripe pear need only be warmed through, while a harder pear must be cooked long enough to soften the flesh. The sweetness of a steamed pear also depends more on ripeness than on variety. Pears vary in texture from grainy to smooth when steamed; Bosc pears have a pronounced grainy texture and Fiorello just a bit less, Comice are buttery smooth, and Anjou and Bartlett fall in between.

Serve steamed pears at room temperature or chilled.

BANANAS

Steam peeled bananas, cut in half lengthwise, on doubled pieces of aluminum foil to make it easy to remove them from the steamer. Or steam them wrapped in aluminum foil (*en papillote*, see page 166), sprinkled with sugar and rum or brandy and dotted with butter—which melt together to sauce the banana in the foil package. Steam bananas for four in a roasting pan with a wire rack. Serve steamed bananas hot or warm.

APPLES

GRANNY SMITH (8 OUNCES)

Whole..10 minutes

Halved..7 minutes

GOLDEN DELICIOUS (8 OUNCES)

Whole..12 to 13 minutes

Halved..10 minutes

MCINTOSH (5 TO 6 OUNCES)

Whole..5 to 6 minutes

Halved..5 minutes

CORTLAND (5 TO 6 OUNCES)

Whole..8 to 9 minutes

Halved..6 to 7 minutes

ROME BEAUTY (12 OUNCES)

Whole..15 minutes

Halved..9 minutes

PEARS

ANJOU, BARTLETT, OR COMICE (ABOUT 8 OUNCES)

Whole..8 to 12 minutes, depending on ripeness

Halved..5 to 10 minutes, depending on ripeness

BOSC (6 TO 7 OUNCES)

Whole..10 minutes

Halved..7 minutes

FIORELLO (4 TO 5 OUNCES)

Whole..5 minutes

GRAPES

Green and red..2 minutes

BANANAS

Medium, halved lengthwise..3 minutes

Medium, halved lengthwise and wrapped *en papillote*..5 minutes

Many of Manière's steamed desserts are egg-based custard-style dishes that he called creams and flans. Some are unmolded before serving, while others, like the Pomelo (Grapefruit) Cream on page 284, are too soft to turn out and are served in their molds. While some of Manière's custards are made with milk, as is traditional, others are more unusual; his White Wine Custard with Honey and Cinnamon (page 282) uses wine instead. His Pomelo Cream is an inspired reincarnation of the old-fashioned, cornstarch-bound blancmange; he transformed this sometimes stodgy dessert into a light, bright-flavored sweet by using grapefruit juice in place of milk.

Egg-bound custards are traditionally cooked in a water bath in the oven to keep the egg from overcooking and turning grainy and watery. But they cook perfectly in a steamer and with much less fuss. Water baths are cumbersome and dangerous to handle because of the risk of boiling water slopping over the side of the pan when moved. What a pleasure to use a steamer instead! It's simple to move the custards in and out of the steamer and it's easier to open a steamer pot to check on the progress of the cooking than to poke one's head into a hot oven.

For desserts that are served in large molds, use decorative porcelain dishes such as quiche or soufflé molds.

CRÈME CARAMEL
Les Oeufs au Lait

This velvety, caramel-coated vanilla custard, well loved throughout Europe and the Americas, is the sort of dessert that goes down easily even when you think you can't possibly eat another bite. The mild bitterness of the caramel offsets the sweet custard, and it's satisfying without being rich. Although it takes only a few minutes to put together, the caramel gives it more finesse than a standard baked custard.

Unmold the custards onto deep plates or shallow bowls to catch the saucy, liquid caramel. Use a vanilla bean, if you can; the flavor really stands out.

(continued)

CARAMEL

½ cup sugar

⅓ cup water

2 cups whole milk

1 vanilla bean or 1 teaspoon vanilla
    extract (see page 297)

⅔ cup sugar

4 large eggs

Aluminum foil

Four 6- to 8-ounce ramekins or 4 Pyrex
    custard cups

Stackable steamer, large steamer pot
    with insert, roasting pan with wire
    rack, or collapsible steamer basket

 Make the caramel and line the ramekins or custard cups with it as directed on pages 294–295.

Pour the milk into a medium saucepan. If using a vanilla bean, rinse it and cut it in half lengthwise. Use a knife to scrape the tiny seeds into the milk, then add the pod. Add the sugar and bring to a boil over medium-high heat.

Meanwhile, with a whisk, lightly beat the eggs in a medium heatproof bowl. Remove the vanilla bean from the milk and whisk the milk into the eggs, pouring slowly at first in a thin steam, and then more rapidly. Whisk in the vanilla extract, if using. Using a liquid measuring cup, fill each ramekin or custard cup with about ¾ cup of the custard. Cover the containers with small squares of aluminum foil, pressing the foil around the rims to seal.

Put the containers on the steamer rack, place over simmering water, cover, and steam until the custard is just set but jiggles in the middle when shaken, about 12 minutes.

Remove the custards from the steamer and let cool. Refrigerate until cold. To serve, unmold the custards onto plates as directed on page 295.

Coconut-caramel flan

Flan Exotique

This flan is silky smooth with a layer of sweet, chewy coconut at the top. The sides are soaked in caramel, adding welcome bitterness, and the whole thing floats in a thin but potent rum-caramel sauce. The dish is effortless to make; the ingredients are simply stirred together.

Unmold the flan onto a deep plate to catch the liquid caramel used to make the sauce.

CARAMEL

⅓ cup sugar

4 large eggs

One 14-ounce can sweetened condensed
    milk

2 cups whole milk

1 cup sweetened shredded coconut

CARAMEL-RUM SAUCE

¼ cup reserved caramel from mold
    (see instructions)

About ¼ cup white rum

Aluminum foil

9-inch round cake pan or Pyrex pie pan

Large stackable steamer, roasting pan
    with wire rack, or collapsible steamer
    basket with removable center post

Make the caramel and line the pan with it as directed on pages 294–295.

Lightly beat the eggs in a medium bowl. Add the condensed milk and whole milk and the coconut and whisk to combine. Pour into the pan and cover with a square of aluminum foil, pressing the foil around the rim of the pan to seal.

Put the pan on the steamer rack, place over simmering water, cover, and steam 20 minutes. Then set the lid ajar and steam 10 more minutes, or until the custard is just set but jiggles in the center when shaken. Let cool, then refrigerate until cold.

To serve, unmold the flan onto a serving plate as directed on page 295, reserving the pan.

Make the sauce: Use a rubber scraper to scrape the liquid caramel out of the pan into a measuring cup. Add the caramel that has collected on the serving plate. You should have about ¼ cup caramel. Stir in an equal amount of rum.

Cut the flan into wedges. Serve each wedge on a plate in a pool of sauce.

COFFEE CUSTARD

Crème au Café

If you like your coffee "regular"—meaning, oddly enough, with milk—as they say in New York, these individual coffee custards are for you; they taste just like a chilled cup of sweetened, "regular" coffee. I like them after a rich meal, particularly one that uses cream or butter; the bitterness of the coffee is refreshing, and the custards, made with milk rather than cream, aren't overly rich in themselves.

While Manière sometimes used whole coffee beans for flavoring (see Mocha Cream with Rum Crème Anglaise, page 280), he used instant coffee in this recipe. If possible, use instant espresso from Medaglio D'Oro. It gives a good, rich coffee flavor but is quicker than using whole coffee beans, and it isn't acrid. There's just enough cocoa in the custard to mellow the acidity of the coffee without turning it mocha.

To make a chocolate custard, see the Variation on page 280.

(continued)

2 cups whole milk

2 tablespoons instant espresso powder or instant coffee

⅔ cup sugar

4 large eggs

1½ tablespoons unsweetened cocoa powder, preferably Dutch processed

Aluminum foil

1½-quart soufflé dish or four 6- to 8-ounce ramekins or 4 Pyrex cups

Large stackable steamer, steamer pot with insert, roasting pan with wire rack, or collapsible steamer basket (with removable center post if making a single mold)

 Combine the milk, espresso or coffee, and sugar in a medium saucepan and bring to a boil.

Meanwhile, combine the eggs and cocoa powder in a medium heatproof bowl and lightly beat with a whisk.

Gradually whisk the milk mixture into the egg mixture, pouring slowly at first in a thin stream, and then more rapidly. Pour the custard mixture into the soufflé dish, if using, or use a liquid measuring cup to pour ¾ cup of the mixture into each individual ramekin or custard cup. Cover the container(s) with a square (or squares) of aluminum foil, pressing the foil around the rim(s) to seal.

Put the container(s) on the steamer rack, place over simmering water, cover, and steam until the custard is just set but jiggles in the center when shaken, about 18 minutes for the soufflé dish or 12 minutes for the small molds.

Remove the custard(s) from the steamer and let cool, then refrigerate until chilled. Serve cold.

Variation

Chocolate Custard: Replace the coffee with ¼ cup unsweetened cocoa, preferably Dutch processed.

MOCHA CREAM WITH RUM CRÈME ANGLAISE

Crème du Perou

This dessert marries the dark, seductive flavors of the tropics—coffee, chocolate, and rum—in a sensual, creamy-textured custard with sauce. The custard is sweetened with caramel instead of sugar so that it has a dark, subtly bitter undertone that speaks to both the coffee and the chocolate; it's rich without being heavy and sweet without being cloying.

While Manière's Coffee Custard (page 279) is flavored with instant coffee, this one uses whole coffee beans, which give a richer, rounder flavor. The beans are warmed in a frying pan, coarsely crushed, then steeped in the milk. Warming the beans develops their flavor—be sure not to burn them.

The custard uses only half a vanilla bean; wrap the remaining half in plastic and refrigerate for another use. Serve any leftover sauce with steamed bananas, pears, or apples (see Cooking Fresh Fruit in the Steamer, page 271) or with the Apple Charlotte on page 290.

MOCHA CREAM

3 cups whole milk

½ vanilla bean or ½ teaspoon vanilla
extract

⅔ cup coffee beans

CARAMEL

½ cup sugar

⅓ cup water

4 ounces bittersweet or semisweet
chocolate, cut into small pieces

2 large eggs

4 large egg yolks

RUM CRÈME ANGLAISE

2 cups whole milk

6 large egg yolks

⅓ cup sugar

¼ cup light rum

Aluminum foil

Six 4-ounce ramekins or 6 Pyrex custard
cups

Stackable steamer with two steaming
compartments or roasting pan with
wire rack

 Make the mocha cream: Pour the milk into a medium saucepan. If using half a vanilla bean, rinse it and cut it in half again, lengthwise. Use a knife to scrape the tiny seeds into the milk, then add the pod. Bring the milk to a boil over medium-high heat. Remove from the heat and set aside.

Meanwhile, put the coffee beans in a frying pan and warm over medium heat until fragrant and shiny; be careful not to burn them. Crush the beans by pulsing them in a food processor, coffee grinder, or blender.

Add the crushed beans to the milk and let stand 20 minutes.

Make the caramel: Prepare a large bowl of ice water. Then make a very light caramel as directed on page 294: When the caramel reaches a light brown color, immediately remove the pan from the heat and immerse the bottom in the ice water for several seconds to stop the cooking and cool the pan. (The caramel will harden in places.) Remove the pan from the water, add the chocolate, and stir with a wooden spoon until the chocolate is partially melted.

Strain the milk through a chinois or a fine strainer lined with cheesecloth into the chocolate mixture. Place over medium heat and cook, stirring with the wooden spoon, until the chocolate and caramel have melted completely.

With a whisk, lightly beat the whole eggs and yolks in a medium heatproof bowl. Whisk the hot milk mixture into the eggs, pouring slowly at first in a thin stream, and then more rapidly. Whisk in the vanilla extract, if using. With a liquid measuring cup, divide the custard mixture among the ramekins or custard cups. Cover each with a small square of aluminum foil and press the foil around the rim to seal.

Put the containers on the steamer rack, place over simmering water, cover, and steam until the custard is set except in the very center (a knife inserted in the center should come out coated with a very thick liquid), 12 to 15 minutes. Let cool, then refrigerate until cold.

Make the crème anglaise: Bring the milk to a boil in a medium saucepan.

Meanwhile, whisk the egg yolks with the sugar in a medium heatproof bowl until frothy and light yellow in color. Whisk in the rum.

Whisk the milk into the egg yolk mixture, pouring slowly at

first in a thin stream, and then more rapidly. Pour the mixture back into the saucepan and cook over low heat, stirring constantly with a wooden spoon and making sure to get into the sides of the pan, until the sauce thickens enough to coat the spoon (leaving a trail when you drag a finger over the back of the spoon). Immediately pour into a bowl and let cool, then refrigerate until cold.

To serve, pour the sauce into a sauceboat. Place each custard in its mold in the center of a dessert plate. Serve the sauce on the side so that each guest can pour it over the top of the custard.

WHITE WINE CUSTARD WITH HONEY AND CINNAMON
Crème Bachique

This honey custard is delightfully original; I've never seen anything quite like it. Made with white wine in place of milk or cream, it tastes like chilled, spiced wine. It's a refreshing end to a large fall or winter meal because the flavors are in keeping with the season, and it's lighter than a traditional custard.

SERVES 8

2½ cups white Hermitage or other white
    Rhône wine
¾ cup honey
Strip of lemon zest, about 1 inch by
    3 inches
One 2-inch piece cinnamon stick
6 large eggs

Aluminum foil
Eight 4-ounce ramekins or 8 Pyrex
    custard cups
Large stackable steamer with two
    steaming compartments or large
    roasting pan with wire rack

 Combine the wine, honey, lemon zest, and cinnamon stick in a medium saucepan and bring to a boil. Reduce the heat and simmer, uncovered, for 10 minutes. Remove from the heat and discard the zest and cinnamon.

With a whisk, lightly beat the eggs in a medium heatproof bowl. Whisk in the hot wine mixture, pouring slowly at first in a thin stream, and then more rapidly. Using a liquid measuring cup, divide the mixture among the ramekins or custard cups. Cover each with a small square of aluminum foil and press the foil around the rim to seal.

Set the containers on the steamer rack, place over simmering water, cover, and steam until the custard is just set but jiggles in the center when shaken, about 10 minutes. Let cool, then refrigerate until chilled. Serve very cold.

CARAMEL ORANGE SCALLOPS "EN SURPRISE"

Coquilles Saint-Jacques en Surprise

This recipe combines two of Manière's passions: his love of the sea and his delight in playing the trickster. We can imagine his gleeful enjoyment of his guests' surprise as they are presented an orange custard disguised in a sea scallop shell. The custards are glazed with a thin shell of caramelized sugar so the identity of the dessert doesn't become apparent until you taste it.

Scallop shells are sold at some specialty food stores. Or you can use porcelain scallop shell–shaped molds or the shallow oval porcelain dishes used for crème brûlée.

True scallop shells will need to be steadied on the steamer rack during steaming so that the liquid custard doesn't run out. Before filling them, set the empty shells on the rack and wedge a small crumpled piece of aluminum foil under the wide curved end of each, opposite the hinge end, angling the shells so that they hold as much liquid as possible. Then carefully pour in the custard mixture and press the foil over the tops.

SERVES 4

---

1 cup whole milk

5 large eggs

⅔ cup granulated sugar

Grated zest of 1 large orange

4 teaspoons superfine sugar

Aluminum foil

4 large sea scallop shells, scallop-shaped
 porcelain molds, or shallow porcelain
 crème brûlée molds

Large stackable steamer with two
 steaming compartments or large
 roasting pan with wire rack

Bring the milk to a boil in a medium saucepan. Remove from the heat.

Combine the eggs and granulated sugar in the bowl of a food processor or in a medium bowl and process or whisk until thick and light-colored. Add the zest and process or whisk to combine. If using a food processor, add the hot milk through the feed tube with the motor running. If using a whisk, whisk in the milk, slowly at first in a thin stream, and then more rapidly.

Put the shells or molds on the steamer rack, using a crumpled piece of aluminum foil under each shell to steady and tip it slightly toward the hinge end (see headnote). Using a liquid measuring cup, divide the custard mixture among the shells or molds. Cover each with a small square of aluminum foil, pressing the foil around the rim to seal. Place over simmering water, cover, and steam 20 minutes.

Preheat the broiler.

Take the custards out of the steamer, remove the foil, and sprinkle the top of each custard evenly with 1 teaspoon of the superfine sugar.

Broil the custards until the tops are caramelized to a light brown, about 5 minutes. Put each custard on a plate and serve hot.

POMELO (GRAPEFRUIT) CREAM

Crème aux Pomelos

Pomelo juice gives this cornstarch-thickened pudding a bright, clean flavor. While *pomelo* is defined as "grapefruit" in my dictionary of French food terms (and grapefruit does make a fine substitute for pomelo in this recipe), a pomelo is in fact a different fruit. In her *Fruit Book,* Jane Grigson writes that *pomelo* means "large citron"; a pomelo and a citron both have thick skins. Pomelos are native to Java and Malaysia and were introduced to Europe in the seventeenth century; the grapefruit is native to the Americas and wasn't known in Europe until the mid–1800s.

I had never tasted a pomelo before eating this dessert. I found them at a specialty food store, imported from Israel, and was delighted by the taste. They're much like grapefruit but sweeter and with a drier texture that makes them wonderfully chewy.

This pudding is served directly from the pan, so use a decorative mold if you have one.

SERVES 4

1⅓ cups pomelo or grapefruit juice
(2 to 3 pomelos or grapefruit)
1½ teaspoons cornstarch
⅔ cup sugar
3 large eggs

Aluminum foil
1½-quart soufflé dish
9-inch or larger stackable steamer or
    steamer pot with insert, roasting pan
    with wire rack, or collapsible steamer
    basket with removable center post

 In a small bowl, combine 1 tablespoon of the pomelo or grapefruit juice and the cornstarch and stir until smooth.

Put the remaining juice in a medium nonaluminum saucepan. Add the sugar, place over medium heat, and cook, stirring, until the sugar melts. Whisk in the cornstarch mixture and remove from the heat.

With a whisk, lightly beat the eggs in a large bowl. Whisk the warm juice into the eggs. Pour the mixture into the soufflé dish and cover with a square of aluminum foil, pressing the foil around the rim to seal.

Put the soufflé dish on the steamer rack, place over simmering water, cover, and steam until the pudding is set and a knife inserted into the center comes out clean, about 35 minutes.

Remove the soufflé dish from the steamer pot and let cool. Refrigerate until chilled. Serve cold.

APRICOT FLAN WITH KIRSCH

Flan d'Abricots

There's nothing complicated here; just apricots, drenched in kirsch (a clear liqueur, or *eau de vie,* made from wild cherries) and blanketed with vanilla custard. Without the kirsch, it's the kind of sweet dessert a child loves. I tried making this with canned apricots in the winter; alas, although the flavor was still superb, the canned fruit doesn't absorb the kirsch as the fresh does, leaving a pool of kirsch underneath the custard.

The flan is flavored with half a vanilla bean; wrap the remaining half in plastic and refrigerate it for another use.

This dessert is served directly from the pan in which it is steamed, so use a decorative Pyrex or porcelain pan if you have one.

SERVES 4

1 pound fresh apricots (about 5 large or
 6 medium), halved and pitted

3 tablespoons kirsch

½ cup sugar

1 cup whole milk

½ vanilla bean or ½ teaspoon vanilla
 extract

1 large whole egg

1 large egg yolk

1½ tablespoons cornstarch

Aluminum foil

8- to 9-inch quiche pan, round cake pan,
 or pie pan

10-inch or larger stackable steamer or
 steamer pot with insert, roasting pan
 with wire rack, or collapsible steamer
 basket with removable center post

 Put the apricot halves in a single layer, cut sides up, in the pan you are using to steam the custard. Sprinkle with the kirsch and 3 tablespoons of the sugar. Let stand 15 minutes to macerate, turning the apricots once or twice during that time.

Meanwhile, put the milk in a medium saucepan. If using half a vanilla bean, cut it in half again, lengthwise. Use a knife to scrape the tiny seeds into the milk, then add the pod. Bring the milk to a boil over medium-high heat.

While the milk heats, in another medium saucepan, combine the whole egg and yolk, the remaining 5 tablespoons sugar, and the cornstarch. Whisk until thick and light-colored.

Remove the vanilla bean, if using, from the milk. Whisk the milk into the egg mixture, pouring slowly at first in a thin stream, and then more rapidly. Place over medium-low heat and cook, whisking constantly and making sure to get into the edges of the pan, until the custard thickens and just comes to a boil. Remove from the heat and add the vanilla extract, if using.

Turn the apricots cut side down in the pan. Pour the custard over the apricots. Cover the pan with a square of aluminum foil, pressing the foil around the rim to seal.

Set the pan on the steamer rack, place over simmering water, cover, and steam until the custard is set, 15 to 20 minutes.

Serve warm, or let cool, refrigerate until chilled, and serve cold.

The following four recipes are for a quartet of unusual desserts. The clafoutis is Manière's version of the French regional puffy, pancake-like pastry made with sour cherries. His is more custard-like than the traditional but sturdier than a true custard because it's thickened with flour. His pumpkin cheesecake is a fluffy, gossamer creation made solely with egg whites; much lighter than a custard, it evaporates in the mouth, leaving a whisper of pumpkin and a burst of lemon. The almond-and-vanilla-flavored semolina pudding is a substantial mouthful on the order of a steamed English pudding, dense with ground almonds and semolina flour and perfumed with the heavenly scent of vanilla bean. The apple charlotte is a vastly simplified version of a French classic; Manière's is a scrumptious thing, something like a buttery apple bread pudding.

CHERRY CLAFOUTIS
Le Clafoutis Limougeot

The traditional clafoutis is a rough peasant dessert from the Limousin region of central France. It's made with the sour cherries of the region, covered with a pancake-like batter and baked. Manière's steamed clafoutis is made with less flour than is traditional and so is soft and creamy.

Traditionally, the fresh cherries for clafoutis aren't pitted because, if they are, the juice bleeds into the batter. Sour cherries, such as morello cherries, are sold in jars at specialty food stores; those I have used are sold pitted. Or you may be able to find canned or frozen sour cherries; some are marketed as "pie cherries." Be sure not to buy the canned sweetened pie filling. Let jarred or canned cherries drain overnight so that they are as dry as possible, and don't add additional liquid to the custard.

A different, very good clafoutis can be made with sautéed apple or pear slices instead of the cherries. Peel, core, and thinly slice apples or pears and sauté them quickly in butter with the extra tablespoon of sugar (for fresh cherries) to caramelize the fruit. Macerate the fruit in a quarter cup of brandy or rum for about fifteen minutes; drain the fruit, saving the rum. Spread the fruit over the bottom of the pan and use the rum to replace one quarter cup of the milk in the batter.

1 pound fresh sour cherries or 2 cups jarred or canned pitted sour cherries in syrup

Unsalted butter, softened, for buttering the pan

5 tablespoons sugar, plus 1 tablespoon if using fresh cherries
¼ cup all-purpose flour
3 large eggs
2 cups whole milk
⅛ teaspoon salt

Aluminum foil
9-inch round cake pan or quiche pan
10-inch or larger stackable steamer or steamer pot with insert, roasting pan with wire rack, or collapsible steamer basket with removable center post

 If using jarred or canned cherries, put them in a strainer over a bowl and drain overnight in the refrigerator.

Lightly butter the pan.

If using fresh cherries, stem and pit them or not, as you like (traditionally they are not pitted because pitted cherries bleed).

Spread the cherries over the bottom of the pan. Sprinkle fresh cherries with 1 tablespoon sugar.

Put 4 tablespoons of the sugar, the flour, eggs, milk, and salt in a food processor or blender. Process or blend until very smooth. Pour the batter over the cherries. Cover the pan with a square of aluminum foil, pressing the foil around the rim to seal.

Put the pan on the steamer rack, place over simmering water, cover, and steam until the clafoutis is set and a knife inserted into the center comes out clean, about 30 minutes. Remove from the steamer and let stand 5 minutes.

Remove the foil and sprinkle the remaining tablespoon sugar over the top of the clafoutis. Serve hot, warm, or cold, cut in wedges.

PUMPKIN CHEESECAKE
Cheese Cake

Although Manière called this a "cheese cake," it's nothing like our rich, dense, American version. His lemony pumpkin-flavored dessert is low-fat, airy, and soufflé-like because it's made with only the beaten whites of the egg. The cake puffs in the steamer and then deflates slightly as it stands.

(continued)

Vegetable oil, if using a nonstick pan;
  unsalted butter, softened, if using a
  standard pan

¾ cup canned pumpkin purée

1 cup (about 7 ounces) ricotta cheese

1 tablespoon potato starch, cornstarch,
  or arrowroot

⅓ cup sugar

Grated zest from ½ lemon (about
  ¼ teaspoon)

4 large egg whites

Aluminum foil

Parchment or waxed paper, if using
  standard cake pan

9-inch round cake pan, preferably
  nonstick

10-inch or larger stackable steamer or
  steamer pot with insert, roasting pan
  with wire rack, or collapsible steamer
  basket with removable center post

 Lightly coat the nonstick pan with vegetable oil, or lightly butter a standard cake pan and line the bottom with a round of buttered parchment or waxed paper.

Put the pumpkin purée in the bowl of a food processor. Add the ricotta cheese; potato starch, cornstarch, or arrowroot; sugar; and lemon zest and process until smooth. Scrape into a large bowl.

In another large bowl, beat the egg whites to stiff peaks. Stir about one quarter of the whites into the pumpkin mixture to lighten it. Then gently fold in the remaining whites. Scrape the mixture into the pan with a rubber spatula and smooth the top. Cover with a square of aluminum foil and press the foil around the rim to seal.

Put the pan on the steamer rack, place over simmering water, cover, and steam 20 minutes. Then set the lid ajar and steam 5 more minutes, or until the cake is set and a knife inserted into the center comes out clean.

Let the cake cool, then refrigerate until chilled.

To serve, invert a serving plate over the pan and quickly reverse the two to unmold the cake. Remove the parchment or waxed paper, if used. Cut the cake into wedges. Serve cold.

SEMOLINA PUDDING WITH PLUM COMPOTE

Couronne de Semoule aux Quetsches

Sabine, a German friend, tells me that her mother made a dessert just like this one in Germany, even down to the plum sauce, but without the almonds. Eaten at room temperature or chilled with the fresh plum sauce, it's dense and moist, rich with almonds and vanilla, and yet very refreshing. It's a dessert to eat late in the summer when the oval, deep purple–skinned Italian plums are abundant. Out of season, Manière served a compote made with dried prunes in place of plums. The pudding gets better as it ages; one to two days in the refrigerator will mellow and marry the flavors.

Semolina is ground durum wheat, a variety of wheat that we speak of as "hard," meaning that it's high in protein. Semolina is light yellow in color and looks like fine yellow cornmeal. It is available in specialty food stores. The amount of sugar needed in the sauce depends on the sweetness of the plums; start with the lesser amount and taste.

S E R V E S   6

Unsalted butter, softened, for buttering
    the pan

1 quart whole milk

1 vanilla bean or 1 teaspoon vanilla
    extract

1 cup finely ground semolina

½ cup sugar

4 large eggs

3 tablespoons unsalted butter

½ cup ground blanched almonds
    (about 1½ ounces)

⅛ teaspoon salt

PLUM COMPOTE

2 pounds Italian plums, halved and pitted

⅓ cup water

1½ to 2 cups sugar, depending on the
    sweetness of the plums

½ teaspoon ground cinnamon

Aluminum foil

8½- by 2¾-inch springform tube pan

10-inch stackable steamer or steamer
    pot with insert, roasting pan with wire
    rack, or collapsible steamer basket
    with removable center post

 Lightly butter the pan.

Put the milk in a large heavy-bottomed saucepan. If using the vanilla bean, rinse it and cut it in half lengthwise. Use a knife to scrape the tiny seeds into the milk, then add the pod. Bring the milk to a boil over medium-high heat.

Remove the vanilla bean and pour in the semolina in a thin stream, stirring constantly. Reduce the heat to medium and cook 10 minutes, stirring constantly and making sure to get into the sides of the pan so the mixture doesn't burn. (The mixture will become stiff, like polenta.)

Stir in the sugar and remove the pan from the heat. Stir in the eggs, one at a time, stirring well after each addition. Add the butter, almonds, salt, and the vanilla extract, if using, and stir well.

Scrape the mixture into the buttered pan. Cover the pan with a square of aluminum foil, pressing the foil around the rim to seal. Put the pan on the steamer rack, place over simmering water, cover, and steam 35 minutes. Then set the lid ajar and steam 10 more minutes, or until the pudding is set and a skewer inserted into the center comes out almost clean, with a few moist bits of the pudding sticking to it. Let cool for 30 minutes before unmolding.

Meanwhile, make the plum compote: Put the plums in a large saucepan and add the water. Bring to a boil, reduce the heat, and simmer, stirring occasionally, until the plums have softened but are still intact, about 10 minutes. Stir in the sugar and cinnamon and simmer about 1 minute. Remove from the heat and let cool.

To unmold the pudding, invert a serving plate over the pan and quickly reverse the two. Cover and refrigerate the pudding until cold.

To serve, spoon some of the compote into the center of the pudding. Serve the remaining compote in a sauceboat on the side. Cut the pudding into thin slices and spoon some of the compote over each slice.

APPLE CHARLOTTE

Charlotte aux Pommes

An apple charlotte is a classic apple dessert made in a charlotte mold, a cylindrical metal mold with gently flaring sides and two roughly heart-shaped handles at the top. Typically the apples for a charlotte are cooked into a thick compote, sweetened and flavored with vanilla and sometimes cinnamon. The mold is lined with ladyfingers or fingers of butter-soaked bread, filled with the compote, and baked. The charlotte is served cold.

With all the cutting and fitting of bread into the mold, a traditional apple charlotte may be too time-consuming a dish for the average busy American cook. So you'll be very happy to find that Manière's version is twice as quick to make as the traditional dessert and a wonderful thing to boot. It's more of a steamed apple bread pudding than a classic charlotte, made with brioche, a rich egg bread, torn into pieces and layered with thinly sliced apples and sugar, moistened with a goodly amount of melted butter. Manière cut the crust off the bread, but you needn't bother. It's so quick and simple, the kind of dessert you can make with a child.

Charlotte molds are available at specialty cookware stores. If you can find one, they're useful for soufflés, puddings, and gelatin desserts as well. If not, you can use a soufflé mold or a Pyrex loaf pan; the charlotte will taste as good but won't be quite as pretty. Make sure to let the charlotte cool for two hours before unmolding, or it may fall apart. Manière served it cold, as is traditional, but I love to eat it when it's still slightly warm; the caramelized flavor of the butter and apples disappears in the chilling.

In France, apple charlotte is served with a sauce made from sieved apricot jam, thinned with a little water. I like it with crème anglaise (see Rum Crème Anglaise, page 281), vanilla ice cream, crème fraîche, or simply cream.

The charlotte steams for one and a half hours. Check the water level a few times during steaming and add water as needed.

SERVES 8

Unsalted butter, softened, for buttering the charlotte mold

One 1-pound loaf brioche or challah
1½ pounds (3 large) Golden Delicious apples, peeled, cored, and quartered
1 cup sugar
8 tablespoons (¼ pound) unsalted butter, melted
Small jar of apricot jam

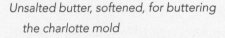 Butter the charlotte mold, loaf pan, or soufflé dish thoroughly with the softened butter. Cut a round or rectangle of parchment or waxed paper to line the bottom and fit it into the container.

Tear the bread into coarse crumbs, as if you were making bread stuffing.

Spread one quarter of the apples over the bottom of the mold or pan. Sprinkle with ¼ cup of the sugar and cover with one quarter of the bread. Press the bread down firmly with the palm of your hand to compress it. Repeat three more times to use all of

Aluminum foil

Parchment or waxed paper

1½-quart charlotte mold, 8- by 4-inch
Pyrex loaf pan, or 1½-quart soufflé
dish

Stackable steamer or steamer pot with
insert if using charlotte mold or soufflé
dish; large stackable steamer, steamer
pot with insert, or roasting pan with
wire rack if using loaf pan

the apples, sugar, and bread, pressing down each layer of bread. (The charlotte mold may seem too small for the amount of apples and bread, but it will all fit, with a mounded top, if you pack it well.) Carefully and slowly pour the melted butter over the top layer of bread crumbs, then gently press again to push down the top layer of bread.

Cover the container with a piece of aluminum foil, pressing the foil around the rim to seal. Set on the steamer rack, place over simmering water, cover, and steam 1½ hours. Remove the charlotte from the steamer and let cool 2 hours. (If you turn the charlotte out too soon, it will fall apart.)

For the sauce, scrape the jam into a saucepan and melt it over low heat. Whisk in a little water to thin the jam—the amount of water needed depends on the thickness of the jam. Strain. Serve slightly warm or at room temperature.

When the charlotte has cooled, invert a serving plate over the top and quickly reverse the two. Serve immediately, or refrigerate until chilled and serve cold.

THREE FRESH PEACH SALADS

While Manière used fruit as an element of several desserts, these three feature fresh peaches with almost no adornment. The fruit is steamed briefly to make peeling easier and then sliced and macerated variously in sweetened red wine, lemon juice, or brandied fresh strawberry purée. These desserts are unabashedly simple, created to celebrate the ripeness of summer, and can be served as is, with cookies or ice cream, or to accompany a cake such as angel food, gingerbread, or poppy seed or pound cake.

The recipes are only as good as the peaches you use. Macerating brings out the perfumed essence of a perfectly ripe peach but won't mask the tasteless chalkiness of unripe fruit. The amount of sugar needed depends on the sweetness of the peaches; start with the lower amount and taste. Taste again just before serving; after chilling, the fruit may need more sugar.

Peaches in Red Wine

Pêches au Vin

SERVES 4

5 small or 4 medium ripe peaches

1 cup red wine, such as Bordeaux or
  Cabernet Sauvignon

¼ to ½ cup sugar, to taste

Stackable steamer, steamer pot with
  insert, or collapsible steamer basket

Peel and pit the peaches as directed on page 294.

Combine the wine and ¼ cup sugar in a serving bowl. Cut the peaches into quarters and add them to the bowl. Cover and refrigerate for 1 hour, gently stirring the peaches occasionally so that they macerate evenly.

Taste for sugar just before serving and add more as needed. Serve cool.

Peaches with Lemon

Pêches au Citron

This simplest of peach desserts can be dressed up by adding a scoop of lemon sorbet and a ginger cookie to each plate.

SERVES 4

5 small or 4 medium ripe peaches

Juice of 1½ medium lemons (3 to 4
  tablespoons)

¼ to ½ cup sugar, to taste

Stackable steamer, steamer pot with
  insert, or collapsible steamer basket

Peel and pit the peaches as directed on page 294. Slice the peaches and put them in a bowl. Sprinkle with the lemon juice and ¼ cup sugar and toss to combine. Taste for sugar and add more if needed. Serve immediately.

PEACHES WITH WILD STRAWBERRIES AND BRANDY

Pêches à la Royale

Manière used *fraises des bois,* tiny, fragrant wild strawberries, for this recipe. I've adapted it to use standard strawberries because the wild are hard to find in America. If you aren't familiar with crème fraîche, this recipe is a good place to try it out; the acidity of the cream is delicious with ripe fruit.

SERVES 4

5 small or 4 medium ripe peaches

¼ cup granulated sugar, or more as
    needed

CRÈME CHANTILLY

¼ cup crème fraîche or ¼ cup heavy
    cream mixed with 1 teaspoon fresh
    lemon juice

3 tablespoons confectioners' sugar

½ teaspoon vanilla extract

6 ounces wild strawberries or ¾ pint
    strawberries (1½ cups), rinsed, hulled,
    and halved

1 tablespoon brandy

Stackable steamer, steamer pot with
    insert, or collapsible steamer basket

 Peel and pit the peaches as directed on page 294. Slice them and put them into a serving bowl. Sprinkle with the ¼ cup granulated sugar and let stand 15 minutes.

Meanwhile, make the crème Chantilly as directed on page 296.

Put the strawberries into the bowl of a food processor. Process 10 seconds. Add the crème Chantilly and brandy and process 10 more seconds. Spread this mixture over the peaches, cover, and refrigerate for 1 hour.

Just before serving, stir gently to combine the peaches with the sauce. Taste for sugar and add more if needed. Serve cool.

While the recipes in this chapter are so easy that anyone can make them, they use a few typically French techniques and ingredients that merit discussion.

✳ PEELING AND PITTING PEACHES

Manière's grandfather used to say, "Peel a peach for a friend, a pear for an enemy," meaning that the skin of many raw pears is delicious, while the furriness of raw peach skin makes it inedible. Peeling a peach can be difficult, but it's child's play with a steamer.

In traditional French cuisine, peaches are peeled just like tomatoes: They're dunked first in boiling water for several seconds and then into an ice bath to loosen the skin. This makes the skin easy to peel off with your fingers or a small knife. Manière used the steamer instead; the steaming time isn't long enough to cook the flesh.

To peel a peach, prepare a bowl of cold water. Make an "X" incision in the bottom of the peach with the tip of the knife. Put the peach on the steamer rack, place over boiling water, cover, adjust the heat as necessary, and steam 2 minutes. Transfer the peach to the bowl of water and let stand until cold. Then pull off the skin with a small knife or your fingers; it should come off easily.

To pit a peach, cut it in half around the seed. Cup half of the peach in each hand and gently twist the halves in opposite directions to pull them apart. Pry out the seed with your fingers.

✳ CARAMEL

Some of Manière's custard desserts, such as Mocha Cream with Rum Crème Anglaise (page 280), Crème Caramel (page 277), and Coconut-Caramel Flan (page 278), use a simple caramel made from sugar and water to flavor the custard or to line the mold. A caramel can range from very light brown and mild-flavored to dark-colored and deep-flavored. Sometimes, as in the recipe for Mocha Cream, Manière specified a light-colored caramel; otherwise, it's up to the cook. Manière wrote that a caramel is easy to make if you follow a few simple rules. Here are his guidelines:

Making a Caramel Manière recommended making caramel with sugar cubes rather than granulated sugar. Cubed sugar is graded by weight in France, and this makes measuring easy for the French, who measure ingredients by weight rather than by volume. I've never had a problem using granulated sugar in Manière's recipes.

Use a small saucepan made of stainless steel or heavy aluminum and make sure that it's very clean.

Put the sugar in the pan (see individual recipes for amounts) and pass the pan quickly under running water to barely moisten the sugar. The exact quantity of water is unimportant, as the water simply helps dissolve the sugar and it boils off in the cooking; caramel can in fact be made with sugar alone. (In the recipes for Crème Caramel and Mocha Cream, Manière also gave specific measurements for water.)

To cook the caramel, put the pan over medium heat, bring to a boil, and boil without stirring, shaking the pan from time to time so that the sugar cooks evenly. The sugar first dissolves in the water to make a clear syrup. Then, as the water boils off and the sugar itself begins to cook, it turns a light caramel color. Watch very carefully once the sugar begins to color at the sides of the pan; it darkens quickly. When the caramel reaches a rich amber color, remove it from the heat and use immediately. Don't let it sit in the pan; even off the heat, the warmth of the pan continues to cook it. If the caramel gets too dark, it will be bitter.

Lining a Mold with Caramel To line a dessert mold, pour the prepared caramel into the mold and then rotate the mold so that the caramel runs over the bottom and sides to coat. Work quickly, because caramel begins to harden as soon as it is removed from the heat.

Then immediately turn the mold over on a rack so the caramel doesn't collect in a thick, hard layer at the bottom. Let it cool; sometimes it cracks as it cools, but it won't affect the final result. When hardened, the caramel-lined mold is ready to be filled with a custard mixture and steamed.

Unmolding To unmold a chilled custard steamed in a caramelized mold, first steam it briefly to remelt the caramel: Cover the mold with a square of aluminum foil, pressing the foil around the rim to seal. Put the mold on the steamer rack, place over boiling water, cover, adjust the heat as necessary, and steam one minute.

Meanwhile, choose a plate deep enough to contain the thin, liquid caramel that will run when the custard is unmolded. Invert the plate over the warmed mold and quickly reverse the two. Remove the mold.

Cleaning Caramel from a Pan To clean hardened caramel from a saucepan, fill the pan with water and boil for five to eight minutes. If the caramel has not completely dissolved, change the water and boil longer.

BASIC CARAMEL SAUCE

A caramel can be turned into a luscious sauce for steamed fruit by adding cream or water to the hot caramel. My favorite sauce is made with cream: For about one cup of sauce, add a cup of heavy cream to a caramel made with a cup of sugar and enough water to dissolve the sugar (see page 295); stand back when adding the cream, because the caramel will sputter and harden. Put the caramel back over low heat to remelt, and serve the sauce warm.

CRÈME CHANTILLY

Crème Chantilly

Crème Chantilly is French whipped cream. The French don't beat cream for as long as we do, so it is soft and cloudlike rather than stiff. It should be smooth, hold a soft peak, and flow from a spoon. Very cold cream whips faster than warmer cream; if the cream is too warm, it won't whip at all.

Traditionally, crème Chantilly is whipped by hand with a whisk or with an electric beater. Manière made it in a food processor: Take the cream out of the refrigerator at the last minute, and don't process too long, or the cream will turn to butter. If the cream thickens too much, add two to three tablespoons of milk to thin it.

Crème Chantilly can be made with crème fraîche (see recipe on page 297), heavy cream, or whipping cream. Crème fraîche thickens more quickly and gains less volume than heavy cream.

MAKES ½ TO ¾ CUP

½ cup very cold crème fraîche or heavy or
   whipping cream
¼ cup confectioners' sugar
1 teaspoon vanilla extract

Pour the cream into the bowl of the food processor. Add the sugar and vanilla and process 5 to 10 seconds. Scrape down the sides and process another 5 to 10 seconds, just until the cream thickens. Refrigerate until ready to use.

HOMEMADE CRÈME FRAÎCHE

Manière used crème fraîche, a thick, tangy, fermented cream with a luscious, rich texture, in many of his recipes. It's available in some specialty food stores and even some supermarkets, but it's very easy to make. Because cream in America has been pasteurized, we need to add a live culture, as there is in buttermilk or sour cream, to the cream and warm it to get the fermentation started. Don't use ultrapasteurized cream; it won't culture.

The time needed to culture the cream depends on the temperature. In summer, it seems to culture practically immediately, while a crème fraîche made in winter takes longer.

Unlike sour cream, crème fraîche can be boiled without separating.

MAKES 1 QUART

1 quart heavy cream (not ultrapasteurized)
¼ cup buttermilk

 In a large saucepan, heat the cream with the buttermilk to tepid (about 98°F on an instant-read thermometer). Pour it into a plastic or glass container, cover, and let stand in a warm place for 8 to 24 hours, until thickened.

Stir the cream well, cover, and refrigerate. The cream will get thicker and tangier as it ages. It lasts for a week to 10 days in the refrigerator.

※ **VANILLA BEANS, VANILLA SUGAR, AND VANILLA EXTRACT**
The French typically use vanilla beans or vanilla-flavored sugar rather than liquid vanilla extract to flavor desserts. The long, skinny, black-podded vanilla beans have an intense perfume when fresh and give any dessert a heavenly flavor. Fresh vanilla beans are soft and plump; the most highly perfumed beans I've ever used came from Tahiti. Buy several at a time, wrap them in plastic, and refrigerate or freeze them; stored this way, the beans last several months.

To use vanilla beans, split them lengthwise and scrape the tiny black seeds into whatever is to be flavored. In Manière's recipes, the beans are used to infuse milk that is boiled for custard; in that case, scrape the seeds into the milk and then add the pod itself. Remove the pod before using the milk. The pods can be rinsed and reused, but they will have much less flavor.

Vanilla sugar is sugar perfumed by vanilla beans: Bury whole vanilla beans in a container of sugar, and use the sugar in desserts.

Vanilla beans are commonly sold in specialty food shops, but if you can't find them, a good vanilla extract works fine in Manière's recipes as well. Vanilla extract is the liquid form of vanilla; the chopped bean is macerated in an alcohol-water mixture to extract the flavor. Buy only pure extract; imitation or artificial vanilla extract is cheaper but has substantially less good flavor. Don't add vanilla extract to boiling-hot mixtures; the heat robs it of flavor. Let the mixture cool slightly before adding the vanilla. My experience is that vanilla extracts vary in potency: Taste the dish and add more if needed.

MAIL ORDER SOURCES

Steamers

Zabar's
2245 Broadway
New York, N.Y. 10024
(212) 787-2000 or
(212) 496-1234

Bridge Kitchenware
214 East 52 Street
New York, N.Y. 10022
(212) 688-4220

Hung Chong Imports, Inc.
14 Bowery
New York, N.Y. 10013
(212) 349-3392

Williams-Sonoma
P.O. Box 7456
San Francisco, CA 94120
(800) 541-2233

AMC Cookware
6593 Powers Avenue
Suite 17
Jacksonville, FL 32217
(800) 766-8262

Sur La Table
84 Pine Street
Pike Place Farmers' Market
Seattle, WA 98101
(800) 243-0852

Poultry

D'Artagnan, Inc.
399 St. Paul Avenue
Jersey City, N.J. 07306
(800) 327-8246

Veal

Summerfield Farm
10044 James Monroe
　Highway
Culpeper, VA 22701
(703) 547-9600

TRANSLATOR'S ACKNOWLEDGMENTS

I'm grateful to many people for their help on this translation-adaptation of Jacques Manière's *Le Grand Livre de la Cuisine à la Vapeur*. First, to Jacques Manière, whose recipes taught me a great deal, not the least of which was to have an eternally open mind. A world of thanks to Barbara Kafka, who inspired, chided, polished, and fed me over the two years I worked on this project. She made me a better thinker, a better writer, and taught me the joy of research. Many thanks also to my wonderful editor, Ann Bramson, who believed in me, was always ready with encouragement and praise, and found a solution to every problem.

I want to thank Brian Buckley and Sabine Renard, who shopped and then worked long days in my steamy kitchen with me, testing and tasting. Sabine's experience with European desserts was invaluable to this project, and if not for Brian's hard work and unfettered enthusiasm, I would doubtless still be testing recipes today.

Friends, cooks, and food writers were endlessly helpful, listening to my questions, giving me their experience, and generally holding my hand. Thanks to Dona Abramson, Katherine Alford, Pam Anderson, Gail Arnold, Jack Bishop, Mark Bittman, Shirley Corriher, Marion Gorman, Paul Grimes, Judy Hill, Peter Kump (who let me teach steaming at his Manhattan cooking school), Ris Lacoste, Tina Ujlaki, the late Greg Usher (who sent me home from Paris with Manière's steamer), Paula Wolfert, Eric Wolff (who did hours of work on the steaming charts), and Nach Waxman and his staff at Kitchen Arts and Letters in Manhattan.

Many of the business people I dealt with were very good to me. Bill Bowers, Mark Conley, and the staff at Jakes Fish Market in Manhattan let me make myself at home in the store and were extraordinarily generous with their fish, their time, and their considerable knowledge; my time spent testing the fish chapter was some of the most enjoyable work I've ever done. Harry Oppenheimer at Oppenheimer Co. and Michel and Eleanor Guiton at the Broadway Butcher, both in Manhattan, and George Faison at D'Artagnan in New Jersey answered myriad questions about meat and poultry; Michel and his staff gave me invaluable information about French butchering. Computer whiz Julian Shapiro fixed my computer, found lost files, and took my desperate phone calls anyway, even when he shouldn't have had to be working.

Judith Sutton's careful and creative copyediting made me do a lot more work after I thought I was done, and made this a lot better book. At William Morrow, Sarah Guralnik and Amy Broderick took care of all the details with great willingness and patience, and Pam Lyons was meticulous in the work she did to shepherd the manuscript through production. Dolores Santo Liquido's illustrations are a wonderful addition to the technical section of the book, and she was a pleasure to work with, even knee-deep in fish trimmings.

Finally, thanks to Clint Fisher, without whose support I would not have had the luxury of time to work on this book, to Joanna, who let me feed her mostly steamed food for a long time, and to Kate Harper and Dick Nodell, who are simply the best.

INDEX

achards de légumes au curry, 59–60

acorn squash, 94, 95

aïoli, salt cod, 144–145

aïoli de morue, 144–145

almonds, radishes, and tomato, cockle salad with, 150–151

alose à l'oseille, 140–141

aluminum foil, as pot lid, 11, 12

anchovy(ies):
   -caper vinaigrette, cod steaks with, 116–117
   olives, and white wine, hot beef "terrine" with, 232–233

Anjou pears, steaming time for, 276

appetizers:
   artichokes à la Grecque, 32–33
   artichokes Henry IV, 34–35
   beef tongue with parsley sauce, 257–258
   celery root flans, 66
   cockle salad with radishes, tomato, and almonds, 150–151
   cucumbers with mint and yogurt, 71–72
   eggplant caviar, 73–74
   fish mousse with mussels, 152–153
   garlic flans, 78–79
   gourmet salad of green beans, chicken livers, shrimp, and mushrooms, 44–45
   grated turnip salad rémoulade, 99–100
   langoustines with Belgian endive and lime, 158–159
   leg of lamb cured in red wine, 243–244
   lobster steamed on a bed of seaweed, 157–158
   marinated vegetables with coriander and thyme, 74–75
   oysters in the shell with spinach and curry, 155
   pike with mint and thyme and a Muscadet butter sauce, 138–139
   Provençal-style marinated peppers, 47–48
   sardines steamed in spicy tomato and garlic sauce, 135
   scallops with a Muscadet butter sauce, 147
   sea scallops in Champagne sauce with mussels and shrimp, 148–149
   spinach and mushroom flans, 93–94
   stuffed zucchini, 96–97
   sweetbread mousse with ham, Madeira, and truffles, 258–259
   warm asparagus with soft-cooked eggs and lemon butter, 40
   warm chick pea salad with spring onions, 85–86
   warm scallop salad with lamb's lettuce and tea-infused vinegar, 149–150
   warm skate salad with red currants, 123–124
   whole steamed shad with sorrel, 140–141

apple(s):
   charlotte, 290–291
   and cider, veal chops with, 238–239
   sauced, 273
   steamed, 272
   steaming times for, 275, 276

apricot:
   flan with kirsch, 285
   sauce, 272

Arctic char, 137
   steaming time for, 114

artichaut de Bretagne, 28

artichauts:
   façon barigoule, 33–34
   à la Grecque, 32–33
   Henri IV, 34–35
   sauce à l', 31–32

artichoke(s), 28–30
   à la Grecque, 32–33
   bottoms, stuffed, 103
   bottoms barigoule, stuffed, 33–34
   Henry IV, 34–35
   mayonnaise, 31
   rack of lamb with spring vegetables, 244–245

asparagus, 36–38
   chicken with rice stuffing and spring vegetables, 189–190
   grilling of, 102
   rack of lamb with spring vegetables, 244–245
   with soft-cooked eggs and lemon butter, warm, 40
   soup, 189
   vinaigrette for, 26

asparagus steamers, 6

asperges tièdes à la coque, 40

"au blanc" sauce, 187

baby artichoke hearts, 28, 30

baby carrots, 56

baking vs. boiling potatoes, 88

balsamic vinaigrette, 24

bamboo steamers, 10, 14

bananas:
   en papillote, 274
   steaming times for, 275, 276

Barbara's warm steamed pineapple, 274
Bartlett pears, steaming time for, 276
basic vinaigrette, 26–27
basil stuffing, for zucchini, 96
basil-tomato sauce:
    fresh, 62
    sole with fresh, 121
baskets, collapsible steamer, 6–7
bâtonnets, 103–104
beans:
    fresh white, Brittany-style, 43
    grilling of, 102
    varieties and preparation of, 41–42
beans, fava:
    chicken with rice stuffing and spring
        vegetables, 189–190
    duck confit with fresh, 201
beans, green:
    chicken liver, shrimp, and
        mushrooms, gourmet salad of,
        44–45
    pickled vegetables with curry, 59–60
    see also haricots verts
béchamel sauce:
    medium, 69
    thick, 58
beef:
    broth, 267
    cuts, 263
    filet mignon with green
        peppercorns, 231–232
    sirloin steak with sunchoke mousse,
        234–235
    skewered, 235–236
    steaming times for, 229
    stuffed cabbage with kasha, 236–237
    "terrine" with olives, anchovies, and
        white wine, hot, 232–233
    tongue with parsley sauce, 257–258
    tournedos "tartare," chopped,
        230–231
beet greens, 79, 80
beets, 45
Belgian endive, 67–68
    langoustines with lime and, 158–159
bell pepper(s), 46
    grilling of, 102
    marinated vegetables with coriander
        and thyme, 74–75
    piperade, 47

Provençal-style marinated, 47–48
red, and paprika cream sauce, fillet
    of veal with, 239–240
sauce, sweet red, spiny lobster stew
    with, 156–157
stuffed, 103
tomatoes, and garlic, tuna with,
    125–126
Belon oysters, 169–170
berries, steamed sauces from, 272
beurre blanc, 120, 127
    herbed, 189
black currants and pears, duck breasts
    with, 199–200
blanching, 100
blanquette de veau, 240–241
blenders, 100
blowfish tails, steaming time for,
    112
blueberry sauce, 272
blue crabs, steaming time for, 115
bluefish, steaming time for, 114
boiling vs. baking potatoes, 88
boning and cutting, of poultry,
    210–212, 218
    and wishbone removal, 206, 214
Bosc pears, steaming time for, 276
bouillinade de pêcheurs, 142–143
brandy, peaches with wild strawberries
    and, 293
Bresse poularde, steamed truffled,
    175–176
Bretagne artichokes, 28
brine, 32
broccoli, 48–49
    flan, 102
    purée, 101
brochetons beurre nantais, 138–139
brochettes d'agneau au cumin, 250–251
brochettes de boeuf, 235–236
broth, 267–268
    see also stock
browning, in broiler vs. oven, 178–179,
    227, 228
Brussels sprouts, 49–50
bulots, in salt cod aïoli, 144
butter, garlic-parsley, chicken with
    onion-raisin jam and, 192–193
butterflying technique, 182, 212
butternut squash, 94, 95, 96

butter sauce:
    beurre blanc I, 120
    beurre blanc II, 127
    Ceylon tea, 119
    chervil, 152–153
    herbed beurre blanc, 189
    lemon, kippers with, 141–142
    lemon, warm asparagus with soft-
        cooked eggs and, 40
    lime, 159
    Muscadet, and mint and thyme, pike
        with, 138–139
    Muscadet, scallops with, 147
    nantais, 158
    saffron-vermouth, 160–161
    sorrel, 141
    tarragon, 254, 255

cabbage, 50–52
    choucroute, 255–256
    with cream and shallots, 53
    kohlrabi, 82–83
    leaves with mint, herring wrapped
        in, 133–134
    parslied, stuffed Guinea hen on a
        bed of, 194–195
    salad, warm sweet-and-sour, 54–55
    smoked haddock with sauerkraut,
        128–129
    stuffed, 103
    stuffed ("green chicken"), 253–255
    stuffed, with kasha, 236–237
cabillaud sauce girondine, 116–117
California artichokes, 28
calves' liver:
    with a ragout of cucumber, spring
        onions, and mint, 260–261
    with onions, parsley, and vinegar,
        259–260
    steaming time for, 229
Canadian rule for cooking fish, 109
cannette à la vapeur de vin, 197–198
caper-anchovy vinaigrette, cod steaks
    with, 116–117
capon:
    butterflying technique and, 182, 212
    carving of, 208–209
    cutting raw, 210–211
    parts, preparation for steaming of,
        209–210

salmonella in, 179–180, 210

steaming time for, 183

whole, preparation for steaming of, 205–208

caramel, 281

-coconut flan, 278–279

crème, 277–278

orange scallops "en surprise," 283

sauce, basic, 295–296

techniques for, 294–295

carp, steaming time for, 114

carré d'agneau printanier, 244–245

carrot(s), 55–56

bâtonnets and julienne, 104

chicken steamed with vegetables and tarragon, 188

chicken with rice stuffing and spring vegetables, 189–190

flan, 102

langoustines with spring vegetables and saffron, 160–161

marinated vegetables with coriander and thyme, 74–75

pickled vegetables with curry, 59–60

rack of lamb with spring vegetables, 244–245

sautéed, with parsley, 56–57

spring, parsley, and garlic, top sirloin of veal with, 242

terrine, 57–58

carving, of poultry, 208–209

catfish, steaming time for, 112

cauliflower, 58–59

flan, 102

Indian-style vegetable cutlets, 61–62

pickled vegetables with curry, 59–60

rack of lamb with spring vegetables, 244–245

caviar, eggplant, 73–74

caviar d'aubergines, 73–74

celery, 63–65

chicken steamed with vegetables and tarragon, 188

grilling of, 102

julienne, 104

pickled vegetables with curry, 59–60

celery root, 64–65

flans, 66–67

and potato purée, 65

Ceylon tea:

–infused vinegar, 120

sole steamed on a bed of, 118–119

vinaigrette, 150

Champagne sauce with mussels and shrimp, sea scallops in, 148–149

charlotte, apple, 290–291

charlotte aux pommes, 290–291

Chartreuse liqueur, 125

charts of basic steaming times, xvi

fish and shellfish, 108–111, 112–115

fruits, 275, 276

meat, 226–227, 228, 229

poultry, 178, 182, 183

vegetables, 22–23

cheese:

Gruyère, gratin of endive with ham and, 68–69

stuffing, pine nut and, 194

white, 16

cheesecake, pumpkin, 287–288

cherry:

apricot flan with kirsch, 285

clafoutis, 286–287

chervil butter sauce, 152–153

chicken, 176, 177

"au blanc," 186–188

boning of, 206, 211–212

butterflying technique and, 182, 212

carving of, 208–209

couscous with lamb and, 247–248

cutting raw, 210–211

en papillote, 213

with fresh ginger and scallions, 185–186

with garlic-parsley butter and onion-raisin jam, 192–193

juices of, 208

parts, preparation for steaming of, 209–210

quarters steamed on a bed of lime flowers, 184–185

with rice stuffing and spring vegetables, 189–190

salmonella bacteria in, 179–180, 210

steamed truffled Bresse *poularde,* 175–176

steamed with vegetables and tarragon, 188

steaming times for, 183

stock, 192

trussing of, 208

whole, preparation for steaming of, 205–208

chicken liver, green beans, shrimp, and mushrooms, gourmet salad of, 44–45

chick pea(s):

couscous, and raisins, skewered lamb with, 250–251

salad with spring onions, warm, 85–86

chicorée frisée, 67

chicories, 67, 68

see also Belgian endive

Chinese eggplant, 72–73

chocolate:

in coffee custard variation, 279–280

mocha cream with rum crème anglaise, 280–282

chou croquant, 53

choucroute, 255–256

chou farci ou poule vert, 253–255

chuck, steaming time for, 229

cider and apples, veal chops with, 238–239

cinnamon and honey, white wine custard with, 282

citrus juice, 272

clafoutis, cherry, 286–287

clafoutis limougeot, le, 286–287

clams, steaming time for, 115

clawed vs. spiny lobsters, 109

cockle(s):

salad with radishes, tomato, and almonds, 150–151

steaming time for, 115

coconut-caramel flan, 278–279

cod:

aïoli, salt, 144–145

with fennel, tomato, and cream, 130

steaks with caper-anchovy vinaigrette, 116–117

steaming time for, 113

coffee:

custard, 279–280

mocha cream with rum crème anglaise, 280–282

collapsible steamer baskets, 6–7

collard greens, 79, 80

Comice pears, steaming time for, 276
compote, plum, semolina pudding
    with, 288–289
concombres à la menthe et au yaourt,
    71–72
confit de canard aux fèves nouvelles, 201
cooking times, 10–11
    see also charts of basic steaming times
coquelets à l'éstragon, 191
coquillage:
    coquilles Saint-Jacques à la vapeur, 147
    coquilles Saint-Jacques en coquilles,
        148–149
    crème de moules "Billy bye," 153–154
    étuvée de langouste à la crème de
        poivrons doux, 156–157
    flan de moules, 152–153
    homard aux algues, 157–158
    huitres à la coque, 155
    langoustines aux endives et citron vert,
        158–159
    langoustines aux petites légumes,
        160–161
    salade de coques aux radis roses,
        150–151
    salade de mâche et de Saint-Jacques au
        vinaigre de thé, 149–150
    salade "un peu folle," 44
coquilles Saint-Jacques en surprise, 283
coral:
    lobster, 170
    sea scallop, 168
coriander, marinated vegetables with
    thyme and, 74–75
corn, 69–70
Cornish game hens:
    with fresh herbs, 191
    steaming time for, 183
Cortland apples, steaming time for, 276
côtelettes de légumes, 61–62
côtes de porc aux graines de moutarde,
    252–253
côtes de veau au cidre, 238–239
coulis de tomate au basilic, 62
courgettes farcies, 96–97
couronne de semoule aux quetsches, 288-
    289
couscous:
    chick peas, and raisins, skewered
        lamb with, 250–251

    with lamb and chicken, 247–248
    steamed, 249
couscousière, 4, 176, 247
crab legs, imitation, 130
crabs, blue, steaming time for, 115
cranberry beans, 42
cream:
    cabbage with shallots and, 53
    fennel, and tomato, pollack with,
        130
    finishing vegetables with, 24
    and herb vinaigrette, fresh, 45
    mocha, with rum crème anglaise,
        280–282
    pomelo (grapefruit), 284
    whipped, 296
cream sauce:
    herbed, 191
    herbed beurre blanc, 189
    red pepper, 156
    red pepper and paprika, fillet of veal
        with, 239–240
    vegetable, 245
    vermouth, 123
cream soups:
    leek and potato, 90–91
    watercress, 81–82
crème:
    d'ail doux, rognons de veau à la,
        262–263
    bachique, 282
    au café, 279–280
    caramel, 277–278
    Chantilly, 296
    de cresson, 81–82
    de moules "Billy bye," 153–154
    à la mustel, 90–91
    du perou, 280–282
    de poivrons doux, étuvée de langouste
        à la, 156–157
    aux pomelos, 284
crème fraîche:
    homemade, 297–298
    as used in recipes, 16
crookneck squash, yellow, 94, 95
croutons, 82
cucumber(s), 70–71
    with mint and yogurt, 71–72
    spring onions, and mint, calves' liver
        with a ragout of, 260–261

currants:
    black, duck breasts with pears and,
        199–200
    red, warm skate salad with, 123–124
curry(ied):
    mussel soup, 153–154
    oysters in the shell with spinach and,
        155
    pickled vegetables with, 59–60
custard:
    coffee, 279–280
    mocha cream with rum crème
        anglaise, 280–282
    white wine, with honey and
        cinnamon, 282
    see also caramel; flan
cutting and boning, of poultry,
    210–212, 218
    and wishbone removal, 206, 214

defrosting, 14
dessert:
    charlotte aux pommes, 290–291
    le clafoutis limougeot, 286–287
    coquilles Saint-Jacques en surprise, 283
    couronne de semoule aux quetsches,
        288–289
    crème au café, 279–280
    crème aux pomelos, 284
    crème bachique, 282
    crème du perou, 280–282
    flan d'abricots, 285
    flan exotique, 278–279
    les oeufs au lait, 277–278
    pêches à la royale, 293
    pêches au citron, 292
    pêches au vin, 292
desserts:
    apple charlotte, 290–291
    apricot flan with kirsch, 285
    caramel orange scallops "en
        surprise," 283
    cherry clafoutis, 286–287
    coconut-caramel flan, 278–279
    coffee custard, 279–280
    crème caramel, 277–278
    crème Chantilly, 296
    homemade crème fraîche, 297–298
    mocha cream with rum crème
        anglaise, 280–282

peaches in red wine, 292

peaches with lemon, 292

peaches with wild strawberries and
brandy, 293

pomelo (grapefruit) cream, 284

pumpkin cheesecake, 287–288

semolina pudding with plum
compote, 288–289

techniques for, 294–295

white wine custard with honey and
cinnamon, 282

see also fruit

dill, whole salmon trout steamed on a
bed of, with a warm mayonnaise,
137–138

Dodin Bouffant, viii, 146

doneness:

fish, 110, 162

lamb, 264, 265

meat, 226, 228

pork, 266

poultry, 179–180, 182

dorade, in salt cod aïoli, 144

Dover sole, 117–118

in langoustines with spring
vegetables and saffron, 160–
161

steaming time for, 112

dressing, *see* mayonnaise; sauce;
vinaigrette

Dublin Bay prawns, 146, 171

duck, duckling, 213–215

breasts with black currants and
pears, 199–200

carving of, 216

confit with fresh fava beans,
201

fat, rendering of, 216

leg "confit," steamed, 217

with pears, red wine–steamed,
197–199

steaming time for, 182, 183

échine de porc à la sauge, 251–252

échine pork cuts, 266

eggplant, 72–73

caviar, 73–74

grilling of, 102

marinated vegetables with coriander
and thyme, 74–75

smothered lamb with, 246

stuffed, 103

eggs:

poached in the steamer, 36

soft-cooked, warm asparagus with
lemon butter and, 40

in stuffing, 102

electric steamers, 7–8

endive:

Belgian, 67–68

with ham and Gruyère cheese,
gratin of, 68–69

langoustines with lime and Belgian,
158–159

endives à la flamande, 68–69

equipment:

asparagus steamers, 6

bamboo steamers, 10, 14

choice of, 11

collapsible steamer baskets, 6–7

electric steamers, 7–8

fish poachers, 8, 10

forks and spoons, 13

pancake turners, 13

pasta cookers, 5, 12

roasting pans, 8–9

stackable steamers, 3–5, 111

steamer inserts, 6

timing consistency and, 10–11

tongs, 13

*escargots de poulet à la confiture d'oignons
et de raisins,* 192–193

escarole, 67, 68

*étuvée de langouste à la crème de poivrons
doux,* 156–157

étuvée d'agneau aux aubergines, 246

evaporation, 12

see also liquids, steaming

fat, duck, rendering of, 216

fava beans, 42

chicken with rice stuffing and spring
vegetables, 189–190

duck confit with fresh, 201

fennel, 76

fans with zucchini and garlic, 77

grilling of, 102

tomato, and cream, pollack with,
130

fenouils à la bohémienne, 77

filet de boeuf au poivre vert, 231–232

filet mignon:

with green peppercorns, 231–232

steaming time for, 229

filets de soles à la vapeur de thé, 118–119

filets de soles au coulis de basilic, 121

filleting and skinning:

of flatfish, 164–165

of roundfish, 163–164

fines herbes, 17

Fiorello pears, steaming time for, 276

first courses, *see* appetizers

fish:

cod steaks with caper-anchovy
vinaigrette, 116–117

Dover sole, in langoustines with
spring vegetables and saffron,
160–161

frozen, 15

measuring thickness of, 110

mosaic of Saint-Pierre with saffron,
126–127

mousse with mussels, 152–153

processed, 130

recipe substitutions for, 108–109

scaling of, 162–163

smoked haddock with sauerkraut,
128–129

sole fillets stuffed with mushrooms,
122–123

sole steamed on a bed of Ceylon
tea, 118–119

sole with fresh tomato-basil sauce,
121

tuna with tomatoes, green pepper,
and garlic, 125–126

using steamers for warming of, 15,
111

warm skate salad with red currants,
123–124

see also shellfish; steaming, of fish

fish, *en papillote,* 129, 132

fresh herring with mustard and
green peppercorns, 132–133

herring wrapped in cabbage leaves
with mint, 133–134

monkfish with zucchini and green
peppercorns, 131–132

pollack with fennel, tomato, and
cream, 130

fish, *en papillote (continued)*
    sardines steamed in spicy tomato and
        garlic sauce, 135
    see also shellfish; steaming, of fish
fish, whole, 136
    fisherman's soup, 142–143
    kippers with lemon butter, 141–142
    pike with mint and thyme and a
        Muscadet butter sauce, 138–139
    salmon trout steamed on a bed of
        dill with a warm mayonnaise,
        137–138
    salt cod aïoli, 144-145
    steamed shad with sorrel, 140–141
    see also steaming, of fish
fisherman's soup, 142–143
fish poachers, 8, 10
flan(s):
    apricot, with kirsch, 285
    celery root, 66–67
    coconut-caramel, 278–279
    garlic, 78–79
    spinach and mushroom, 93–94
    vegetable, 102
flan:
    d'abricots, 285
    d'ail, 78–79
    de céleri, petits, 66–67
    d'épinards aux champignons, 93–94
    exotique, 278–279
    de moules, 152–153
flatfish, skinning and filleting of, 164–165
flounder, 117, 118
    gray sole, 113
    in stackable steamers, 111
flowers, lime, chicken quarters steamed
    on a bed of, 184–185
fluke, 118
foie:
    d'agneau aux oignons, 259–260
    de veau au ragoût de concombres et aux
        oignons nouveaux à la menthe,
        260–261
foil trays, steaming on, 163
food processors, 100
formidable choucroute garnie, 255–256
fowl, *see* poultry
French potato salad, 89
fromage blanc, 16
frozen foods, 14, 15, 171

fruit:
    apple charlotte, 290–291
    apricot flan with kirsch, 285
    caramel orange scallops "en
        surprise," 283
    cherry clafoutis, 286–287
    coconut-caramel flan, 278–279
    peaches in red wine, 292
    peaches with lemon, 292
    peaches with wild strawberries and
        brandy, 293
    peeling and pitting of, 294
    poaching vs. steaming of, 271–272
    pomelo (grapefruit) cream, 284
    pumpkin cheesecake, 287–288
    sauces, 272–273
    semolina pudding with plum
        compote, 288-289
    steaming times for, 275, 276
fruite saumonée à la mayonnaise chaude,
    137–138

game hens, Cornish:
    with fresh herbs, 191
    steaming time for, 183
garlic, 77–78
    fennel fans with zucchini and, 77
    flans, 78–79
    lemon sauce, 134
    -parsley butter and onion-raisin jam,
        chicken with, 192–193
    pork with sage and, 251–252
    sauce, sweet, veal kidneys with,
        262–263
    spring carrots, and parsley, top
        sirloin of veal with, 242
    tomatoes, and green pepper, tuna
        with, 125–126
    and tomato sauce, sardines steamed
        in spicy, 135
garniture de carottes sautées, 56–57
giblets, 205
ginger:
    chicken with scallions and fresh,
        185–186
    smothered goose with onions and,
        202–203
globe artichokes, whole, 29
Golden Delicious apples, steaming
    time for, 276

goose:
    butterflying technique and, 182, 212
    with ginger and onions, smothered,
        202–203
    juices of, 208
    parts, preparation for steaming of,
        209–210
    salmonella in, 179–180, 210
    steaming time for, 183
    whole, preparation for steaming of,
        205–208
gourmet salad of green beans, chicken
    liver, shrimp, and mushrooms,
    44–45
Grand Livre de la Cuisine à la Vapeur, Le
    (Manière), xi
graniteware, 9
Granny Smith apples, steaming time
    for, 276
grapefruit (pomelo) cream, 284
grapes:
    steamed, 274
    steaming time for, 276
gratin, 67–68
    of endive with ham and Gruyère
        cheese, 68–69
gray sole, 113, 117, 118
green asparagus, 37
green beans, 41–42
    chicken liver, shrimp, and
        mushrooms, gourmet salad of,
        44–45
    pickled vegetables with curry, 59–60
    see also haricots verts
"green chicken" (stuffed cabbage),
    253–255
green grapes, steaming time for, 276
green pepper, tomatoes, and garlic,
    tuna with, 125–126
    see also bell pepper
green peppercorns:
    filet mignon with, 231–232
    fresh herring with mustard and,
        132–133
    and zucchini, monkfish with,
        131–132
greens, 67–68, 79–80
green shell peas, 86, 87
    with pearl onions and mint, 87–88
grenadins de veau sauce paprika, 239–240

grilling, of vegetables, 102
grondin, in salt cod aïoli, 144
grouper, steaming time for, 113
Gruyère cheese, gratin of endive with
    ham and, 68–69
Guinea hen(s):
    butterflying technique and, 182, 212
    carving of, 208–209
    cutting raw, 210–211
    juices of, 208
    parts, preparation for steaming of,
        209–210
    salmonella in, 179–180, 210
    steaming time for, 183
    stuffed, on a bed of parslied
        cabbage, 194–195
    trussing of, 208
    warm salad of, with wild
        mushrooms, 196–197
    whole, preparation for steaming of,
        205–208
gurnard, in salt cod aïoli, 144

haddock, smoked, with sauerkraut,
    128–129
haddock sur choucroute, 128–129
halibut, steaming time for, 113
ham:
    gratin of endive with Gruyère
        cheese and, 68–69
    Madeira, and truffles, sweetbread
        mousse with, 258–259
    hard-shell clams, steaming time for,
        115
harengs:
    en feuilles de chou, 133–134
    frais à la moutarde et au poivre vert,
        132–133
*haricots frais (blancs ou flageolets verts)
    écosses "Bretonne,"* 43
haricots verts, 41–42
    Indian-style vegetable cutlets, 61–62
    langoustines with spring vegetables
        and saffron, 160–161
    rack of lamb with spring vegetables,
        244–245
    see also green beans
herbes de Provence, 234
herbs, herbed:
    beurre blanc, 189

cream sauce, 191
and cream vinaigrette, fresh, 45
fresh vs. dried, 17
steaming of fish on, 161
herring:
    with mustard and green
        peppercorns, fresh, 132–133
    wrapped in cabbage leaves with
        mint, 133–134
hollandaise, 38–39
homard aux algues, 157–158
homard vs. *langouste* lobster, 170
homemade crème fraîche, 297–298
honey and cinnamon, white wine
    custard with, 282
hothouse cucumbers, 70, 71
    with mint and yogurt, 71–72
huitres à la coque, 155

Idaho Russet potatoes, 88, 89
Indian-style vegetable cutlets, 61–62
ingredients, quality of, 15–16
Izarra liqueur, 125

jam, onion-raisin, chicken with garlic-
    parsley butter and, 192–193
jambon d'agneau à la bourguignonne,
    243–244
Jerusalem artichokes, 97
John Dory:
    with saffron, mosaic of, 126–127
    steaming time for, 113
juice, *see* liquids, steaming
julienne, 103–104

Kafka, Barbara, xi
kale, 79, 80
    and spinach sauce, 102
kasha, stuffed cabbage with, 236–237
kidneys, veal:
    steaming time for, 229
    with sweet garlic sauce, 262–263
kippers, with lemon butter, 141–142
kippers au beurre citronné, 141–142
kitchen knives, vs. scissors, 208
kohlrabi, 82–83

lamb:
    tongue with parsley sauce, 257–258
    broth, 267

with couscous, chick peas, and
    raisins, skewered, 250–251
couscous with chicken and,
    247–248
cuts of, 263–265
doneness of, 264, 265
with eggplant, smothered, 246
leg of, cured in red wine, 243–244
rack of, with spring vegetables,
    244–245
spinach and kale sauce for, 102
steaming times for, 229
sweetbread mousse with ham,
    Madeira, and truffles, 258–259
lamb's lettuce, warm scallop salad with
    tea-infused vinegar and, 149–150
langouste vs. *homard* lobsters, 170
langoustines:
    with Belgian endive and lime,
        158–159
    with spring vegetables and saffron,
        160–161
    technique for, 171
langoustines:
    aux endives et citron vert, 158–159
    aux petites légumes, 160–161
langues de porc (ou d'agneau) sauce persil,
    257–258
leek(s), 84–85
    chicken steamed with vegetables and
        tarragon, 188
    grilling of, 102
    julienne, 104
    and potato soup, cream of, 90–91
leg cuts, of lamb, 265
leg of lamb cured in red wine,
    243–244
lemon(s):
    butter, kippers with, 141–142
    butter, warm asparagus with soft-
        cooked eggs and, 40
    garlic sauce, 134
    mousseline sauce, 39
    mustard vinaigrette, 124
    peaches with, 292
    pickled vegetables with curry, 59–60
    rack of lamb with spring vegetables,
        244–245
    vinaigrette, 24
lemon sole, 117, 118

lettuce:
  lamb's, warm scallop salad with tea-infused vinegar and, 149–150
  squab stuffed with spinach and steamed in, 204–205
lieu jaune au fenouil, 130
lima beans, 42
lime:
  flowers, chicken quarters steamed on a bed of, 184–185
  langoustines with Belgian endive and, 158–159
liquids, steaming, 208
  for broth, 267–268
  flavor imparted by, 13
  for macerated fruit, 273
  quantities and evaporation rates in, 12
  for soup, 167–168
  for stock, 220–221
  replenishing of, 182, 228
liver, calves':
  with a ragout of cucumber, spring onions, and mint, 260–261
  with onions, parsley, and vinegar, 259–260
  steaming time for, 229
liver, chicken, 205–206
  green beans, shrimp, and mushrooms, gourmet salad of, 44–45
  steaming time for, 183
liver, lobster, 170
lobster(s):
  clawed vs. spiny, 109
  steamed on a bed of seaweed, 157–158
  steaming time for, 115
  stew with sweet red pepper sauce, spiny, 156–157
  technique for, 170–171
  see also langoustines
lotte aux courgettes en papillotes, 131
Lyness, Stephanie, vii, ix

macerated fruit, 273
mâche, warm scallop salad with tea-infused vinegar and, 149–150
McIntosh apples, steaming time for, 276
mackerel, steaming time for, 114

Madeira, ham, and truffles, sweetbread mousse with, 258–259
magrets aux grains de cassis, 199–220
mahi-mahi, steaming time for, 113
main dishes:
  beef tongue with parsley sauce, 257–258
  calves' liver with a ragout of cucumber, spring onions, and mint, 260–261
  calves' liver with onions, parsley, and vinegar, 259–260
  chicken "au blanc," 186–188
  chicken quarters steamed on a bed of lime flowers, 184–185
  chicken steamed with vegetables and tarragon, 188
  chicken with fresh ginger and scallions, 185–186
  chicken with garlic-parsley butter and onion-raisin jam, 192–193
  chicken with rice stuffing and spring vegetables, 189–190
  chopped beef tournedos "tartare," 230–231
  choucroute, 255–256
  cod steaks with caper-anchovy vinaigrette, 116–117
  cornish game hens with fresh herbs, 191
  couscous with lamb and chicken, 247–248
  duck breasts with black currants and pears, 199–200
  duck confit with fresh fava beans, 201
  filet mignon with green peppercorns, 231–232
  fillet of veal with red pepper and paprika cream sauce, 239–240
  fisherman's soup, 142–143
  fresh herring with mustard and green peppercorns, 132–133
  gratin of endive with ham and Gruyère cheese, 68–69
  "green chicken" (stuffed cabbage), 253–255
  herring wrapped in cabbage leaves with mint, 133–134

hot beef "terrine" with olives, anchovies, and white wine, 232–233
kippers with lemon butter, 141–142
langoustines with Belgian endive and lime, 158–159
langoustines with spring vegetables and saffron, 160–161
leg of lamb cured in red wine, 243–244
lobster steamed on a bed of seaweed, 157–158
monkfish with zucchini and green peppercorns, 131
mosaic of Saint-Pierre with saffron, 126–127
pike with mint and thyme and a Muscadet butter sauce, 138–139
pollack with fennel, tomato, and cream, 130
pork with garlic and sage, 251–252
pork with whole-grain mustard, 252–253
rack of lamb with spring vegetables, 244–245
red wine–steamed duckling with pears, 197–198
salt cod aïoli, 144–145
scallops with a Muscadet butter sauce, 147
sirloin steak with sunchoke mousse, 234–235
skewered beef, 235–236
skewered lamb with couscous, chick peas, and raisins, 250–251
smoked haddock with sauerkraut, 128–129
smothered goose with ginger and onions, 202–203
smothered lamb with eggplant, 246
sole fillets stuffed with mushrooms, 122–123
sole steamed on a bed of Ceylon tea, 118–119
sole with fresh tomato-basil sauce, 121
spiny lobster stew with sweet red pepper sauce, 156–157
squab stuffed with spinach and steamed in lettuce, 204–205

stuffed artichoke bottoms barigoule, 33–34
stuffed cabbage with kasha, 236–237
stuffed guinea hen on a bed of parslied cabbage, 194–195
stuffed zucchini, 96–97
top sirloin of veal with spring carrots, parsley, and garlic, 242
tuna with tomatoes, green pepper, and garlic, 125–126
veal blanquette, 240–241
veal chops with cider and apples, 238–239
veal kidneys with sweet garlic sauce, 262–263
warm salad of Guinea hen with wild mushrooms, 196–197
warm skate salad with red currants, 123–124
whole salmon trout steamed on a bed of dill with a warm mayonnaise, 137–138
whole steamed shad with sorrel, 140–141
Manière, Jacques, vii–ix, xi, xii, xv
marinade, for hot beef "terrine" with olives, anchovies, and white wine, 233
mayonnaise, 27
    artichoke, 31
    salt cod aïoli, 144–145
    sherry vinegar, 151
    whole salmon trout steamed on a bed of dill with a warm, 137–138
measurement conversions, 18
meat, 225–226
    beef cuts, 263
    beef tongue with parsley sauce, 257–258
    broth, 267–268
    browning of, 228
    calves' liver with a ragout of cucumber, spring onions, and mint, 260–261
    calves' liver with onions, parsley, and vinegar, 259–260
    chopped beef tournedos "tartare," 230–231
    choucroute, 255–256

couscous with lamb and chicken, 247–248
doneness of, 226, 228
filet mignon with green peppercorns, 231–232
fillet of veal with red pepper and paprika cream sauce, 239–240
French vs. American cuts, 228
gratin of endive with ham and Gruyère cheese, 68–69
"green chicken" (stuffed cabbage), 253–255
hot beef "terrine" with olives, anchovies, and white wine, 232–233
lamb cuts, 263–264
leg of lamb cured in red wine, 243–244
pork cuts, 265
pork with garlic and sage, 251–252
pork with whole-grain mustard, 252–253
rack of lamb with spring vegetables, 244–245
sirloin steak with sunchoke mousse, 234–235
skewered beef, 235–236
skewered lamb with couscous, chick peas, and raisins, 250–251
smothered lamb with eggplant, 246
steaming times for, 226–227, 228–229
stews, 268
stuffed cabbage with kasha, 236–237
sweetbread mousse with ham, Madeira, and truffles, 258–259
tongue cuts, 267
top sirloin of veal with spring carrots, parsley, and garlic, 242
veal blanquette, 240–241
veal chops with cider and apples, 238–239
veal cuts, 265
veal kidneys with sweet garlic sauce, 262–263
méli-mélo de légumes à la Grecque, 74–75
metal steamers, 10–11
microwave reheating and defrosting, 14
mini carrots, 56

mint:
    cucumber and spring onions, calves' liver with a ragout of, 260–261
    cucumbers with yogurt and, 71–72
    herring wrapped in cabbage leaves with, 133–134
    peas with pearl onions and, 87–88
    pike with thyme and a Muscadet butter sauce and, 138–139
mocha cream with rum crème anglaise, 280–282
molds, 295
monkfish:
    fillet, 110
    en papillote, 167
    steaming time for, 112
    with zucchini and green peppercorns, 131–132
mosaic of Saint-Pierre with saffron, 126–127
mosaïque de Saint-Pierre aux pistils de safron, 126–127
moules de bouchot, 169
mousse:
    fish, with mussels, 152–153
    sunchoke, sirloin steak with, 234–235
    sweetbread, with ham, Madeira, and truffles, 258–259
Muscadet butter sauce:
    and mint and thyme, pike with, 138–139
    scallops with, 147
mushroom(s):
    green beans, chicken liver, and shrimp, gourmet salad of, 44–45
    sole fillets stuffed with, 122–123
    and spinach flans, 93–94
    wild, warm salad of Guinea hen with, 196–197
mussel(s):
    fish mousse with, 152–153
    sea scallops in Champagne sauce with shrimp and, 148–149
    soup, curried, 153–154
    steaming time for, 115
    technique for, 169
mustard:
    fresh herring with green peppercorns and, 132–133
    lemon vinaigrette, 124

mustard (*continued*)
    pork with whole-grain, 252–253
    -vinegar red wine vinaigrette, 24
mustard greens, 79, 80

nantais butter sauce, 158
Napa cabbage, 50
navets nouveaux en rémoulade, 99–100
neck cut, of lamb, 264
Norway lobster, 171
nutrition, and steaming, 100

ocean perch, steaming time for, 113
oeufs au lait, les, 277–278
offal, 266–267
oie à l'étuvée, 202–203
olives:
    anchovies, and white wine, hot beef
        "terrine" with, 232–233
    pitting of, 233
onion(s):
    chicken with rice stuffing and spring
        vegetables, 189–190
    langoustines with spring vegetables
        and saffron, 160–161
    leeks, 84–85
    marinated vegetables with coriander
        and thyme, 74–75
    parsley, and vinegar, calves' liver
        with, 259–260
    pearl, 84
    peas with mint and pearl, 87–88
    rack of lamb with spring vegetables,
        244–245
    -raisin jam, chicken with garlic-
        parsley butter and, 192–193
    scallions, 83
    smothered goose with ginger and,
        202–203
    spring, 83
    spring, cucumber, and mint,
        calves' liver with a ragout of,
        260–261
    warm chick pea salad with spring,
        85–86
open-lid technique, 110
orange caramel scallops "en surprise,"
    283
orange roughy, steaming time for,
    113

oven vs. broiler browning, 178–179,
    227, 228
oysters, 169–170
    in the shell with spinach and curry,
        155
    steaming time for, 115

Pactole, Le, vii
pain de carottes, 57–58
papillote, en:
    fish, 166–167
    poultry, 213
    see also specific ingredients
paprika and red pepper cream sauce,
    fillet of veal with, 239–240
parfait de ris d'agneau ou de veau,
    258–259
parsley(ied):
    cabbage, stuffed Guinea hen on a
        bed of, 194–195
    -garlic butter and onion-raisin jam,
        chicken with, 192–193
    onions, and vinegar, calves' liver
        with, 259–260
    sauce, beef tongue with, 257–258
    sautéed carrots with, 56–57
    spring carrots, and garlic, top sirloin
        of veal with, 242
pasta:
    couscous with lamb and chicken,
        247–248
    skewered lamb with couscous, chick
        peas, and raisins, 250–251
    steamed couscous, 249
pasta cookers, 5, 6, 12
pastis liqueur, 125
paupiettes de choux à la kacha, 236–237
paupiettes de soles farcies aux champignons,
    122–123
pavé de rumsteak à la mousse de
    topinambours, 234–235
peaches:
    with lemon, 292
    macerated, 273
    peeling and pitting of, 294
    in red wine, 292
    with wild strawberries and brandy,
        293
pearl onions, 84
    peas with mint and, 87–88

pears:
    duck breasts with black currants and,
        199–200
    red wine–steamed duckling with,
        197–199
    steamed, 272
    steaming times for, 275, 276
peas, 86–87
    chicken with rice stuffing and spring
        vegetables, 189–190
    Indian-style vegetable cutlets, 61–
        62
    langoustines with spring vegetables
        and saffron, 160–161
    with pearl onions and mint, 87–88
    rack of lamb with spring vegetables,
        244–245
pêches:
    au citron, 292
    à la royale, 293
    au vin, 292
pencil asparagus, 38
pepper(s), bell, 46
    grilling of, 102
    marinated vegetables with coriander
        and thyme, 74–75
    piperade, 47
    Provençal-style marinated, 47–48
    red, and paprika cream sauce, fillet
        of veal with, 239–240
    sauce, sweet red, spiny lobster stew
        with, 156–157
    stuffed, 103
    tomatoes, and garlic, tuna with,
        125–126
peppercorns, green:
    filet mignon with, 231–232
    fresh herring with mustard and,
        132–133
    and zucchini, monkfish with,
        131–132
Pernod liqueur, 125
persillade, 242, 260
petits flans de céleri, 66–67
petits pois à la menthe, 87–88
petrale sole, 117
pickled vegetables with curry, 59–60
pigeons farcis, 204–205
pike:
    fish mousse with mussels, 152–153

with mint and thyme and a
Muscadet butter sauce, 138–139
steaming time for, 113
pineapple, Barbara's warm steamed,
274
pine nut and cheese stuffing, 194
pintade farcie sur chou croquant, 194–195
Piot, Michel, ix
piperade, 47
plum compote, semolina pudding
with, 288–289
poaching vs. steaming of fruits,
271–272
pod peas, 86, 87
with pearl onions and mint, 87–88
pois chiches aux oignons nouveaux, 85–86
poisson:
aïoli de morue, 144–145
alose à l'oseille, 140–141
brochetons beurre nantais, 138–139
cabillaud sauce girondine, 116–117
filets de soles à la vapeur de thé,
118–119
filets de soles au coulis de basilic, 121
flan de moules, 152–153
fruite saumonée à la mayonnaise chaude,
137–138
haddock sur choucroute, 128–129
harengs en feuilles de chou, 133–134
*harengs frais à la moutarde et au poivre
vert,* 132–133
kippers au beurre citronné, 141–142
lieu jaune au fenouil, 130
lotte aux courgettes en papillotes, 131
*mosaïque de Saint-Pierre aux pistils de
safron,* 126–127
*paupiettes de soles farcies aux
champignons,* 122–123
salade de raie tiède aux groseilles,
123–124
sardines en papillotes, 135
thon à la luzienne, 125–126
poivrade à la Grecque, 32–33
poivronnade Provençale, 47–48
pollack, 109
with fennel, tomato, and cream, 130
pomelo (grapefruit) cream, 284
pommes de terre au Gruyère, 91
pompano, steaming time for, 114
porgy, steaming time for, 113

pork:
beef tongue with parsley sauce,
257–258
broth, 267
choucroute, 255–256
cuts of, 266
doneness of, 266
with garlic and sage, 251–252
gratin of endive with ham and
Gruyère cheese, 68–69
"green chicken" (stuffed cabbage),
253–255
steaming times for, 229
stuffed cabbage with kasha, 236–237
sweetbread mousse with ham,
Madeira, and truffles, 258–259
with whole-grain mustard, 252–
253
potato(es), 88–90
bâtonnets and julienne, 104
and celery purée, 65
grilling of, 102
Indian-style vegetable cutlets, 61–
62
and leek soup, cream of, 90–91
salad, French, 89
twice-cooked, 91
poularde, poulet:
"au blanc," 186–187
*à la confiture d'oignons et de raisins,
escargots de,* 192–193
farcie aux petits légumes, 189–190
au pot dit "ilot," 185–186
steamed truffled Bresse, 175–176
à la vapeur de légumes, 188
à la vapeur de tilleul, 184–185
poultry:
boning of, 206, 211–212, 214, 218
butterflying technique and, 182,
212
carving of, 208–209, 216
chicken "au blanc," 186–188
chicken quarters steamed on a bed
of lime flowers, 184–185
chicken steamed with vegetables and
tarragon, 188
chicken with fresh ginger and
scallions, 185–186
chicken with garlic-parsley butter
and onion-raisin jam, 192–193

chicken with rice stuffing and spring
vegetables, 189–190
Cornish game hens with fresh herbs,
191
couscous with lamb and chicken,
247–248
cutting raw, 210–211, 214–215
duck breasts with black currants and
pears, 199–200
duck confit with fresh fava beans,
201
fat, rendering of, 216
juices of, 208
red wine–steamed duckling with
pears, 197–199
salmonella in, 179–180, 210
skin, browning of, 178
skin, removal of, 209, 215–216
smothered goose with ginger and
onions, 202–203
squab stuffed with spinach and
steamed in lettuce, 204–205
steamed duck leg "confit," 217
stuffed Guinea hen on a bed of
parslied cabbage, 194–195
trussing of, 207, 208
warm salad of Guinea hen with wild
mushrooms, 196–197
see also steaming, of poultry
preservatives, in shellfish, 168–169
Provençal-style marinated peppers,
47–48
pudding, semolina, with plum
compote, 288–289
pumpkin cheesecake, 287–288
pumpkin squash, 94, 95, 96
purée, 100–101
artichoke, 28–29
broccoli, 101
celery root and potato, 65
vegetable soups and sauces, 101–
102
purée de céleri et pomme de terre, 65

quail, steaming time for, 183
quasi de veau aux carottes nouvelles,
242

rabbit, 219–220
steaming time for, 182, 183

rack of lamb, 264
    with spring vegetables, 244–245
radishes, tomato, and almonds, cockle
    salad with, 150–151
raisin(s):
    couscous, and chick peas, skewered
        lamb with, 250–251
    -onion jam and garlic-parsley butter,
        chicken with, 192–193
raspberry sauce, 272–273
ravigote, sauce, 27
recette de base pour les oeufs pochés, 36
red asparagus, 37
red bream fish, 144
red currants, warm skate salad with,
    123–124
red grapes, steaming time for, 276
red pepper:
    and paprika cream sauce, fillet of
        veal with, 239–240
    sauce, sweet, spiny lobster stew with,
        156–157
    see also bell pepper
red-skinned potatoes, 88
red wine:
    leg of lamb cured in, 243–244
    peaches in, 292
    –steamed duckling with pears,
        197–199
    vinegar-mustard vinaigrette, 24
reheating, 14
rémoulade, grated turnip salad, 99–100
rex sole, 117
Ricard liqueur, 125
rice cookers, 7–8
rice stuffing and spring vegetables,
    chicken with, 189–190
roasting pans, 8–9
roe:
    lobster, 170
    sea scallop, 168
rognons de veau à la crème d'ail doux,
    262–263
Rome Beauty apples, steaming time
    for, 276
roundfish, skinning and filleting of,
    163–164
rum crème anglaise, mocha cream
    with, 280–282
rutabaga flan, 102

sabayon, 39
saffron:
    langoustines with spring vegetables
        and, 160–161
    mosaic of Saint-Pierre with,
        126–127
    -vermouth sauce, 160–161
sage, pork with garlic and, 251–252
Saint-Pierre with saffron, mosaic of,
    126–127
salad:
    cockle, with radishes, tomato, and
        almonds, 150–151
    French potato, 89
    of green beans, chicken liver,
        shrimp, and mushrooms,
        gourmet, 44–45
    of Guinea hen with wild
        mushrooms, warm, 196–197
    rémoulade, grated turnip, 99–100
    warm chick pea, with spring onions,
        85–86
    warm scallop, with lamb's lettuce
        and tea-infused vinegar, 149–150
    warm skate, with red currants,
        123–124
    warm sweet-and-sour cabbage,
        54–55
salade:
    de coques aux radis roses, 150–151
    de mâche et de Saint-Jacques au vinaigre
        de thé, 149–150
    navets nouveaux en rémoulade, 99–100
    "un peu folle," 44–45
    de pintade "soir d'été," 196–197
    pois chiches aux oignons nouveaux,
        85–86
    de raie tiède aux groseilles, 123–124
    tiède de chou vert, sauce à l'aigre-doux,
        54–55
salmonella bacteria, 179–180, 210
salmon trout, 109–110
    steaming time for, 114, 115
    whole, steamed on a bed of dill with
        a warm mayonnaise, 137–138
salt cod aïoli, 144–145
sardines:
    steamed in spicy tomato and garlic
        sauce, 135
    steaming time for, 115

sauce:
    for apples, 273
    artichoke mayonnaise, 31
    "au blanc," 187
    basic caramel, 295–296
    black currant, 200
    Champagne, sea scallops in, with
        mussels and shrimp, 148–149
    fresh tomato-basil, 62
    fresh tomato-basil, sole with, 121
    fruit, 272–273
    garlic lemon, 134
    green peppercorn, 232
    herbed cream, 191
    hollandaise, 38–39
    lemon mousseline, 39
    medium béchamel, 69
    mustard, 253
    Normande, 239
    parsley, beef tongue with, 257–258
    ravigote, 27
    red pepper and paprika cream, fillet
        of veal with, 239–240
    rémoulade, 100
    saffron-tomato, 127
    spicy tomato and garlic, sardines
        steamed in, 135
    spinach and kale, 102
    sweet garlic, veal kidneys with,
        262–263
    sweet red pepper, spiny lobster stew
        with, 156–157
    thick béchamel, 58
    tomato and green pepper, 126
    for veal blanquette, 241
    vegetable cream, 245
    vegetable purée, 101–102
    vermouth cream, 123
sauce, butter:
    beurre blanc I, 120
    beurre blanc II, 127
    Ceylon tea, 119
    chervil, 152–153
    herbed beurre blanc, 189
    lemon, 40
    lime, 159
    nantais, 158
    pike with mint and thyme and a
        Muscadet, 138–139
    saffron-vermouth, 160–161

scallops with a Muscadet, 147
sorrel, 141
tarragon, 254, 255
sauce à l'artichaut, 31
sauce mousseline au citron, 39
sauerkraut, 255–256
smoked haddock with, 128–129
Savoy cabbage, 50
scaling, of fish, 162–163
scallions, 83
chicken with fresh ginger and,
185–186
langoustines with spring vegetables
and saffron, 160–161
rack of lamb with spring vegetables,
244–245
scallop(s):
in Champagne sauce with mussels
and shrimp, 148–149
fish mousse with mussels, 152–153
imitation, 130
with a Muscadet butter sauce, 147
salad with lamb's lettuce and tea-
infused vinegar, warm, 149–150
steaming time for, 115
technique for, 171
in warm salad with red currants,
125
scampi, 171
scissors, vs. kitchen knives, 208
scorching, prevention of, 12
scorpion fish, steaming time for, 113
sea bass, steaming time for, 113
seafood, *see* fish; shellfish
sea robin, 144
steaming time for, 113
sea scallops:
in Champagne sauce with mussels
and shrimp, 148–149
fish mousse with mussels, 152–153
steaming time for, 115
technique for, 168–169
in warm salad with red currants, 125
see also scallop(s)
sea snails, in salt cod aïoli, 144–145
seaweed:
lobster steamed on a bed of,
157–158
as taste enhancer, 146, 161
semiconserves, 59

semolina pudding with plum compote,
288–289
shad:
steaming time for, 115
whole steamed, with sorrel,
140–141
shallots, cabbage with cream and, 53
shell beans, 42
shelled green peas, 86, 87
with pearl onions and mint, 87–88
shellfish:
cockle salad with radishes, tomato,
and almonds, 150–151
curried mussel soup, 153–154
en papillote, 108
fish mousse with mussels, 152–153
gourmet salad of green beans,
chicken liver, shrimp, and
mushrooms, 44
langoustines with Belgian endive
and lime, 158–159
langoustines with spring vegetables
and saffron, 160–161
lobster steamed on a bed of
seaweed, 157–158
oysters in the shell with spinach and
curry, 155
recipe substitutions for, 108–109
scallops with a Muscadet butter
sauce, 147
sea scallops in Champagne sauce
with mussels and shrimp, 148–149
shucking of, 168, 170
spiny lobster stew with sweet red
pepper sauce, 156–157
warm scallop salad with lamb's
lettuce and tea-infused vinegar,
149–150
see also fish; steaming, of shellfish
shelling, of lobster, 170–171
sherry vinegar:
mayonnaise, 151
vinaigrette, 196, 197
shin, steaming time for, 229
"shortened" leg of lamb, 265
shoulder cuts, lamb, 263–264
shrimp:
green beans, chicken liver, and
mushrooms, gourmet salad of,
44–45

imitation, 130
sea scallops in Champagne sauce
with mussels and, 148–149
steaming time for, 115
technique for, 171
shucking:
of oysters, 170
of sea scallops, 168
side dishes:
cabbage with cream and shallots, 53
carrot terrine, 57–58
celery root and potato purée, 65
celery root flans, 66–67
fennel fans with zucchini and garlic,
77
fresh white beans Brittany-style, 43
garlic flans, 78–79
peas with pearl onions and mint,
87–88
pickled vegetables with curry, 59–60
sautéed carrots with parsley, 56–57
spinach and mushroom flans, 93–94
steamed couscous, 249
twice-cooked potatoes, 91
sirloin steak:
steaming time for, 229
with sunchoke mousse, 234–235
skate:
fillets, in stackable steamers, 111
salad with red currants, warm,
123–124
steaming time for, 113
skin, poultry:
browning of, 178
removal of, 209, 215–216
skinning and filleting:
of flatfish, 164–165
of roundfish, 163–164
snails, in salt cod aïoli, 144–145
snapper, steaming time for, 114
snow peas, 86, 87
soft-shell clams, steaming time for, 115
sole, 117–118
fillets stuffed with mushrooms,
122–123
with fresh tomato-basil sauce, 121
in langoustines with spring
vegetables and saffron, 160–161
steamed on a bed of Ceylon tea,
118–119

sorrel, whole steamed shad with, 140–141

soup:
asparagus, 189
broth, 267–268
cream of leek and potato, 90–91
cream of watercress, 81–82
curried mussel, 153–154
fisherman's, 142–143
steaming liquid as, 167–168
vegetable purée, 101

spaghetti squash, 94
spinach, 92
basic steamed, 92–93
and kale sauce, 102
and mushroom flans, 93–94
oysters in the shell with curry and, 155
squab stuffed with, and steamed in lettuce, 204–205

spiny lobster, 109, 170
stew with sweet red pepper sauce, 156–157
see also lobster

spring carrots, parsley, and garlic, top sirloin of veal with, 242

spring onions, 83
cucumber, and mint, calves' liver with a ragout of, 260–261
rack of lamb with spring vegetables, 244–245
warm chick pea salad with, 85–86

spring vegetables:
chicken with rice stuffing and, 189–190
langoustines with saffron and, 160–161
rack of lamb with, 244–245

squab:
boning of, 206, 218
steaming time for, 183
stuffed with spinach and steamed in lettuce, 204–205

squash, 94–96
bâtonnets and julienne, 104
fennel fans with zucchini and garlic, 77
grilling of, 102
marinated vegetables with coriander and thyme, 74–75

monkfish with zucchini and green peppercorns, 131–132
stuffed zucchini, 96–97, 103

stackable steamers, 3–5, 111

steak, beef:
filet mignon with green peppercorns, 231–232
sirloin, with sunchoke mousse, 234–235
steaming time for, 229

steak, fish, 15, 110, 165–166
see also fish

steamers, see equipment

steaming, of fish:
Canadian rule for, 109
darker-colored, moderately fatty and fatty fish, 114–115
and doneness, 110, 162
fillets, steaks, and large chunks, 165–166
on a flavorful bed, 161
on a foil tray, 163
lean, white-fleshed fish, 112–114
lid-ajar technique for, 110
en papillote, 166–167
soup from, 167–168
in stackable steamers, 111
and recipe substitutions, 108–109
steaks and fillets, 110
whole fish and large chunks, 109–110, 161–162
see also fish; fish, en papillote; fish, whole

steaming, of fruit:
chart of basic times for, 275, 276
vs. poaching, 271–272

steaming, of poultry, 176–177
chart of basic times for, 178, 182, 183
duck, 214–215
parts, 209–212
whole, 205–208

steaming, of shellfish:
chart of basic times for, 109, 115
langoustines, 171
lobsters, 170–171
mussels, 169
oysters, 169–170
scallops, 168–169
shrimp, 171

steaming techniques:
flavoring, 13–14
food warming, 15, 110, 180, 227
for frozen fish fillets and steaks, 15
placing ingredients in and out of steamers, 12–13
reheating and defrosting, 14
for vegetables in quantity, 24–25
for vegetable varieties steamed together, 25–26

stewing, 100
stews, meat, 268

stock:
chicken, 192
duck, 217
poultry, 220–221
veal, 241

straightneck squash, 94

strawberry(ies):
peaches with brandy and wild, 293
sauce, 272–273

stuffing:
basil, for zucchini, 96
cheese and pine nut, 194
garlic-parsley butter, 192–193
kasha, 236
pork, 254, 255
rice, chicken with spring vegetables and, 189–190
spinach, 204
of vegetables, 102–103

sugar snap peas, 86, 87
summer squash, 94–95
sunchoke(s), 97
mousse, sirloin steak with, 234–235
surimi, 130
sweet-and-sour cabbage salad, warm, 54–55
sweetbread mousse with ham, Madeira, and truffles, 258–259
Swiss chard, 79, 80
swordfish, steaming time for, 114

Table au Pays de Brillat-Savarin, La (Tendret), 175
tarragon:
butter sauce, 254, 255
chicken steamed with vegetables and, 188

tea:
    -infused vinegar, Ceylon, 120
    -infused vinegar, warm scallop salad
        with lamb's lettuce and, 149–150
    sole steamed on a bed of Ceylon,
        118–119
temperature, and doneness:
    fish, 110, 162
    lamb, 264, 265
    meat, 226, 228
    pork, 266
    poultry, 179–180, 182
Tendret, Lucien, 175
terrine chaude de boeuf à la façon des
        mariniers du Rhône, 232–233
thermometers, instant-read, 110
    see also temperature, and doneness
thon à la luzienne, 125–126
thyme:
    marinated vegetables with coriander
        and, 74–75
    pike with mint and a Muscadet
        butter sauce and, 138–139
tilefish, steaming time for, 114
timing, *see* charts of basic steaming
        times
tomalley, lobster, 170
tomatoes:
    fennel, and cream, pollack with,
        130
    green pepper, and garlic, tuna with,
        125–126
    piperade, 47
    radishes, and almonds, cockle salad
        with, 150–151
tomato sauce:
    basil-, fresh, 62
    basil-, sole with fresh, 121
    concassé, 98
    garlic and, sardines steamed in spicy,
        135
    green pepper and, 126
    saffron-, 127
tongue, beef:
    with parsley sauce, 257–258
    steaming time for, 229
top sirloin of veal with spring carrots,
        parsley, and garlic, 242
tournedoes hachés tartare, 230–231
trichinosis, 228, 266

trout:
    salmon, steaming time for, 115
    whole, steamed on a bed of dill with
        a warm mayonnaise, 137–138
truffles, ham, and Madeira, sweetbread
        mousse with, 258–259
trussing, of poultry, 208
tuna:
    steaming time for, 114
    with tomatoes, green pepper, and
        garlic, 125–126
turkey:
    butterflying technique and, 182, 212
    juices of, 208
    parts, preparation for steaming of,
        209–210, 219
    salmonella in, 179–180
    steaming time for, 183
    whole, preparation for steaming of,
        205–208, 219
turnip(s), 98–99
    bâtonnets and julienne, 104
    chicken steamed with vegetables and
        tarragon, 188
    chicken with rice stuffing and spring
        vegetables, 189–190
    flan, 102
    langoustines with spring vegetables
        and saffron, 160–161
    pickled vegetables with curry, 59–60
    rack of lamb with spring vegetables,
        244–245
    salad rémoulade, grated, 99–100
twice-cooked potatoes, 91

Vanel, Lucien, 175
Vanel, Mémée, 175, 176
vanilla beans, vanilla sugar, and vanilla
        extract, 297–298
veal:
    blanquette, 240–241
    broth, 267–268
    chops with cider and apples,
        238–239
    cuts of, 266
    kidneys with sweet garlic sauce,
        262–263
    with red pepper and paprika cream
        sauce, fillet of, 239–240
    steaming times for, 229

sweetbread mousse with ham,
        Madeira, and truffles, 258–259
    top sirloin of, with spring carrots,
        parsley, and garlic, 242
vegetable(s):
    chicken steamed with tarragon and,
        188
    chicken with rice stuffing and
        spring, 189–190
    cream sauce, 245
    cutlets, Indian-style, 61–62
    langoustines with saffron and spring,
        160–161
    marinated, with coriander and
        thyme, 74–75
    pickled, with curry, 59–60
    rack of lamb with spring, 244–245
    steaming of fish on, 161
    stuffed, 102–103
    techniques for, 23, 100–104
    see also specific vegetables
vermouth sauce:
    cream, 123
    -saffron, 160–161
viande:
    blanquette de veau, 240–241
    brochettes de boeuf, 235–236
    brochettes d'agneau au cumin, 250–251
    carré d'agneau printanier, 244–245
    chou farci ou poule vert, 253–255
    côtes de porc aux graines de moutarde,
        252–253
    côtes de veau au cidre, 238–239
    échine de porc à la sauge, 251–252
    endives à la flamande, 68
    étuvée d'agneau aux aubergines, 246
    filet de boeuf au poivre vert, 231–232
    foie d'agneau aux oignons, 259–260
    foie de veau au ragoût de concombres et
        aux oignons nouveaux à la menthe,
        260–261
    formidable choucroute garnie, 255-256
    grenadins de veau sauce paprika,
        239–240
    jambon d'agneau à la bourguignonne,
        243–244
    langues de porc (ou d'agneau) sauce
        persil, 257–258
    parfait de ris d'agneau ou de veau,
        258–259

viande (continued)

    paupiettes de choux à la kacha,
        236–237

    pavé de rumsteak à la mousse de
        topinambours, 234–235

    quasi de veau aux carottes nouvelles,
        242

    rognons de veau à la crème d'ail doux,
        262–263

    terrine chaude de boeuf à la façon des
        mariniers du Rhône, 232–233

    tournedos hachés tartare, 230–231

vinaigre de thé, 120

vinaigrette, 24

    basic, 26–27

    caper-anchovy, cod steaks with,
        116–117

    Ceylon tea, 150

    curry, 60

    fresh herb and cream, 45

    lemon mustard, 124

    sherry vinegar, 196, 197

    sweet-and-sour, 54

vinegar:

    Ceylon tea–infused, 120

    -mustard red wine vinaigrette, 24

    onions, and parsley, calves' liver
        with, 259–260

    sherry mayonnaise, 151

    sherry vinaigrette, 196, 197

    tea-infused, warm scallop salad with
        lamb's lettuce and, 149–150

violet artichokes, 28

volaille:

    canette à la vapeur de vin, 197–198

    confit de canard aux fèves nouvelles,
        201

    coquelets à l'éstragon, 191

escargots de poulet à la confiture
    d'oignons et de raisins, 192–193

magrets aux grains de cassis, 199–200

oie à l'étuvée, 202–203

pigeons farcis, 204–205

pintade farcie sur chou croquant,
    194–195

poularde à la vapeur de légumes, 188

poularde farcie aux petits légumes,
    189–190

poulet à la vapeur de tilleul, 184–185

poulet "au blanc," 186–187

poulet au pot dit "ilot," 185–186

salade de pintade "soir d'été," 196–
    197

water, *see* liquids, steaming

watercress, 79, 81

    soup, cream of, 81–82

wax beans, 41–42

waxy potatoes, 88, 89

weakfish, steaming time for, 114

whelks, in salt cod aïoli, 144–145

whipped cream, 296

white asparagus, 37

white beans, fresh, Brittany-style, 43

white cheese, 16

white wine:

    olives, and anchovies, hot beef
        "terrine" with, 232–233

    wine custard with honey and
        cinnamon, 282

whiting:

    fish mousse with mussels, 152–153

    steaming time for, 114

wine, red:

    leg of lamb cured in, 243–244

    peaches in, 292

–steamed duckling with pears,
    197–199

vinegar-mustard vinaigrette, 24

wine, white:

    custard with honey and cinnamon,
        282

    olives, and anchovies, hot beef
        "terrine" with, 232–233

    pike with mint and thyme and a
        Muscadet butter sauce, 138–139

    scallops with a Muscadet butter
        sauce, 147

    sweetbread mousse with ham,
        Madeira, and truffles, 258–259

winter squash, 94, 95

wire racks, 9

wishbone, removal of, 206, 214

woks, 10

wolffish, steaming time for, 113

yellow crookneck squash, 94, 95

yogurt, cucumbers with mint and,
    71–72

Yukon Gold potatoes, 88

zucchini, 94, 95

    bâtonnets and julienne, 104

    fennel fans with garlic and, 77

    grilling of, 102

    marinated vegetables with coriander
        and thyme, 74–75

    monkfish with green peppercorns
        and, 131–132

    stuffed, 96–97, 103